Professional Examinations

Paper F6

Taxation
(Finance Act 2014)

EXAM KIT

For June 2015 to March 2016 examination sittings

KAPLAN

PUBLISHING

British Library Cataloguing-in-Publication Data

A catalogue record for this book is available from the British Library.

Published by:

Kaplan Publishing UK

Unit 2 The Business Centre

Molly Millar's Lane

Wokingham

Berkshire

RG41 2QZ

ISBN: 978-1-78415-046-4

Acknowledgements

The past ACCA examination questions are the copyright of the Association of Chartered Certified Accountants. The original answers to the questions from June 1994 onwards were produced by the examiners themselves and have been adapted by Kaplan Publishing.

We are grateful to the Chartered Institute of Management Accountants and the Institute of Chartered Accountants in England and Wales for permission to reproduce past examination questions. The answers have been prepared by Kaplan Publishing.

CONTENTS

Section

Key features in this edition

In addition to providing a wide ranging bank of real past exam questions, we have also included in this edition:

- An analysis of all of the recent examination papers.

- Paper specific information and advice on exam technique.

- Our recommended approach to make your revision for this particular subject as effective as possible. This includes step by step guidance on how best to use our Kaplan material (Complete text, pocket notes and exam kit) at this stage in your studies.

- A wealth of past real examination questions adapted to the new examination style with enhanced tutorial answers and packed with specific key answer tips, technical tutorial notes and exam technique tips from our experienced tutors.

- Complementary online resources including full tutor debriefs and question assistance to point you in the right direction when you get stuck.

June and December 2014 – Real examination questions

The real June 2014 and December 2014 exam papers are available on **My**Kaplan at:

www.mykaplan.co.uk

You will find a wealth of other resources to help you with your studies on the following sites:

www.mykaplan.co.uk

www.accaglobal.com/en/student.html

Quality and accuracy are of the utmost importance to us so if you spot an error in any of our products, please send an email to mykaplanreporting@kaplan.com with full details, or follow the link to the feedback form in **My**Kaplan.

Our Quality Coordinator will work with our technical team to verify the error and take action to ensure it is corrected in future editions.

INDEX TO QUESTIONS AND ANSWERS

INTRODUCTION

The new syllabus has been introduced with effect from June 2015 and, although there has been some reordering of topics the syllabus content remains, for the most part unchanged from the 2014 exams. However the format of the exam has changed significantly, with multiple choice (objective test) questions introduced into the F6 exam for the first time, and shorter long-form questions than were seen in previous exams.

As a result of these changes to the F6 exam format, the majority of past exam questions are too long in their original format to be representative of F6 questions going forward. The questions contained in this exam kit are therefore based on past exam questions but it has been necessary to adapt them to ensure that they are representative of questions that could be seen in the examinations from June 2015 onwards. The adaptations have been made to reflect the new style of paper, new legislative changes in recent Finance Acts, Tax law rewrites and IAS terminology. We have included the new topics brought into the syllabus in some questions.

The questions within the kit are past ACCA exam questions, and the more recent questions (from 2005) are labelled as such in the index. Note that if a question within this kit has been changed in any way from the original version, this is indicated in the end column of the index below with the mark *(A)*.

Also included are the marking schemes for past ACCA examination questions to assist you in understanding where marks are earned and the amount of time to spend on particular tasks. Note that if a question has been changed from the original version, it will have also been necessary to change the original ACCA marking scheme. Therefore, if a question is marked as 'ADAPTED' you should assume that this also applies to the marking scheme.

The new Section A multiple choice questions included in this kit have been generated based on the style of questions in the sample assessment and to provide as broad coverage of the syllabus as possible. The questions in the real exam will be two marks each, but some will be slightly longer and some slightly shorter. The questions should take approximately 3.6 minutes each, and this will average out over 15 questions in the exam. The majority of the questions in this kit are worth 2 marks, however some are longer than for tutorial purposes in order to maximise the syllabus coverage.

KEY TO THE INDEX

PAPER ENHANCEMENTS

We have added the following enhancements to the answers in this exam kit:

Key answer tips

All answers include key answer tips to help your understanding of each question.

Tutorial note

All answers include more tutorial notes to explain some of the technical points in more detail.

Tutor's top tips

For selected questions, we 'walk through the answer' giving guidance on how to approach the questions with helpful 'tips from a top tutor', together with technical tutor notes.

These answers are indicated with the 'footsteps' icon in the index.

ONLINE ENHANCEMENTS

Timed question with Online tutor debrief

For selected questions, we recommend that they are to be completed in full exam conditions (i.e. properly timed in a closed book environment).

In addition to the examiner's technical answer, enhanced with key answer tips and tutorial notes in this exam kit, online you can find an answer debrief by a top tutor that:

- works through the question in full
- points out how to approach the question
- how to ensure that the easy marks are obtained as quickly as possible, and
- emphasises how to tackle exam questions and exam technique.

These questions are indicated with the 'clock' icon in the index.

Online question assistance

Have you ever looked at a question and not known where to start, or got stuck part way through?

For selected questions, we have produced 'Online question assistance' offering different levels of guidance, such as:

- ensuring that you understand the question requirements fully, highlighting key terms and the meaning of the verbs used
- how to read the question proactively, with knowledge of the requirements, to identify the topic areas covered
- assessing the detailed content of the question body, pointing out key information and explaining why it is important
- help in devising a plan of attack

With this assistance, you should then be able to attempt your answer confident that you know what is expected of you.

These questions are indicated with the 'signpost' icon in the index.

Online question enhancements and answer debriefs will be available from Spring 2015 on **My**Kaplan at:

www.mykaplan.co.uk

PRACTICE SECTION A QUESTIONS

PRACTICE SECTION B QUESTIONS

CHARGEABLE GAINS

ANALYSIS OF PAST EXAM PAPERS

The table below summarises the key topics that have been tested in recent exams.

Key:

Q   The question references are to the number of the question in this edition of the exam kit.

✓   Refers to Q2 from the December 2012 exam, which has not been included in the kit due to similarity to other recent questions.

*   Refers to topics that were included in these questions when originally set, but with the adaptation of the question to the new style exam, this topic element has been removed from this question in the kit

	Jun 2011	Dec 2011	Jun 2012	Dec 2012	June 2013	Dec 2013
Ethics						
Ethics of non-disclosure						Q78
Money laundering						Q78
Income tax						
Exempt income	Q20		Q27	✓		
Basic income tax computation	Q20	Q7	Q4	✓	Q31	
				Q15	Q54*	
Gift Aid donation		Q7		✓		
Reduction of personal allowance	Q20	Q7		✓		
Personal age allowance		Q7				
Property income		Q8	Q4	✓	Q31*	
					Q54*	
Furnished holiday lettings		Q8		✓	Q31*	
Rent-a-room relief		Q8				
NISAs				Q53*		
Residence						
Employed individual						
Factors indicating employment						
Salary and bonus	Q20		Q4			
Exempt benefits						
Car and fuel benefit		Q7*			Q31*	Q22
Living accommodation			Q4			
Beneficial loan					Q31	
Use of assets			Q4			
Mileage allowance					Q31	
Self-employed individual						
Adjustment to profits	Q20					Q22
Capital allowances			Q4	✓	Q16	Q22
Basis of assessment rules	Q21	Q7		✓	Q16	Q17
Partnerships – allocation	Q21		Q4			
Pre-trading expenditure						Q17

	Jun 2011	Dec 2011	Jun 2012	Dec 2012	June 2013	Dec 2013
Pensions						
Pension income		Q7			Q31*	
Occupational pension		Q7*			Q31	
Personal pension contributions	Q42*	Q7		Q53	Q31	
Annual allowance				Q53	Q31	
Income tax losses						
Relief against income			Q27			Q17
Opening year loss relief			Q27			
Terminal loss relief			Q27			
Tax savings			Q27			
Ongoing losses						Q17
Relief against gains						Q17
National Insurance contributions						
Class 1	Q21	Q7*	Q4*	Q15	Q31	Q22
Class 1A			Q4*		Q31	Q22
Class 2	Q21	Q7	Q4*			
Class 4	Q21	Q7	Q4*			
Capital gains						
Chargeable person			Q44			
Basic CGT computation			Q44		Q45 Q54	Q46
Enhancement				Q49		
Exempt assets		Q43				
Chattels		Q43				
Part disposal		Q43		Q49		
Shares	Q42			Q49	Q45	Q46
Takeover	Q42					
Wasting asset		Q43				
Insurance for damaged assets				Q49		
Husband and wife		Q43				Q46
Capital losses				Q15*		
Planning re disposal date						Q46
Reliefs						
Entrepreneurs' relief	Q42		Q44 Q27		Q45	Q46*
Principal private residence relief		Q43*				Q46
Gift relief		Q43			Q45	Q46*
Rollover relief			Q44*		Q45*	

	Jun 2011	Dec 2011	Jun 2012	Dec 2012	June 2013	Dec 2013
Self-assessment – individual						
Payments on account	Q20*			✓		
Filing dates						Q22
Compliance checks						Q22
Interest and penalties	Q20*					
Inheritance tax						
PETs	Q50		Q52	Q53	Q54	Q55
CLTs	Q50	Q51		Q53		Q55
Exemptions			Q52*		Q54	Q55
Diminution in value						Q55
Estate computation	Q50		Q52		Q54	
After tax inheritance						Q55
Due dates	Q50*				Q54*	Q55*
Transfer of nil rate band			Q52			
Corporation tax						
Residence			Q44			
Definition of accounting periods		Q63*				
Adjustment to profits	Q61	Q63	Q64	Q77	Q65	Q66
Capital allowances	Q61	Q63	Q64	Q77	Q65	Q66
					Q16	
Lease premiums	Q61*		Q64*			Q66*
Basic TTP computation	Q61		Q64	Q77	Q73	Q66
				Q15		
Property income	Q61*					Q66
Interest income	Q61	Q63*		Q77		Q66
Chargeable gains	Q61*		Q64	Q49		
			Q44*			
Long period of account			Q64		Q16	
Straddling 31 March liability comp			Q64			
Corporation tax losses						
Capital losses				Q49*		
Groups						
Associated companies			Q64	Q77	Q73	
Group relief		Q51*			Q73	
Capital gains group			Q64			Q66*
Self-assessment – companies						
Due dates and interest				Q77		Q66
Quarterly instalments	Q61					
iXBRL				Q77		

	Jun 2011	Dec 2011	Jun 2012	Dec 2012	June 2013	Dec 2013
Value added tax						
Registration	Q84		Q86			Q78
VAT return computation		Q63*			Q87	
Tax point			Q86		Q87	
Due dates	Q84*					Q78*
VAT invoices	Q84					Q78
Default surcharge					Q87	
Errors in a VAT return	Q84					
Transfer of going concern		Q63*				
Overseas supplies	Q84			Q85		
VAT Groups					Q87	
Annual accounting scheme	Q84*			Q85		
Cash accounting scheme				Q85		
Flat rate scheme			Q86			
Net after tax cost comparison				Q15		

ANALYSIS OF MOST RECENT EXAM

The table below summarises the key topics that have been tested in the most recent exam.

Note that the references are to the number of the question in the original exam. This exam can be found, with enhanced 'walk through answers', updated in line with legislation relevant to your exam sitting, on **My**Kaplan at: www.mykaplan.co.uk

	Jun 14
Income tax	
Basic income tax computation	Q1,Q4
Property income	Q1
Savings income	Q1
Dividend income	Q1
Child benefit tax charge	Q1
Employed individual	
Salary and bonus	Q1
Car and fuel benefit	Q1
Living accommodation	Q1
Use of assets	Q1
Self-employed individual	
Adjustment to profit	Q4
Capital allowances	Q1
Basis of assessment rules	Q1
Cash basis	Q4
Pensions	
Personal pension contributions	Q1
Annual allowance	Q1
National insurance contributions	
Class 2	Q4
Class 4	Q4
Capital gains	
Basic CGT computation	Q3
Enhancement	Q3
Part disposal	Q3
Shares	Q3
Reliefs	
Entrepreneurs' relief	Q3
Gift relief	Q3
Rollover relief	Q3
Self-assessment – individual	
Payments on account	Q4
Filing dates	Q4

	Jun 14
Corporation tax	
Adjustment to profits	Q2
Capital allowances	Q2
Basic TTP computation	Q2
Interest income	Q2
Chargeable gains	Q2
Qualifying charitable donations	Q2
Corporation tax losses	
Trading losses	Q2
Groups	
Associated companies	Q2
Group relief	Q2
Self-assessment – companies	
PAYE Real time information	Q2
Value added tax	
VAT return computation	Q2
Tax point	Q2
Inheritance tax	
PETs	Q5
CLTs	Q5
IHT planning	Q5
Estate computation	Q5

EXAM TECHNIQUE

- Decide in advance whether you will attempt Section A or Section B first so that you are not wasting time on this decision in the real exam.
  - This is a personal choice and you have time on the revision phase to try out different approaches, for example, if you sit mock exams.
  - A common approach is to tackle the multiple choice questions first, so they are out of the way and you can focus on Section B.
  - Others may prefer to tackle the longer Section B questions first, as they will take longer than the individual questions in section A.

  You should complete at least one mock exam under exam conditions to try out your chosen approach in advance.

  Whatever your approach though, you must make sure that you leave enough time to attempt all questions fully and be very strict with yourself in timing each question.

- Use the allocated **15 minutes reading and planning time** at the beginning of the exam:
  - read the Section B questions and examination requirements carefully, and
  - begin planning your Section B answers.

  See the Paper Specific Information for advice on how to use this time for this paper.

- **Divide the time** you spend on questions in proportion to the marks on offer:
  - there are 1.8 minutes available per mark in the examination
  - within that, try to allow time at the end of each question to review your answer and address any obvious issues

  Whatever happens, always keep your eye on the clock and **do not over run on any part of any question!**

- Spend the last **five minutes** of the examination:
  - reading through your answers, and
  - **making any additions or corrections**.

- If you **get completely stuck** with a question:
  - leave space in your answer book, and
  - **return to it later.**

- Stick to the question and **tailor your answer** to what you are asked.
  - pay particular attention to the verbs in the question.

- If you do not understand what a question is asking, **state your assumptions**.

  Even if you do not answer in precisely the way the examiner hoped, you should be given some credit, if your assumptions are reasonable.

- You should do everything you can to make things easy for the marker.

  The marker will find it easier to identify the points you have made if your **answers are legible**.

- **Section A multiple choice questions:**
  - Decide whether you want to attempt these at the start of the exam or at the end.
  - You should spend no longer than 54 minutes (1.8 × 30 marks) on Section A.
  - No credit for workings will be given in these questions; the answers will either be correct (2 marks) or incorrect (0 marks).

- – Work steadily. Rushing leads to careless mistakes and questions are designed to include answers which result from careless mistakes.

    - – If you don't know the answer, eliminate those options you know are incorrect and see if the answer becomes more obvious.

    - – Remember that only one answer to a multiple-choice question can be correct and there is no negative marking for an incorrect answer. After you have eliminated the options that you know to be wrong, if you are still unsure, guess.

- **Section B written questions:**

    - – Your answer should have:

        - – a clear structure

        - – a brief introduction, a main section and a conclusion.

    - – Be concise.

    - – It is better to write a little about a lot of different points than a great deal about one or two points.

- **Section B Computations:**

    - – It is essential to include all your workings in your answers.

    - – Many computational questions require the use of a standard format e.g. income tax computations, corporation tax computations and capital gains.

    - – Be sure you know these formats thoroughly before the exam and use the layouts that you see in the answers given in this book and in model answers.

- **Section B Reports, memos and other documents:**

    - – Some questions ask you to present your answer in the form of a report, a memo, a letter or other document.

    - – Make sure that you use the correct format – there could be easy marks to gain here.

PAPER SPECIFIC INFORMATION

THE EXAM

FORMAT OF THE EXAM

The exam will be in **TWO sections**, and will be predominantly computational.

Section A will be 15 multiple choice questions, each worth 2 marks.

Section B will consist of four 10 mark questions and two 15 mark questions.

All questions are compulsory.

		Number of marks
Section A:	15 multiple choice questions of 2 marks each	30
Section B:	Four 10 mark questions covering any area of the syllabus	40
	Two 15 mark questions, one focusing on income tax and one on corporation tax	30
		———
Total:		100

Total time allowed: 3 hours plus 15 minutes reading and planning time.

Note that:

- Section A questions can be drawn from any area of the syllabus.

- The two 15 mark Section B questions could include a small number of marks in respect of other taxes.

- There is no set order for the Section B questions. In the specimen paper the 10 mark questions appeared before the 15 mark questions, but the examiner could change the order.

Any of the questions might include the consideration of issues relating to the minimisation or deferral of tax liabilities.

PASS MARK

The pass mark for all ACCA Qualification examination papers is 50%.

SECTION A QUESTIONS

Note that Section A questions should take an average of 3.6 minutes each, and the questions in this kit generally reflect this, however some may take longer. They have been left as longer questions as they are good for tutorial purposes and provide good practice for your revision. However, remember that in the examination all multiple choice questions will be worth only two marks each.

READING AND PLANNING TIME

Remember that all three hour paper based examinations have an additional 15 minutes reading and planning time.

ACCA GUIDANCE

ACCA guidance on the use of this time is as follows:

> This additional time is allowed at the beginning of the examination to allow candidates to read the questions and to begin planning their answers before they start to write in their answer books.
>
> This time should be used to ensure that all the information and, in particular, the exam requirements are properly read and understood.
>
> During this time, candidates may only annotate their question paper. They may not write anything in their answer booklets until told to do so by the invigilator.

KAPLAN GUIDANCE

As all questions are compulsory, there are no decisions to be made about choice of questions, other than in which order you would like to tackle them.

Therefore, in relation to F6, we recommend that you take the following approach with your reading and planning time:

- There is very little information to consider for each Section A multiple choice question and there should be no need to plan your answers so don't waste your reading and planning time on Section A – go straight to Section B.

- **Skim through Section B** of the paper, assessing the level of difficulty of each question.

- **Write down** on the question paper next to the mark allocation **the amount of time you should spend on each part.** Do this for each part of every question.

- **Decide the order** in which you think you will attempt each question in Section B:

  A common approach is to tackle the question you think is the easiest and you are most comfortable with first.

  Others may prefer to tackle the longest questions first, or conversely leave them to the last.

  It is usual however for students to tackle their least favourite topic and/or the most difficult question in their opinion last.

  Whatever your approach, you must make sure that you leave enough time to attempt all questions fully and be very strict with yourself in timing each question.

- **For each Section B question** in turn, read the requirements and then the detail of the question carefully.

  Always read the requirement first as this enables you to **focus on the detail of the question with the specific task in mind**.

  For Section B computational questions:

  Highlight key numbers/information and key words in the question, scribble notes to yourself on the question paper to remember key points in your answer.

  Jot down pro formas required if applicable.

  For Section B written questions:

  Take notice of the format required (e.g. letter, memo, notes) and identify the recipient of the answer. You need to do this to judge the level of financial sophistication required in your answer and whether the use of a formal reply or informal bullet points would be satisfactory.

  Plan your beginning, middle and end and the key areas to be addressed and your use of titles and sub-titles to enhance your answer.

  For all Section B questions:

  Spot the easy marks to be gained in a question and parts which can be performed independently of the rest of the question. For example, writing down due dates of payment of tax, due dates for making elections, laying out basic pro formas correctly.

  Make sure that you do these parts first when you tackle the question.

  Don't go overboard in terms of planning time on any one question – you need a good measure of the whole paper and a plan for all of the Section B questions at the end of the 15 minutes.

  By covering all questions you can often help yourself as you may find that facts in one question may remind you of things you should put into your answer relating to a different question.

- With your plan of attack in mind, **start answering your chosen question** with your plan to hand, as soon as you are allowed to start.

- As mentioned in the 'Exam Technique' section earlier, you should decide in advance of the real exam whether to attempt Section A or Section B first.

 Always keep your eye on the clock and do not over run on any part of any question!

DETAILED SYLLABUS

The detailed syllabus and study guide written by the ACCA can be found at:

www.accaglobal.com/en/student.html

KAPLAN'S RECOMMENDED REVISION APPROACH

QUESTION PRACTICE IS THE KEY TO SUCCESS

Success in professional examinations relies upon you acquiring a firm grasp of the required knowledge at the tuition phase. In order to be able to do the questions, knowledge is essential.

However, the difference between success and failure often hinges on your exam technique on the day and making the most of the revision phase of your studies.

The **Kaplan complete text** is the starting point, designed to provide the underpinning knowledge to tackle all questions. However, in the revision phase, pouring over text books is not the answer.

Kaplan Online knowledge checks help you consolidate your knowledge and understanding and are a useful tool to check whether you can remember key topic areas.

Kaplan pocket notes are designed to help you quickly revise a topic area, however you then need to practice questions. There is a need to progress to full exam standard questions as soon as possible, and to tie your exam technique and technical knowledge together.

The importance of question practice cannot be over-emphasised.

The recommended approach below is designed by expert tutors in the field, in conjunction with their knowledge of the examiner and the recent real exams.

The approach taken for the fundamental papers is to revise by topic area. However, with the professional stage papers, a multi topic approach is required to answer the scenario based questions.

You need to practice as many questions as possible in the time you have left.

OUR AIM

Our aim is to get you to the stage where you can attempt exam standard questions confidently, to time, in a closed book environment, with no supplementary help (i.e. to simulate the real examination experience).

Practising your exam technique on real past examination questions, in timed conditions, is also vitally important for you to assess your progress and identify areas of weakness that may need more attention in the final run up to the examination.

In order to achieve this we recognise that initially you may feel the need to practice some questions with open book help and exceed the required time.

The approach below shows you which questions you should use to build up to coping with exam standard question practice, and references to the sources of information available should you need to revisit a topic area in more detail.

Remember that in the real examination, all you have to do is:

- attempt all questions required by the exam
- only spend the allotted time on each question, and
- get them at least 50% right!

Try and practice this approach on every question you attempt from now to the real exam.

EXAMINER COMMENTS

We have included the examiner's comments to the recent examination questions in this kit for you to see the main pitfalls that students fall into with regard to technical content.

However, too many times in the general section of the report, the examiner comments that students had failed due to:

- 'misallocation of time'
- 'running out of time' and
- showing signs of 'spending too much time on an earlier question and clearly rushing the answer to a subsequent question'.

Good exam technique is vital.

KAPLAN'S PAPER F6 REVISION PLAN

Stage 1: Assess areas of strengths and weaknesses

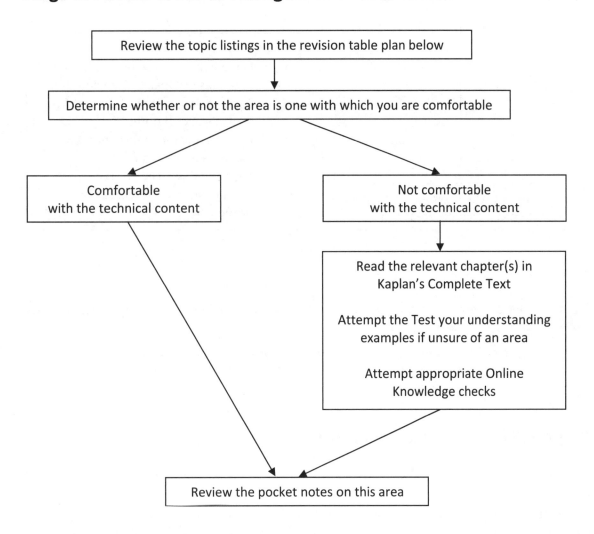

Review the topic listings in the revision table plan below

Determine whether or not the area is one with which you are comfortable

Comfortable
with the technical content

Not comfortable
with the technical content

Read the relevant chapter(s) in
Kaplan's Complete Text

Attempt the Test your understanding
examples if unsure of an area

Attempt appropriate Online
Knowledge checks

Review the pocket notes on this area

Stage 2: Practice questions

Follow the order of revision of topics as recommended in the revision table plan below and attempt the questions in the order suggested. Note that although the plan is organised into different subject areas, the real exam questions will cover more than one topic, and therefore some parts of the exam questions set below will be on topics covered later in the revision plan.

For each topic listed below you must also practice a selection of multiple choice questions covering that topic. Do bear in mind that some of the questions in this kit will take longer than 3.6 minutes each.

Try to avoid referring to text books and notes and the model answer until you have completed your attempt.

Try to answer the question in the allotted time.

Review your attempt with the model answer and assess how much of the answer you achieved in the allocated exam time.

Fill in the self-assessment box below and decide on your best course of action.

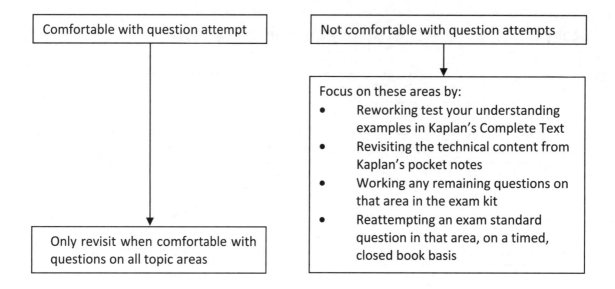

Note that:

    The 'footsteps questions' give guidance on exam techniques and how you should have approached the question.

    The 'clock questions' have an online debrief where a tutor talks you through the exam technique and approach to that question and works the question in full.

Stage 3: Final pre-exam revision

We recommend that you **attempt at least one three hour mock examination** containing a set of previously unseen exam standard questions.

It is important that you get a feel for the breadth of coverage of a real exam without advanced knowledge of the topic areas covered – just as you will expect to see on the real exam day.

Ideally this mock should be sat in timed, closed book, real exam conditions and could be:

* a mock examination offered by your tuition provider and/or
* the specimen paper in the back of this exam kit and/or
* the last real examination paper (available shortly afterwards on **My**Kaplan with 'enhanced walk through answers' and a full 'tutor debrief').

THE DETAILED REVISION PLAN

Topic	Complete Text Chapter	Pocket note Chapter	Questions to attempt	Tutor guidance	Date attempted	Self assessment
			Section B			
Personal income tax computation	2	1		Review the layout of an income tax computation and rates of tax.		
				Section B in the exam will include at least one question focusing on income tax, and it is crucial that you are comfortable with the pro forma.		
				Various aspects of income tax will also inevitably be tested in Section A and it is important to practice a cross-section of these questions.		
– Residence	2	1	30(a) 39(a)	The rules to determine whether an individual is resident in the UK are relatively complex. Revise the rules from the pocket notes and practice these two questions.		
– Employment income and assessable benefits	4	2	2 4 5 14	A popular exam topic, almost guaranteed to form part of the exam. There are many questions on this area. Start with Q2 which is a basic warm up question covering a number of employment benefits. Build up to Q4 and Q5 which are more demanding past exam questions on this area. Q14 tests the rules for determining whether an individual is employed or self-employed and the consequences of this decision.		

Topic	Complete Text Chapter	Pocket note Chapter	Questions to attempt	Tutor guidance	Date attempted	Self assessment
			Section B			
– Property income	3	1	8	This is a detailed question solely on property income which is an excellent test of your retention of these rules. However, be aware that this topic often appears as part of an income tax computation, where property is just one of a few sources of income for an individual.		
– Badges of trade	5	3	19	Revise the badges of trade rules from the pocket notes, before attempting this question. Note that although you are not required to apply the rules to a particular scenario in this question, you may be asked to do so in the exam. The consequences of the decision are however covered and this question demonstrates the importance of the badges of trade and how an individual is taxed as a consequence.		
– Adjusted trading profit, including capital allowances and cash basis	5 & 6	3 & 4	13 20 11	An adjustment of profits calculation is almost certain to be tested in the exam, although it may form part of a sole trader/partnership or corporation tax question. Q13 tests many of the typical adjustments you may see, and having practiced this question you can then attempt Q20 to time. Q11 tests the cash basis of assessment.		
– Basis of assessment	7	5	12 16	You may benefit from practicing the test your under-standings from the complete text before attempting these questions. The opening year rules are commonly tested and these questions provide good practice.		

KAPLAN PUBLISHING

Topic	Complete Text Chapter	Pocket note Chapter	Questions to attempt	Tutor guidance	Date attempted	Self assessment
			Section B			
– National insurance	11	8	33(b)	National insurance has regularly formed part of a longer question, and can provide easy marks to a well-prepared student. It is also likely to be tested in Section A. This question covers NICs for both an employee and a self-employed individual.		
– Trading losses for individuals	9	7	26 25 23	These questions cover the range of ways losses can be tested – in an ongoing business, losses in the opening years and losses on cessation. Q26 also tests the cap on income tax reliefs. In the current climate, losses are topical and it is important to be familiar with each of the reliefs.		
– Partnerships	8	6	30(b)	The allocation of profits between partners is a relatively straightforward computation, but does require practice.		
– Pensions	10	8	32 34	Like National Insurance, pensions is a topic which is likely to form a small part of a longer question, however the two questions listed here provide excellent practice of the various ways this topic could be tested.		
– Tax admin for individuals	12	9	35 36	Administration has rarely appeared as a standalone question (apart from in June 2010); and has been regularly tested at the end of a longer income tax question. Under the new syllabus it is more likely to appear as a standalone question and/or in Section A, so you need to be prepared for this. It is vital to learn the dates for submission and payment as well as the potential penalties and interest.		

Topic	Complete Text Chapter	Pocket note Chapter	Questions to attempt	Tutor guidance	Date attempted	Self assessment
			Section B			
Consolidation of income tax			18 29	Having revised all of the above topics, attempt Q18 and Q29 which are recent questions incorporating many aspects of the taxation of individuals. Don't forget to practice a number of MCQs on income tax if you haven't already done so.		
Inheritance tax (IHT)	17	13	50 51 52	IHT can be tested in both Section A and B and therefore it is important to study this area. Use your pocket notes to revise the key facts and techniques. Warm up with Q50 then practice questions 51 and 52.		
Corporation tax computation	18	14	–	Review the layout of a corporation tax computation and the rates of tax. One of the 15 mark Section B questions will focus on CT, and it is crucial that you are comfortable with the pro forma. There may also be further Section B questions and certainly some Section A questions as well. You should also ensure you know how to calculate the tax liability for an accounting period which straddles 31 March 2014 as this is highly examinable.		
– Adjustment of profits and capital allowances	19	14	57 66	It is important to be comfortable with the differences between sole traders and companies for adjustments to profits and capital allowances. Use Q57 to check that you are clear about these differences, then attempt Q66, which is classic example of this type of question.		

KAPLAN PUBLISHING

Topic	Complete Text Chapter	Pocket note Chapter	Questions to attempt	Tutor guidance	Date attempted	Self assessment
			Section B			
– Property income	19	14	75(a)	There are minor but important differences between taxing property income for individuals and companies. This question covers property income for a company, and also covers loss relief, which you could leave until you revise that area, or have a go and see what you remember!		
– Long periods of account	19	14	58 62	In order to deal with a long period of account, you need to learn the rules regarding apportioning different types of income between the two periods. Having revised these rules from the pocket notes, practice them using these questions.		
– Corporation tax losses	21	16	70	Many students are daunted by loss questions, however a systematic approach is all that is required and practice is key. Remind yourself of the layout required using the pocket notes, and practice the test your understandings from the complete text if you are not confident, before attempting Q70.		
– Groups	22	17	69 72	Groups are often tested as part of a Corporation tax question. Q69 tests group relief and Q72 tests the rules for determining a capital gains group and the number of associates.		
– Tax admin for a company	23	18	60	It has been rare to see a standalone question on administration in the exam (apart from in June 2010), however there were often easy marks available as part of other questions. Under the new syllabus it is more likely to appear as a standalone question and/or in Section A. It is therefore very important to learn the submission and payment dates as well as the penalty and interest rules.		

Topic	Complete Text Chapter	Pocket note Chapter	Questions to attempt	Tutor guidance	Date attempted	Self assessment
			Section B			
Chargeable gains for individuals	13	10	–	Chargeable gains could appear in any question in Section B and these questions will usually test a wide variety of the topics below. They are also likely to be tested in Section A. Revise the basic computation using the pocket notes before looking at the detailed areas.		
Chattels, shares, PPR, Entrepreneurs relief	14 & 16	11 & 12	38 43	These questions demonstrate how various aspects of capital gains will be tested in one question. Few of these areas are technically challenging, however, it is important that you can tackle them all.		
– Deferral reliefs	16	12	39 41	Recognising which deferral reliefs apply and whether they are available in full is important These questions cover all these reliefs and provide excellent practice.		
Chargeable gains for companies	20	15	48	Remind yourself of the different gains rules for companies, and test your understanding using Q48.		
– Quoted shares	15 & 20	11 & 15	49	A brief revision of the share pool and matching rules from the pocket notes may be useful. Then attempt Q49 which tests the capital gains rules for companies, including share pooling and also bonus issues and rights issues.		
Value added tax	24 & 25	19	78 80 84 86	Start by reviewing the examiner's VAT article. Under the new exam format, you should expect VAT to be tested in both Sections A and B so it is important that you practice VAT questions from both sections.		

Topic	Complete Text Chapter	Pocket note Chapter	Questions to attempt	Tutor guidance	Date attempted	Self assessment
			Section B			
Scenario style exam questions	N/A	20	6 7 15 20	These questions test a range of subjects and the tax rules covered are not complex, however, the style of questions differs from the others in the kit. Look at the different styles of question using the chapter in the pocket notes, and then ensure you are comfortable with the different question styles by practicing each of these questions.		

Note that not all of the Section B questions in the exam kit are referred to in the programme above.

We have recommended an approach to build up from the basics to exam standard Section B questions using a selection of the exam kit questions. The remaining questions are available in the kit for additional practice for those who require more questions on some areas.

It is also vital that you practice Section A questions on all topics.

TAX RATES AND ALLOWANCES

Throughout this exam kit:

1   **Calculations and workings need only to be made to the nearest £.**

2   **All apportionments should be made to the nearest month.**

3   **All workings should be shown in Section B.**

The tax rates and allowances below will be reproduced in the examination paper for Paper F6 in the 2014 examination sittings. In addition, other specific information necessary for candidates to answer individual questions will be given as part of the question.

INCOME TAX

		Normal rates	Dividend rates
		%	%
Basic rate	£1 – £31,865	20	10
Higher rate	£31,866 – £150,000	40	32.5
Additional rate	£150,001 and above	45	37.5

A starting rate of 10% applies to savings income where it falls within the first £2,880 of taxable income.

Personal allowances

Personal allowance

Born on or after 6 April 1948	£10,000
Born between 6 April 1938 and 5 April 1948	£10,500
Born before 6 April 1938	£10,660

Income limit

Personal allowance	£100,000
Personal allowance (born before 6 April 1948)	£27,000

Residence status

Days in UK	Previously resident	Not previously resident
Less than 16	Automatically not resident	Automatically not resident
16 to 45	Resident if 4 UK ties (or more)	Automatically not resident
46 to 90	Resident if 3 UK ties (or more)	Resident if 4 UK ties
91 to 120	Resident if 2 UK ties (or more)	Resident if 3 UK ties (or more)
121 to 182	Resident if 1 UK tie (or more)	Resident if 2 UK ties (or more)
183 or more	Automatically resident	Automatically resident

Child benefit income tax charge

Where income is between £50,000 and £60,000, the charge is 1% of the amount of child benefit received for every £100 of income over £50,000.

Car benefit percentage

The relevant base level of CO_2 emissions is 95 grams per kilometre.

The percentage rates applying to petrol cars with CO_2 emissions up to this level are:

75 grams per kilometre or less	5%
76 to 94 grams per kilometre	11%
95 grams per kilometre	12%

Car fuel benefit

The base level figure for calculating the car fuel benefit is £21,700.

New Individual Savings Accounts (NISAs)

The overall investment limit is £15,000.

Pension scheme limits

Annual allowance	– 2014/15	£40,000
	– 2011/12 to 2013/14	£50,000

The maximum contribution that can qualify for tax relief without any earnings is £3,600.

Authorised mileage allowance: cars

Up to 10,000 miles	45p
Over 10,000 miles	25p

Capital allowances: rates of allowance

Plant and machinery

Main pool	18%
Special rate pool	8%

Motor cars

New cars with CO_2 emissions up to 95 grams per kilometre	100%
CO_2 emissions between 96 and 130 grams per kilometre	18%
CO_2 emissions above 130 grams per kilometre	8%

Annual investment allowance

Rate of allowance	100%
Expenditure limit	£500,000

Cap on income tax reliefs

Unless otherwise restricted, reliefs are capped at the higher of £50,000 or 25% of income.

CORPORATION TAX

Financial year	2012	2013	2014
Small profits rate	20%	20%	20%
Main rate	24%	23%	21%
Lower limit	£300,000	£300,000	£300,000
Upper limit	£1,500,000	£1,500,000	£1,500,000
Standard fraction	1/100	3/400	1/400

Marginal relief

$$\text{Standard fraction} \times (U - A) \times N/A$$

VALUE ADDED TAX

Standard rate of VAT	20%
Registration limit	£81,000
Deregistration limit	£79,000

INHERITANCE TAX: Tax rates

£1 – £325,000		Nil
Excess –	Death rate	40%
–	Lifetime rate	20%

Inheritance tax: Taper relief

Years before death:	Percentage reduction
Over 3 but less than 4 years	20%
Over 4 but less than 5 years	40%
Over 5 but less than 6 years	60%
Over 6 but less than 7 years	80%

CAPITAL GAINS TAX

Rates of tax	– Lower rate	18%
	– Higher rate	28%
Annual exempt amount		£11,000
Entrepreneurs' relief –	Lifetime limit	£10,000,000
	– Rate of tax	10%

NATIONAL INSURANCE CONTRIBUTIONS
(not contracted out rates)

Class 1	Employee	£1 – £7,956 per year	Nil
		£7,957 – £41,865 per year	12%
		£41,866 and above per year	2%
Class 1	Employer	£1 – £7,956 per year	Nil
		£7,957 and above per year	13.8%
Class 1A			13.8%
Class 2		£2.75 per week	
		Small earnings exception limit	£5,885
Class 4		£1 – £7,956 per year	Nil
		£7,957 – £41,865 per year	9%
		£41,866 and above per year	2%

RATES OF INTEREST (assumed)

Official rate of interest:	3.25%
Rate of interest on underpaid tax:	3%
Rate of interest on overpaid tax:	0.5%

TIME LIMITS AND ELECTION DATES

Income tax

Election/claim	Time limit	For 2014/15
Agree the amount of trading losses to carry forward	4 years from the end of the tax year in which the loss arose	5 April 2019
Current and prior year set-off of trading losses against total income (and chargeable gains)	12 months from 31 January following the end of the tax year in which the loss arose	31 January 2017
Three year carry back of trading losses in the opening years	12 months from 31 January following the end of the tax year in which the loss arose	31 January 2017
Three year carry back of terminal trading losses in the closing years	4 years from the end of the last tax year of trading	5 April 2019

National Insurance Contributions

Class 1 primary and secondary – pay days	17 days after the end of each tax month under PAYE system (14 days if not paid electronically)	22nd of each month
Class 1 A NIC – pay day	22 July following end of tax year (19 July if not paid electronically)	22 July 2015
Class 2 NICs – pay days	Monthly direct debit or six monthly invoicing	31 January 2015 & 31 July 2015
Class 4 NICs – pay days	Paid under self-assessment with income tax	

Capital gains tax

Replacement of business asset relief for individuals (Rollover relief)	4 years from the end of the tax year: – in which the disposal occurred or – the replacement asset was acquired whichever is later	5 April 2019 for 2013/14 sale and 2014/15 acquisition
Holdover relief of gain on the gift of a business asset (Gift relief)	4 years from the end of the tax year in which the disposal occurred	5 April 2019
Entrepreneurs' relief	12 months from 31 January following the end of the tax year in which the disposal occurred	31 January 2017
Determination of principal private residence	2 years from the acquisition of the second property	

Self-assessment – individuals

Election/claim	Time limit	For 2014/15
Pay days for income tax and Class 4 NIC	1st instalment: 31 January in the tax year	31 January 2015
	2nd instalment: 31 July following the end of tax year	31 July 2015
	Balancing payment: 31 January following the end of tax year	31 January 2016
Pay day for CGT	31 January following the end of tax year	31 January 2016
Filing dates If return issued by 31 October in the tax year	Paper return: 31 October following end of tax year	31 October 2015
	Electronic return: 31 January following end of tax year	31 January 2016
If return issued after 31 October in the tax year	3 months from the date of issue of the return	
Retention of records Business records	5 years from 31 January following end of the tax year	31 January 2021
Personal records	12 months from 31 January following end of the tax year	31 January 2017
HMRC right of repair	9 months from date the return was filed	
Taxpayers right to amend a return	12 months from 31 January following end of the tax year	31 January 2017
Taxpayers claim for overpayment relief	4 years from the end of the tax year	5 April 2019
HMRC can open an enquiry	12 months from submission of the return	
HMRC can raise a discovery assessment – No careless or deliberate behaviour	4 years from the end of the tax year	5 April 2019
– Tax lost due to careless behaviour	6 years from the end of the tax year	5 April 2021
– Tax lost due to deliberate behaviour	20 years from the end of the tax year	5 April 2035
Taxpayers right of appeal against an assessment	30 days from the assessment – appeal in writing	

Corporation tax

Election/claim	Time limit
Replacement of business asset relief for companies (Rollover relief)	4 years from the end of the chargeable accounting period: — in which the disposal occurred or — the replacement asset was acquired whichever is later
Agree the amount of trading losses to carry forward	4 years from the end of the chargeable accounting period in which the loss arose
Current year set-off of trading losses against total profits (income and gains), and 12 month carry back of trading losses against total profits (income and gains)	2 years from the end of the chargeable accounting period in which the loss arose
Surrender of current period trading losses to other group companies (Group relief)	2 years after the claimant company's chargeable accounting period
Election for transfer of capital gain or loss to another company within the gains group	2 years from the end of the chargeable accounting period in which the disposal occurred by the company actually making the disposal

Self-assessment – companies

Election/claim	Time limit
Pay day for small and medium companies	9 months and one day after the end of the chargeable accounting period
Pay day for large companies	Instalments due on 14th day of: — Seventh, Tenth, Thirteenth, and Sixteenth month **after the start** of the chargeable accounting period
Filing dates	Later of: — 12 months from the end of the chargeable accounting period — 3 months from the issue of a notice to deliver a corporation tax return
Companies claim for overpayment relief	4 years from the end of the chargeable accounting period
HMRC can open an enquiry	12 months from the actual submission of the return
Retention of records	6 years from the end of the chargeable accounting period

Value added tax

Election/claim	Time limit
Compulsory registration	
Historic test:	
− Notify HMRC	30 days from end of the month in which the threshold was exceeded
− Charge VAT	Beginning of the month, one month after the end of the month in which the threshold was exceeded
Future test:	
− Notify HMRC	30 days from the date it is anticipated that the threshold will be exceeded
− Charge VAT	the date it is anticipated that the threshold will be exceeded (i.e. the beginning of the 30 day period)
Compulsory deregistration	30 days from cessation
Filing of VAT return and payment of VAT	One month and seven days after the end of the return period

Section 1

PRACTICE SECTION A QUESTIONS

INCOME TAX AND NATIONAL INSURANCE

INCOME TAX BASICS AND EMPLOYMENT INCOME

1   Said is a professional translator and has made the following investments during the tax year 2014/15:

   (i)   £400 in shares in the company he works for

   (ii)   £1,000 in a New Individual Savings Account

   (iii)   £800 in a National Savings and Investments Investment Account

   (iv)   £500 purchasing a National Savings and Investments Certificate

   Which of the above investments will generate income which is exempt from income tax for the tax year 2014/15?

   A   All of the above

   B   (i) (ii) and (iv) only

   C   (ii) (iii) and (iv) only

   D   (i) only

2   Fiona is a sole trader and was born on 13 October 1972. During 2014/15 she had taxable trading income of £105,000 and received dividend income of £1,350. Fiona makes a gift aid donation of £2,000 (gross) during 2014/15.

   What amount of personal allowance will Fiona be entitled to for the tax year 2014/15?

   A   £7,750

   B   £7,825

   C   £8,000

   D   £6,750

3 Sabrina was born on 15 January 1937 and during the tax year 2014/15 she received dividends of £1,800 and rental income of £29,500. During the tax year 2014/15 Sabrina also made a gift aid donation of £500 (gross).

By what amount will the personal age allowance for Sabrina be reduced for the tax year 2014/15?

A £1,900

B £2,000

C £660

D £10,000

4 Ifram, a management consultant, is in the process of completing his tax return for the tax year 2014/15 and has asked your advice regarding the following interest payments he has made during the year:

(i) Interest paid on a loan he incurred to purchase a laptop for use in his employment

(ii) Interest paid on the mortgage for his principal private residence

(iii) Interest paid on an amount he borrowed to finance the acquisition of 2,000 shares in a quoted company.

(iv) Interest paid on a loan he took to invest capital in a partnership in order to become a partner.

Which of the Ifram's interest payments represent qualifying interest and are deductible from his total income?

A (i) only

B (iii) and (iv)

C (i), (ii) and (iv)

D (i) and (iv) only

5 Petra had trading income of £56,500 and no other income for 2014/15. She made an annual charitable donation to Oxfam of £400 under the gift aid scheme. She received child benefit of £1,066 during 2014/15 in respect of her son, Kostas.

What child benefit tax charge, if any, will be added to Petra's income tax liability for 2014/15?

A £692

B £639

C £650

D £Nil

6   Bao spends 37 days travelling in the UK during the tax year 2014/15. He has never been resident in the UK prior to 2014/15.

Minh arrives in the UK from Vietnam on 10 November 2014 to work full time in the UK.

Who will be treated as UK resident in the tax year 2014/15?

A   Bao and Minh

B   Neither of them

C   Bao only

D   Minh only

7   **Which of the following forms of savings income are received gross?**

(i)   Unquoted loan stock interest

(ii)   NS&I investment account interest

(iii)   Gilt edged security interest

(iv)   NS&I direct saver account interest

A   (ii) and (iii) only

B   (ii) and (iv) only

C   (i) and (iii)

D   (ii), (iii) and (iv)

8   James has the following income in 2014/15:

	£
Rental income	12,200
Bank interest	8,300
Gilt edged security interest	1,500
Interest on a NISA account	1,200

The figures for interest income are the amounts received.

What is James's income tax payable for 2014/15?

A   £672

B   £740

C   £372

D   £2,747

9   Harrison received dividends of £9,900 in 2014/15 and had no other income during the year.

What is Harrison's income tax payable/(repayable) for 2014/15?

A   £100

B   £Nil

C   (£775)

D   (£1,000)

10   Maisy has a cottage which she lets out furnished for an annual rent of £9,600, payable monthly in advance.

She incurred the following expenditure, which was paid for on the dates shown:

		£
April 2014	Council tax (for the year to 31 March 2015)	900
September 2014	Replacement of broken window	300
October 2014	Insurance for the year ended 30 September 2015 (previous year £480)	540
May 2015	Redecoration (work completed in March 2015)	450

What is Maisy's property business profit for 2014/15?

A   £6,480

B   £6,540

C   £6,570

D   £7,020

11   Hannah grants a 23 year lease on a warehouse to Mandy for £42,000 on 1 September 2014.

What is the property business income assessable on Hannah for 2014/15?

A   £18,480

B   £23,520

C   £24,500

D   £42,000

12   Sanjay was employed on an annual salary of £36,000 until 31 October 2014, when he had a pay rise of 5%. His salary is paid at the end of every month. He is also paid a bonus on 1 April each year based upon his performance to the end of the previous calendar year.

On 1 April 2014 he received a bonus of £2,800, and on 3 April 2015 he received a bonus of £3,300.

What is Sanjay's assessable employment income for 2014/15?

A   £39,550

B   £42,850

C   £39,900

D   £40,050

13   Katie earned an annual salary of £55,000 throughout the 2014/15 tax year. She used her own car for business travel, and she travelled 14,500 business miles during 2014/15.

What is Katie's assessable employment income assuming her employer paid her 43p per business mile?

A   £55,610

B   £54,390

C   £54,710

D   £55,290

14   Christos, a higher rate taxpayer, is provided with the following benefits in 2014/15 by his employer:

(i)   Free use of the staff canteen at lunchtime for 200 days a year. The canteen is available to all staff and the average cost of preparing a meal is £4.

(ii)   £40 per week of child care vouchers which he uses with an approved childcare provider.

(iii)   £3 per week for the additional household costs incurred when he works from home.

What is the assessable value of his benefits in 2014/15?

A   £Nil

B   £624

C   £2,080

D   £3,036

15   Jo is provided with non-job related accommodation by her employer, which the employer purchased 35 years ago at a cost of £72,000. The property has an annual value of £2,600, and had a market value of £245,000 when first made available to Jo 8 years ago. Jo pays £250 per month to her employer to live in the property.

What is the assessable benefit for Jo in 2014/15?

A   £Nil

B   £5,125

C   £5,222

D   £2,600

16   Thiago is provided with a new diesel company car on 6 May 2014 which he used for both business and private use during 2014/15. The car has a list price of £28,000 and CO_2 emissions of 198 grams per kilometre.

What is Thiago's car benefit for 2014/15?

A   £8,213

B   £8,960

C   £9,800

D   £8,983

17   Woojin was provided with a loan of £100,000 on 6 April 2014 by his employer. He paid back £40,000 of the loan on 6 August 2014.

What is Woojin's loan benefit for 2014/15?

A   £2,600

B   £2,383

C   £2,492

D   £2,275

18 On 6 April 2012 Ritvik was provided, by his employer, with the use of a home cinema system which cost £8,500. On 6 April 2014 he purchased the home cinema system from his employer for £1,500 even though the market value was £2,400

What is Ritvik's benefit in respect of the cinema system for 2014/15?

A   £900

B   £5,300

C   £5,100

D   £3,600

INCOME TAX BASICS AND INCOME FROM SELF-EMPLOYMENT

19 Wilson is a sole trader. When calculating his trading profits Wilson has deducted the following expenses:

(i)   Gifts of food hampers for 10 customers costing £450

(ii)   Christmas party for 3 staff members costing £630

(iii) Legal fees of £150 in respect of the acquisition of a 20 year lease

(iv)   Employee parking fine whilst on business of £30

What amount needs to be added back when calculating Wilson's tax adjusted trading profits?

A   £600

B   £1,230

C   £1,260

D   £480

20 Haniful has taken goods from his business for personal use. The goods cost £850 and have a selling price of £1,100.

Haniful has made no entry in his accounts in respect of this.

When calculating tax adjusted trading profits how much must be added to Haniful's accounting profits?

A   £850

B   £1,100

C   £250

D   £1,950

21 Fleur runs a sole trader business and has a year end of 31 December.

On 1 January 2014 Fleur paid a £25,000 premium for a 20 year lease on an office.

What amount can be deducted in respect of the lease premium when calculating Fleur's tax adjusted trading profits for the year ended 31 December 2014?

A £25,000

B £15,500

C £1,250

D £775

22 **Which one of the following assets bought by a sole trader will be allocated to the main pool for capital allowances purposes?**

A Delivery van costing £12,500 with 25% private use by the owner of the business

B Laptop computer costing £4,500 with 15% private use by the owner of the business

C Motor car with CO_2 emissions of 115 g/km costing £17,500 with 25% private use by one of the employees

D Motor car with CO_2 emissions of 135 g/km costing £16,500 used solely for business purposes by the owner of the business

23 Andrew prepares accounts for the eight months to 31 March 2015. The tax written down value of the main pool on 1 August 2014 was £18,000.

On 15 January 2015 he purchased a new motor car with CO_2 emissions of 95 g/km costing £12,260. It is used solely for business purposes by Andrew.

What are the maximum capital allowances Andrew may claim for the eight month period ended 31 March 2015?

A £15,500

B £14,420

C £10,333

D £12,260

24 Ronald has always prepared his accounts to 31 March. On the 31 March 2015 Ronald ceased trading. The tax written down of the general pool at 1 April 2014 was £15,000.

On 1 January 2015 Ronald purchased a laptop solely for business use costing £4,500.

On 31 March 2015 all the items in the general pool were sold for £14,550 apart from the laptop which was retained by Ronald. The market value of the laptop at 31 March 2015 was £4,150. None of the items in the general pool was sold for more than its original cost.

What are the capital allowances/(balancing charge) for the year ended 31 March 2015?

A £144

B £450

C (£300)

D £800

25 Jacinta started trading on 1 August 2014 and prepares accounts to 31 December each year. Her trading profits for the first two periods are as follows:

5 months ended 31 December 2014   £10,500
y/e 31 December 2015   £24,000

What is the trading income assessment for Jacinta for 2014/15?

A   £10,500

B   £16,500

C   £24,500

D   £24,000

26 Lee decides to cease trading on 31 January 2015 after trading for many years. His tax adjusted profits for recent years have been:

y/e 30 April 2013	£40,000
y/e 30 April 2014	£10,000
p/e 31 January 2015	£14,000

Lee has overlap profits of £3,000 brought forward from the commencement of trade.

What is Lee's trading income assessment for 2014/15?

A   £11,000

B   £14,000

C   £21,000

D   £24,000

PARTNERSHIPS

27 Elizabeth and Henry have been in partnership for many years, preparing accounts to 31 December each year.

Until 30 June 2014 Henry received a salary of £10,000 per annum and the remaining profit was shared in the ratio 70:30 to Elizabeth and Henry respectively.

From 1 July 2014 Henry continued to receive his salary but the profit sharing ratio was adjusted to 80:20 to Elizabeth and Henry respectively.

The adjusted trading profits for the accounting year ended 31 December 2014 are £80,000.

What is the trading income assessed on Henry for 2014/15?

A   £17,500

B   £20,000

C   £24,000

D   £27,500

TRADING LOSSES

28   Brooke has been trading as a sole trader for a number of years. Her recent tax adjusted trading profits/(losses) have been:

y/e 31 August 2012   £45,000

y/e 31 August 2013   £(75,000)

y/e 31 August 2014   £1,000

Brooke is expecting to make trading profits in the foreseeable future of approximately £5,000 per annum.

Brooke also receives dividends of £8,100 each tax year.

What is the amount of trading loss carried forward to 2015/16 assuming that Brooke claims to use the loss in the most efficient way?

A   £24,000

B   £20,000

C   £11,000

D   £21,000

29   Sabine started to trade as a sole trader on 1 November 2012. Her tax adjusted trading profits/(losses) for the first two years are:

y/e 31 October 2013   £(25,000)

y/e 31 October 2014   £5,000

Sabine was employed until 31 March 2012 earning £45,000 per annum.

How much, if any, of the loss can be offset against Sabine's employment income in 2009/10?

A   £25,000

B   £10,417

C   £14,583

D   £Nil

PENSIONS AND NIC

30   Hamid runs a sole trader business, in which he employs an employee who earns £20,000 per annum and is provided with a company car for private and business use.

Which classes of NIC will make up the total NIC cost borne by Hamid?

A   Class 2 and 4 only

B   Class 1 secondary and 1A only

C   Classes 2 and 4, Class 1 secondary and Class 1A only

D   Classes 2 and 4, Class 1 primary and secondary and Class 1A

31 Efe is an employee of Mulch Ltd, and is paid an annual salary of £60,000. During 2014/15 he also receives an annual bonus of £3,000 and childcare vouchers of £20 per week.

How much Class 1 primary NICs is Efe required to pay for the tax year 2014/15?

A £4,492

B £4,512

C £4,432

D £6,605

32 Bob is an employee of Dibbit Ltd, and is paid an annual salary of £50,000. He makes contributions of £3,000 into the company's occupational pension scheme each year.

In 2014/15 he drove 12,000 business miles in his own car for which he was paid 50p per mile by Dibbit Ltd.

How much Class 1 secondary NICs is Dibbit Ltd required to pay in respect of Bob's earnings for the tax year 2014/15?

A £5,802

B £5,885

C £5,940

D £5,526

33 Kolo is an employee of Lapsang Ltd. He is paid a salary of £20,000 and has use of a company car for private purposes throughout 2014/15. The car has a list price of £15,000 and CO_2 emissions of 129g. No petrol is provided for private mileage.

How much Class 1A NIC is payable?

A £2,700

B £373

C £3,133

D £393

34 Mohammed, age 35, runs a sole trader business. In the year ended 5 April 2015 his accounting profit and tax adjusted trading profit were £5,400 and £6,800 respectively.

Nicole is aged 75 and receives the state retirement pension. She also has a sole trader business. In the year ended 5 April 2015 her accounting profit and tax adjusted trading profit were £5,900 and £5,200.

Who will be required to pay Class 2 NIC for 2014/15?

A Neither of them

B Mohammed only

C Nicole only

D Both of them

35 Marion runs a sole trader business. Her accounting profit is £300,000 for the year ended December 2014, and when adjusted for tax it is £280,000.

How much Class 4 NIC is Marion required to pay in the tax year 2014/15?

A   £7,815

B   £8,215

C   £8,832

D   £8,531

36 Isaac is self-employed and for the year ended 31 March 2015 he paid £40,000 into his personal pension plan. Isaac's relevant earnings for 2014/15 were £90,000.

By how much will Isaac's basic rate band be extended for 2014/15?

A   £3,600

B   £90,000

C   £40,000

D   £50,000

37 Padma became a member of a personal pension scheme on 6 April 2011 and has made gross personal pension contributions as follows:

2011/12   £23,000

2012/13   £40,000

2013/14   £55,000

Padma's tax adjusted trading income in 2014/15 is £300,000.

What is the maximum gross personal pension contribution that Padma can make in 2014/15 without incurring an annual allowance charge?

A   £77,000

B   £40,000

C   £72,000

D   £42,000

38 Griff is employed by Gargoyle plc on an annual salary of £50,000. In addition Griff lets out qualifying furnished holiday accommodation which generates taxable income of £5,000 per annum and a warehouse, to a local business, which generates taxable income of £8,000 per annum.

In 2014/15 he made a £4,000 (gross) donation to a national charity under the Gift Aid scheme.

What are Griff's net relevant earnings for 2014/15?

A   £51,000

B   £63,000

C   £59,000

D   £55,000

ADMINISTRATION AND ETHICS

39 Which of the following is true of tax evasion?

A   Tax evasion means using the taxation regime to ones' own advantage by arranging your affairs to minimise your tax liability

B   Tax evasion is legal and does not involve misleading HMRC

C   Tax evasion utilises loopholes in tax legislation

D   Tax evasion encompasses any attempt to avoid or reduce tax by illegal means

40 Which of the following is true of a tax adviser?

A   A tax adviser can only disclose any information about the client with the clients' consent

B   A tax adviser must not assist a client to plan or commit any offence

C   If a tax adviser becomes aware that a client has committed a tax irregularity they must disclose it to HMRC

D   A tax adviser acting for a client has no duties and responsibilities towards HM Revenue & Customs

41   Philip is a sole trader and is married to Harriet. Harriet is in employment. They jointly own a residential investment property which is rented out unfurnished.

Until which date(s) must Philip and Harriet keep the records which support their tax returns for 2014/15?

	Philip	Harriet
A	31 January 2021	31 January 2021
B	31 January 2021	31 January 2017
C	31 January 2017	31 January 2017
D	31 January 2020	31 January 2020

42   Jeanette's income tax and capital gains tax liabilities for 2014/15 were £25,000 and £5,000 respectively. Income tax of £5,400 was deducted at source and she made payments on account totalling £18,000 for 2014/15.

What is the balancing payment Jeanette should pay on 31 January 2016?

A   £16,400

B   £6,600

C   £12,000

D   £1,600

43   Belinda paid the balancing payment of income tax of £7,400 for 2014/15 on 10 March 2016.

Which of the following statements is/are correct?

(1)   Belinda will have to pay interest on late paid tax from 31 January to 9 March 2016.

(2)   Belinda will have to pay a 5% penalty because the payment is more than 7 days late.

(3)   Belinda will have to pay a 5% penalty because the payment is more than 30 days late.

A   (1) and (2)

B   (1) and (3)

C   (1) only

D   (2) only

44   Florence filed her 2014/15 tax return, showing income tax payable of £6,500 on 15 August 2016.

In addition to the initial £100 late filing penalty, what is the maximum further penalty that she can be charged for filing the tax return late?

A   £1,225

B   £325

C   £900

D   £5,450

45   Welan Ltd pays its employees monthly on the 15th of every month.

Which of the following statements is/are correct?

(1)   Under the Real Time Information PAYE system, Welan Ltd must submit income tax and NIC information in respect of the monthly salary payments to HM Revenue & Customs electronically by the 15th day of each month.

(2)   Welan Ltd must pay the income tax and NIC due on the monthly salary payments to HM Revenue & Customs electronically by the 22nd of the month following the month the salaries are paid.

(3)   Welan Ltd must provide each employee with a year-end summary form (P60) for 2014/15 by 6 July 2015.

A   (2) and (3) only

B   (1) and (2) only

C   All of them

D   (1) and (3) only

CHARGEABLE GAINS

INDIVIDUALS – CAPITAL GAINS TAX

46 Massita is planning to dispose of several assets in 2014/15 and wants to avoid any capital gains tax liability. He is unsure which of his assets to sell and which to retain.

Which of the following assets would potentially realise a chargeable gain?

A   Qualifying corporate bonds

B   Gilt-edged securities

C   Main residence that she has always lived in

D   A van used in her trade, on which she has claimed capital allowances and which would be sold for £22,000 and realise a profit.

47 Lexie sold an investment property for £340,000 in 2014/15 incurring legal expenses of £2,500. She had acquired the building for £150,000 in 2005.

Lexie has capital losses brought forward of £80,000 and has taxable income of £54,000 for 2014/15. She sold no other assets in 2014/15.

What is Lexie's capital gains tax liability?

A   £27,720

B   £27,020

C   £30,100

D   £17,370

48 Jackson acquired a holiday villa for £115,000 on 1 May 2004. He gave it to his wife Sophia on 30 September 2009 when it was worth £100,000. Sophia sold the villa for £165,000 on 1 July 2014.

Sophia had no other capital disposals In 2014/15 and has capital losses brought forward of £5,000. Her taxable income for 2014/15 is £60,000.

What is Sophia's capital gains tax payable in 2014/15?

A   £6,120

B   £9,520

C   £10,920

D   £13,720

49   Aiden bought 30 acres of land on 1 March 2008 for £300,000.

On 1 January 2010 he sold 10 acres of the land for £150,000. At this time the remaining land was worth £250,000.

On 1 March 2015 Aiden sold the remaining acres for £425,000.

Aiden's taxable income for 2014/15 is £80,000 and he has no other capital disposals during the tax year.

What is Aiden's capital gains tax payable for 2014/15?

A   £31,920

B   £63,420

C   £66,500

D   £73,920

50   Noah sold two paintings at an auction on 14 May 2014 for £4,000 and £7,200 respectively. He had purchased the two paintings for £1,000 each on 22 May 2003.

What is Noah's total chargeable gain arising on the sale of the paintings?

A   £2,000

B   £5,000

C   £6,200

D   £9,200

51   Liam purchased an antique glass vase for £22,000 on 30 March 2000, incurring legal fees of £800.

The market for antique glassware has since slumped and Liam sold the vase for £5,500 on 1 January 2015 incurring auctioneer fees of £300.

What is Liam's allowable loss on this disposal?

A   £16,000

B   £16,800

C   £17,100

D   £17,600

52   On 1 June 2002 Aaliyah purchased a copyright at a cost of £35,000. The copyright had an estimated useful life of 20 years.

Aaliyah sold the copyright on 1 June 2014 for £44,000.

What is the chargeable gain arising on this sale?

A   £9,000

B   £19,000

C   £23,000

D   £30,000

53 Cooper purchased a holiday home for £142,000 on 1 October 2008. The property was damaged in a fire on 1 January 2010.

Cooper received compensation of £60,000 from his insurance company on 31 January 2010. He spent £70,000 on restoring the home in March 2010 and it was worth £180,000 after restoration. Cooper made an election such that a part disposal did not arise in 2009/10.

Cooper sold the holiday home for £230,000 on 1 March 2015.

What is Cooper's chargeable gain on the sale?

A   £18,000

B   £88,000

C   £148,000

D   £78,000

54 Madison gave 10,000 shares in Miles plc to her daughter during 2014/15.

The shares were quoted in the Stock Exchange Official List at 120p – 132p per share on the day of the sale. On the same day there were recorded bargains of 136p, 132p and 122p.

What figure will be used for the proceeds in the capital gain calculation?

A   123p

B   129p

C   130p

D   132p

55 Clarissa has disposed of the following shares and securities during 2014/15:

(1)   8½% Exchequer Stock for £8,000 which was purchased in 2012 for £2,500.

(2)   20,000 shares in Martin plc sold to her sister for £7,000.

    The market value of the shares on the day of the sale was £12,300.

    The shares were purchased for £8,000 in February 2012.

What is Madison's total chargeable gain on these disposals in 2014/15?

A   £4,500

B   £4,300

C   £5,500

D   £9,800

56 Emily had the following transactions in the shares of Elijah Plc:

		Number of shares	Cost £	Proceeds £
1 June 2014	Purchase	22,000	88,000	
1 October 2014	Purchase	2,000	7,440	
1 October 2014	Sale	20,000		59,000
23 October 2014	Purchase	3,000	10,800	

In what order will Emily's share purchases be matched to the 20,000 shares sold on 1 October 2014?

A   All 20,000 shares to the purchase on 1 June 2014

B   All 20,000 shares to the share pool as at 1 October 2014

C   2,000 shares to the purchase on 1 October 2014 and the balance of 18,000 shares to the share pool as at 1 October 2014

D   2,000 shares to the purchase on 1 October 2014, 3,000 shares to the purchase on 23 October 2014 and the balance of 15,000 shares to the share pool as at 1 October 2014

57 Carter sold 5,000 shares in Brody Ltd on 28 February 2015 for £25,000.

He had purchased shares in Brody Ltd as follows:

21 April 1996   9,000 shares for £27,050

30 April 2010   2,600 shares for £9,750

10 March 2015   500 shares for £2,050

What is Carter's chargeable gain on the disposal of the Brody Ltd shares?

A   £8,674

B   £8,946

C   £9,138

D   £9,972

58 Caleb had the following transactions in Harper plc shares:

26 April 2003   Purchased 40,000 shares in Harper plc for £200,000

19 May 2006   Harper plc announced a 1:4 rights issue at £4 per share. Elijah took up his rights in full

3 May 2010   Harper plc announced a 1:5 bonus issue

25 March 2015   Elijah sold 12,500 shares for £175,000

What is the allowable cost for capital gains tax purposes of the shares disposed of on 25 March 2015?

A   £62,500

B   £53,333

C   £50,000

D   £41,667

59   Hunter purchased 50,000 shares in Grayson Ltd for £90,000 on 30 May 2004.

On 1 November 2014 Grayson Ltd was taken over by Riley plc. Grayson Ltd shareholders received £3 cash and 2 Riley plc ordinary £1 shares for every Grayson Ltd share.

Immediately after takeover Riley Plc shares were worth £1.20 each.

What is Hunter's chargeable gain as a result of the takeover?

A   £Nil

B   £150,000

C   £100,000

D   £180,000

60   Zofia sold her only home after 17 years of ownership. She lived in it for the first year and last eight years of ownership. She did not live in it for the middle eight years.

Under which of the following circumstances would the entire eight year period when she did not live in the property qualify as deemed occupation?

A   She was employed abroad

B   She was self-employed abroad

C   She was working in a different part of the UK

D   She was travelling

61   Masuma sold her only home and realised a gain before reliefs of £120,000. She had used six of the ten rooms herself and let out the other four for the duration of her ownership.

What is her chargeable gain, assuming she claims all available reliefs?

A   £Nil

B   £8,000

C   £48,000

D   £72,000

62   The four shareholders of Elephant Ltd are selling their shares. They own the share capital as follows:

Amin: 32%
Ben: 32%
Camilla: 32%
Dimitri: 4%

All shares have equal voting rights. Amin does not work for the company. Ben works part time and Camilla and Dimitri work full time for the company. Camilla only joined Elephant Ltd six months ago and has owned her shares for three months, whereas the others have owned their shares for five years.

Who will qualify for entrepreneurs' relief on the sale of their shares?

A   Amin

B   Ben

C   Camilla

D   Dimitri

63   In October 2014 Bhavin sold his furniture business which he had run for nine years as a sole trader, realising a chargeable gain of £13,250,000.

Bhavin is a higher rate tax payer and has not previously claimed any Entrepreneurs' relief.

What is Bhavin's capital gains tax liability for 2014/15 assuming he has made no other gains during the tax year and claims all available reliefs?

A   £906,920

B   £1,906,920

C   £1,908,900

D   £1,910,000

64   **The disposal of which of the following assets qualifies for rollover relief?**

A   A portable sewing machine used by a sole trader in his business

B   Shares in an individual's personal trading company

C   Land used by a sole trader in his business

D   Shares in the company of which the individual is an employee

65   In October 2003 Hitesh sold a factory for £230,574 and realised a gain of £31,083.

In May 2004 he bought a warehouse for £231,211. He then sold the warehouse in December 2014 for £270,213.

Both of the buildings were used for the purposes of his sole trader business.

What is the chargeable gain arising on the disposal of the warehouse assuming all available reliefs are claimed?

A   £31,083

B   £39,002

C   £59,085

D   £70,085

66   Lionel owns 50% of the ordinary share capital in Giraffe Ltd and 2% of the ordinary share capital in Zebra plc. Both are trading companies and Lionel has 50% and 2% of the voting rights respectively.

Which of the following would be a qualifying asset for the purposes of gift relief?

A   Part of Lionel's shareholding in Giraffe Ltd, representing 2% of the total ordinary share capital in Giraffe Ltd

B   A building owned by Lionel and used in the trade of Zebra plc

C   Lionel's entire holding of Zebra plc shares

D   A building owned by Lionel and held by Giraffe Ltd as an investment property

COMPANIES – CHARGEABLE GAINS

67 Forrest Ltd bought a warehouse for £250,000 in December 2005, incurring £20,000 legal fees in connection with the acquisition. The company spent £100,000 on an extension in March 2008. The warehouse was sold for £800,000 in May 2014.

Assume the relevant RPIs are as follows:

December 2005	194.1
March 2008	212.1
May 2014	255.6

What is the chargeable gain arising on the sale of the warehouse?

A   £323,910

B   £323,942

C   £330,250

D   £330,288

68 Harrop Ltd sold two assets in the year ended 31 December 2014.

(i)   Two acres of land which it had acquired for £20,000 in May 1986 were sold for £45,000 in October 2014.

(ii)   A storage unit which it had acquired for £80,000 in June 1995 was sold for £75,000 in October 2014.

Assume the relevant RPIs are as follows:

May 1986	97.85
June 1995	149.8
October 2014	257.6

What is the company's allowable loss for the year ended 31 December 2014, assuming it sold no other assets?

A   £70,260

B   £12,660

C   £5,000

D   £70,222

69 In the year ended 30 June 2014 Lompy Ltd had a tax adjusted trading profit of £800,200 and property income of £45,000. It also realised a chargeable gain of £25,000 and a capital loss of £80,000 on assets that were used for the purposes of the property business.

In the year ended 30 June 2013 it had a tax adjusted trading profit of £520,000 and chargeable gains of £9,000.

How much, if any, of the capital loss arising in the year ended 30 June 2014 is carried forward to the year ended 30 June 2015?

A   £55,000

B   £10,000

C   £46,000

D   £Nil

70   Rimbo Ltd had the following transactions in the shares of Profitable Ltd, an investment company:

		Number	£
April 1992	Purchase	25,000	33,000
June 2014	Sale	8,000	26,000

Assume the relevant RPIs are as follows:

April 1992	138.8
June 2014	256.0

What is the amount of the indexed cost available on the sale of the shares in June 2014?

A   £19,477

B   £10,560

C   £60,865

D   £27,865

71   On 1 October 2014 Smooth Ltd sold a factory for £850,000, which gives rise to a gain of £250,000.

On 1 November 2013 the company had purchased an immovable specialised machine for £900,000. The machine is expected to be used by the company for at least 25 years.

The company prepares accounts to 31 December.

The company wishes to defer the gain arising on the sale of the factory by making a rollover relief election in respect of the acquisition of the machine.

Which of the following statements is/are correct?

(i)   The £250,000 gain which could be deferred as a result of the acquisition of the machine will become chargeable on 1 October 2024.

(ii)   The company must make a rollover relief election by 31 December 2018.

A   Both of them

B   (i) only

C   (ii) only

D   Neither of them

INHERITANCE TAX

72 Mario made the following gifts during 2014/15:

(i) On 7 May 2014 he gifted 100,000 shares in Lahm Ltd to his wife. The shares have been valued at that date at £500,000

(ii) On 10 August 2014 he gifted 50,000 shares in Hummells Ltd to a discretionary trust. The shares have been valued at that date at £75,000

(iii) On 6 October 2014 he gifted £2,000 to his son on the occasion of his marriage.

(iv) On 9 February 2015 he gifted £300 to his daughter.

Which of the above gifts are exempt transfers for inheritance tax purposes?

A (i) and (ii)

B (ii) and (iii)

C (i) and (iii) only

D (i), (iii) and (iv)

73 Shola made the following lifetime gifts during the 2014/15 tax year. He has previously made no other gifts.

(i) 18 August 2014   Gross chargeable transfer into a trust of £200,000

(ii) 27 September 2014   £30,000 to his daughter

(iii) 29 December 2014   £275,000 into a trust – Shola will pay any tax arising

What is the lifetime inheritance tax liability in relation to the lifetime gift on 29 December 2014?

A £30,000

B £36,000

C £28,800

D £37,500

74 Christiano made the following gifts during his lifetime, and agreed to pay any inheritance tax that arose as a result of the second gift.

(i) a gift into a discretionary trust on 18 February 2013 – the gross chargeable transfer was £274,000

(ii) £150,000 into a discretionary trust on 20 May 2014

The nil rate band for 2012/13 was £325,000.

How much lifetime tax is paid by Christiano in respect of the gift on 20 May 2014?

A £24,000

B £Nil

C £23,250

D £24,750

75   Sully gave £210,000 to a discretionary trust on 1 May 2014.

The only other gifts that Sully has made are:

(i)   On 1 June 2013 £2,000 to his nephew on the occasion of his marriage

(ii)   On 1 August 2013 £200,000 into a discretionary trust.

For inheritance tax purposes, how much nil rate band is available to set against the gift on 1 May 2014?

A   £130,000

B   £125,000

C   £131,000

D   £129,000

76   Amir died on 1 February 2015. During his lifetime, he made two gifts:

(i)   On 30 November 2007 he gave £200,000 to his son

(ii)   On 15 June 2008 he gave £350,000 to his daughter

What is the chargeable amount of the above gifts (i.e. value before the deduction of the nil rate band) which becomes chargeable as a result of Amir's death?

	30 November 2007	**15 June 2008**
A	£194,000	£347,000
B	£Nil	£344,000
C	£194,000	£344,000
D	£Nil	£347,000

77   Edin died on 16 July 2014. He made one lifetime transfer on 10 November 2009 into a discretionary trust. He paid the lifetime tax of £52,250 and the gross chargeable transfer value of the gift was £586,250.

How much inheritance tax is due on the lifetime gift as a result of Edin's death?

A   £10,450

B   £62,700

C   £52,250

D   £104,500

78   Fabrice died on 20 January 2015. During his lifetime he made the following transfers:

(i)   20 February 2004   £300,000 to his son

(ii)   22 March 2007   £400,000 to a discretionary trust

(iii)   30 September 2013   half share in the family home, worth £250,000 to his daughter

(iv)   24 December 2014   £800,000 to his wife

On which gifts will inheritance tax be payable as a result of Fabrice's death?

A   (i), (ii) & (iii)

B   (iii) only

C   (ii) only

D   None of them

79   Fred died on 8 July 2014.

His estate consisted of the following assets:

- a house worth £545,000 on which there is an outstanding endowment mortgage of £145,000, and

- a life insurance policy with a market value of £300,000, however the proceeds paid to the executors from the policy were £350,000.

Under the terms of Fred's will £400,000 was left to his wife with the remainder of his estate to his son.

What is the gross chargeable value of Fred's death estate for inheritance tax purposes?

A   £350,000

B   £445,000

C   £895,000

D   £495,000

80   Olivier died on 22 November 2014.

His estate comprised the following assets and liabilities:

- A house worth £400,000 (with an outstanding repayment mortgage of £85,000)

- Chattels worth £70,000

- Cash in a NISA of £20,000

- An outstanding gambling debt of £500 owed to a friend.

He leaves his whole estate to his children.

What is the gross chargeable value of Olivier's death estate for inheritance tax purposes?

A   £404,500

B   £385,000

C   £405,000

D   £384,500

81 Joel dies on 20 December 2014, and leaves an estate worth £1,101,000 to his daughter.

During his lifetime, Joel made a gift to his son on 8 August 2013, with a gross chargeable transfer value of £124,000.

How much inheritance tax is payable on Joel's death estate?

A   £310,400

B   £180,000

C   £440,400

D   £360,000

82 Dominic owned 7,500 shares in Halder Ltd. On 1 July 2014 he gave 3,000 shares to his son.

The company has an issued share capital of 10,000 shares.

The values of different shareholdings in the shares on 1 July 2014 are as follows:

Holding	Value per share
Up to 25%	£5
26% to 50%	£8
51% to 74%	£13
75% or more	£20

What is the transfer of value for inheritance tax purposes on the gift of the shares to his son?

A   £28,000

B   £114,000

C   £24,000

D   £60,000

83 On 15 August 2010 Elvis transferred £500,000 into a discretionary trust.

On 15 August 2014 Elvis died leaving an estate worth £3,000,000 to his neighbour.

When is the tax due in respect of the chargeable lifetime transfer?

	Lifetime tax	Additional tax on death
A	30 April 2011	28 February 2015
B	28 February 2011	28 February 2015
C	15 February 2011	15 February 2015
D	30 April 2011	30 April 2015

84 Melvin died on 6 March 2015 leaving an estate worth £2,000,000. His estate included a holiday home in the UK worth £400,000 which he left to his sister. He left the rest of his estate to his daughter.

Who pays the tax and who suffers the inheritance tax payable on the estate?

	Pays tax	Suffers tax
A	Daughter	Daughter
B	Executors	Sister on home and daughter on residue
C	Executors	Daughter
D	Daughter	Executors

85 Which of the following statements are correct?

(i) An advantage of giving an appreciating asset away during lifetime is that the increase in value up to the date of death will not be subject to inheritance tax.

(ii) For capital gains tax purposes lifetime gifts are taxable but gifts on death are not.

(iii) On a lifetime gift taper relief will reduce the amount chargeable on death provided the donor survives for more than three years after the date of the gift.

A (ii) and (iii) only

B (i) and (iii) only

C (i) and (ii) only

D All of them

86 Willow died on 1 February 2008 with an estate valued at £280,000. She left £120,000 to her son and the remainder to her husband Stanley.

Stanley died on 1 March 2015 with an estate valued at £800,000 which he left to his son.

Neither Willow nor Stanley had made any lifetime gifts.

What is the nil rate band available to Stanley's estate assuming all beneficial elections are made?

The nil rate band in 2007/08 was £300,000.

A £325,000

B £505,000

C £346,667

D £520,000

CORPORATION TAX

CORPORATION TAX BASICS AND ADMINISTRATION

87 Which of these options identify when a chargeable accounting period will come to an end?

(i) At the end of a company's period of account

(ii) The end of the tax financial year

(iii) Twelve months after the beginning of the accounting period

(iv) The date the company begins or ceases to trade

A (i) and (ii) only

B All of them

C (i), (iii) and (iv) only

D (i) and (iii) only

88 In the year ended 31 March 2015, Easter Ltd had £100,000 of tax adjusted trading profits before capital allowances, interest receivable of £5,000 and dividends received from non-associated companies of £4,500. It also made charitable donations to Oxfam of £3,200. Capital allowances for the year were £2,000.

What are Easter Ltd's taxable total profits for the year ended 31 March 2015?

A   £103,800

B   £99,800

C   £104,800

D   £99,000

89 You have been given some work to complete, which includes a draft calculation of taxable total profits for a client, Trains Ltd.

Your manager has asked you to check the following calculation and make any corrections necessary.

Year ended 31 December 2014	£
Tax adjusted trading profit	50,000
Property business profit	6,000
Dividends received (net) from Track Ltd	5,400
Interest received	1,800
Taxable total profits	63,200

The amount of interest receivable for the year was £2,000. In addition the company realised a chargeable gain of £12,000.

The company owns 25% of the shares of Track Ltd.

What is the correct amount of taxable total profits for Trains Ltd for the year ended 31 December 2014?

A   £58,000

B   £70,000

C   £76,000

D   £69,800

90 In the year ended 31 March 2015 Biscuit Ltd had tax adjusted trading profits of £1,200,000. In addition, Biscuit Ltd had property income of £250,000, received dividends from non-associated companies of £52,200 and paid a qualifying donation to a national charity of £7,000.

What is the corporation tax liability of Biscuit Ltd for the year ended 31 March 2015?

A   £315,210

B   £303,018

C   £304,500

D   £303,030

91 Shed Ltd had a tax adjusted trading profit for the year ended 31 March 2015 of £250,000. The company also received dividends from non-associated companies of £405,000.

During the year the company sold a painting they had held as an investment for £110,000 realising a chargeable gain of £60,000. The directors had not been expecting the painting to sell for more than £50,000 so they decided to donate the excess proceeds of £60,000 to charity.

What is the corporation tax payable by Shed Ltd for the year ended 31 March 2015?

A £51,786

B £146,286

C £51,694

D £64,345

92 Custard Ltd started trading on 1 August 2014 and prepared its first set of accounts to 31 March 2015. The company's taxable total profits for the period to 31 March 2015 are £190,000.

Custard Ltd received dividends from non-associated companies of £27,000.

What is the corporation tax liability of Custard Ltd for the period ended 31 March 2015?

A £38,216

B £37,136

C £38,000

D £38,186

93 Bourbon Ltd prepares annual accounts to 31 January. In the year ended 31 January 2015, the company had the following income:

	£
Trading income	1,450,000
Franked investment income	55,000

What is the corporation tax liability of Bourbon Ltd for the year ended 31 January 2015?

A £304,500

B £309,333

C £309,166

D £321,067

94 In the year ended 30 June 2014, Chelsea Ltd made a trading profit per the accounts of £25,050.

Included in the accounts was £1,000 spent on a Christmas party for their 5 employees, £530 spent on entertaining clients and £2,000 for car lease payments.

The leased car has CO_2 emissions of 145g/km and has been leased by the company since 1 July 2013. During the year the car was used by one of the company's directors who drove 4,000 personal miles and 16,000 business miles in the car.

What is the tax adjusted trading profit for Chelsea Ltd for the year ended 30 June 2014?

A £25,980

B £26,880

C £25,580

D £25,880

95 During the year ended 31 March 2015, Swiss Ltd purchased a new car for £8,000, which has CO_2 emissions of 90g/km. It is used by an employee 30% of the time for private purposes and 70% of the time for business purposes.

On 1 April 2014, Swiss Ltd had a tax written down value brought forward on the main pool of £35,000.

What are the maximum capital allowances that Swiss Ltd could claim in the year ended 31 March 2015?

A £7,740

B £14,300

C £11,900

D £7,308

96 During the year ended 31 December 2014 Scotch Ltd rented out an unfurnished office building.

It was let from 1 August 2013 for an annual rent of £15,000, payable annually in advance, until 31 July 2014, when the tenant moved out. The office building was then unoccupied until 1 November 2014.

In August 2014 the company spent £500 replacing damaged fitted units in the kitchen area.

On 1 November 2014 a new tenant moved into the property. Under the new rental agreement annual rent of £8,000 is payable in advance on 1 November.

What is the property business profit to be included in Scotch Ltd's taxable total profits for the year ended 31 December 2014?

A £9,583

B £11,583

C £10,083

D £8,333

RELIEF FOR TRADING LOSSES

97 Toulon Ltd started trading on 1 April 2013. Its results for the first two accounting periods are as follows:

Year ended 31 March	2014	2015
	£	£
Tax adjusted trading (loss)/profit	(100,000)	20,000
Interest income	12,000	13,000
Chargeable gain	15,000	–
Qualifying charitable donations paid	(8,000)	(9,000)

What is the amount of loss carried forward at 31 March 2015 assuming the company makes a current year loss relief claim?

A £73,000

B £61,000

C £53,000

D £40,000

98 Hobart Ltd has had the following recent results:

Year ended 31 March	2014	2015
	£	£
Tax adjusted trading profit/(loss)	40,000	(50,000)
Property business profits	15,000	17,000
Chargeable gain	–	4,000
Qualifying charitable donations paid	(6,000)	(14,000)

What are Hobart Ltd's taxable total profits, if any, in the year ended 31 March 2014 assuming the company makes a claim to carry back the loss to y/e 31 March 2014?

A £20,000

B £NII

C £6,000

D £9,000

99 Tasman Ltd has had the following recent results:

	Year ended 30 June 2013	9 months ended 30 June 2014	Year ended 31 March 2015
	£	£	£
Tax adjusted trading profit/(loss)	40,000	22,000	(60,000)
Interest income	4,000	3,000	5,000

What is the amount of loss, if any, which is available to carry forward as at 31 March 2015 assuming Tasman Ltd claims to use the trading loss as soon as possible?

A £Nil

B £30,000

C £19,000

D £28,000

100 Darwin Ltd ceased to trade on 31 March 2015. Its recent results have been as follows:

Year ended	31.3.2012	31.3.2013	31.3.2014	31.3.2015
	£	£	£	£
Tax adjusted trading profit/(loss)	45,000	32,000	10,000	(100,000)
Chargeable gain	5,000	–	9,000	14,000

What are the company's taxable total profits for the year ended 31 March 2012 assuming the company makes a terminal loss relief claim?

A   £Nil

B   £6,000

C   £1,000

D   £15,000

101 Adelaide Ltd has had the following recent results:

Year ended 31 March	2013	2014	2015
	£	£	£
Tax adjusted trading profit	16,000	20,000	25,000
Property business profit/(loss)	5,000	(65,000)	10,000
Qualifying charitable donations paid	(800)	(900)	(1,100)

What is the amount of the unused property business loss as at 31 March 2015?

A   £50,000

B   £10,000

C   £12,000

D   £55,000

WITH GROUP ASPECTS

102 Telephone Ltd prepares accounts to 31 March each year. As at 1 April 2014 Telephone Ltd owned 62% of Desk Ltd, 75% of Chair Ltd, 55% of Table Ltd (a dormant company) and 100% of Window Inc (resident overseas). Telephone Ltd acquired 60% of the share capital of Curtain Ltd on 1 January 2015.

What is the total number of associated companies for the purposes of calculating the corporation tax liability of Telephone Ltd for the year ended 31 March 2015?

A   2

B   3

C   4

D   5

103 Novak Ltd owns 80% of Roger Ltd, 60% of Rafael Ltd and 55% of Andy Ltd which is a dormant company.

In 2015 the company changed its year end and drew up a seven month set of accounts to 31 March 2015.

Which of the following are the correct corporation tax profits limits used to determine the tax rate for Novak Ltd for the seven month period to 31 March 2015?

A   £75,000 and £375,000

B   £43,750 and £218,750

C   £100,000 and £500,000

D   £58,333 and £291,667

104 Computer Ltd owns 75% of Chair Ltd, 60% of Bin Ltd and 100% of Paper Inc. Paper Inc owns 75% of Cardboard Ltd. All companies are resident in the UK except Paper Inc which is resident in the US.

Computer Ltd suffered a trading loss in the year ending 31 March 2015.

Which companies could Computer Ltd's trading loss be surrendered to?

A   Chair Ltd, Paper Inc and Cardboard Ltd only

B   Chair Ltd, Bin Ltd, Paper Ltd and Cardboard Ltd

C   Chair Ltd and Cardboard Ltd only

D   Chair Ltd only

105 Battery Ltd owns 100% of Watch Ltd. During the year ended 31 March 2015 Battery Ltd had a trading loss of £100,000. During the 6 month period ended 30 June 2015 Watch Ltd had trading income of £50,000 and property income of £30,000.

What is the maximum loss that Watch Ltd can claim from Battery Ltd for the period ended 30 June 2015?

A   £50,000

B   £25,000

C   £40,000

D   £80,000

106 Brazil Ltd owns 100% of Germany Ltd and 75% of Holland Ltd. Germany Ltd owns 65% of Belgium Ltd and Holland owns 75% of Russia Ltd.

Which companies form a capital gains group for corporation tax purposes?

A   Brazil Ltd, Germany Ltd and Holland Ltd

B   Brazil Ltd, Germany Ltd, Holland Ltd, Belgium Ltd and Russia Ltd

C   Brazil Ltd, Germany Ltd, Holland Ltd and Russia Ltd

D   Brazil Ltd, Germany Ltd, Holland Ltd and Belgium Ltd

107   Apple Ltd owns 75% of Grape Ltd. In the year ended 31 March 2015 Apple Ltd transferred a property with a market value of £300,000 to Grape Ltd. The original cost of the asset was £100,000 and the indexation allowance to the date of transfer was £50,000.

What is the deemed acquisition cost for chargeable gains purposes for Grape Ltd?

A   £150,000

B   £100,000

C   £Nil

D   £300,000

108   Hound Ltd started to trade on 1 June 2014 and prepared its first set of accounts for the 15 month period to 31 August 2015.

On which date(s) must Hound Ltd submit a corporation tax return in respect of the 15 month period of account?

A   1 March 2016 and 1 June 2016

B   31 August 2016 only

C   31 May 2015 and 31 August 2016

D   31 May 2015 only

109   The following companies all pay corporation tax at the small profits rate.

(i)   W Ltd – prepared accounts for the year ended 30 June 2014

(ii)   X Ltd – prepared accounts for the 15 months ended 30 September 2014

(iii)   Y Ltd – prepared accounts for the year ended 31 March 2014

(iv)   Z Ltd – prepared accounts for the 8 months to 30 June 2014

Which of the above companies have a due date in respect of corporation tax of 1 April 2015?

A   W Ltd, X Ltd and Z Ltd only

B   W Ltd and Z Ltd only

C   All of them

D   X Ltd and Y Ltd only

110   Gerber Ltd has been a large company for the purposes of paying its corporation tax liability for a number of years.

In 2014 it changed its accounting date and prepared an 8 month set of accounts to 31 December 2014.

When is the final corporation tax instalment in respect of the 8 month accounting period ended 31 December 2014 due?

A   14 February 2015

B   14 April 2015

C   14 May 2015

D   14 August 2015

VALUE ADDED TAX

111   Fred, is a sole trader and has made the following sales, all of which are standard rated:

	£
January 2015	2,000
February 2015	3,500
March 2015	4,000
April 2015	3,200
May 2015	1,400
June 2015	90,000
July 2015	5,000
August 2015	4,000

All of the sales in June 2015 relate to an order which was received on 1 June 2015 for goods to be delivered by 30 June 2015.

When must Fred start charging VAT to his customers?

A   1 June 2015

B   1 July 2015

C   30 June 2015

D   1 August 2015

112   Layla started trading on 4 January 2014.

Taxable supplies for 2014 are as follows:

3 months to 31 March	£3,000 per month
3 months to 30 June	£9,000 per month
3 months to 30 September	£30,000 per month
3 months to 31 December	£50,000 per month

What is the effective date of registration for VAT, assuming that Layla waits until her turnover exceeds the registration limit before registering?

A   1 February 2015

B   1 October 2014

C   1 July 2014

D   1 September 2014

113   Betty, a retailer, decides to voluntarily register for VAT.

Which of the following statements is true?

A   Betty can reclaim VAT on a car that she purchased six months ago, which she uses for both private and business purposes

B   Betty cannot reclaim input VAT on the petrol purchased for the car prior to her VAT registration

C   Betty can reclaim input VAT on a van purchased for the business two years ago

D   Betty can reclaim input VAT on accountancy services she purchased one year ago in connection with setting up the business

114 Fergus owns shares in a number of companies as set out below.

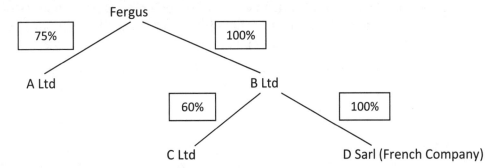

D Sarl's only place of business is in France.

Which of the above companies can be in a VAT group?

A   All of them

B   A only

C   B and D only

D   A, B, and C only

115 Vikram ceased trading on 17 June 2014.

By what date should he have notified HM Revenue & Customs that he had ceased to make taxable supplies?

A   17 June 2014

B   16 July 2014

C   30 July 2014

D   30 June 2014

116 Padma Ltd received an order for a handbag on 20 October 2014. The handbag was delivered to the customer on 20 December 2014 and Padma Ltd sent the invoice for £1,000 on 15 January 2015, which the customer paid on 5 February 2015.

What is the tax point of the transaction for VAT?

A   20 October 2014

B   20 December 2014

C   15 January 2015

D   5 February 2015

117 Barney buys a machine on 25 July 2014 which is advertised in the manufacturer's brochure for sale at £2,000 plus VAT. He manages to negotiate a reduction in price of 10% and the manufacturer also offers him a further discount of 5% on the discounted price if he pays within 30 days. As Barney is short of funds he doesn't pay until 31 August 2014.

How much VAT will Barney be charged on the invoice for the machine?

A   £342

B   £400

C   £360

D   £285

118 West Ltd is registered for VAT and makes standard rated supplies.

The company incurs the following costs:

(i)   £650 (VAT inclusive) on entertaining new suppliers based in France

(ii)   £3,000 (VAT inclusive) on car leasing costs. The car has CO_2 emission of 120 g/km and is used by a director for both private (20% of the time) and business purposes.

How much input VAT can the company recover on the above costs?

A   £358

B   £250

C   £108

D   £400

119 Tobias is VAT registered and only makes standard rated supplies.

In the quarter to 31 March 2015 he had the following transactions:

(i)   Sales of £30,000 and purchases of goods for resale of £15,000. Both figures are VAT inclusive.

(ii)   On 31 March 2015 he wrote off two irrecoverable debts in his VAT account. The first for £800 (VAT inclusive) was due for payment on 1 June 2014 and despite being chased has still not been paid. The second for £1,000 (VAT inclusive) relates to a company that Tobias has recently been informed has gone into liquidation. The debt was due for payment on 1 December 2014.

(iii) He gave samples of his products to a potential customer which he would normally sell for £100 (VAT exclusive).

How much VAT is payable by Tobias for the quarter ended 31 March 2015 assuming he makes all available claims?

A   £2,187

B   £2,387

C   £2,200

D   £2,367

120 Blessing is VAT registered.

In the quarter to 31 March 2015 she had the following transactions:

(i) Standard rated supplies of £40,000 and zero rated supplies of £8,000. Blessing offers a 5% discount to customers who pay their invoices with 10 days. In the quarter 40% of her customers took advantage of the early settlement discount.

(ii) Standard rated purchases and expenses of £22,000 (VAT inclusive). The expenses included the total cost of fuel for her car of £1,200 (VAT inclusive) which she uses 20% for private purposes. The relevant VAT scale charge for the car is £485.

How much VAT is payable by Blessing for the quarter ended 31 March 2015 assuming he makes all available claims?

A   £4,054

B   £4,254

C   £4,014

D   £4,030

121 **A less detailed VAT invoice can be provided when the consideration for the supply is less than how much?**

A   £100

B   £200

C   £250

D   £500

122 **Which of the following is not required on a less detailed VAT invoice?**

A   Date of supply

B   Description of goods and services

C   Rate of VAT in force at time

D   Amount of VAT payable

123 Having always filed VAT returns on time, Chimney Ltd's VAT return for the quarter ended 31 October 2014 was submitted on 13 December 2014 along with the VAT due. For the quarter ended 31 January 2015 the return and VAT of £26,000 was filed on 23 March 2015.

What are the VAT consequences when the 31 January 2015 VAT return is filed late?

A   A surcharge liability period will run for the 12 months until 31 January 2016 but no penalty will be charged

B   A surcharge liability period will run for the 12 months until 31 January 2016 and a penalty of £520 will be charged

C   A surcharge liability period will run for the 12 months until 23 March 2015 but no penalty will be charged

D   A surcharge liability period will run for the 12 months until 23 March 2015 and a penalty of £520 will be charged

124 For the VAT quarter ended 30 June 2014 Beach Ltd has a taxable turnover of £380,000. It subsequently finds it has under declared output tax of £8,000 on its VAT return for that quarter.

What of the following statements is correct?

A   Beach Ltd can correct the error on the next VAT return and will be charged a penalty for an incorrect VAT return only

B   Beach Ltd can correct the error on the next VAT return and will be charged a penalty for an incorrect return and default interest

C   Beach Ltd must separately notify HM Revenue & Customs of the error and will be charged a penalty for an incorrect return only

D   Beach Ltd must separately notify HM Revenue & Customs of the error and will be charged a penalty for an incorrect return and default interest

125 Which of the following statements concerning the cash accounting scheme are correct?

(i)   Input tax cannot be claimed until the invoice is paid which delays recovery of input VAT.

(ii)   Traders using the scheme do not have to pay output VAT to HMRC until they receive it from customers.

(iii)   To join the scheme the trader's expected taxable turnover (excluding VAT) for the next twelve months must not exceed £150,000.

(iv)   The cash accounting scheme cannot be used where a trader issues an invoice in advance of supplying goods.

A   All of them

B   (i) and (ii) only

C   (ii) and (iii) only

D   (i), (ii) and (iv) only

126 Jano operates the annual accounting scheme. In the year ended 30 September 2013 he had a VAT liability of £3,600. In his year ended 30 September 2014 he estimated his VAT liability to be £4,115.

What is the amount of his balancing payment for the VAT year to 30 September 2014?

A   £875

B   £515

C   £411

D   £Nil

127 Petr has standard rated sales of £80,000 excluding VAT, zero-rated sales of £15,000 and exempt sales of £10,000 for the quarter ended 30 June 2014. He has standard rated expenses including VAT of £8,400. Petr uses the flat rate scheme for VAT and the flat rate for his business is 13%.

What is Petr's VAT liability for the quarter ended 30 June 2014?

A   £11,388

B   £13,650

C   £14,638

D   £15,730

128 A UK VAT registered trader making standard rated supplies purchased goods worth £10,000 (VAT exclusive) from a VAT registered trader in France (an EU country). The goods would be classed as standard rated if they were supplied in the UK. The standard rate in France is 5%.

What is the net effect on the VAT position of the UK trader?

A   £Nil

B   £2,000 to pay to HM Revenue & Customs

C   £2,000 to reclaim from HM Revenue & Customs

D   £500 to pay to HM Revenue & Customs

Section 2

PRACTICE SECTION B QUESTIONS

INCOME TAX AND NATIONAL INSURANCE

Tutorial note

Income tax will be the focus of a 15 mark Section B question.

You should also expect Income tax to be tested in both the Section A multiple choice questions and potentially in the Section B 10 mark questions.

You should expect NIC to be tested in both the Section A multiple choice questions and also in the Section B questions. There is however no set minimum or maximum number of marks for NIC.

INCOME TAX BASICS AND EMPLOYMENT INCOME

1   SALLY BURTON (ADAPTED) *Online question assistance*

Sally was born on 6 February 1948. The following information is available for 2014/15:

Sally Burton

(1)   Sally is employed by Burton plc as a part time manager working 3 days a week in one of the company's nationwide chain of retail clothing shops. She is paid a gross annual salary of £12,000 from which PAYE of £2,400 was deducted by her employer.

(2)   On 6 June 2014 Sally was provided with a petrol powered motor car which has a list price of £17,118. Sally made a capital contribution of £2,000 towards the cost of the motor car when it was first provided. The official CO_2 emission rate for the motor car is 172 grams per kilometre. Burton plc paid for all of the motor car's maintenance costs of £2,400 during 2014/15 as well as car parking costing £1,200. Her employer did not provide any fuel for private journeys.

(3)   Burton plc has provided Sally with living accommodation since 2013. The property was purchased in 2006 for £105,000, and was valued at £120,000 when first provided to Sally. It has an annual value of £1,632. Sally was not required by her job to live in the accommodation provided by her employer. Sally was required to reimburse her employer £75 each month for the use of the accommodation.

(4)   In addition to her employment income, Sally received interest of £1,000 on the maturity of a NS&I savings certificate during the tax year 2014/15. This was the actual cash amount received.

(5)   During 2014/15 Sally received building society interest of £1,800. This was the actual cash amount received.

(6)   On 5 April 2015 Sally granted a 15 year lease on a property she owns in return for a premium of £10,680.

Required:

Calculate Sally's income tax payable for 2014/15.   **(15 marks)**

 Online question assistance

2   VIGOROUS PLC (ADAPTED)

Vigorous plc runs a health club. The company has three employees who received benefits during 2014/15, and it therefore needs to prepare forms P11D for them. Each of the three employees is paid an annual salary of £60,000.

The following information is relevant:

Andrea Lean

(1)   Andrea was employed by Vigorous plc throughout 2014/15.

(2)   Throughout 2014/15 Vigorous plc provided Andrea with a petrol powered company motor car with a list price of £19,400. The official CO_2 emission rate for the motor car is 250 grams per kilometre. Vigorous plc paid for all of the motor car's running costs of £6,200 during 2014/15, including petrol used for private journeys. During 2014/15 Andrea paid £150 per month to Vigorous plc for the private use of the motor car.

(3)   Vigorous plc has provided Andrea with living accommodation since 1 November 2012. The property was purchased on 1 January 2010 for £130,000. The company spent £14,000 improving the property during March 2011, and a further £8,000 was spent on improvements during May 2014.

The value of the property on 1 November 2012 was £170,000, and it has an annual value of £7,000. The furniture in the property cost £6,000 during November 2012. Andrea personally pays for the annual running costs of the property amounting to £4,000.

Ben Slim

(1)   Ben commenced employment with Vigorous plc on 1 July 2014.

(2)   On 1 July 2014 Vigorous plc provided Ben with an interest free loan of £120,000 so that he could purchase a new main residence. He repaid £20,000 of the loan on 1 December 2014.

(3)   During 2014/15 Vigorous plc paid £9,300 towards the cost of Ben's relocation. His previous main residence was 125 miles from his place of employment with the company. The £9,300 covered the cost of disposing of Ben's old property and of acquiring his new property.

(4)   On 1 July 2014 Ben joined the company's childcare scheme which provides employees with childcare vouchers of £60 per week to buy care from an approved child carer. Ben received vouchers to provide care for 36 weeks in 2014/15.

Chai Trim

(1)   Chai was employed by Vigorous plc throughout 2014/15.

(2)   During 2014/15 Vigorous plc provided Chai with a two-year old company van, which was available for private use. The van was unavailable during the period 1 August to 30 September 2014. Chai paid for fuel for all private journeys.

(3)   Vigorous plc has provided Chai with a television for her personal use since 6 April 2012. The television cost Vigorous plc £800 in April 2012. On 6 April 2014 the company sold the television to Chai for £150, although its market value on that date was £250.

(4)   Throughout 2014/15 Vigorous plc provided Chai with free membership of its health club. The normal annual cost of membership is £800. This figure is made up of direct costs of £150, fixed overhead costs of £400 and profit of £250. The budgeted membership for the year has been exceeded, but the health club has surplus capacity.

Required:

(a)   **Calculate the benefit figures that Vigorous plc will have to include on the forms P11D for Andrea, Ben, and Chai for 2014/15.** **(12 marks)**

(b)   **Explain how the income tax liability in respect of benefits is collected by HM Revenue & Customs.** **(3 marks)**

(Total: 15 marks)

3   **ALI PATEL (ADAPTED)**   *Walk in the footsteps of a top tutor*

You should assume that today's date is 15 March 2014.

Ali Patel, who was born on 23 January 1978, has been employed by Box plc since 1 January 2011, and is currently paid an annual salary of £29,000. On 6 April 2014 Ali is to be temporarily relocated for a period of 12 months from Box plc's head office to one of its branch offices. He has been offered two alternative remuneration packages:

First remuneration package

(1)   Ali will continue to live near Box plc's head office, and will commute on a daily basis to the branch office using his private motor car.

(2)   He will be paid additional salary of £500 per month.

(3)   Box plc will pay Ali an allowance of 38 pence per mile for the 1,600 miles that Ali will drive each month commuting to the branch office.

Ali's additional cost of commuting for 2014/15 will be £1,800.

Second remuneration package

(1)   Box plc will provide Ali with rent-free living accommodation near the branch office.

(2)   The property will be rented by Box plc at a cost of £800 per month. The annual value of the property is £4,600.

(3)   Ali will rent out his main residence near Box plc's head office, and this will result in property business income of £6,000 for 2014/15.

Required:

(a) Calculate Ali's income tax liability and Class 1 national insurance contributions for 2014/15, if he:

   (i) accepts the first remuneration package offered by Box plc; (6 marks)

   (ii) accepts the second remuneration package offered by Box plc. (5 marks)

(b) Advise Ali as to which remuneration package is the most beneficial from a financial perspective.

   Your answer should be supported by a calculation of the amount of income, net of all costs including income tax and Class 1 national insurance contributions, which he would receive for 2014/15 under each alternative. (4 marks)

(Total: 15 marks)

4 **FLICK PICK (ADAPTED)** *Walk in the footsteps of a top tutor*

 Timed question with Online tutor debrief

Flick Pick was born on 29 April 1990. On 6 April 2014 she commenced employment with 3D Ltd as a film critic and was employed throughout 2014/15. On 1 January 2015 she commenced in partnership with Art Reel running a small cinema, preparing accounts to 30 April. The following information is available for the tax year 2014/15:

Employment

(1) During the tax year 2014/15 Flick was paid a gross annual salary of £23,700.

(2) Throughout the tax year 2014/15 3D Ltd provided Flick with living accommodation. The company had purchased the property in 2005 for £89,000, and it was valued at £144,000 on 6 April 2014. The annual value of the property is £4,600. The property was furnished by 3D Ltd during March 2014 at a cost of £9,400.

Partnership

(1) The partnership's tax adjusted trading profit for the four-month period ended 30 April 2015 is £29,700. This figure is before taking account of capital allowances.

(2) The only item of plant and machinery owned by the partnership is a motor car that cost £15,000 on 1 February 2015. The motor car has a CO_2 emission rate of 150 grams per kilometre. It is used by Art, and 40% of the mileage is for private journeys.

(3) Profits are shared 40% to Flick and 60% to Art. This is after paying an annual salary of £6,000 to Art.

Property income

(1) Flick owns a freehold house which is let out furnished. The property was let throughout the tax year 2014/15 at a monthly rent of £660.

(2) During the tax year 2014/15 Flick paid council tax of £1,320 in respect of the property, and also spent £2,560 on replacing damaged furniture.

(3) Flick claims the wear and tear allowance.

Required:

(a)   Calculate Flick Pick's taxable income for the tax year 2014/15.   **(11 marks)**

(b)   List the advantages and disadvantages for the partnership of choosing 30 April as its accounting date rather than 5 April.   **(4 marks)**

(Total: 15 marks)

 Calculate your allowed time, allocate the time to the separate parts...................

5   JOE JONES (ADAPTED) *Walk in the footsteps of a top tutor*

On 31 December 2014 Joe Jones resigned as an employee of Firstly plc, and on 1 January 2015 commenced employment with Secondly plc. Joe was employed by both companies as a financial analyst.

The following information is available for the tax year 2014/15:

Employment with Firstly plc

(1)   From 6 April 2014 to 31 December 2014 Joe was paid a salary of £12,400 per month. In addition to his salary, Joe was paid a bonus of £12,000 on 12 May 2014. He had become entitled to this bonus on 22 March 2014.

(2)   Joe contributed 6% of his monthly gross salary of £12,400 into Firstly plc's HM Revenue and Customs' registered occupational pension scheme.

(3)   During the period 6 April 2014 to 31 December 2014 Firstly plc paid gym membership fees of £1,050 for Joe.

Employment with Secondly plc

(1)   From 1 January 2015 to 5 April 2015 Joe was paid a salary of £16,200 per month.

(2)   During the period 1 January 2015 to 5 April 2015 Joe contributed a total of £3,000 (gross) into a personal pension scheme.

(3)   During the period 1 January 2015 to 5 April 2015 Joe used Secondly plc's company gym which is only open to employees of the company. The cost to Secondly plc of providing this benefit to Joe was £340.

(4)   During the period 1 January 2015 to 5 April 2015 Secondly plc provided Joe with a mobile telephone costing £560. The company paid for all of Joe's business and private telephone calls.

Joe was born on 4 October 1980.

Required:

(a)   Calculate Joe Jones' taxable income for the tax year 2014/15.   **(7 marks)**

(b)   (i)   For each of the PAYE forms P45, P60 and P11D, briefly describe the circumstances in which the form will be completed, state who will provide it, the information to be included, and the dates by which they should have been provided to Joe Jones for the tax year 2014/15.   **(6 marks)**

Your answer should be confined to the details that are relevant to Joe Jones.

(ii)   State how and when Secondly plc must submit information to HM Revenue & Customs (HMRC) regarding Joe's income tax and NIC on his employment income and state the date by which Secondly plc must pay the income tax and NIC due in respect of Joe to HMRC.

Secondly plc makes all payments of tax electronically.   **(2 marks)**

(Total: 15 marks)

6   SAMMI SMITH (ADAPTED) *Walk in the footsteps of a top tutor*

You should assume that today's date is 20 March 2014.

Sammi Smith is a director of Smark Ltd. The company has given her the choice of being provided with a leased company motor car or alternatively being paid additional director's remuneration and then privately leasing the same motor car herself.

Company motor car

The motor car will be provided throughout the tax year 2014/15, and will be leased by Smark Ltd at an annual cost of £26,540. The motor car will be petrol powered, will have a list price of £81,858, and will have an official CO_2 emission rate of 305 grams per kilometre.

The lease payments will cover all the costs of running the motor car except for fuel. Smark Ltd will not provide Sammi with any fuel for private journeys.

Additional director's remuneration

As an alternative to having a company motor car, Sammi will be paid additional gross director's remuneration of £26,000 during the tax year 2014/15. She will then privately lease the motor car at an annual cost of £26,540.

Other information

The amount of business journeys that will be driven by Sammi will be immaterial and can therefore be ignored.

Sammi's current annual director's remuneration is just in excess of £45,000. Smark Ltd prepares its accounts to 5 April, and pays corporation tax at the main rate of 21%. The lease of the motor car will commence on 6 April 2014.

Required:

(a)   Advise Sammi Smith of the income tax and national insurance contribution implications for the tax year 2014/15 if she

(1)   is provided with the company motor car, and

(2)   receives additional director's remuneration of £26,000.   **(5 marks)**

(b)   Advise Smark Ltd of the corporation tax and national insurance contribution implications for the year ended 5 April 2015 if the company

(1)   provides Sammi Smith with the company motor car, and

(2)   pays Sammi Smith additional director's remuneration of £26,000.

You should ignore value added tax (VAT).   **(5 marks)**

(c)   Determine which of the two alternatives is the most beneficial from each of the respective points of view of Sammi Smith and Smark Ltd.   **(5 marks)**

(Total: 15 marks)

7   PHILIP & CHARLES (ADAPTED) *Walk in the footsteps of a top tutor*

Philip and Charles are father and son. The following information is available for the tax year 2014/15:

Philip Wind

Philip was born on 1 October 1935. During the tax year 2014/15 he received pensions of £13,500.

In addition to his pension income, Philip received building society interest of £11,680 during the tax year 2014/15. This was the actual cash amount received.

Charles Wind

Charles was born on 30 March 1965. He is self-employed as an architect, and his tax adjusted trading profit for the year ended 31 December 2014 was £109,400.

During the tax year 2014/15 Charles made a gift aid donation of £800 (gross) to a national charity.

Required:

(a)   Calculate the respective income tax liabilities for the tax year 2014/15 of:

    (i)   Philip Wind   **(4 marks)**

    (ii)   Charles Wind   **(4 marks)**

(b)   Calculate the respective national insurance contributions, if any, suffered by Philip and Charles for the tax year 2014/15.   **(4 marks)**

(c)   Explain to Charles, with supporting calculations, how his income tax liabilities for the tax year 2014/15 would have been reduced if he had contributed £8,600 (gross) into a personal pension scheme during the tax year 2014/15.   **(3 marks)**

(Total: 15 marks)

8   LETICIA STONE *Walk in the footsteps of a top tutor*

Leticia Stone owns three properties which are let out. The following information relates to the tax year 2014/15:

Property one

This is a freehold house that qualifies as a trade under the furnished holiday letting rules. Leticia purchased this property on 1 July 2014 for £282,000. The purchase price included £4,600 for furniture and kitchen equipment.

Leticia borrowed £220,000 to purchase this property. During the period 1 July 2014 to 5 April 2015 she made loan repayments totalling £14,300, of which £12,700 was in respect of loan interest.

The property was let for 22 weeks at £425 per week during the period 1 July 2014 to 5 April 2015.

Due to a fire, £12,200 was spent on replacing the roof of the house during March 2015. Only £10,900 of this was paid for by Leticia's property insurance.

During the tax year 2014/15 Leticia drove 1,170 miles in her motor car in respect of the furnished holiday letting business. She uses HM Revenue and Customs' authorised mileage rates to calculate her expense deduction. The mileage was for the following purposes:

	Miles
Purchase of property	160
Running the business on a weekly basis	880
Property repairs	130

The other expenditure on this property for the period 1 July 2014 to 5 April 2015 amounted to £3,770, and this is all allowable.

Property two

This is a leasehold shop that is let out unfurnished. The property was acquired on 1 May 2014 and was immediately let to a tenant, with Leticia receiving a premium of £45,000 for the grant of a five-year lease. During the period 1 May 2014 to 5 April 2015 Leticia received four quarterly rental payments of £2,160 per quarter, payable in advance.

Leticia pays a monthly rent of £1,360 for this property, but did not pay a premium when she acquired it.

Property three

This is a freehold house that is let out unfurnished. The property was let from 6 April 2014 to 31 January 2015 at a monthly rent of £580. On 31 January 2015 the tenant left, owing three months' rent. Leticia recovered two months of the outstanding rent by retaining the tenant's security deposit, but was unable to recover the balance.

On 1 March 2015 a new tenant paid Leticia a security deposit of £1,200, being two months' rent, although the new tenancy did not commence until 15 April 2015.

During the tax year 2014/15 Leticia paid loan interest of £9,100 in respect of a loan that was taken out to purchase this property.

Other expenditure

The other expenditure on properties two and three for the tax year 2014/15 amounted to £36,240, and this is all allowable.

Furnished room

During the tax year 2014/15 Leticia rented out one furnished room of her main residence. During the year she received rent of £3,170, and incurred allowable expenditure of £4,840 in respect of the room. Leticia always uses the most favourable basis as regards the tax treatment of the furnished room.

Required:

(a) Calculate Leticia Stone's property business loss for the tax year 2014/15.

Your answer should separately identify the furnished holiday letting loss.

(13 marks)

(b) Advise Leticia Stone as to the possible ways in which her property business loss for the tax year 2014/15 can be relieved. **(2 marks)**

(Total: 15 marks)

9   KIM BAXTER (ADAPTED) *Walk in the footsteps of a top tutor*

(1)   Kim, born on 1 December 1963, is employed as a sales person by Sharp-Suit plc, a clothing manufacturing company. During the tax year 2014/15 she was paid a gross annual salary of £21,689.

(2)   On 1 June 2014 Sharp-Suit plc provided Kim with an interest free loan of £14,250 so that she could purchase a new motor car.

(3)   During the period from 1 June 2014 to 5 April 2015 Kim used her private motor car for business and private purposes. She received no reimbursement from Sharp-Suit plc for any of the expenditure incurred.

Kim's mileage during this period included the following:

	Miles
Normal daily travel between home and permanent workplace	3,400
Travel between permanent workplace and Sharp-Suit plc's customers	11,200
Travel between home and a temporary workplace for one month	1,300

(4)   During the tax year 2014/15 Kim paid interest of £140 (gross) on a personal loan taken out on 1 January 2014 to purchase a laptop computer for use in her employment with Sharp-Suit plc. She also made a charitable contribution of £800 under the Gift Aid scheme, which she does every year.

Kim's husband Richard, born on 13 March 1960, stays at home to look after their children while Kim is at work. Richard has no income.

Building society deposit account

Kim has savings of £12,500 in a building society deposit account.

During the tax year 2014/15 Kim received building society interest totalling £600 from this account. This was the actual cash amount received.

Required:

(a)   Calculate Kim's income tax liability for the tax year 2014/15.

You should ignore any capital allowances that Kim might be entitled to.   **(6 marks)**

(b)   Explain to Kim how her overall income tax liability could be reduced if she were to either:

(i)   transfer her building society deposit account into a New Individual Savings Account (NISA); or   **(2 marks)**

(ii)   transfer her building society deposit account to Richard.   **(2 marks)**

Assume that 2014/15 rates and allowances continue to apply.

(Total: 10 marks)

INCOME TAX BASICS AND INCOME FROM SELF-EMPLOYMENT

10   CAROL COURIER (ADAPTED)

For the purposes of this question you should assume that today's date is 15 March 2014.

Carol Courier was born on 13 March 1975. She is employed by Quick-Speed plc as a delivery driver, and is paid a salary of £37,500 p.a. She contributes 5% of her gross salary into Quick-Speed plc's HM Revenue & Customs registered occupational pension scheme.

As an alternative to being employed, Quick-Speed plc have offered Carol the opportunity to provide delivery services to the company on a self-employed basis.

The details of the proposed arrangement for the year ended 5 April 2015 are as follows:

(1)   Carol will commence being self-employed on 6 April 2014.

(2)   Her income from Quick-Speed plc is expected to be £43,500.

(3)   Carol will also provide delivery services to other clients. Her income from these contracts is expected to be £8,000.

(4)   Carol will lease a delivery van and 100% of the mileage will be for business purposes. The cost of leasing and running the van will be £4,400.

(5)   When she is unavailable Carol will have to provide a replacement driver to deliver for Quick-Speed plc. This will cost her £2,800.

(6)   Carol will contribute £3,000 (gross) into a personal pension scheme during 2014/15. This will provide her with the same benefits as the occupational pension scheme provided by Quick-Speed plc.

Required:

(a)   Assuming that Carol does not accept the offer from Quick-Speed plc and continues to be employed by the company, calculate her income tax and Class 1 NIC liability for 2014/15. **(5 marks)**

(b)   Assuming that Carol accepts the offer to provide delivery services to Quick-Speed plc on a self-employed basis from 6 April 2014 onwards, calculate her Income tax, Class 2 NIC and Class 4 NIC liability for 2014/15. **(6 marks)**

(c)   Advise Carol as to whether it will be beneficial to accept the offer to provide delivery services to Quick-Speed plc on a self-employed basis.

Your answer should be supported by a calculation of the amount by which Carol's income for 2014/15 (net of outgoings, income tax and NIC) will increase or decrease if she accepts the offer. **(4 marks)**

(Total: 15 marks)

11   IDRIS WILLIAMS   *Walk in the footsteps of a top tutor*

(a)   Idris Williams has opened a small bed and breakfast and is considering whether to prepare his accounts to 5 April or 30 June.

Required:

Advise Idris of the advantages for tax purposes of choosing an accounting date of either 5 April or 30 June. **(4 marks)**

(b)   Idris commenced trade on 6 April 2014 and has decided to prepare his first set of accounts to 5 April 2015.

The following information is available regarding his statement of profit and loss for the first year of trading:

	Notes	£	£
Revenue	(1)		49,910
Less: Food, utilities and other household goods	(2)		(17,660)
			————
Gross profit			32,250
Expenses:			
Depreciation	(3)	1,250	
Motor expenses	(4)	9,340	
Other expenses	(5)	1,485	
		———	(12,075)
			————
Net profit			20,175
			————

Notes:

(1)   Revenue includes £10,275 which is still receivable at 5 April 2015.

(2)   Idris paid for 95% of his purchases by 5 April 2015 and the remainder in May 2015. There is no closing inventory at 5 April 2015.

Idris is also living in part of the bed and breakfast and £4,500 of the purchases relate to Idris's personal use.

(3)   The depreciation charge relates to furniture bought in the period for £3,500 and a motor car purchased on 6 April 2014 for £9,000. The motor car has CO_2 emissions of 105 g/km.

(4)   The motor expenses of £9,340 relate to Idris' car and in the period he drove 13,000 business miles and 20,000 miles in total.

(5)   The other expenses are all allowable for tax purposes. £400 of these expenses were unpaid at 6 April 2015.

The cash basis private use adjustment for one occupant in a business premises for a 12 month period is £4,200.

Required:

(i)   **Calculate Idris' tax adjusted trading profit for the year ended 5 April 2015, assuming he uses the normal accruals basis.**   **(4 marks)**

(ii)   **State why Idris is entitled to use the cash basis and calculate Idris' tax adjusted trading profit for the year ended 5 April 2015, assuming he uses the cash basis.**   **(6 marks)**

(iii) **State which basis would be more beneficial for Idris for 2014/15.**   **(1 mark)**

(Total: 15 marks)

12 FOO DEE (ADAPTED)

On 31 December 2014 Foo Dee resigned as an employee of Gastronomic-Food plc and on 1 January 2015 Foo commenced self-employment running her own restaurant, preparing accounts to 30 September.

The following information is available for 2014/15:

Employment

(1) During the period 6 April 2014 to 31 December 2014 Foo's total gross salary from her employment with Gastronomic-Food plc was £38,000.

(2) Foo used her private motor car for both business and private purposes during the period from 6 April 2014 to 31 December 2014. She received no reimbursement from Gastronomic-Food plc for any of the expenditure incurred.

Foo's total mileage during this period was 15,000 miles, made up as follows:

	Miles
Normal daily travel between home and permanent workplace	4,650
Travel between home and permanent workplace in order to turn off a fire alarm at work	120
Travel between permanent workplace and Gastronomic-Food plc's suppliers	750
Travel between home and a temporary workplace for two months	3,800
Private travel	5,680
	———
	15,000
	———

(3) While Foo is at work, her mother cares for her two children on an informal basis. Gastronomic-Food plc paid £55 per week for 39 weeks towards the cost of this.

(4) Foo contributed 6% of her gross salary of £38,000 into Gastronomic-Food plc's HM Revenue & Customs' registered occupational pension scheme.

Self-employment

(1) Foo's statement of profit or loss for her restaurant business for the nine-month period ended 30 September 2015 is as follows:

	£	£
Gross profit		202,054
Depreciation	3,500	
Motor expenses (Note 2)	4,200	
Property expenses (Note 3)	12,800	
Other expenses (all allowable)	50,700	
	———	
		(71,200)
		———
Net profit		130,854
		———

(2) During the period 1 January 2015 to 30 September 2015 Foo drove a total of 6,000 miles, of which 2,000 were for private journeys.

(3) Foo purchased her restaurant on 1 January 2015. She lives in a flat that is situated above the restaurant, and one-quarter of the total property expenses of £12,800 relate to this flat.

(4)   On 1 January 2015 Foo purchased a motor car with CO_2 emissions of 115 grams per kilometre for £14,600 (see note 2 above) and equipment for £81,200.

Required:

(a)   **Calculate Foo's taxable employment income for 2014/15.**   **(5 marks)**

(b)   **Calculate Foo's tax adjusted trading profit for the nine-month period ended 30 September 2015.**

       Assume that the current tax rates and allowances apply throughout.   **(5 marks)**

                                                                     (Total: 10 marks)

13   SAM WHITE (ADAPTED) *Walk in the footsteps of a top tutor*

(1)   Sam is self-employed running a retail clothing shop. Sam was born on 22 August 1967. His statement of profit or loss for the year ended 5 April 2015 is as follows:

	Note	£	£
Gross profit			190,300
Depreciation		7,600	
Motor expenses	2	8,800	
Patent royalties	3	700	
Professional fees	4	1,860	
Other expenses	5	71,340	
		──────	(90,300)
Net profit			100,000

(2)   During the year ended 5 April 2015 Sam drove a total of 25,000 miles, of which 5,000 miles were driven when he visited his suppliers in Europe. The balance of the mileage is 25% for private journeys and 75% for business journeys in the United Kingdom.

(3)   During the year ended 5 April 2015 Sam paid patent royalties of £700 (gross) in respect of specialised technology that he uses when altering clothes for customers.

(4)   The figure for professional fees consists of £1,050 for legal fees in connection with an action brought against a supplier for breach of contract and £810 for accountancy. Included in the figure for accountancy is £320 in respect of personal capital gains tax advice for the tax year 2014/15.

(5)   The figure for other expenses of £71,340 includes £560 for gifts to customers of food hampers costing £35 each and £420 for gifts to customers of pens carrying an advertisement for the clothing shop costing £60 each.

(6)   Sam uses one of the eight rooms in the couple's house as an office for when he works at home. The total running costs of the house for the year ended 5 April 2015 were £5,120. This cost is not included in the expenses in the statement of profit or loss of £90,300.

(7)   Sam uses his private telephone to make business telephone calls. The total cost of the private telephone for the year ended 5 April 2015 was £1,600, and 25% of this related to business telephone calls. The cost of the private telephone is not included in the expenses in the statement of profit or loss of £90,300.

(8)   During the year ended 5 April 2015 Sam took goods out of the clothing shop for his personal use without paying for them and no entry has been made in the accounts to record this. The goods cost £820, and had a selling price of £1,480.

(9)   The tax written down values for capital allowance purposes at 6 April 2014 were:

General pool	£14,800
Motor car bought January 2014	£20,200

The motor car is used by Sam (see note 2) and has an official CO_2 emission rate of 190 g/km.

Calculate Sam's tax adjusted trading profit for the year ended 5 April 2015.

Your computation should start with the net profit of £100,000 and should list all the items referred to in Notes (1) to (8), indicating with a zero (0) any items that do not require adjustment.   **(10 marks)**

14   ANDREW ZOOM *Walk in the footsteps of a top tutor*

Andrew Zoom, born on 30 November 1990, is a cameraman who started working for Slick-Productions Ltd on 6 April 2014. The following information is available in respect of the year ended 5 April 2015:

(1)   Andrew received gross income of £50,000 from Slick-Productions Ltd.

He works a set number of hours each week and is paid an hourly rate for the work that he does. When Andrew works more than the set number of hours he is paid overtime.

(2)   Andrew is under an obligation to accept the work offered to him by Slick-Productions Ltd, and the work is carried out under the control of the company's production manager. He is obliged to do the work personally, and this is all performed at Slick-Productions Ltd's premises.

(3)   All of the equipment that Andrew uses is provided by Slick-Productions Ltd.

Andrew has several friends who are cameramen, and they are all treated as self-employed. He therefore considers that he should be treated as self-employed as well in relation to his work for Slick-Productions Ltd.

Required:

(a)   **List those factors that indicate that Andrew Zoom should be treated as an employee in relation to his work for Slick-Productions Ltd rather than as self-employed.**

You should confine your answer to the information given in the question. (4 marks)

(b)   **Calculate Andrew Zoom's income tax liability and national insurance contributions for the tax year 2014/15 if he is treated:**

(i)   **As an employee in respect of his work for Slick-Productions Ltd;**

You are not required to calculate the employer's National Insurance contributions.   **(3 marks)**

(ii)   **As self-employed in respect of his work for Slick-Productions Ltd.   (3 marks)**

(Total: 10 marks)

15   SOPHIA WONG (ADAPTED) *Walk in the footsteps of a top tutor*

You should assume that today's date is 15 March 2014.

(a)   Sophia Wong was born on 7 June 1975 and is self-employed as a lawyer. For the year ended 5 April 2015 Sophia has forecast that her tax adjusted trading profit will be £80,000.

This will be her only income for the tax year 2014/15, and Sophia's total income tax liability and National Insurance contributions (NIC) for this year if she continues to trade on a self-employed basis will be as follows:

	£
Income tax	21,627
Class 2 NIC	143
Class 4 NIC	3,815
	———
	25,585
	———

Sophia understands that she could save tax and NIC if she instead traded as a limited company, and she is therefore considering incorporating her business on 6 April 2014. The forecast taxable total profits of the new limited company for the year ended 5 April 2015 are unchanged at £80,000 (before taking account of any director's remuneration).

Required:

Assuming that Sophia Wong incorporates her business on 6 April 2014, advise her whether or not there will be an overall saving of tax and National Insurance contributions (NIC) for the tax year 2014/15 if she withdraws all of the profits from the new company as:

(i)   **director's remuneration (after allowing for employer's Class 1 NIC, gross director's remuneration will be £73,021); or**   **(6 marks)**

(ii)   **dividends (after allowing for corporation tax, net dividends will be £64,000).**
                                                                        (5 marks)

Notes:

(1)   **For both alternatives, you are expected to calculate the corporation tax liability (if any) of the new limited company for the year ended 5 April 2015, the income tax payable by Sophia Wong, and the Class 1 NIC (if any) payable by Sophia and the new company.**

(2)   **You should assume that the rates of corporation tax remain unchanged.**

(b)   Since receiving your advice in (a) above Sophia has unexpectedly received a very generous offer to buy her business. This coincided with discussions she has been having with a major law firm who are interested in employing her.

She has therefore now decided not to incorporate her business but instead to sell it to an unconnected third party for £200,000, to be received in cash on 1 May 2014. The only chargeable asset of Sophia Wong's business is goodwill and this is valued at £150,000. The goodwill has a nil cost.

On 15 April 2014 Sophia sold a necklace realising a chargeable gain of £11,053.

Sophia will not make any other disposals during the tax year 2014/15. She will take a long holiday before starting her new job and her taxable income (after deduction of the personal allowance) for the tax year 2014/15 will be £20,000.

Required:

Calculate Sophia Wong's capital gains tax liability for 2014/15 assuming she sells her business on 1 May 2014 for £200,000 cash and she makes any beneficial elections.

State the deadline(s) for making any elections you have identified as being beneficial.

(4 marks)

(Total: 15 marks)

16   JOHN AND LIAN (ADAPTED) *Walk in the footsteps of a top tutor*

(a)   John Higgins left employment on 30 April 2014 and started an unincorporated business on 1 June 2014. He will prepare his first set of accounts for the 12 months to 31 May 2015 and expects to make a taxable profit of £80,000.

Prior to starting the business his only income was from his employment and his income tax liability was paid at source through the Pay As You Earn (PAYE) system.

Required:

(i)   State the date by which John must notify HM Revenue & Customs that he is chargeable to income tax in respect of his trading income if he does not receive a notice to complete a tax return.

(ii)   State the date that John must keep records which relate to his tax return for 2014/15.

(iii)   State the first date by which John will first be required to pay an amount of income tax in relation to the taxable profits arising from his business.

(3 marks)

(b)   Lian Zhang commenced in self-employment on 1 May 2012. She prepared accounts to 30 April and her trading profits for the first two years of trading were as follows:

	Tax adjusted trading profits before capital allowances	*Capital allowances*
	£	£
Year ended 30 April 2013	62,300	11,900
Year ended 30 April 2014	75,400	38,200

In 2015 Lian was offered an employment contract with a large company which she decided to accept. She ceased trading and prepared her final set of accounts for the 14-month period to 30 June 2015.

Lian's tax adjusted trading profit (before capital allowances) for the 14-month period ended 30 June 2015 will be £61,500.

The tax written down value of her capital allowances main pool at 1 May 2014 was £14,400. She acquired a new machine on 1 June 2014 for £12,000 and sold all of the plant and machinery which was still owned by the business on 30 June 2015 for £22,000. No item was sold for more than its original cost.

Required:

Calculate the amount of trading profit that will be assessed on Lian Zhang for each of the tax years 2012/13, 2013/14, 2014/15 and 2015/16.

You should assume that the capital allowance rates for the tax year 2014/15 apply throughout. **(7 marks)**

(Total: 10 marks)

17 FANG, HONG AND KANG *Walk in the footsteps of a top tutor*

(a) Fang commenced self-employment on 1 August 2012. She has a trading profit of £45,960 for the year ended 31 July 2013, and a trading profit of £39,360 for the year ended 31 July 2014.

Required:

(i) **Calculate the amount of trading profit which will have been assessed on Fang for each of the tax years 2012/13, 2013/14 and 2014/15, and state the amount of any overlap profit.** **(3 marks)**

(ii) **Explain how Fang would have obtained relief for trading expenditure incurred prior to 1 August 2012 and for computer equipment which Fang already owned which was brought into business use on 1 August 2012.**
(2 marks)

(b) Hong has been in self-employment since 2003, preparing accounts to 5 April. For the year ended 5 April 2015 she made a trading loss of £45,800, and has claimed this against her total income and chargeable gain for the tax year 2013/14.

For the year ended 5 April 2014 Hong made a trading profit of £29,700. She also has a property business profit of £3,900 for the tax year 2013/14. Hong has an unused trading loss of £2,600 brought forward from the tax year 2012/13.

During the tax year 2013/14 Hong disposed of an investment property and this resulted in a chargeable gain (before the annual exempt amount) of £17,800. Hong has unused capital losses of £6,200 brought forward from the tax year 2011/12.

Required:

After taking account of the loss relief claims made, calculate Hong's taxable income and taxable gain for the tax year 2013/14, and state the amount of any trading loss carried forward.

You should assume that the tax allowances for the tax year 2014/15 apply throughout. **(5 marks)**

(c) Kang, Ling and Ming have been in partnership since 2005, preparing accounts to 30 June. Ming left the partnership on 31 October 2013. Profits have always been shared equally.

The partnership had a trading profit of £148,800 for the year ended 30 June 2013, and a profit of £136,800 for the year ended 30 June 2014. Each partner has unused overlap profits brought forward of £29,400.

Required:

Calculate the trading income assessments of Kang, Ling and Ming for each of the tax years 2013/14 and 2014/15. **(5 marks)**

(Total: 15 marks)

18 NA STYLE (ADAPTED) *Walk in the footsteps of a top tutor*

Na Style, born on 22 July 1970, commenced self-employment as a hairdresser on 1 January 2012. She had tax adjusted trading profits as follows:

	£
Six months ended 30 June 2012	25,200
Year ended 30 June 2013	21,600
Year ended 30 June 2014	30,665

Other information

(1) During 2014/15 Na received dividends of £1,080, building society interest of £560, interest of £310 from a new individual savings account (NISA), interest of £1,100 on the maturity of a NS&I savings certificate, and interest of £370 from government stocks (gilts). These were the actual cash amounts received in each case.

(2) Na's payments on account of income tax in respect of the tax year 2014/15 totalled £3,200.

Required:

(a) **Calculate the amount of trading profits that will have been assessed on Na Style for the tax years 2011/12 to 2014/15 inclusively, clearly identifying the amount of any overlap profits.** **(6 marks)**

(b) (i) **Calculate the income tax payable by Na Style for the tax year 2014/15.**

(6 marks)

(ii) **Calculate Na Style's balancing payment for the tax year 2014/15 and her payments on account for the tax year 2015/16, stating the relevant due dates.**

You should ignore National Insurance contributions. **(3 marks)**

(Total: 15 marks)

19 SIMON HOUSE (ADAPTED) *Walk in the footsteps of a top tutor*

On 1 May 2014 Simon House purchased a derelict freehold house for £127,000. Legal fees of £1,800 were paid in respect of the purchase.

Simon then renovated the house at a cost of £50,600, with the renovation being completed on 10 August 2014. He immediately put the house up for sale, and it was sold on 31 August 2014 for £260,000. Legal fees of £2,600 were paid in respect of the sale.

Simon financed the transaction by a bank loan of £150,000 that was taken out on 1 May 2014 at an annual interest rate of 6%. The bank loan was repaid on 31 August 2014.

Simon had no income or capital gains for the tax year 2014/15 except as indicated above. He was born on 1 January 1955.

Simon has been advised that whether or not he is treated as carrying on a trade will be determined according to the 'badges of trade', which include:

(1) Subject matter of the transaction.

(2) Length of ownership.

(3) Frequency of similar transactions.

(4) Work done on the property.

(5) Circumstances responsible for the realisation.

(6) Motive.

Required:

(a) **Briefly explain the meaning of each of the six 'badges of trade' listed in the question.**

   You are not expected to quote from decided cases. **(3 marks)**

(b) **Calculate Simon House's income tax liability and his Class 2 and Class 4 national insurance contributions for the tax year 2014/15, if he is treated as carrying on a trade in respect of the disposal of the freehold house.** **(8 marks)**

(c) **Calculate Simon House's capital gains tax liability for the tax year 2014/15, if he is not treated as carrying on a trade in respect of the disposal of the freehold house.** **(4 marks)**

   (Total: 15 marks)

20 BAYLE DEFENDER (ADAPTED) *Walk in the footsteps of a top tutor*

You should assume that today's date is 20 November 2014.

Bayle Defender, born on 23 June 1980, is self-employed as a lawyer. She is also a director of Acquit & Appeal Ltd. The following information is available for the tax year 2014/15:

Self-employment

(1) Bayle's statement of profit or loss for the year ended 30 September 2014 is as follows:

	Note	£	£
Revenue	2		324,100
Expenses			
Gifts and donations	3	8,680	
Lease of motor car	4	10,360	
Professional fees	5	3,240	
Property expenses	6	46,240	
Travel expenses	7	16,770	
Other expenses	8	66,410	
		———	(151,700)
Net profit			172,400

(2) Revenue includes £2,800 received during May 2014 in respect of an impairment loss that Bayle had written off when calculating her trading profit for the year ended 30 September 2012.

(3) Gifts and donations are as follows:

	£
Gifts to customers (clocks costing £110 each and displaying Bayle's name)	3,300
Gifts to customers (bottles of champagne costing £40 each, displaying Bayle's name)	2,480
Donations to political parties	2,900
	8,680

(4) The lease commenced on 1 May 2014, and is in respect of a motor car with CO_2 emissions of 144 grams per kilometre. There is no private use of the motor car.

(5) The figure of £3,240 for professional fees is in respect of accountancy services, of which £600 is for inheritance tax planning advice.

(6) Bayle lives in an apartment that is situated above her office, and two-fifths of the total property expenses of £46,240 relate to this apartment.

(7) The figure of £16,770 for travel expenses includes £220 for parking fines and £300 for a speeding fine incurred by Bayle.

(8) The figure for other expenses of £66,410 includes £670 for Bayle's professional subscription to the Law Society, and £960 for her golf club membership fee.

Director's remuneration

(9) Bayle will be paid gross director's remuneration of £42,000 by Acquit & Appeal Ltd during the tax year 2014/15.

(10) In addition to her director's remuneration, Bayle received two bonus payments of £6,000 from Acquit & Appeal Ltd during June 2014, both of which were in respect of the year ended 31 December 2013.

Bayle became entitled to the first bonus payment of £6,000 on 10 March 2014, and to the second bonus payment of £6,000 on 20 April 2014.

(11) Acquit & Appeal Ltd deducts PAYE at a flat rate of 45% from all of Bayle's earnings.

Other information

(12) During the tax year 2014/15 Bayle will receive dividends of £9,900, interest of £5,240 on the maturity of a savings certificate issued by National Savings & Investments (NS&I), and interest of £3,600 from government stocks (gilts).

These are the actual cash amounts that will be received.

(13) Bayle's payments on account of income tax in respect of the tax year 2014/15 will total £53,400.

Required:

(a) Calculate Bayle Defender's tax adjusted trading profit for the year ended 30 September 2014.

Your computation should commence with the net profit figure of £172,400, and you should also list all of the items referred to in Notes (2) to (8) indicating by the use of zero (0) any items that do not require adjustment. **(7 marks)**

(b) Calculate the income tax payable by Bayle Defender for the tax year 2014/15.

(8 marks)

(Total: 15 marks)

21 TIM BURR (ADAPTED) *Walk in the footsteps of a top tutor*

Tim Burr, born on 15 November 1957, is a self-employed tree surgeon. His business has grown rapidly over the last few years and Tim is struggling to keep up with his workload.

On 1 December 2014, he is planning to bring a newly qualified tree surgeon, Hazel Grove into his business. Hazel will either be taken on as an employee, being paid a gross monthly salary of £3,300, or join Tim as a partner, receiving a 20% share of the new partnership's profits.

Tim has forecast that his tax adjusted trading profit will be £216,000 for the year ended 30 September 2015, and £240,000 for the year ended 30 September 2016.

Hazel was born on 26 August 1999 and does not have any other income for the tax year 2014/15.

Required:

(a) Assuming that Hazel Grove is employed from 1 December 2014, calculate the total amount of National Insurance contributions that will be paid by Tim Burr and Hazel Grove, if any, in respect of her earnings for the tax year 2014/15.

You are not expected to calculate the National Insurance contributions that will be paid in respect of Tim Burr's earnings. **(4 marks)**

(b) Assuming that Hazel Grove becomes a partner from 1 December 2014:

(i) Calculate her trading income assessments for the tax years 2014/15 and 2015/16.

You are not expected to calculate any overlap profits. **(4 marks)**

(ii) Calculate the total amount of National Insurance contributions that will be paid by Tim Burr and Hazel Grove, if any, in respect of her trading income assessment for the tax year 2014/15.

You are not expected to calculate the National Insurance contributions that will be paid in respect of Tim Burr's trading income assessment. **(2 marks)**

(Total: 10 marks)

22   RICHARD FEAST (ADAPTED) *Walk in the footsteps of a top tutor*

(a)   On 6 April 2014, Richard Feast, born on 4 April 1968, commenced in self-employment, running a restaurant. Richard's statement of profit or loss for the year ended 5 April 2015 is as follows:

	Notes	£	£
Gross profit			73,440
Expenses			
Motor expenses	1	7,660	
Property expenses	2	16,200	
Repairs and renewals	3	6,420	
Other expenses	4	10,960	
		———	(41,240)
Net profit			32,200

Note 1 – Motor expenses

	£
Cost of running Richard's motor car	4,710
Cost of running a motor car used by the restaurant's chef	2,670
Parking fines incurred by Richard	280
	———
	7,660

Richard's motor car is used 70% for private journeys, and the chef's motor car is used 20% for private journeys.

Note 2 – Property expenses

Richard lives in an apartment which is situated above the restaurant, and one-fifth of the total property expenses of £16,200 relate to this apartment.

Note 3 – Repairs and renewals

	£
Decorating the restaurant	5,100
Decorating the apartment	1,320
	———
	6,420

The property was in a usable state when it was purchased.

Note 4 – Other expenses

The figure of £10,960 for other expenses includes legal fees of £2,590 in connection with the purchase of the restaurant property. The remaining expenses are all allowable.

Additional information: Plant and machinery

The following motor cars were purchased during the year ended 5 April 2015:

	Date of purchase	Cost £	CO_2 emission rate
Motor car (1)	6 April 2014	14,000	124 grams per kilometre
Motor car (2)	6 April 2014	16,800	123 grams per kilometre

Motor car (1) is used by Richard, and motor car (2) is used by the restaurant's chef.

Required:

Calculate Richard Feast's tax adjusted trading profit for the year ended 5 April 2015.

Notes:

1   Your computation should commence with the net profit figure of £32,200, and should list all of the items referred to in Notes (1) to (4), indicating by the use of zero (0) any items which do not require adjustment.

2   In answering this part of the question you are not expected to take account of any of the information provided in parts (b) or (c) below.

(7 marks)

(b)   Richard's only employee is a chef who is employed throughout the 2014/15 tax year on a gross annual salary of £46,000. The chef was provided with a petrol powered motor car (see the plant and machinery information in part (a) above) throughout the tax year. The list price of the motor car is the same as its cost. Richard did not provide any fuel for private journeys.

Required:

Calculate the employers' Class 1 and Class 1A National Insurance contributions which Richard Feast would have incurred in respect of the chef's earnings and benefit for the tax year 2014/15.

You are not expected to calculate the National Insurance contributions suffered by the employees or by Richard in respect of his self-employment.   (3 marks)

(c)   Richard has not previously filed a self-assessment tax return, and therefore wants to know when he will have to file his return for the tax year 2014/15. He is not sure whether to file a paper tax return or to file the return online.

As this will be his first self-assessment tax return, Richard is concerned that HM Revenue and Customs might carry out a compliance check.

Required:

(i)   Advise Richard Feast of the latest dates by which his self-assessment tax return for the tax year 2014/15 should be filed in order to avoid a penalty.

(2 marks)

(ii)   State the period during which HM Revenue and Customs will have to notify Richard Feast if they intend to carry out a compliance check in respect of his self-assessment tax return for the tax year 2014/15, and the possible reasons why such a check would be made.

You should assume that Richard will file his tax return by the filing date.

(3 marks)

(Total: 15 marks)

TRADING LOSSES

23 NORMA (ADAPTED)

Norma, who had been in business as a confectioner since 1 May 2010, disposed of the business and retired on 31 May 2014. She does not intend to start any other business, but will be employed part-time from 1 June 2014 on an annual salary of £11,400.

Her trading profits/(losses), as adjusted for taxation were:

	£	
Period ended 31.12.10	21,000	Profit
Year ended 31.12.11	17,000	Profit
Year ended 31.12.12	15,500	Profit
Year ended 31.12.13	8,835	Profit
Period ended 31.5.14	(11,000)	Loss

Norma has received bank interest of £2,000 (gross) each year since April 2010. In addition she realised a taxable gain (i.e. after the annual exempt amount), of £35,000 in June 2013.

Norma was born on 8 October 1949.

Required:

(a)   Calculate Norma's taxable income and gains for each tax year that she was in business before any relief for the loss arising in the period ended 31 May 2014.

(b)   Explain the options available to Norma to utilise the loss and explain the effect on her tax liability of the loss relief claims identified.

Assume that rates and allowances for 2014/15 apply throughout.   **(15 marks)**

24 LEONARDO

Leonardo commenced to trade as an art dealer on 1 September 2011. His trading results, adjusted for income tax, are:

	£	
1.9.11 to 31.5.12	40,500	Profit
1.6.12 to 31.5.13	(54,000)	Loss
1.6.13 to 31.5.14	(27,000)	Loss
1.6.14 to 31.5.15	11,000	Profit

Leonardo does not foresee making any significant profits in the next 2 or 3 years.

Leonardo has not had any other income in any of the years in question, or earlier.

Required:

(a)   Show how his trading loss can be utilised most effectively, giving your reasons.

(8 marks)

(b)   State by what date(s) the claims you are proposing in part (a) should be submitted to HM Revenue & Customs.   **(2 marks)**

(Total: 10 marks)

25   DEE ZYNE (ADAPTED) *Walk in the footsteps of a top tutor*

On 5 July 2014 Dee Zyne resigned as an employee of Trendy-Wear plc. The company had employed her as a fashion designer since 2004. On 6 July 2014 Dee commenced self-employment running her own clothing business, preparing accounts to 5 April.

The following information is available for 2014/15.

Self-employment

(1)   Dee's tax adjusted trading loss for the period 6 July 2014 to 5 April 2015 was £11,440. This figure is before taking account of the information in Note (2) and capital allowances.

(2)   During the period 6 July 2014 to 5 April 2015 Dee paid patent royalties of £500 (gross) in respect of specialised technology that she uses in her clothing business.

(3)   Dee purchased the following assets during the period ended 5 April 2015:

		£
10 July 2014	Computer	1,257
16 August 2014	Office furniture	2,175
13 November 2014	Motor car (1)	10,400
21 January 2015	Motor car (2)	17,800

Motor car (1) purchased on 13 November 2014 has CO_2 emissions of 105 grams per kilometre, is used by an employee, and 15% of the mileage is for private purposes.

Motor car (2) purchased on 21 January 2015 has CO_2 emissions of 135 grams per kilometre, is used by Dee, and 20% of the mileage is for private purposes.

Other information

(1)   Dee's employment income for the period 6 April 2014 – 5 July 2014 was £28,875.

(2)   Dee's total income for each of the years 2008/09 to 2013/14 was £80,000.

Required:

(a)   Calculate Dee's tax adjusted trading loss for 2014/15.   **(6 marks)**

(b)   Describe the ways in which Dee could have relieved her trading loss for 2014/15 against total income, and explain which of these claims would have been most beneficial.

You should assume that the tax rates for 2014/15 apply throughout.   **(4 marks)**

(Total: 10 marks)

26   SAMANTHA FABRIQUE (ADAPTED)

Samantha Fabrique, born on 13 July 1976, has been a self-employed manufacturer of clothing since 2003. She has the following gross income and chargeable gains for the tax years 2013/14 to 2015/16:

	2013/14	2014/15	2015/16
	£	£	£
Trading profit/(loss)	21,600	(81,900)	10,500
Building society interest	52,100	3,800	1,500
Chargeable gains/(loss)	53,300	(3,400)	11,300

The chargeable gains do not qualify for Entrepreneurs' relief.

Required:

(a) State the factors that will influence an individual's choice of loss relief claims.

(3 marks)

(b) Calculate Samantha's taxable income and taxable gains for each of the tax years 2013/14, 2014/15 and 2015/16 on the assumption that she relieves the trading loss of £81,900 for the tax year 2014/15 on the most favourable basis.

Explain your reasoning behind relieving the loss on the most favourable basis.

You should assume that the tax allowances for the tax year 2014/15 apply throughout.

(12 marks)

(Total: 15 marks)

---

27 MICHAEL AND SEAN *Walk in the footsteps of a top tutor*

(a) The UK Government uses tax policies to encourage certain types of activity.

Required:

Briefly explain how the UK Government's tax policies encourage:

(i) Individuals to save;   (1 mark)

(ii) Individuals to support charities;   (1 mark)

(iii) Entrepreneurs to build their own businesses and to invest in plant and machinery.

(2 marks)

(b) You are a trainee chartered certified accountant and your manager has asked for your help regarding two taxpayers who have both made trading losses.

Michael

Michael commenced in self-employment on 1 July 2013, preparing accounts to 5 April. His results for the first two periods of trading were as follows:

	£
Nine-month period ended 5 April 2014 – Trading loss	(24,600)
Year ended 5 April 2015 – Trading profit	7,100

For tax years 2009/10 to 2011/12, Michael had the following employment income:

	£
2009/10	44,500
2010/11	16,800
2011/12	50,600

Michael did not have any income during the period 6 April 2012 to 30 June 2013.

Sean

Sean has been in self-employment since 2004, but ceased trading on 31 December 2014. He has always prepared accounts to 31 December. His results for the final five years of trading were as follows:

	£
Year ended 31 December 2010 – Trading profit	21,300
Year ended 31 December 2011 – Trading profit	14,400
Year ended 31 December 2012 – Trading profit	18,900
Year ended 31 December 2013 – Trading profit	3,700
Year ended 31 December 2014 – Trading loss	(23,100)

For each of the tax years 2010/11 to 2014/15 Sean has property business profits of £10,500. Sean has unused overlap profits brought forward of £3,600.

Required:

For each of the two taxpayers Michael and Sean, identify the loss relief claims that are available to them, and explain which of the available claims would be the most beneficial.

Notes:

(1) **You should clearly state the amount of any reliefs claimed and the rates of income tax saved. However, you are not expected to calculate any income tax liabilities.**

(2) **You should assume that the tax rates and allowances for the tax year 2014/15 apply throughout.**

The following mark allocation is provided as guidance for this requirement:

Michael	**(5 marks)**
Sean	**(6 marks)**

(Total: 15 marks)

PARTNERSHIPS

28 PETER, QUINTON AND ROGER (ADAPTED)

Peter and Quinton commenced in partnership on 1 January 2012. Roger joined as a partner on 1 January 2013, and Peter resigned as a partner on 31 December 2014. Profits and losses have always been shared equally.

The partnership's tax adjusted profits and losses are as follows:

	£	
Year ended 31 December 2012	40,000	Profit
Year ended 31 December 2013	90,000	Profit
Year ended 31 December 2014	(30,000)	Loss

All of the partners were in employment prior to becoming partners, and each of them has investment income. None of the partners has any capital gains.

Required:

(a) **Briefly explain the basis by which trading profits are assessed on partners when they join a partnership.**   **(2 marks)**

(b) **Calculate the trading income assessments of Peter, Quinton and Roger for 2011/12, 2012/13 and 2013/14.**   **(6 marks)**

(c) **State the possible ways in which Peter, Quinton and Roger can relieve their share of the trading loss for 2014/15.**

   Your answer should include a calculation of the amount of loss available for relief to each partner.   **(7 marks)**

(Total: 15 marks)

29   AE, BEE, CAE, AND DEE (ADAPTED) *Walk in the footsteps of a top tutor*

(a)   Ae and Bee commenced in partnership on 1 July 2012 preparing accounts to 30 June. Cae joined as a partner on 1 July 2014. Profits have always been shared equally.

The partnership's trading profits since the commencement of trading have been:

	£
Year ended 30 June 2013	54,000
Year ended 30 June 2014	66,000
Year ended 30 June 2015	87,000

Required:

Calculate the trading income assessments of Ae, Bee and Cae for each of the tax years 2012/13, 2013/14 and 2014/15.   **(5 marks)**

(b)   Dee has been self-employed for many years. The business has been loss making for the last two years. In the year ended 5 April 2016 she is planning to bring her sister, Eae, into the business as a partner, in an attempt to turn the business around. She anticipates that the business will make a small loss in the year ended 5 April 2016, but will make growing profits going forward.

Dee's losses have been as follows:

	£
Year ended 5 April 2014	5,000
Year ended 5 April 2015	165,000

Dee has savings income of £85,000 each year.

Required:

(i)   **Explain how the loss in the year ended 5 April 2015 can be relieved, assuming Dee always claims relief for her losses as soon as possible.**   **(3 marks)**

(ii)   **Explain the claims available to Eae to obtain relief for her share of any trading losses in the year ended 5 April 2016.**   **(2 marks)**

(Total: 10 marks)

30   AUY MAN AND BIM MEN (ADAPTED) *Walk in the footsteps of a top tutor*

Auy Man and Bim Men have been in partnership since 6 April 2004 as management consultants. The following information is available for the tax year 2014/15:

Personal information

Auy was born on 3 July 1982. During the tax year 2014/15 she spent 190 days in the United Kingdom (UK). Auy was resident in the UK during 2013/14.

Bim was born on 4 January 1959. During the tax year 2014/15 she spent 100 days in the UK. Bim also spent 100 days in the UK in each of the previous five tax years, and was treated as resident in the UK during each of the previous three years. Bim's time in the UK is spent living in her holiday home in the Lake District.

Statement of profit or loss for the year ended 5 April 2015

The partnership's summarised statement of profit or loss for the year ended 5 April 2015 is:

	Notes	£	£
Sales			143,880
Expenses:			
Depreciation		3,400	
Other expenses	1	1,800	
Wages and salaries	2	50,900	
		———	(56,100)
Net profit			87,780

Notes:

(1)   The figure of £1,800 for other expenses includes £720 for entertaining employees. The remaining expenses are all allowable.

(2)   The figure of £50,900 for wages and salaries includes the annual salary of £4,000 paid to Bim (see the profit sharing note below).

Plant and machinery

On 6 April 2014 the tax written down values of the partnership's plant and machinery were:

	£
Main pool	3,100
Motor car (1)	18,000

The following transactions took place during the year ended 5 April 2015:

		Cost
		£
8 May 2014	Purchased motor car (2)	11,600
21 November 2014	Purchased motor car (3)	14,200
14 January 2015	Purchased motor car (4)	8,700

Motor car (1) was purchased in March 2012 and has a CO_2 emission rate of 175 grams per kilometre. It is used by Auy, and 70% of the mileage is for business journeys.

Motor car (2) is a new car purchased on 8 May 2014 has a CO_2 emission rate of 85 grams per kilometre. It is used by Bim, and 70% of the mileage is for business journeys.

Motor car (3) purchased on 21 November 2014 has a CO_2 emission rate of 105 grams per kilometre. Motor car (4) purchased on 14 January 2015 has a CO_2 emission rate of 140 grams per kilometre. These two motor cars are used by employees of the business.

Profit sharing

Profits are shared 80% to Auy and 20% to Bim. This is after paying an annual salary of £4,000 to Bim, and interest at the rate of 5% on the partners' capital account balances.

The capital account balances are:

	£
Auy Man	56,000
Bim Men	34,000

Required:

(a) Explain why both Auy Man and Bim Men will each be treated for tax purposes as resident in the United Kingdom for the tax year 2014/15. **(2 marks)**

(b) Calculate the partnership's tax adjusted trading profit for the year ended 5 April 2015, and the trading income assessments of Auy Man and Bim Men for the tax year 2014/15.

Your computation should commence with the net profit figure of £87,780, and should also list all of the items referred to in Notes (1) and (2) indicating by the use of zero (0) any items that do not require adjustment. **(10 marks)**

(c) Calculate the Class 4 National Insurance contributions payable by Auy Man and Bim Men for the tax year 2014/15. **(3 marks)**

(Total: 15 marks)

PENSIONS AND NIC

31 JOHN BEACH (ADAPTED) *Walk in the footsteps of a top tutor*

John Beach was born on 19 August 1953. The following information is available for the tax year 2014/15:

(1) John has been employed by Surf plc as a sales director since 1 December 1994. During the tax year 2014/15, he was paid gross director's remuneration of £184,000.

(2) During the tax year 2014/15, John contributed £28,000 into Surf plc's HM Revenue and Customs' registered occupational pension scheme. The company contributed a further £10,000 on his behalf. Both John and Surf plc have made exactly the same contributions for the previous five tax years.

(3) During the period 6 April to 31 October 2014, John used his private motor car for both private and business journeys. He was reimbursed by Surf plc at the rate of 60p per mile for the following mileage:

	Miles
Normal daily travel between home and Surf plc's offices	1,180
Travel between Surf plc's offices and the premises of Surf plc's clients	4,270
Travel between home and the premises of Surf plc's clients (none of the clients' premises were located near the offices of Surf plc)	510
Total mileage reimbursed by Surf plc	5,960

(4) During 2011 Surf plc provided John with a loan which was used to purchase a yacht. The amount of loan outstanding at 6 April 2014 was £84,000. John repaid £12,000 of the loan on 31 July 2014, and then repaid a further £12,000 on 31 December 2014. He paid loan interest of £1,270 to Surf plc during the tax year 2014/15. The taxable benefit in respect of this loan is calculated using the average method.

(5) Surf plc gave John an engraved gold watch costing £465 on 1 December 2014 in recognition of his long service with the company.

(6) During the tax year 2014/15, John made personal pension contributions up to the maximum amount of available annual allowances, including any unused amounts brought forward from previous years. These contributions were in addition to the contributions he made to Surf plc's occupational pension scheme (see Note (2)). John has not made any personal pension contributions in previous tax years.

Required:

(a) Calculate John Beach's income tax liability for the tax year 2014/15. **(11 marks)**

(b) Calculate the Class 1 and Class 1A National Insurance contributions that will have been suffered by John Beach and Surf plc in respect of John's earnings and benefits for the tax year 2014/15. **(4 marks)**

(Total: 15 marks)

32 DUKE AND EARL UPPER-CRUST (ADAPTED)

Duke and Earl Upper-Crust, born on 29 August 1970, are twin brothers.

Duke is employed by the High-Brow Bank plc as a financial adviser. During the tax year 2014/15 Duke was paid a gross salary of £114,000. He also received a bonus of £40,000 on 15 March 2015. On 31 March 2015 Duke made a contribution of £35,000 (gross) into a personal pension scheme. He is not a member of High-Brow Bank plc's occupational pension scheme.

Earl is self-employed as a financial consultant. His trading profit for the year ended 5 April 2015 was £34,000. During 2014/15 Earl has made contributions of £40,000 (gross) into a personal pension scheme.

Neither Duke nor Earl has any other income.

In previous years Duke and Earl Upper-Crust had the same level of income as in 2014/15. Duke paid £45,000 (gross) into his pension scheme and Earl paid £10,000 (gross).

Required:

(a) Calculate Duke and Earl's income tax liabilities for the tax year 2014/15, together with the net amounts that Duke and Earl will have paid to their personal pension companies. **(9 marks)**

(b) Explain the effect of the pension scheme annual allowance limit, and the tax implications if contributions are made in excess of this limit. **(2 marks)**

(c) Advise Duke and Earl of the maximum additional amounts that they could have contributed into personal pension schemes for the tax year 2014/15 for which they would get tax relief and which would not incur an annual allowance charge, and the date by which any qualifying contributions would have had to have been paid. **(4 marks)**

(Total: 15 marks)

33 VANESSA AND SERENE (ADAPTED) *Walk in the footsteps of a top tutor*

Vanessa Serve and Serene Volley, born on 28 June 1982 and 11 July 1979 respectively, are sisters. The following information is available for the tax year 2014/15:

Vanessa Serve

(1) Vanessa is self-employed as a tennis coach. Her tax adjusted trading profit for the year ended 31 March 2015 is £52,400. However, this figure is before taking account of capital allowances.

(2) The only item of plant and machinery owned by Vanessa is her motor car. This was bought in May 2013 and has an official CO_2 emission rate of 100 grams per kilometre. At 1 April 2014 it had a tax written down value of £10,400.

   During the year ended 31 March 2015 Vanessa drove a total of 20,000 miles, of which 6,000 were for private journeys.

(3) Vanessa contributed £6,400 (gross) into a personal pension scheme during the tax year 2014/15.

(4) In addition to her self-employed income, Vanessa received interest of £1,100 from an NS&I investment account during the tax year 2014/15. This was the actual cash amount received.

Serene Volley

(1) Serene is employed as a sports journalist by Backhand plc, a newspaper publishing company.

   During the tax year 2014/15 she was paid a gross annual salary of £26,400. Income tax of £3,016 was deducted from this figure under PAYE.

(2) Throughout the tax year 2014/15 Backhand plc provided Serene with a diesel powered motor car which has a list price of £24,700. The official CO_2 emission rate for the motor car is 87 grams per kilometre.

   The company did not provide Serene with any fuel for private journeys.

(3) Serene contributed 5% of her gross salary of £26,400 into Backhand plc's HM Revenue and Customs' registered occupational pension scheme.

(4) In addition to her employment income, Serene received interest of £1,200 on the maturity of a NS&I Savings Certificate during the tax year 2014/15. This was the actual cash amount received.

Required:

(a) **Calculate the income tax payable by both Vanessa and Serene for the tax year 2014/15.** **(11 marks)**

(b) **Calculate the national insurance contributions payable by both Vanessa and Serene for the tax year 2014/15.** **(4 marks)**

(Total: 15 marks)

34   ANN, BASIL AND CHLOE (ADAPTED) *Walk in the footsteps of a top tutor*

You are a trainee accountant and your manager has asked for your help regarding three taxpayers who have all made personal pension contributions during the tax year 2014/15.

Ann Peach

Ann, born on 31 May 1984, is self-employed as an estate agent. Her trading profit for the year ended 5 April 2015 was £38,000. Ann made contributions of £42,000 (gross) into a personal pension scheme during the tax year 2014/15.

Basil Plum

Basil, born on 15 September 1972, is employed by the Banana Bank plc as a fund manager. During the tax year 2014/15 Basil was paid a gross salary of £120,000.

Basil has made contributions into a personal pension plan totalling £40,000 (gross) each year for the last four years. In 2014/15 he also makes total gross contributions of £40,000.

He is not a member of Banana Bank plc's occupational pension scheme but the bank contributed to Basil's personal pension in 2014/15.

Chloe Pear

Chloe Pear, born on 24 December 1960, lets out unfurnished property. For the tax year 2014/15 her property business profit was £23,900. Chloe made contributions of £8,200 (gross) into a personal pension scheme during the tax year 2014/15.

Neither Ann nor Basil nor Chloe has any other income.

Required:

(a)   **For each of the three taxpayers Ann Peach, Basil Plum and Chloe Pear, state, giving reasons, the amount of personal pension contributions that will have qualified for tax relief for the tax year 2014/15, and calculate their income tax liabilities for that year.**

Marks are allocated as follows:

Ann Peach 3 marks; Basil Plum 5 marks; and Chloe Pear 2 marks.   (10 marks)

(b)   **Explain the tax consequences of Banana Bank plc contributing £100,000 into Basil's personal pension in 2014/15 and the purpose of the annual allowance.   (5 marks)**

(Total: 15 marks)

SELF-ASSESSMENT

35   PI CASSO

 Timed question with Online tutor debrief

Pi Casso has been a self-employed artist since 2003, preparing her accounts to 30 June.

Pi's tax liabilities for the tax years 2012/13, 2013/14 and 2014/15 are as follows:

	2012/13	2013/14	2014/15
	£	£	£
Income tax liability	3,240	4,100	2,730
Class 2 National Insurance contributions	138	140	143
Class 4 National Insurance contributions	1,240	1,480	990
Capital gains tax liability	–	4,880	–

No income tax has been deducted at source.

Required:

(a)   Prepare a schedule showing the payments on account and balancing payments that Pi will have made or will have to make during the period from 1 July 2014 to 31 March 2016, assuming that Pi makes any appropriate claims to reduce her payments on account.

Your answer should clearly identify the relevant due date of each payment.

(7 marks)

(b)   State the implications if Pi had made a claim to reduce her payments on account for the tax year 2014/15 to £Nil.   (2 marks)

(c)   Advise Pi of the latest date by which her self-assessment tax return for the tax year 2014/15 should be submitted if she wants HM Revenue and Customs (HMRC) to prepare the self-assessment tax computation on her behalf.   (3 marks)

(d)   State the date by which HMRC will have to notify Pi if they intend to enquire into her self-assessment tax return for the tax year 2014/15 and the possible reasons why such an enquiry would be made.   (3 marks)

(Total: 15 marks)

 Calculate your allowed time, allocate the time to the separate parts.....................

36 ERNEST VADER (ADAPTED) *Walk in the footsteps of a top tutor*

You should assume that today's date is 30 June 2016.

You are a trainee Chartered Certified Accountant and are dealing with the tax affairs of Ernest Vader.

Ernest's self-assessment tax return for the tax year 2014/15 was submitted to HM Revenue & Customs (HMRC) on 15 May 2015, and Ernest paid the resulting income tax liability by the due date of 31 January 2016. However, you have just discovered that during the tax year 2014/15 Ernest disposed of a freehold property, the details of which were omitted from his self-assessment tax return. The capital gains tax liability in respect of this disposal is £18,000, and this amount has not been paid.

Ernest has suggested that since HMRC's right to initiate a compliance check into his self-assessment tax return for the tax year 2014/15 expired on 15 May 2016, no disclosure should be made to HMRC of the capital gain.

Required:

(a) Briefly explain the difference between tax evasion and tax avoidance, as well as the general anti-abuse rule and how HMRC would view the situation if Ernest Vader does not disclose his capital gain. **(4 marks)**

(b) Briefly explain from an ethical viewpoint how you, as a trainee Chartered Certified Accountant, should deal with the suggestion from Ernest Vader that no disclosure is made to HMRC of his capital gain. **(3 marks)**

(c) Explain the penalties which your firm, as tax agents, could be liable to, if a compliance check is commenced by HMRC and the firm fails to supply the information requested by HMRC. **(2 marks)**

(d) Assuming that HMRC discover the capital gain and raise an assessment in respect of Ernest Vader's capital gains tax liability of £18,000 for the tax year 2014/15, and that this amount is then paid on 31 July 2016:

    (i) Calculate the amount of interest that will be payable;

    You should assume that the rates for the tax year 2014/15 continue to apply. **(2 marks)**

    (ii) Advise Ernest Vader as to the amount of penalty that is likely to be charged as a result of the failure to notify HMRC, and how this could have been reduced if the capital gain had been disclosed. **(4 marks)**

(Total: 15 marks)

CHARGEABLE GAINS

Tutorial note

You should expect chargeable gains to be tested in both the Section A multiple choice questions and also in the Section B 10 mark questions.

There is however no set minimum or maximum number of marks for chargeable gains.

INDIVIDUALS – CAPITAL GAINS TAX

37   MICHAEL CHIN (ADAPTED) *Online question assistance*

Michael Chin made the following gifts of assets to his daughter, Mika, during 2014/15:

(1)   On 30 June 2014 Michael gave Mika a business that he had run as a sole trader since 1 January 2010. The market value of the business on 30 June 2014 was £250,000, made up as follows:

	£
Goodwill	60,000
Freehold property	150,000
Net current assets	40,000
	———
	250,000
	———

The goodwill has been built up since 1 January 2010, and had a nil cost. The freehold property had cost £86,000 on 20 May 2012. Michael used 75% of this property for business purposes, but the other 25% has never been used for business purposes.

(2)   On 8 December 2014 Michael gave Mika his entire holding of 50,000 50p ordinary shares (a 60% holding) in Minnow Ltd, an unquoted trading company. The market value of the shares on that date was £180,000.

Michael had originally purchased the shares on 5 January 2014 for £87,500. On 8 December 2014 the market value of Minnow Ltd's chargeable assets was £250,000, of which £200,000 was in respect of chargeable business assets. Michael has never been employed by Minnow Ltd.

(3)   On 28 February 2015 Michael gave Mika a painting. On that date the painting was valued at £7,500. He had originally acquired the painting on 1 June 2013 for £4,000.

(4)   On 15 March 2015 Michael gave Mika an antique necklace. On that date the necklace was valued at £4,000. Michael had acquired the necklace for £2,000 on 1 April 2013.

Where possible, Michael and Mika have elected to hold over any gains arising.

Michael incurred a capital loss of £16,800 during 2012/13, and made a chargeable gain of £12,100 during 2013/14. Michael's taxable income in 2014/15 is £41,250.

Required:

Calculate Michael's capital gains tax liability for 2014/15, clearly showing the amount of any gains that can be held over. Ignore Entrepreneurs' relief.

You should assume that the annual exempt amount for 2014/15 applies throughout.

(10 marks)

 Online question assistance

---

38 DAVID AND ANGELA BROOK (ADAPTED) *Walk in the footsteps of a top tutor*

David and Angela Brook are a married couple. They disposed of the following assets during the tax year 2014/15:

Jointly owned property

(1) On 29 July 2014 David and Angela sold a classic Ferrari motor car for £34,400. The motor car had been purchased on 17 January 2003 for £27,200.

(2) On 30 September 2014 David and Angela sold a house for £381,900. The house had been purchased on 1 October 1994 for £86,000.

David and Angela occupied the house as their main residence from the date of purchase until 31 March 1998. The house was then unoccupied between 1 April 1998 and 31 December 2001 due to Angela being required by her employer to work elsewhere in the United Kingdom.

From 1 January 2002 until 31 December 2008 David and Angela again occupied the house as their main residence. The house was then unoccupied until it was sold on 30 September 2014.

Throughout the period 1 October 1994 to 30 September 2014 David and Angela did not have any other main residence.

David Brook

On 5 May 2014 David transferred his entire shareholding of 20,000 £1 ordinary shares in Bend Ltd, an unquoted trading company, to Angela. On that date the shares were valued at £64,000. David's shareholding had been purchased on 21 June 2012 for £48,000.

Angela Brook

On 7 July 2014 Angela sold 15,000 of the 20,000 £1 ordinary shares in Bend Ltd that had been transferred to her from David. The sale proceeds were £62,400.

Neither David nor Angela has ever worked for Bent Ltd. Angela has taxable income of £31,310 for the tax year 2014/15. David does not have any taxable income.

Required:

Compute David and Angela's respective capital gains tax liabilities for the tax year 2014/15.

(10 marks)

39 WILSON BIAZMA (ADAPTED)

Wilson Biazma is resident in the United Kingdom for tax purposes. He is a higher rate taxpayer.

He disposed of the following assets during the tax year 2014/15:

(1) On 21 July 2014 Wilson sold a freehold office building for £246,000. The office building had been purchased on 3 January 1995 for £104,000. Wilson has made a claim to rollover the gain on the office building against the replacement cost of a new freehold office building that was purchased on 14 January 2014 for £136,000. Both office buildings have always been used entirely for business purposes in a wholesale business run by Wilson as a sole trader.

(2) On 26 July 2014 Wilson sold a retail business that he had run as a sole trader since 1 June 2009. The disposal proceeds for the business were £200,000.

The only chargeable asset of the business was goodwill and this was valued at £120,000 on 26 July 2014. The goodwill has a nil cost.

Required:

(a) Briefly explain the automatic UK residence tests and state how a person's residence status establishes whether or not they are liable to capital gains tax. **(4 marks)**

(b) Calculate Wilson's capital gains tax liability for 2014/15, clearly identifying the effects of the reliefs claimed in respect of disposals (1) and (2). **(6 marks)**

(Total: 10 marks)

40 BILL DING *Walk in the footsteps of a top tutor*

Bill Ding has run a construction company, High Rise Ltd since he purchased the entire shareholding for £112,000 in 1998. He has worked for the company since purchase.

Bill has decided to retire and on 17 August 2014 Bill made a gift of his entire holding of High Rise Ltd shares to his daughter, Belle, who also works for the company. The market value of the shares on that date was £260,000.

On 17 August 2014 the market value of High Rise Ltd's chargeable assets was £180,000, of which £150,000 was in respect of chargeable business assets. Bill and his daughter have elected to hold over the gain on this gift of a business asset.

Belle plans to sell the shares in High Rise Ltd on 31 March 2015, when they are expected to be worth £265,000 in order to fund a new business venture.

Neither Bill nor Belle has made any previous disposals chargeable to capital gains tax, and both are higher rate taxpayers.

Required:

(a) Calculate the gains arising and capital gains tax liabilities for Bill and Belle on the gift of High Rise Ltd shares to Belle and the subsequent sale by Belle.

Assume that Bill and Belle make a joint claim for gift relief, and state the due date for this claim. **(5 marks)**

(b) Recalculate the gains arising and capital gains tax liabilities for Bill and Belle, assuming a joint claim for gift relief is not made. **(3 marks)**

(c) Briefly conclude, including a calculation of the tax saving, on which route would be preferable for Bill and Belle. **(2 marks)**

(Total: 10 marks)

41 BO AND CHARLES (ADAPTED) *Walk in the footsteps of a top tutor*

You are a trainee accountant and your manager has asked for your help regarding two taxpayers who have disposed of assets during the tax year 2014/15.

(a) Bo Neptune

On 31 July 2014 Bo made a gift to his son of his entire holding of 50,000 £1 ordinary shares (a 100% holding) in Botune Ltd, an unquoted trading company. The market value of the shares on that date was £210,000. The shares had been purchased by Bo on 22 January 2008 for £94,000. Bo and his son have elected to hold over the gain as a gift of a business asset.

Required:

(i) Calculate Bo Neptune's chargeable gain, if any, for the tax year 2014/15, and the base cost of his son's 50,000 £1 ordinary shares in Botune Ltd. **(3 marks)**

(ii) Explain how your answer to (i) above would have differed if the shares in Botune Ltd had instead been sold to Bo Neptune's son for £160,000.

(2 marks)

You should ignore Entrepreneurs' relief.

(b) Charles Orion

On 30 September 2014 Charles sold a house for £282,000, resulting in a chargeable gain of £172,000. The house had been purchased on 1 October 2002.

He occupied the house as his main residence from the date of purchase until 31 March 2004. Charles then moved in with his girlfriend and the house was unoccupied between 1 April 2004 and 30 September 2014.

Throughout the period 1 October 2002 to 30 September 2014 Charles did not have any other main residence.

Required:

(i) Calculate Charles Orion's chargeable gain, if any, for the tax year 2014/15.

(2 marks)

(ii) Explain how your answer to (i) above would have differed if Charles Orion had rented out his house during the period 1 April 2004 to 30 September 2014. **(3 marks)**

(Total: 10 marks)

42   ALPHABET LTD (ADAPTED) *Walk in the footsteps of a top tutor*

On 15 October 2014 Alphabet Ltd, an unquoted trading company, was taken over by XYZ plc. Prior to the takeover Alphabet Ltd's share capital consisted of 100,000 £1 ordinary shares and under the terms of the takeover the shareholders received either cash of £6 per share or one £1 ordinary share in XYZ plc for each £1 ordinary share in Alphabet Ltd.

The following information is available regarding three shareholders of Alphabet Ltd:

Aloi

Aloi has been the managing director of Alphabet Ltd since the company's incorporation on 1 January 2004, and she accepted XYZ plc's cash alternative of £6 per share in respect of her shareholding of 60,000 £1 ordinary shares in Alphabet Ltd. Aloi had originally subscribed for 50,000 shares in Alphabet Ltd on 1 January 2004 at their par value, and purchased a further 10,000 shares on 20 May 2006 for £18,600.

On 6 February 2015 Aloi sold an investment property, and this disposal resulted in a chargeable gain of £22,600.

For the tax year 2014/15 Aloi has taxable income of £60,000.

Bon

Bon has been the sales director of Alphabet Ltd since 1 February 2014, having not previously been an employee of the company. She accepted XYZ plc's share alternative of one £1 ordinary share for each of her 25,000 £1 ordinary shares in Alphabet Ltd. Bon had purchased her shareholding on 1 February 2014 for £92,200.

On 4 March 2015 Bon made a gift of 10,000 of her £1 ordinary shares in XYZ plc to her brother. On that date the shares were quoted on the Stock Exchange at £7.10 – £7.18. There were no recorded bargains. Holdover relief is not available in respect of this disposal.

For the tax year 2014/15 Bon has taxable income of £55,000.

Cherry

Cherry has been an employee of Alphabet Ltd since 1 May 2005. She accepted XYZ plc's share alternative of one £1 ordinary share for each of her 3,000 £1 ordinary shares in Alphabet Ltd. Cherry had purchased her shareholding on 20 June 2006 for £4,800.

On 13 November 2014 Cherry sold 1,000 of her £1 ordinary shares in XYZ plc for £6,600.

Cherry died on 5 April 2015, and her remaining 2,000 £1 ordinary shares in XYZ plc were inherited by her daughter. On that date these shares were valued at £15,600.

For the tax year 2014/15 Cherry had taxable income of £12,000.

Required:

(a)   State why Bon and Cherry did not meet the qualifying conditions for Entrepreneurs' relief as regards their shareholdings in Alphabet Ltd.   **(2 marks)**

(b)   Calculate the capital gains tax liabilities of Aloi, Bon, and Cherry for the tax year 2014/15.

In each case, the taxable income is stated after the deduction of the personal allowance.   **(8 marks)**

(Total: 10 marks)

43   JORGE JUNG (ADAPTED) *Walk in the footsteps of a top tutor*

Jorge Jung disposed of the following assets during the tax year 2014/15:

(1)   On 30 September 2014 Jorge sold a copyright for £8,200. The copyright had been purchased on 1 October 2012 for £7,000 when it had an unexpired life of 10 years.

(2)   On 6 October 2014 Jorge sold a painting for £5,400. The painting had been purchased on 18 May 2010 for £2,200.

(3)   On 29 October 2014 Jorge sold a motor car for £10,700. The motor car had been purchased on 21 December 2012 for £14,600.

(4)   On 3 December 2014 Jorge sold two acres of land for £92,000. Jorge's father-in-law had originally purchased three acres of land on 4 August 2002 for £19,500.

The father-in-law died on 17 June 2009, and the land was inherited by Jorge's wife. On that date the three acres of land were valued at £28,600. On 1 December 2009 Jorge's wife incurred legal fees of £500 defending her title to the land. Jorge's wife transferred the land to Jorge on 14 November 2012. On that date the three acres of land were valued at £39,000. The market value of the unsold acre of land as at 3 December 2014 was £38,000.

(5)   On 14 January 2015 Jorge sold 5,000 £1 ordinary shares in Futuristic Ltd, an unquoted trading company, to his sister for £40,000. The market value of the shares on that date was £64,800. The shares had been purchased on 21 March 2010 for £26,300. Jorge and his sister have elected to hold over the gain as a gift of a business asset.

Required:

Calculate Jorge Jung's taxable gains for the tax year 2014/15.   **(10 marks)**

44   WINSTON KING (ADAPTED) *Walk in the footsteps of a top tutor*

 Timed question with Online tutor debrief

(a)   'Tax is charged when there is a chargeable disposal of a chargeable asset by a chargeable person.'

Required:

(i)   **State which individuals are subject to capital gains tax on the disposal of chargeable assets situated in the United Kingdom;**   **(1 mark)**

(ii)   **State which companies are subject to corporation tax on the disposal of chargeable assets situated in the United Kingdom.**   **(1 mark)**

(b)   Winston King was born on 15 August 1959. On 19 May 2014 he disposed of a painting, and this resulted in a chargeable gain of £45,860. For the tax year 2014/15 Winston has taxable income of £22,400 after the deduction of the personal allowance.

Winston has £1,500 of capital losses brought forward from 2013/14.

Winston is considering the sale of a business that he has run as a sole trader since 1 July 2007. The business will be sold for £260,000, and this figure, along with the respective cost of each asset, is made up as follows:

	Sale proceeds	Cost
	£	£
Freehold shop	140,000	80,000
Freehold warehouse	88,000	102,000
Net current assets	32,000	32,000
	———	
	260,000	
	———	

The assets have all been owned for more than one year. The freehold warehouse has never been used by Winston for business purposes.

Where possible, Winston will claim Entrepreneurs' relief in respect of this disposal.

Required:

(i) **Assuming that Winston King does not sell his sole trader business, calculate his capital gains tax liability for the tax year 2014/15;** **(4 marks)**

(ii) **Calculate Winston King's capital gains tax liability for the tax year 2014/15 if he sold his sole trader business on 25 March 2015.** **(4 marks)**

(Total: 10 marks)

 Calculate your allowed time, allocate the time to the separate parts...................

---

45 GINGER AND NIGEL (ADAPTED) *Walk in the footsteps of a top tutor*

You should assume that today's date is 1 March 2015.

(a) Ginger has a holding of 10,000 £1 ordinary shares in Nutmeg Ltd, an unquoted trading company, which she had purchased on 13 February 2006 for £2.40 per share. The current market value of the shares is £6.40 per share, but Ginger intends to sell some of the holding to her daughter at £4.00 per share during March 2015. Ginger and her daughter will elect to hold over any gain as a gift of a business asset.

For the tax year 2014/15, Ginger will not make any other disposals, and has therefore not utilised her annual exempt amount.

Required:

Explain how many £1 ordinary shares in Nutmeg Ltd Ginger can sell to her daughter for £4.00 per share during March 2015 without incurring any capital gains tax liability for the tax year 2014/15.

Your answer should be supported by appropriate calculations. **(4 marks)**

(b) Innocent and Nigel, a married couple, both have shareholdings in Cinnamon Ltd, an unquoted trading company with a share capital of 100,000 £1 ordinary shares.

Innocent has been the managing director of Cinnamon Ltd since the company's incorporation on 1 July 2006, and she currently holds 20,000 shares (with matching voting rights) in the company. These shares were subscribed for on 1 July 2006 at their par value.

Nigel has never been an employee or a director of Cinnamon Ltd, and he currently holds 3,000 shares (with matching voting rights) in the company. These shares were purchased on 23 April 2010 for £46,200.

Either Innocent or Nigel will sell 2,000 of their shares in Cinnamon Ltd during March 2015 for £65,000, but they are not sure which of them should make the disposal. For the tax year 2014/15, both Innocent and Nigel have already made disposals which will fully utilise their annual exempt amounts, and they will each have taxable income of £80,000.

Required:

Calculate the capital gains tax saving if the disposal of 2,000 shares in Cinnamon Ltd during March 2015 is made by Innocent rather than Nigel. **(6 marks)**

(Total: 10 marks)

46   MARLON AND LEROY (ADAPTED) *Walk in the footsteps of a top tutor*

(a)   On 12 February 2015, Marlon sold a house for £497,000, which he had owned individually. The house had been purchased on 22 October 1999 for £146,000. Marlon incurred legal fees of £2,900 in connection with the purchase of the house, and legal fees of £3,700 in connection with the disposal.

Throughout the period of ownership the house was occupied by Marlon and his wife, Alvita, as their main residence. One-third of the house was always used exclusively for business purposes by the couple. Entrepreneurs' relief is not available in respect of this disposal.

For the tax year 2014/15 Marlon is a higher rate taxpayer, but Alvita did not have any taxable income. Neither of them made any other disposals of assets during the year.

Required:

(i)   Calculate Marlon's chargeable gain for the tax year 2014/15. **(3 marks)**

(ii)   Calculate the amount of capital gains tax which could have been saved if Marlon had transferred 50% ownership of the house to Alvita prior to its disposal. **(2 marks)**

(b)   On 2 April 2015, Leroy sold 12,000 £1 ordinary shares in Jerk-Chic plc for £83,400.

He has had the following transactions in the shares of the company:

1 March 2006	Purchased 20,000 shares for £19,800
20 July 2010	Purchased 8,000 shares for £27,800
23 October 2014	Made a gift of 4,000 shares

The gift of 4,000 shares on 23 October 2014 was to Leroy's daughter. On that date the shares were quoted on the Stock Exchange at £7.80 – £8.20. There were no recorded bargains. Holdover relief is not available in respect of this disposal.

Neither disposal of Jerk-Chic plc shares during the tax year 2014/15 qualifies for Entrepreneurs' relief.

For the tax year 2014/15 Leroy is a higher rate taxpayer, and will remain so for the tax year 2015/16. Leroy regularly makes disposals of other investments, so no annual exempt amount is available for either of the tax years 2014/15 or 2015/16.

Required:

(i) Calculate the chargeable gains arising from Leroy's disposals of Jerk-Chic plc shares during the tax year 2014/15. **(4 marks)**

(ii) State why it would have been beneficial if Leroy had delayed the sale of the 12,000 shares in Jerk-Chic plc until 6 April 2015. **(1 mark)**

(Total: 10 marks)

COMPANIES – CHARGEABLE GAINS

47 FORWARD LTD (ADAPTED)

Forward Ltd sold the following assets during the year ended 31 March 2015:

(1) On 31 May 2014 Forward Ltd sold a freehold office building for £290,000. The office building had been purchased on 15 July 1995 for £148,000. The retail price index (RPI) for July 1995 was 149.1, and for May 2014 it was 255.6.

Forward Ltd purchased a replacement freehold office building on 1 June 2014 for £260,000.

(2) On 30 November 2014 Forward Ltd sold 5,000 £1 ordinary shares in Backward plc for £62,500. Forward Ltd had originally purchased 9,000 shares in Backward plc on 20 April 1989 for £18,000, and purchased a further 500 shares on 1 November 2014 for £6,500. Assume the retail price index for April 1989 was 114.3, and for November 2014 it was 258.0. Forward Ltd has never owned more than 1% of the shares in Backward plc.

Forward Ltd purchased 10,000 £1 ordinary shares in Sideways plc on 1 December 2014 for £65,000.

Where possible, Forward Ltd has claimed to roll over any gains arising.

Forward Ltd's only other income for the year ended 31 March 2015 is its tax adjusted trading profit of £78,000. There are no associated companies.

Required:

(a) Calculate Forward Ltd's corporation tax liability for the year ended 31 March 2015, and state by when this should be paid.

Your answer should clearly identify the amount of any gains that have been rolled over. Capital allowances should be ignored. **(7 marks)**

(b) Explain how Forward Ltd's rollover relief claim would have altered if on 1 June 2014 it had acquired a leasehold office building on a 15-year lease for £300,000, rather than purchasing the freehold office building for £260,000. **(3 marks)**

(Total: 10 marks)

48   HAWK LTD (ADAPTED) *Walk in the footsteps of a top tutor*

Hawk Ltd sold the following asset during the year ended 31 March 2015:

On 30 April 2014 a freehold office building was sold for £260,000. The office building had been purchased on 2 July 1994 for £81,000, and had been extended at a cost of £43,000 during May 2006.

Hawk Ltd incurred legal fees of £3,200 in connection with the purchase of the office building, and legal fees of £3,840 in connection with the disposal. The office building has always been used by Hawk Ltd for business purposes.

The relevant retail prices indexes (RPIs) are as follows:

July 1994	144.0
May 2006	197.7
April 2014	255.2

Hawk Ltd's only other income for the year ended 31 March 2015 was a trading profit of £250,000.

Hawk Ltd does not have any associated companies.

Required:

(a)   Calculate Hawk Ltd's corporation tax liability for the year ended 31 March 2015.

(6 marks)

(b)   Advise Hawk Ltd of:

(i)   The minimum amount that will have to be reinvested in qualifying replacement business assets in order for the company to claim the maximum possible amount of rollover relief in respect of its chargeable gain for the year ended 31 March 2015.   **(1 mark)**

(ii)   The period during which the reinvestment must take place.   **(1 mark)**

(iii)   The amount of corporation tax that will be deferred if the maximum possible amount of rollover relief is claimed for the year ended 31 March 2015.

(2 mark)

(Total: 10 marks)

49   ACEBOOK LTD (ADAPTED) *Walk in the footsteps of a top tutor*

Acebook Ltd sold the following assets during the year ended 31 December 2014:

(1)   On 10 March 2014 Acebook Ltd sold its entire shareholding of 50p ordinary shares in Oogle plc for £3.20 per share. The company had originally purchased 8,000 shares in Oogle plc on 28 June 2006 for £25,200.

On 31 October 2009 Oogle plc made a 2 for 1 bonus issue. Then, on 14 February 2011, Oogle plc made a 1 for 5 rights issue. Acebook Ltd took up its allocation under the rights issue in full, paying £4.30 for each new share issued.

The company has never owned more than 1% of the shares of Oogle plc.

Indexation factors are as follows:

June 2006 to October 2009	0.088
June 2006 to February 2011	0.165
June 2006 to March 2014	0.284
October 2009 to February 2011	0.071
October 2009 to March 2014	0.180
February 2011 to March 2014	0.102

(2) On 30 June 2014 three acres of land were sold for £192,000. Acebook Ltd had originally purchased four acres of land, and the indexed cost of the four acres on 30 June 2014 was £196,000. The market value of the unsold acre of land as at 30 June 2014 was £53,000. During June 2014 Acebook Ltd spent £29,400 clearing and levelling all four acres of land. The land has never been used for business purposes.

(3) On 1 October 2014 an investment property owned by Acebook Ltd was destroyed in a fire. The indexed cost of the property on that date was £138,400. Acebook Ltd received insurance proceeds of £189,000 on 20 October 2014, and on 31 October 2014 the company paid £172,400 for a replacement investment property. Acebook Ltd has made a claim to defer the gain arising from the receipt of the insurance proceeds.

Required:

Calculate Acebook Ltd's chargeable gains for the year ended 31 December 2014.

(10 marks)

INHERITANCE TAX

Tutorial note

You should expect inheritance tax to be tested in both the Section A multiple choice questions and also in the Section B 10 mark questions.

There is however no set minimum or maximum number of marks for inheritance tax.

50 JIMMY (ADAPTED) *Walk in the footsteps of a top tutor*

Jimmy died on 14 February 2015. He had made the following gifts during his lifetime:

(1) On 2 August 2013 Jimmy made a cash gift of £50,000 to his grandson as a wedding gift when he got married.

(2) On 14 November 2013 Jimmy made a cash gift of £800,000 to a trust. Jimmy paid the inheritance tax arising from this gift.

At the date of his death Jimmy owned the following assets:

(1) His main residence valued at £260,000.

(2) A life assurance policy on his own life. On 14 February 2015 the policy had an open market value of £182,000, and proceeds of £210,000 were received following Jimmy's death.

Under the terms of his will Jimmy left all of his estate to his daughter.

The nil rate band for the tax year 2013/14 is £325,000.

Required:

(a) **Explain why it is important to differentiate between potentially exempt transfers and chargeable lifetime transfers for inheritance tax purposes.**   **(2 marks)**

(b) **Calculate the inheritance tax that will be payable as a result of Jimmy's death.**

(8 marks)

(Total: 10 marks)

51 ETHEL AND BLU (ADAPTED) *Walk in the footsteps of a top tutor*

(a) Ethel Brown started to run a small bed and breakfast business as a sole trader on 6 April 2014. She prepared her first accounts for the year to 5 April 2015.

She has read in the newspapers about a new cash basis of accounting and new HMRC flat rate expense adjustments which are intended to simplify tax accounting for small businesses.

In the year to 5 April 2015 she has the following transactions:

(1) Payments of £25,000 in respect of food, utilities and other household costs. She lives in part of the bed and breakfast premises with her husband and two children and 35% of the food, utilities and other household costs relate to their private use. The HMRC flat rate private use adjustment for four occupants of business premises is £7,800.

(2) On 1 June 2014 Ethel paid a car dealer £14,000 by cheque for a car with CO_2 emissions of 125g/km. She also made payments totalling £3,000 related to the running costs of the car for the year. She has used the car 40% of the time for private purposes and she drove 11,000 business miles during the year.

(3) On 1 March 2015 she acquired an item of kitchen equipment for £350 on credit terms. She paid the supplier's invoice on 15 April 2015.

Required:

Prepare brief notes which you can use to advise Ethel on how the transactions in Notes (1) to (3) should be treated for tax purposes in the accounts for the year to 5 April 2015 assuming that she opts to prepare her accounts using the cash basis and the HMRC flat rate expense adjustments.

Your should ignore VAT   **(4 marks)**

(b) On 15 January 2015 Blu Reddy made a gift of 200,000 £1 ordinary shares in Purple Ltd, an unquoted investment company, to a trust. Blu paid the inheritance tax arising from this gift.

Before the transfer Blu owned 300,000 shares out of Purple Ltd's issued share capital of 500,000 £1 ordinary shares.

On 15 January 2015 Purple Ltd's shares were worth £2 each for a holding of 20%, £3 each for a holding of 40%, and £4 each for a holding of 60%.

Blu has not made any previous gifts.

Required:

Calculate the inheritance tax that will be payable as a result of Blu Reddy's gift to the trust, and the additional inheritance tax that would be payable if Blu were to die on 31 May 2019.

You should ignore annual exemptions, and should assume that the nil rate band for the tax year 2014/15 remains unchanged. (6 marks)

(Total: 10 marks)

52   NING GAO (ADAPTED)   *Walk in the footsteps of a top tutor*

 Timed question with Online tutor debrief

You should assume that today's date is 15 March 2015.

Ning Gao, aged 71, owns the following assets:

(1)   Two properties respectively valued at £674,000 and £442,000. The first property has an outstanding repayment mortgage of £160,000, and the second property has an outstanding endowment mortgage of £92,000.

(2)   Vintage motor cars valued at £194,400.

Ning owes £22,400 in respect of a personal loan from a bank, and she has also verbally promised to pay legal fees of £4,600 incurred by her nephew.

Under the terms of her will Ning has left all of her estate to her children.

Ning's husband died on 12 March 2005, and 70% of his inheritance tax nil rate band was not used.

On 7 November 2014 Ning made a gift of £220,000 to her son. This figure is after deducting all available exemptions.

The nil rate band for the tax year 2004/05 is £263,000.

Required:

(a)   Advise Ning Gao as to how much nil rate band will be available when calculating the inheritance tax payable in respect of her estate were she to die on 20 March 2015. (3 marks)

(b)   (i)   Calculate the inheritance tax that would be payable in respect of Ning Gao's estate were she to die on 20 March 2015, and state who will be responsible for paying the tax; (5 marks)

        (ii)   Advise Ning Gao as to whether the inheritance tax payable in respect of her estate would alter if she were to live for either another six or another seven years after 20 March 2015, and if so by how much.

        You should assume that both the value of Ning Gao's estate and the nil rate band will remain unchanged. (2 marks)

(Total: 10 marks)

 Calculate your allowed time, allocate the time to the separate parts.....................

53   ROSIE AND TOM (ADAPTED) *Walk in the footsteps of a top tutor*

You should assume that today's date is 15 February 2015.

(a)   Rosie Rohan, born on 31 July 1973, is the managing director of Hornburg plc. During the tax year 2014/15 Rosie was paid gross director's remuneration of £220,000.

She has made the following gross personal pension contributions:

Tax year	Pension contribution
	£
2011/12	41,000
2012/13	26,000
2013/14	Nil

Rosie was a member of a pension scheme for the tax year 2013/14.

Required:

Advise Rosie Rohan of the total amount of pension scheme annual allowances that she has available for the tax year 2014/15, the method by which tax relief will be given for any personal pension contributions that she makes during that year, and the tax implications if she makes contributions in excess of the available annual allowances.

Note:

1   You are not expected to calculate Rosie Rohan's income tax liability.

2   You are not expected to consider the situation where pension contributions do not attract tax relief.   (5 marks)

(b)   Tom Tirith, born on 25 September 1942, made a cash gift of £200,000 to his daughter on 20 December 2013. He is now going to make a cash gift of £450,000 to a trust on 20 February 2015. The nil rate band for the tax year 2013/14 is £325,000.

Required:

(i)   **Calculate the lifetime inheritance tax that will be payable in respect of Tom Tirith's gift of £450,000 to a trust if:**

(1)   **the trust pays the tax arising from the gift; or**

(2)   **Tom pays the tax arising from the gift,**

and in the case of (2) only state the value of the gross chargeable transfer.

The total marks will be split equally between each part.   (3 marks)

(ii)   **Explain how your answer would be different if, instead of making a cash gift to his daughter on 20 December 2013, Tom made the same gift to a trust.**

You are not required to do calculations for requirement (b)(ii).   (2 marks)

(Total: 10 marks)

54 PERE JONES (ADAPTED) *Walk in the footsteps of a top tutor*

On 23 August 2009, Pere Jones made a gift of a house valued at £420,000 to his son, Phil Jones. This was a wedding gift when Phil got married.

Pere Jones

Pere died on 20 March 2015 aged 76, at which time his estate was valued at £880,000. Under the terms of his will, Pere divided his estate equally between his wife and his son, Phil. Pere had not made any gifts during his lifetime except for the gift of the house to Phil.

The nil rate band for the tax year 2009/10 is £325,000.

Phil Jones

Phil was born on 13 August 1966. The house which he received as a wedding gift from Pere, his father, was always let out unfurnished until it was sold on 5 April 2015.

The following income and outgoings relate to the property for the tax year 2014/15:

	£
Sale proceeds	504,000
Cost of new boundary wall around the property (there was previously no boundary wall)	(5,300)
Cost of replacing the property's chimney	(2,800)
Legal fees paid in connection with the disposal	(8,600)
Property insurance	(2,300)

Phil has earnings from employment of £80,000 in 2014/15.

Required:

(a) Calculate the inheritance tax that will be payable as a result of Pere Jones' death;

(6 marks)

(b) Calculate Phil Jones' capital gains tax liability for the tax year 2014/15.   (4 marks)

(Total: 10 marks)

55 AFIYA (ADAPTED) *Walk in the footsteps of a top tutor*

Afiya died on 29 November 2014. She had made the following gifts during her lifetime:

(1) On 14 September 2013, Afiya made a gift of 6,500 £1 ordinary shares in Cassava Ltd, an unquoted investment company, to her daughter.

Before the transfer Afiya owned 8,000 shares out of Cassava Ltd's issued share capital of 10,000 £1 ordinary shares. On 14 September 2013, Cassava Ltd's shares were worth £3 each for a holding of 15%, £7 each for a holding of 65%, and £8 each for a holding of 80%.

(2) On 27 January 2014, Afiya made a cash gift of £400,000 to a trust. Afiya paid the inheritance tax arising from this gift.

On 29 November 2014, Afiya's estate was valued at £620,000. Under the terms of her will Afiya left £150,000 to her husband, a specific legacy of £40,000 to her sister, and the residue of the estate to her children.

The nil rate band for the tax year 2013/14 is £325,000.

Required:

(a) Calculate the inheritance tax which will be payable as a result of Afiya's death.

(7 marks)

(b) State the due dates of payment for the inheritance tax arising from the gift made to the trust on 27 January 2014.

Your answer should cover both the lifetime inheritance tax paid and the additional tax payable as a result of Afiya's death. **(2 marks)**

(c) Calculate the amount of the inheritance which will be received by Afiya's children.

(1 mark)

(Total: 10 marks)

CORPORATION TAX

Tutorial note

Corporation tax will be the focus of a 15 mark Section B question.

You should also expect corporation tax to be tested in both the Section A multiple choice questions and potentially in the Section B 10 mark questions.

CORPORATION TAX BASICS AND ADMINISTRATION

56   ARABLE LTD (ADAPTED)

Arable Ltd commenced trading on 1 April 2014 as a manufacturer of farm equipment, preparing its first accounts for the nine-month period ended 31 December 2014. The following information is available:

Trading profit

The tax adjusted trading profit is £601,611. This figure is before taking account of capital allowances and any deduction arising from the premium paid in respect of leasehold property.

Plant and machinery

Arable Ltd purchased the following assets in respect of the nine-month period ended 31 December 2014.

		£
20 April 2014	Delivery lorries	418,350
12 May 2014	Motor car (1)	11,200
14 May 2014	Motor car (2)	14,600
17 May 2014	Motor car (3)	13,000

Motor car (1) purchased on 12 May 2014 for £11,200 has a CO_2 emission rate of 106 grams per kilometre. Motor car (2) purchased on 14 May 2014 for £14,600 has a CO_2 emission rate of 138 grams per kilometre. Motor car (3), purchased on 17 May 2014 for £13,000, is a new car and has CO_2 emissions of 79 grams per kilometre.

The company will not make any short life asset elections.

Leasehold property

On 1 April 2014 Arable Ltd acquired a leasehold office building. A premium of £75,000 was paid for the grant of a 15-year lease. The office building was used for business purposes by Arable Ltd throughout the period ended 31 December 2014.

Freehold property

On 1 August 2014 Arable Ltd acquired the freehold of a second office building. This office building was empty until 30 September 2014, and was then let to a tenant. On that date Arable Ltd received a premium of £50,000 for the grant of a five-year lease, and annual rent of £14,800 which was payable in advance.

Loan interest received

Loan interest of £6,000 was received on 30 September 2014, and £3,000 was accrued at 31 December 2014. The loan was made for non-trading purposes.

Dividends received

During the period ended 31 December 2014 Arable Ltd received dividends of £18,000 from Ranch plc, an unconnected UK company. This figure was the actual cash amount received.

Other information

Arable Ltd has two associated companies.

Required:

Calculate Arable Ltd's corporation tax liability for the nine-month period ended 31 December 2014. **(15 marks)**

57 ZOOM PLC (ADAPTED) *Online question assistance*

Zoom plc is a manufacturer of photographic equipment. The company had taxable total profits of £858,835 for the year ended 31 March 2015.

The statement of profit or loss of Zoom plc for the year ended 31 March 2015 shows:

	£	£
Operating profit (Note 1)		828,900
Income from investments		
Bank interest (Note 3)	10,420	
Loan interest (Note 4)	22,500	
Dividends (Note 5)	49,500	
	———	82,420
		———
		911,320
Interest payable (Note 6)		(46,000)
		———
Profit before taxation		865,320
		———

Note 1 – Operating profit

Depreciation of £59,227 has been deducted in arriving at the operating profit of £828,900.

Note 2 – Plant and machinery

On 1 April 2014 the tax written down values of plant and machinery were as follows:

	£
General pool	19,600
Short life asset	20,200

The following transactions took place during the year ended 31 March 2015:

		Cost/Proceeds £
19 July 2014	Purchased computer	12,300
29 July 2014	Sold short life asset	(19,200)
30 July 2014	Purchased motor car	16,600
3 August 2014	Sold a lorry	(9,800)
28 February 2015	Sold equipment (original cost £1,900)	(1,000)

The motor car purchased on 30 July 2014 for £16,600 has a CO_2 emission rate of 140 grams per kilometre.

The short life asset sold on 29 July 2014 for £19,200 originally cost £31,500 in May 2012. The lorry sold on 3 August 2014 for £9,800 originally cost £17,200.

Note 3 – Bank interest received

The bank interest was received on 31 March 2015. The bank deposits are held for non-trading purposes.

Note 4 – Loan interest receivable

The loan was made for non-trading purposes on 1 July 2014. Loan interest of £15,000 was received on 30 December 2014, and interest of £7,500 was accrued at 31 March 2015.

Note 5 – Dividends received

The dividends were all received from unconnected UK companies. The figure of £49,500 is the actual cash amount received.

Note 6 – Interest payable

The interest is in respect of a loan note that has been used for trading purposes. Interest of £23,000 was paid on 30 September 2014 and again on 31 March 2015.

Required:

(a) Calculate the amount of capital allowances that Zoom plc can claim for the year ended 31 March 2015.   **(10 marks)**

(b) Prepare a computation for the year ended 31 March 2015 reconciling Zoom plc's profit before taxation with its taxable total profits.

Your reconciliation should commence with the profit before taxation figure of £865,320, clearly identify the tax adjusted trading profit and the amount of property business profit, and end with the figure of £858,835 for taxable total profits.

You should list all of the items referred to in Notes (1)–(6) that are relevant, indicating by use of zero (0) any items that do not require adjustment.   **(5 marks)**

(Total: 15 marks)

 Online question assistance

58 DO-NOT-PANIC LTD (ADAPTED)

Do-Not-Panic Ltd is a United Kingdom resident company that installs burglar alarms.

The company commenced trading on 1 January 2014 and its results for the fifteen-month period ended 31 March 2015 are summarised as follows:

(1)   The trading profit as adjusted for tax purposes is £437,500. This figure is before taking account of capital allowances.

(2)   Do-Not-Panic Ltd purchased equipment for £24,000 on 20 February 2015.

(3)   On 21 December 2014 Do-Not-Panic Ltd disposed of some investments and this resulted in a capital loss of £4,250. On 28 March 2015 the company made a further disposal and this resulted in a chargeable gain of £42,000.

(4)   Franked investment income of £25,000 was received on 22 February 2015.

Do-Not-Panic Ltd has no associated companies.

Required:

Calculate Do-Not-Panic Ltd's corporation tax liabilities in respect of the fifteen-month period ended 31 March 2015 and advise the company by when these should be paid.

(10 marks)

59 CRASH BASH LTD (ADAPTED) *Walk in the footsteps of a top tutor*

Crash-Bash Ltd commenced trading on 1 May 2014 as a manufacturer of motor cycle crash helmets in the United Kingdom. The company is incorporated overseas, although its directors are based in the United Kingdom and hold their board meetings in the United Kingdom.

Crash-Bash Ltd prepared its first accounts for the nine-month period ended 31 January 2015. The following information is available:

Trading profit

The tax adjusted trading profit based on the draft accounts for the nine-month period ended 31 January 2015 is £1,002,924.

This figure is before making any adjustments required for:

(1)   Capital allowances.

(2)   Advertising expenditure of £12,840 incurred during April 2014. This expenditure has not been deducted in arriving at the tax adjusted trading profit for the period ended 31 January 2015 of £1,002,924.

Plant and machinery

The accounts for the nine-month period ended 31 January 2015 showed the following additions and disposals of plant and machinery:

		Cost
		£
2 May 2014	Purchased machinery	381,250
28 June 2014	Purchased a motor car	13,200

The motor car purchased on 28 June 2014 for £13,200 was a new car and has a CO_2 emission rate of 79 grams per kilometre.

Dividends received

During the period ended 31 January 2015 Crash-Bash Ltd received a dividend of £14,250 from a 100% owned subsidiary company, Safety Ltd and received dividends of £36,000 from Flat-Out plc, an unconnected company. These figures were the actual cash amount received.

Other information

With the exception of Safety Ltd, Crash-Bash Ltd does not have any associated companies.

Required:

(a) Explain why Crash-Bash Ltd is treated as being resident in the UK. **(2 marks)**

(b) Calculate Crash-Bash Ltd's corporation tax liability for the nine-month period ended 31 January 2015. **(9 marks)**

(c) State the date by Crash-Bash Ltd's self-assessment corporation tax return for the year ended 31 January 2015 should be submitted, and advise the company of the penalties that will be due if the return is submitted eight months late.

You should assume that the company pays its corporation tax liability at the same time that the self-assessment tax return is submitted. **(4 marks)**

(Total: 15 marks)

60 QUAGMIRE LTD *Walk in the footsteps of a top tutor*

For the year ended 31 January 2015 Quagmire plc had taxable total profits of £1,200,000 and franked investment income of £200,000.

For the year ended 31 January 2014 the company had taxable total profits of £1,600,000 and franked investment income of £120,000.

Quagmire plc's profits accrue evenly throughout the year. Quagmire plc has one associated company.

Required:

(a) Explain why Quagmire plc will have been required to make quarterly instalment payments in respect of its corporation tax liability for the year ended 31 January 2015. **(3 marks)**

(b) Calculate Quagmire plc's corporation tax liability for the year ended 31 January 2015, and explain how and when this will have been paid. **(3 marks)**

(c) Explain how your answer to part (b) above would differ if Quagmire plc did not have an associated company.

Your answer should include a calculation of the revised corporation tax liability for the year ended 31 January 2015. **(4 marks)**

(Total: 10 marks)

61   MOLTEN METAL PLC (ADAPTED)   *Walk in the footsteps of a top tutor*

Molten-Metal plc is a manufacturer of machine tools. The following information is available for the year ended 31 March 2015:

Trading profit

The tax adjusted trading profit for the year ended 31 March 2015 is £2,090,086. This figure is **before** making any deductions required for:

(1)   Interest payable.

(2)   Capital allowances.

(3)   Any revenue expenditure that may have been debited to the company's capital expenditure account in error.

Interest payable

During the year ended 31 March 2015 Molten-Metal plc paid loan stock interest of £22,500. Loan stock interest of £3,700 was accrued at 31 March 2015, with the corresponding accrual at 1 April 2014 being £4,200. The loan is used for trading purposes.

The company also incurred a loan interest expense of £6,800 in respect of a loan that is used for non-trading purposes.

Capital expenditure account

The following items of expenditure have been debited to the capital expenditure account during the year ended 31 March 2015:

1 May 2014	Purchase of a second-hand freehold office building for £378,000. This figure included £83,000 for a ventilation system and £10,000 for a lift. Both the ventilation system and the lift are integral to the office building.
	During May 2014 Molten-Metal plc spent a further £97,400 on repairs. The office building was not usable until these repairs were carried out, and this fact was represented by a reduced purchase price.
26 June 2014	Purchase of machinery for £390,000. During June 2014 a further £7,000 was spent on building alterations that were necessary for the installation of the machinery.
8 August 2014	A payment of £41,200 for the construction of a new decorative wall around the company's premises.
27 August 2014	Purchase of movable partition walls for £22,900. Molten-Metal plc uses these to divide up its open plan offices, and the partition walls are moved around on a regular basis.
11 March 2015	Purchase of two motor cars each costing £17,300. Each motor car has a CO_2 emission rate of 120 grams per kilometre. One motor car is used by the factory manager, and 60% of the mileage is for private journeys. The other motor car is used as a pool car.

Written down value

On 1 April 2014 the tax written down value of plant and machinery in Molten-Metal plc's general pool was £87,800.

Interest receivable

Molten-Metal plc made a loan for non-trading purposes on 1 August 2014. Loan interest of £9,800 was received on 31 January 2015, and £3,100 was accrued at 31 March 2015.

The company also received bank interest of £2,600 during the year ended 31 March 2015. The bank deposits are held for non-trading purposes.

Quarterly instalment payments

Molten-Metal plc makes quarterly instalment payments in respect of its corporation tax liability. The first three instalment payments for the year ended 31 March 2015 totalled £298,200.

Required:

(a)   **Calculate Molten-Metal plc's corporation tax liability for the year ended 31 March 2015.**   **(13 marks)**

(b)   **Calculate the final quarterly instalment payment that will have to be made by Molten-Metal plc for the year ended 31 March 2015, and state when this will be due.**   **(2 marks)**

(Total: 15 marks)

62   STRETCHED LTD (ADAPTED)

Stretched Ltd has always prepared its accounts to 31 December, but has decided to change its accounting date to 31 March. The company's results for the 15-month period ended 31 March 2015 are as follows:

(i)   The tax adjusted trading profit is £642,500. This figure is before taking account of capital allowances.

(ii)   Until January 2015 the company has never been entitled to capital allowances as all assets were leased. However, on 15 January 2015 the company bought office equipment for £132,500.

(iii)   There is a property business profit of £45,000 for the 15-month period ended 31 March 2015.

(iv)   On 15 April 2014 the company disposed of some investments, and this resulted in a chargeable gain of £44,000. On 8 February 2015 the company made a further disposal, and this resulted in a capital loss of £6,700.

(v)   Franked investment income of £30,000 was received on 10 September 2014.

(vi)   A qualifying charitable donation of £5,000 was made on 31 March 2015.

As at 1 January 2014 Stretched Ltd had unused trading losses of £273,000, and unused capital losses of £3,000.

Stretched Ltd has no associated companies.

Required:

(a)   Calculate Stretched Ltd's corporation tax liabilities in respect of the 15-month period ended 31 March 2015, and advise the company by when these should be paid.   **(13 marks)**

(b)   State the advantages for tax purposes of a company having an accounting date of 31 March instead of 31 December.   **(2 marks)**

                                                                                                          (Total: 15 marks)

63   STARFISH LTD (ADAPTED) *Walk in the footsteps of a top tutor*

Starfish Ltd, a retailer of scuba diving equipment, was incorporated on 15 October 2010, and commenced trading on 1 December 2010. The company initially prepared accounts to 31 March, but changed its accounting date to 31 December by preparing accounts for the nine-month period ended 31 December 2014. Starfish Ltd ceased trading on 31 March 2015, and a resolution was subsequently passed to commence winding up procedures.

Starfish Ltd's results for each of its periods of account up to 31 December 2014 are:

	Tax adjusted trading profit/(loss)	Bank interest	Qualifying charitable donations
	£	£	£
Four-month period ended 31 March 2011	(12,600)	600	(800)
Year ended 31 March 2012	64,200	1,400	(1,000)
Year ended 31 March 2013	53,900	1,700	(900)
Year ended 31 March 2014	14,700	0	(700)
Nine-month period ended 31 December 2014	49,900	0	(600)

The company's summarised statement of profit or loss for its final three-month period of trading ended 31 March 2015 is as follows:

	Notes	£	£
Gross profit			16,100
Expenses			
Depreciation		34,400	
Donations	1	1,650	
Impairment loss	2	2,000	
Other expenses	3	168,050	
			(206,100)
Loss before taxation			(190,000)

Note 1 – Donations

Donations were made as follows:	£
Donation to a political party	300
Qualifying charitable donation	1,350
	1,650

Note 2 – Impairment loss

On 31 March 2015 Starfish Ltd wrote off an impairment loss of £2,000 in respect of a trade debt.

Note 3 – Other expenses

Other expenses are as follows:

	£
Entertaining customers	3,600
Entertaining employees	1,840
Counselling services provided to employees who were made redundant	8,400
Balance of expenditure (all allowable)	154,210
	168,050

Note 4 – Plant and machinery

On 1 January 2015 the tax written down values of the company's plant and machinery were:

	£
General pool	23,600
Special rate pool	13,200

On 10 January 2015 Starfish Ltd purchased a laptop computer for £3,120. This figure is inclusive of value added tax (VAT).

On 31 March 2015 the company sold all of the items included in the general pool for £31,200, and the laptop computer for £1,800.

The only item in the special rate pool was a car which had been acquired for £16,000 and which was sold on 31 March 2015 for £9,600. The car was used by the managing director, and 20% of the mileage was for private journeys.

Starfish Ltd is registered for VAT. All of the above figures are inclusive of VAT where applicable. None of the items included in the general pool was sold for more than its original cost, and all of the items in the general pool were standard rated.

Required:

(a)   Calculate Starfish Ltd's tax adjusted trading loss for the three-month period ended 31 March 2015.

Your computation should commence with the loss before taxation figure of £190,000, and should also list all of the items referred to in notes (1) to (4) indicating by the use of zero (0) any items that do not require adjustment.

(10 marks)

(b)   Assuming that Starfish Ltd claims relief for its trading losses on the most beneficial basis, calculate the company's taxable total profits for the four-month period ended 31 March 2011, the years ended 31 March 2012, 2013 and 2014 and the nine-month period ended 31 December 2014.   (5 marks)

(Total: 15 marks)

64   HEAVY LTD (ADAPTED) *Walk in the footsteps of a top tutor*

Heavy Ltd runs a music publishing business. On 1 April 2014 Heavy Ltd acquired 100% of the ordinary share capital of Soft Ltd, a company that runs a music recording studio. Neither company has any other associated companies.

Heavy Ltd has prepared accounts for the year ended 31 July 2015. The following information is available:

(1)   The operating profit for the year ended 31 July 2015 is £433,100. Depreciation of £12,880 and a health and safety fine of £9,000 have been deducted in arriving at this figure.

(2)   On 1 August 2014 the tax written down values of Heavy Ltd's plant and machinery were as follows:

	£
General pool	900
Short life asset (1) – machine acquired May 2012	15,100
Short life asset (2) – plant acquired August 2012	13,200
Special rate pool	21,700

The following purchases and disposals of plant and machinery took place during the year ended 31 July 2015:

		Cost/(Proceeds)
		£
23 March 2015	Purchased office equipment	22,400
24 April 2015	Purchased new motor car	16,000
19 July 2015	Sold short life asset (2)	(4,600)
28 July 2015	Sold all the items included in the special rate pool	(12,300)

The motor car purchased on 24 April 2015 has CO_2 emissions of 90 grams per kilometre and is used by the managing director of Heavy Ltd, and 60% of the mileage is for private journeys. Short life asset (2) sold on 19 July 2015 originally cost £19,200.

(3)   On 18 May 2015 Heavy Ltd sold a freehold office building to Soft Ltd for £113,600. The indexed cost of the office building on that date was £102,800.

(4)   During the year ended 31 July 2015 Heavy Ltd received the following dividends:

Company paying the dividend:	£
An unconnected UK company	27,000
Soft Ltd	6,300

These figures were the actual cash amounts received.

Required:

Calculate Heavy Ltd's corporation tax liability for the year ended 31 July 2015.

Assume that tax rates and allowances for FY2014 continue into the future.   (15 marks)

65 GREENZONE LTD (ADAPTED) *Walk in the footsteps of a top tutor*

Greenzone Ltd runs a business providing environmental guidance. The company's summarised statement of profit or loss for the year ended 31 March 2015 is as follows:

	Note	£	£
Gross profit			404,550
Operating expenses			
Depreciation		28,859	
Repairs and renewals	1	28,190	
Other expenses	2	107,801	
		———	(164,850)
			———
Operating profit			239,700
			———

Note 1 – Repairs and renewals

Repairs and renewals are as follows:

	£
Repainting the exterior of the company's office building	8,390
Extending the office building in order to create a new reception area	19,800
	———
	28,190
	———

Note 2 – Other expenses

Other expenses are as follows:

	£
Entertaining UK customers	3,600
Entertaining overseas customers	1,840
Political donations	740
Donation to a charity where Greenzone Ltd received free advertising in the charity's newsletter.	
This was not a qualifying charitable donation	430
Gifts to customers	
pens costing £30 each, not displaying Greenzone Ltd's name	660
clocks costing £65 each and displaying Greenzone Ltd's name	910
Balance of expenditure (all allowable)	99,621
	———
	107,801
	———

Note 3 – Plant and machinery

On 1 April 2014 the tax written down values of Greenzone Ltd's plant and machinery were as follows:

	£
General pool	48,150
Special rate pool	9,200

The following motor cars were purchased during the year ended 31 March 2015:

	Date of purchase	Cost	CO_2 emission rate
		£	
New motor car (1)	10 April 2014	10,800	92 grams per kilometre
Motor car (2)	10 June 2014	20,400	120 grams per kilometre

The following motor cars were sold during the year ended 31 March 2014:

	Date of sale	Proceeds	Original cost
		£	£
Motor car (3)	8 March 2015	9,100	8,500
Motor car (4)	8 March 2015	12,400	18,900

The original cost of motor car (3) has previously been added to the general pool, and the original cost of motor car (4) has previously been added to the special rate pool.

Required:

Calculate Greenzone Ltd's tax adjusted trading profit for the year ended 31 March 2015.

Your computation should commence with the operating profit figure of £239,700, and should also list all of the items referred to in Notes (1) and (2), indicating by the use of zero (0) any items that do not require adjustment. **(10 marks)**

66   SOFTAPP LTD (ADAPTED) *Walk in the footsteps of a top tutor*

Softapp Ltd is a software developer. The company's summarised statement of profit or loss for the year ended 31 March 2015 is as follows:

	Note	£
Operating profit	1	1,013,000
Other income		
Income from property	2	36,700
Loan interest receivable	3	8,100
Profit on disposal of shares	4	64,900
Finance costs		
Interest payable	5	(67,200)
		————
Profit before taxation		1,055,500
		————

Note 1 – Operating profit

Depreciation of £8,170 and amortisation of leasehold property of £2,500 have been deducted in arriving at the operating profit of £1,013,000.

Note 2 – Income from property

Since 1 November 2014, Softapp Ltd has let out one floor of a freehold office building which is surplus to requirements (see Note 5).

The income from property figure of £36,700 is made up of the following income and expenditure:

Date received/(paid):		£
23 October 2014	Advertising for tenants	(600)
25 October 2014	Security deposit of two months' rent	10,400
25 October 2014	Rent for the quarter ended 31 January 2015	15,600
1 November 2014	Insurance for the year ended 31 October 2015	(1,200)
2 February 2015	Rent for the quarter ended 30 April 2015	15,600
20 March 2015	Repairs following a flood	(12,800)
4 April 2015	Insurance claim in respect of the flood damage	9,700
		————
		36,700
		————

Note 3 – Loan interest receivable

The loan was made for non-trading purposes on 1 July 2014. Loan interest of £5,600 was received on 31 December 2014, and interest of £2,500 was accrued at 31 March 2015.

Note 4 – Profit on disposal of shares

The profit on disposal of shares is in respect of the sale of Softapp Ltd's entire (2%) shareholding in Networked plc on 28 February 2015. The disposal resulted in a chargeable gain of £61,300. This figure is after taking account of indexation.

Note 5 – Interest payable

The interest payable is made up as follows:

(i)   £42,200 in respect of the company's 4% debenture loan stock. Interest of £21,100 was paid on 30 September 2014 and again on 31 March 2015. The loan stock was used to finance the company's trading activities.

(ii)   £25,000 in respect of a loan to acquire the freehold office building. The building has five floors, one of which is let out (see Note 2).

Additional information

Plant and machinery

The tax written down value of Softapp Ltd's plant and machinery as at 1 April 2014 was £Nil.

During October 2014 Softapp Ltd had an extension constructed adjacent to its existing freehold office building, which is used by the company's employees as a staff room.

The total cost is made up as follows:

	£
Integral to the building	
Building costs of extension	61,000
Heating system	93,600
Ventilation system	75,600
Not integral to the building	
Furniture and furnishings	338,400
Refrigerator and microwave cooker	1,400
	————
	570,000
	————

The full annual investment allowance is available to Softapp Ltd.

Subsidiary company

Softapp Ltd owns 100% of the ordinary share capital of Byte-Size Ltd.

Required:

Calculate Softapp Ltd's corporation tax liability for the year ended 31 March 2015 and state the date it is due for payment.

Your computation should commence with the operating profit figure of £1,013,000.

(15 marks)

RELIEF FOR TRADING LOSSES

67   HALF-LIFE LTD (ADAPTED)

Half-Life Ltd commenced trading on 1 April 2011 and ceased trading on 30 June 2015.

The company's results for all its periods of trading are as follows:

	y/e 31.3.12	y/e 31.3.13	y/e 31.3.14	p/e 30.6.14	y/e 30.6.15
	£	£	£	£	£
Tax adjusted profit/(loss)	224,000	67,400	38,200	(61,700)	(308,800)
Property business profit	8,200	12,200	6,500	4,400	–
Chargeable gains	–	–	5,600	–	23,700
Qualifying charitable donations	(1,200)	(1,000)	–	–	(700)

Half-Life Ltd does not have any associated companies.

Required:

(a)   **Assuming that Half-Life Ltd claims the maximum possible relief for its trading losses, calculate the company's taxable total profits for the years ended 31 March 2012, 2013 and 2014, the period ended 30 June 2014, and the year ended 30 June 2015.**

Your answer should clearly identify the amounts of any losses and qualifying charitable donations that are unrelieved. (9 marks)

(b)   **State the dates by which Half-Life Ltd must make the loss relief claims in part (a).** (2 marks)

(c)   **Calculate the amount of corporation tax that will be repaid to Half-Life Ltd as a result of making the loss relief claims in part (a).**

The corporation tax rates for FY 2011 were 20% and 26%, with a marginal relief fraction of 3/200. The upper and lower limits were the same as in FY 2014.

(4 marks)

(Total: 15 marks)

68   LOSER LTD (ADAPTED)

Loser Ltd 's results for the year ended 30 June 2012, the nine month period ended 31 March 2013, the year ended 31 March 2014 and the year ended 31 March 2015 are:

	y/e 30.6.12 £	p/e 31.3.13 £	y/e 31.3.14 £	y/e 31.3.15 £
Trading profit/(loss)	86,600	(25,700)	27,300	(78,300)
Property business profit	–	4,500	8,100	5,600
Qualifying charitable donations	(1,400)	(800)	(1,200)	(1,100)

Loser Ltd does not have any associated companies.

Required:

(a)   **State the factors that will influence a company's choice of loss relief claims.**

(3 marks)

(b)   **Assuming that Loser Ltd claims relief for its losses as early as possible, compute the company's taxable total profits for the year ended 30 June 2012, the period ended 31 March 2013, the year ended 31 March 2014 and the year ended 31 March 2015.**

Your answer should clearly identify the amount of any losses that are unrelieved.

(5 marks)

(c)   **Explain how your answer to (b) above would have differed if Loser Ltd had ceased trading on 31 March 2015.**   **(2 marks)**

(Total: 10 marks)

69   SOFA LTD (ADAPTED)   *Online question assistance*

(a)   Sofa Ltd is a manufacturer of furniture.

The company's summarised statement of profit or loss for the year ended 31 March 2015 is as follows:

	Note	£	£
Gross profit			162,210
Operating expenses			
Depreciation		150,820	
Professional fees	1	19,900	
Repairs and renewals	2	22,800	
Other expenses	3	304,000	
			(497,520)
Operating loss			(335,310)
Profit from sale of fixed assets			
Disposal of shares	4		4,300
Income from investments			
Bank interest	5		8,400
			(322,610)
Interest payable	6		(31,200)
Loss before taxation			(353,810)

Note 1 – Professional fees

Professional fees are as follows:

	£
Accountancy and audit fee	3,400
Legal fees in connection with the issue of share capital	7,800
Legal fees in connection with the renewal of a ten year property lease	2,900
Legal fees in connection with the issue of a loan note (see Note 6)	5,800
	19,900

Note 2 – Repairs and renewals

The figure of £22,800 for repairs and renewals includes £9,700 for constructing a new wall around the company's premises and £3,900 for repairing the wall of an office building after it was damaged by a lorry. The remaining expenses are all fully allowable.

Note 3 – Other expenses

The figure of £304,000 for other expenses includes £1,360 for entertaining suppliers; £700 for entertaining employees; £370 for counselling services provided to an employee who was made redundant; and a fine of £420 for infringing health and safety regulations. The remaining expenses are all fully allowable.

Note 4 – Profit on disposal of shares

The profit on the disposal of shares of £4,300 is in respect of a shareholding that was sold on 29 October 2014.

Note 5 – Bank interest received

The bank interest was received on 31 March 2015. The bank deposits are held for non-trading purposes.

Note 6 – Interest payable

Sofa Ltd issued a loan note on 1 July 2014, and this was used for trading purposes. Interest of £20,800 was paid on 31 December 2014, and £10,400 was accrued at 31 March 2015.

Note 7 – Plant and machinery

On 1 April 2014 the tax written down values of plant and machinery were as follows:

	£
General pool	16,700
Special rate pool	16,400

There were no acquisitions or disposals of plant and machinery during the year.

Required:

Calculate Sofa Ltd's tax adjusted trading loss for the year ended 31 March 2015.

Your answer should commence with the loss before taxation figure of £353,810, and should list all of the items referred to in Notes (1) to (7) indicating by the use of zero (0) any items that do not require adjustment.

You should assume that the company claims the maximum available capital allowances. **(10 marks)**

(b)   Sofa Ltd has three subsidiary companies:

Settee Ltd

Sofa Ltd owns 100% of the ordinary share capital of Settee Ltd. For the year ended 30 June 2014 Settee Ltd had taxable total profits of £240,000, and for the year ended 30 June 2015 will have taxable total profits of £90,000.

Couch Ltd

Sofa Ltd owns 60% of the ordinary share capital of Couch Ltd. For the year ended 31 March 2015 Couch Ltd had taxable total profits of £64,000.

Futon Ltd

Sofa Ltd owns 80% of the ordinary share capital of Futon Ltd. Futon Ltd commenced trading on 1 January 2015, and for the three-month period ended 31 March 2015 had taxable total profits of £60,000.

Required:

Advise Sofa Ltd as to the maximum amount of group relief that can potentially be claimed by each of its three subsidiary companies in respect of its trading loss for the year ended 31 March 2015.

For the purposes of answering this part of the question, you should assume that Sofa Ltd's tax adjusted trading loss for the year ended 31 March 2015 is £200,000.

(5 marks)

(Total: 15 marks)

 Online question assistance

---

70   VOLATILE LTD (ADAPTED) *Walk in the footsteps of a top tutor*

Volatile Ltd commenced trading on 1 January 2010. The company's recent results are:

	y/e 31 Dec 2012 £	p/e 30 Sept 2013 £	y/e 30 Sept 2014 £
Trading profit/(loss)	15,200	78,700	(101,800)
Property business profit	6,500	–	–
Chargeable gains	–	–	9,700
Qualifying charitable donations	(1,200)	(1,000)	(800)

Required:

(a)   **State the factors that will influence a company's choice of loss relief claims.**
       You are not expected to consider group relief.   **(3 marks)**

(b)   **Assuming that Volatile Ltd claims relief for its trading losses as early as possible, calculate the company's taxable total profits for the year ended 31 December 2012, nine month period ended 30 September 2013, and year ended 30 September 2014.**

       Your answer should also clearly identify the amount of any unrelieved trading losses as at 30 September 2014.   **(7 marks)**

(Total: 10 marks)

WITH GROUP ASPECTS

71 ANIMAL LTD (ADAPTED)

Animal Ltd is the holding company for a group of companies.

The results of each group company for the year ended 31 March 2015 are as follows:

	Tax adjusted trading profit/(loss)	Property business income	Franked Investment Income
	£	£	£
Animal Ltd	450,000	5,000	20,000
Bat Ltd	65,000	15,000	–
Cat Ltd	85,000	–	–
Dog Ltd	100,000	–	–
Elk Ltd	–	–	–
Fox Ltd	60,000	–	5,000
Gnu Ltd	(200,000)	–	–

Animal Ltd owned 100% of each subsidiary company's ordinary share capital throughout the year ended 31 March 2015 with the following exceptions:

(1) Animal Ltd only owned 90% of Bat Ltd's ordinary share capital.

(2) Animal Ltd's shareholding in Cat Ltd was disposed of on 31 December 2014. The tax adjusted trading profit of £85,000 is for the year ended 31 March 2015.

(3) Animal Ltd's shareholding in Dog Ltd was acquired on 1 January 2015. The tax adjusted trading profit of £100,000 is for the year ended 31 March 2015.

Elk Ltd was a dormant company throughout the year ended 31 March 2015.

Required:

(a) Explain the group relationship that must exist in order that group relief can be claimed. **(3 marks)**

(b) Explain why there are six associated companies in the Animal Ltd group of companies. Your answer should identify the six associated companies. **(3 marks)**

(c) Assuming that relief is claimed for Gnu Ltd's trading loss of £200,000 in the most beneficial manner; calculate the taxable total profits of Animal Ltd, Bat Ltd, Cat Ltd, Dog Ltd and Fox Ltd for the year ended 31 March 2015.

Explain your strategy for claiming group relief in the most beneficial manner.

(9 marks)

(Total: 15 marks)

72 MUSIC PLC (ADAPTED)

Music plc is the holding company for a group of companies. The group structure is as follows:

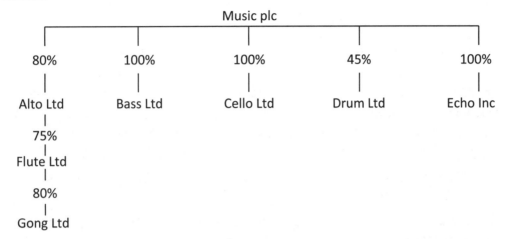

Music plc's shareholding in Bass Ltd was disposed of on 31 December 2014, and the shareholding in Cello Ltd was acquired on 1 January 2015. The other shareholdings were all held throughout the year ended 31 March 2015.

Echo Inc is resident overseas. The other companies are all resident in the United Kingdom.

For the year ended 31 March 2015 Music plc had a tax adjusted trading profit of £92,000. During the year Music plc received franked investment income of £15,000 from an unconnected company, bank interest of £12,000 and a dividend of £5,400 from Bass Ltd.

As at 31 March 2014 Music plc had unused capital losses of £32,000. On 5 January 2015 the company sold a freehold office building, and this resulted in a further capital loss of £65,000.

Alto Ltd sold a freehold warehouse on 10 March 2015, and this resulted in a capital gain of £120,000. An election has been made so that the gain is treated as Music plc's gain.

Year ending 31 March 2016

Music plc is considering acquiring a property which it will rent out for £10,000 per annum. The company will take out a new non-trade related bank loan of £100,000 at a 10% interest rate to partly fund the acquisition. Legal fees will be £300.

Required:

(a)   **State, giving appropriate reasons, which companies in the Music plc group of companies form a group for capital gains purposes.**   **(5 marks)**

(b)   **Explain why Music plc has six associated companies.**

      Your answer should identify the six associated companies.   **(3 marks)**

(c)   **Calculate Music plc's corporation tax liability for the year ended 31 March 2015.**
                                                                            (4 marks)

(d)   **Explain how the interest costs, legal fees and rent receivable will be treated for tax purposes if Music plc acquires a property in the year ended 31 March 2016.**

                                                                            (3 marks)

                                                                  (Total: 15 marks)

73   **DEUTSCH LTD (ADAPTED)** *Walk in the footsteps of a top tutor*

Deutsch Ltd has held shares in four trading companies throughout the year ended 31 March 2015. All four companies prepare accounts to 31 March.

The following information is available for the year ended 31 March 2015:

	Eins Ltd	Zwei Ltd	Drei Ltd	Vier Co
Residence	UK	UK	UK	Overseas
Percentage shareholding	60%	40%	90%	70%
Trading profit/(loss)	£(74,800)	£68,900	£(64,700)	£22,600
Dividends paid to Deutsch Ltd	£36,180	£35,100	£29,400	£Nil

The dividend figures are the actual cash amounts received by Deutsch Ltd during the year ended 31 March 2015.

In the year ended 31 March 2015 Deutsch Ltd had a tax adjusted trading profit of £277,700 and no other income or gains.

Required:

(a)   State, giving reasons, which of the four trading companies will be treated as being associated with Deutsch Ltd;   **(2 marks)**

(b)   Calculate the maximum amount of group relief that Deutsch Ltd can claim for the year ended 31 March 2015;   **(2 marks)**

(c)   Calculate Deutsch Ltd's corporation tax liability for the year ended 31 March 2015.

        You should assume that Deutsch Ltd will claim the maximum possible amount of group relief.   **(5 marks)**

(d)   State the date by which Deutsch Ltd and the other group companies must make an election for group relief in respect of the year ended 31 March 2015   **(1 mark)**

                                                        (Total: 10 marks)

74   **GASTRON LTD (ADAPTED)** *Walk in the footsteps of a top tutor*

Gastron Ltd, a United Kingdom resident company, is a luxury food manufacturer. The following information is available for the year ended 31 March 2015.

Note 1 – Trading profits

Gastron Ltd has trading profits of £516,792 after capital allowances for the year ended 31 March 2015.

Note 2 – Income from property

Gastron Ltd lets out the whole of an unfurnished freehold office building that is surplus to requirements. The office building was let from 1 April 2014 to 31 December 2014 at a monthly rent of £1,800, payable in advance. On 31 December 2014 the tenant left owing two months' rent which Gastron Ltd was unable to recover. During January 2015 the company spent £3,700 decorating the property. The office building was then re-let from 1 February 2015 at a monthly rent of £1,950, on which date the new tenant paid six months' rent in advance.

Note 3 – Bank interest received

Bank interest of £12,400 was received on 31 March 2015. The bank deposits are held for non-trading purposes.

Note 4 – Dividends received

During the year ended 31 March 2015 Gastron Ltd received dividends of £36,000 from Tasteless plc, an unconnected UK company, and dividends of £18,000 from Culinary Ltd, a 100% UK subsidiary company (see Note 6). Both figures are the actual cash amounts received.

Note 5 – Profit on disposal of shares

On 14 October 2014 the company disposed of a 1% shareholding in a company. The disposal resulted in a chargeable gain of £74,800. This figure is after taking account of indexation.

Note 6 – Subsidiary company

Gastron Ltd owns 100% of the ordinary share capital of Culinary Ltd. On 13 February 2015 Culinary Ltd sold a freehold factory and this resulted in a capital loss of £66,000. For the year ended 31 March 2015 Culinary Ltd made no other disposals and paid corporation tax at the small profits rate of 20%.

Required:

(a) Calculate Gastron Ltd's corporation tax liability for the year ended 31 March 2015, on the basis that no election is made between Gastron Ltd and Culinary Ltd in respect of capital gains. **(7 marks)**

(b) State the date by which Gastron Ltd's corporation tax liability for the year ended 31 March 2015 should be paid, and advise the company of the interest that will be due if the liability is not paid until 31 August 2016. **(3 marks)**

(c) Explain the group relationship that must exist in order for two or more companies to form a group for capital gains purposes. **(2 marks)**

(d) State the time limit for Gastron Ltd and Culinary Ltd to make a joint election such that Culinary Ltd is treated as making the chargeable gain on the disposal of shares (see Note 6), and explain why such an election will be beneficial. **(3 marks)**

(Total: 15 marks)

75   MICE LTD (ADAPTED) *Walk in the footsteps of a top tutor*

You should assume that today's date is 28 March 2015.

Mice Ltd commenced trading on 1 July 2011 as a manufacturer of computer peripherals.

The company prepares accounts to 31 March, and its results for the first three periods of trading were as follows:

	Period ended 31 March 2012	Year ended 31 March 2013	Year ended 31 March 2014
	£	£	£
Trading profit	83,200	24,700	51,200
Property business profit	2,800	7,100	12,200
Qualifying charitable donations	(1,000)	(1,500)	–

The following information is available in respect of the year ended 31 March 2015:

Trading loss

Mice Ltd expects to make a trading loss of £180,000.

Business property income

Mice Ltd lets out three office buildings that are surplus to requirements.

The first office building is owned freehold. The property was let throughout the year ended 31 March 2015 at a quarterly rent of £3,200, payable in advance. Mice Ltd paid business rates of £2,200 and insurance of £460 in respect of this property for the year ended 31 March 2015. During June 2014 Mice Ltd repaired the existing car park for this property at a cost of £1,060, and then subsequently enlarged the car park at a cost of £2,640.

The second office building is owned leasehold. Mice Ltd pays an annual rent of £7,800 for this property, but did not pay a premium when the lease was acquired. On 1 April 2014 the property was sub-let to a tenant, with Mice Ltd receiving a premium of £18,000 for the grant of an eight-year lease. The company also received the annual rent of £6,000 which was payable in advance. Mice Ltd paid insurance of £310 in respect of this property for the year ended 31 March 2015.

The third office building is also owned freehold. Mice Ltd purchased the freehold of this building on 1 January 2015, and it will be empty until 31 March 2015. The building is to be let from 1 April 2015 at a monthly rent of £640, and on 15 March 2015 Mice Ltd received three months' rent in advance.

On 1 January 2015 Mice Ltd paid insurance of £480 in respect of this property for the year ended 31 December 2015, and during February 2015 spent £680 on advertising for tenants. Mice Ltd paid loan interest of £1,800 in respect of the period 1 January 2015 to 31 March 2015 on a non-trade related loan that was taken out to purchase this property.

Loan interest received

On 1 July 2014 Mice Ltd made a loan for non-trading purposes. Loan interest of £6,400 was received on 31 December 2013, and £3,200 will be accrued at 31 March 2015.

Dividend received

On 15 October 2014 Mice Ltd received a dividend of £7,400 (net) from a 3% shareholding in USB Ltd.

Chargeable gain

On 20 December 2014 Mice Ltd sold its 3% shareholding in USB Ltd. The disposal resulted in a chargeable gain of £10,550, after taking account of indexation.

Required:

(a) Calculate Mice Ltd's property business profit for the year ended 31 March 2015.

(8 marks)

(b) Assuming that Mice Ltd claims relief for its trading loss as early as possible, calculate the company's taxable total profits for the nine-month period ended 31 March 2012, and each of the years ended 31 March 2013, 2014 and 2015. (7 marks)

(Total: 15 marks)

76   NEUNG LTD (ADAPTED) *Walk in the footsteps of a top tutor*

Neung Ltd is a UK resident company that runs a business providing financial services. The company's summarised statement of profit or loss for the year ended 31 March 2015 is:

	Note	£
Operating profit	1	877,300
Income from investments		
Loan interest	2	37,800
Dividends	3	54,000
		————
Profit before taxation		969,100
		————

Note 1 – Operating profit

Depreciation of £11,830 and amortisation of leasehold property of £7,000 have been deducted in arriving at the operating profit of £877,300.

Note 2 – Loan interest receivable

The loan was made for non-trading purposes on 1 July 2014. Loan interest of £25,200 was received on 31 December 2014, and interest of £12,600 was accrued at 31 March 2015.

Note 4 – Dividends received

Neung Ltd holds shares in four UK resident companies as follows:

	Percentage shareholding	Status
Second Ltd	25%	Trading
Third Ltd	60%	Trading
Fourth Ltd	100%	Dormant
Fifth Ltd	100%	Trading

During the year ended 31 March 2015 Neung Ltd received a dividend of £37,800 from Second Ltd, and a dividend of £16,200 from Third Ltd. These figures were the actual cash amounts received.

Fifth Ltd made a trading loss of £15,700 for the year ended 31 March 2015.

Additional information

Leasehold property

On 1 April 2014 Neung Ltd acquired a leasehold office building, paying a premium of £140,000 for the grant of a 20-year lease. The office building was used for business purposes by Neung Ltd throughout the year ended 31 March 2015.

Plant and machinery

On 1 April 2014 the tax written down values of Neung Ltd's plant and machinery were:

	£
General pool	4,800
Short life asset	22,800
Special rate pool	12,700

The company purchased the following assets during the year ended 31 March 2015:

		£
19 July 2014	Motor car [1]	15,400
12 December 2014	Motor car [2]	28,600
20 December 2014	Ventilation system	562,000

The short life asset is a specialised piece of machinery which was purchased on 1 January 2014. Motor car [1] purchased on 19 July 2014 has a CO_2 emission rate of 212 grams per kilometre. Motor car [2] purchased on 12 December 2014 has a CO_2 emission rate of 118 grams per kilometre.

The ventilation system purchased on 20 December 2014 for £562,000 is integral to the freehold office building in which it was installed.

Required:

Calculate Neung Ltd's corporation tax liability for the year ended 31 March 2015.

You should assume that the whole of the annual investment allowance is available to Neung Ltd, that the company wishes to maximise its capital allowances claim, and that any favourable claims are made in respect of group losses. **(15 marks)**

77 CLUELESS LTD (ADAPTED) *Walk in the footsteps of a top tutor*

 Timed question with Online tutor debrief

(a) You are a trainee accountant and your manager has asked you to correct a corporation tax computation that has been prepared by the managing director of Clueless Ltd, a company which manufactures children's board games.

The corporation tax computation is for the year ended 31 March 2015 and contains a significant number of errors:

Clueless Ltd – Corporation tax computation for the year ended 31 March 2015

	£
Trading profit (working 1)	453,782
Loan interest received (working 2)	32,100
	———
	485,882
Dividends received (working 3)	28,700
	———
	514,582
	———
Corporation tax (£514,582 × 21%)	108,062
	———

Working 1 – Trading profit

	£
Profit before taxation	382,610
Depreciation	15,740
Donations to political parties	400
Qualifying charitable donations paid	900
Gifts to customers	
pens costing £40 each and displaying Clueless Ltd's name	920
food hampers costing £45 each and displaying Clueless Ltd's name	1,650
Capital allowances (working 4)	51,562
Trading profit	453,782

Working 2 – Loan interest received

	£
Loan interest receivable	32,800
Accrued at 1 April 2014	10,600
Accrued at 31 March 2015	(11,300)
Loan interest received	32,100

The loan was made for non-trading purposes.

Working 3 – Dividends received

	£
From unconnected companies	20,700
From a 100% UK subsidiary company	8,000
Dividends received	28,700

These figures were the actual cash amounts received.

Working 4 – Capital allowances

	General pool £	Motor car £	Special rate pool £	Allowances £
TWDV brought forward	12,400		13,500	
Additions				
Machinery	42,300			
Motor car		11,800		
	54,700			
Annual investment allowance	(54,700)			54,700
Disposal proceeds			(9,300)	
			4,200	
Balancing allowance			(4,200)	(4,200)
WDA (18%)		(2,124) × 50%		1,062
TWDV carried forward	0	9,676		
Total allowances				51,562

Notes:

(1)   The motor car has a CO_2 emission rate of 145 grams per kilometre. This motor car is used by the sales manager and 50% of the mileage is for private journeys.

(2)   All of the items included in the special rate pool at 1 April 2014 were sold for £9,300 during the year ended 31 March 2015. The original cost of these items was £16,200.

Other information

From your files, you note that Clueless Ltd has one associated company (the 100% UK subsidiary company mentioned in Working 3).

Required:

Prepare a corrected version of Clueless Ltd's corporation tax computation for the year ended 31 March 2015.

You should indicate by the use of zero any items in the computation of the trading profit for which no adjustment is required.   **(11 marks)**

(b)   The managing director of Clueless Ltd understands that the company has to file its self-assessment corporation tax returns online, and that the supporting accounts and tax computations have to be filed using the inline eXtensible Business Reporting Language (iXBRL). The managing director is interested in the options regarding how the company can produce documents in this format.

Required:

(i)   **State the date by which Clueless Ltd's self-assessment corporation tax return for the year ended 31 March 2015 should be filed;**   **(1 mark)**

(ii)   **Explain the options available to Clueless Ltd regarding the production of accounts and tax computations in the iXBRL format.**   **(3 marks)**

(Total: 15 marks)

 Calculate your allowed time, allocate the time to the separate parts.....................

VALUE ADDED TAX

Tutorial note

You should expect VAT to be tested in both the Section A multiple choice questions and also in the Section B 10 mark questions.

There is however no set minimum or maximum number of marks for VAT.

78   CANDY APPLE (ADAPTED)   *Walk in the footsteps of a top tutor*

Candy Apple began a business selling luxury sweets on 6 April 2014. Her sales since the commencement of trading have been as follows:

April to July 2014	£10,500 per month
August to November 2014	£14,000 per month
December 2014 to March 2015	£21,500 per month

These figures are stated exclusive of value added tax (VAT). Candy's sales are all standard rated.

As a trainee Chartered Certified Accountant you have advised Candy in writing that she should be registered for VAT, but she has refused to register because she thinks her net profit is insufficient to cover the additional cost which would be incurred.

Required:

(a)   Explain from what date Candy Apple was required to be compulsorily registered for value added tax (VAT) and the VAT implications of continuing to trade after this date without registering.

You are not expected to explain the VAT penalties arising from late VAT registration.   **(4 marks)**

(b)   Briefly explain from an ethical viewpoint the issues you, as a trainee Chartered Certified Accountant, should consider in order for your firm to deal with Candy Feast's refusal to register for VAT.   **(2 marks)**

(c)   State the circumstances in which a business can issue a simplified (or less detailed) VAT invoice, when such an invoice should be issued, and FIVE pieces of information which such an invoice must show where the supply is entirely standard rated.

(4 marks)

(Total: 10 marks)

79   ASTUTE LTD (ADAPTED)

(a)   Astute Ltd registered for VAT on 1 July 2014. The company has annual standard rated sales of £350,000. This figure is inclusive of VAT. As a result of bookkeeping problems Astute Ltd has been late in submitting its VAT returns to date.

Required:

Advise Astute Ltd of the conditions that it must satisfy before being permitted to use the VAT annual accounting scheme, and the advantages of joining the scheme.

(4 marks)

(b)   Clever Ltd registered for VAT on 1 June 2014. The company has annual standard rated sales of £250,000. This figure is inclusive of VAT. The company pays its expenses on a cash basis, but allows customers three months' credit when paying for sales. Several of Clever Ltd's customers have recently defaulted on the payment of their debts.

Required:

Advise Clever Ltd of the conditions that it must satisfy before being permitted to use the VAT cash accounting scheme, and the advantages of joining the scheme.

(4 marks)

(c)   Talent Limited holds 100% of the shares in Gifted Limited. Talent Limited and Gifted Limited trade with each other.

Required:

Advise Talent Limited and Gifted Limited whether they can be group registered for VAT purposes and one advantage of a VAT group registration.   **(2 marks)**

(Total: 10 marks)

80   VICTOR STYLE (ADAPTED)   *Online question assistance*

Victor Style has been a self-employed hairdresser since 1 January 2012.

His sales from the date of commencement of the business to 31 December 2014 were £5,800 per month.

On 1 January 2015 Victor increased the prices that he charged customers, and from that date his sales have been £9,500 per month. Victor's sales are all standard rated.

Concerned about the registration thresholds, Victor voluntarily registered for VAT on 1 January 2015.

As all of his customers are members of the general public, it was not possible to increase prices any further as a result of registering for VAT.

Victor's standard rated expenses are £400 per month.

Where applicable, the above figures are inclusive of VAT.

Required:

(a) Calculate the total amount of VAT payable by Victor during the year ended 31 December 2015. **(3 marks)**

(b) Advise Victor why it would have been beneficial to have used the VAT flat rate scheme from 1 January 2015.

Your answer should include a calculation of the amount of VAT that Victor would have saved for the year ended 31 December 2015 by joining the scheme.

The flat rate scheme percentage for hairdressing for Victor in the year ended 31 December 2015 is 13%. **(3 marks)**

(c) Calculate the effect on Victor's net profit for the year ended 31 December 2015 as a consequence of the price increase on 1 January 2015 and subsequent VAT registration. **(4 marks)**

(Total: 10 marks)

 Online question assistance

81 LITHOGRAPH LTD (ADAPTED)

Lithograph Ltd runs a printing business, and is registered for VAT. Because its annual taxable turnover is only £250,000, the company uses the annual accounting scheme so that it only has to prepare one VAT return each year. The annual VAT period is the year ended 31 December.

Year ended 31 December 2014

The total amount of VAT payable by Lithograph Ltd for the year ended 31 December 2014 was £10,200.

Year ended 31 December 2015

The following information is available:

(1) Sales invoices totalling £250,000 were issued to VAT registered customers, of which £160,000 were for standard rated sales and £90,000 were for zero-rated sales.

(2) Purchase invoices totalling £45,000 were received from VAT registered suppliers, of which £38,000 were for standard rated purchases and £7,000 were for zero-rated purchases.

(3) Standard rated expenses amounted to £28,000. This includes £3,600 for entertaining overseas customers.

(4) On 1 January 2015 Lithograph Ltd purchased a motor car costing £18,400 for the use of its managing director. The manager director is provided with free petrol for private mileage, and the cost of this is included in the standard rated expenses in Note (3). The car has CO_2 emissions of 210 g/km and the relevant annual scale charge is £2,008. Both figures are inclusive of VAT.

(5) During the year ended 31 December 2015 Lithograph Ltd purchased machinery for £24,000, and sold office equipment for £8,000. Input VAT had been claimed when the office equipment was originally purchased.

(6)   On 31 December 2015 Lithograph Ltd wrote off £4,800 due from a customer as an impaired debt. The debt was in respect of an invoice that was due for payment on 31 May 2015.

Unless stated otherwise all of the above figures are exclusive of VAT.

Required:

(a)   **Calculate the monthly payments on account of VAT that Lithograph Ltd will have made in respect of the year ended 31 December 2015, and state in which months these will have been paid.** **(2 marks)**

(b)   (i)   **Calculate the total amount of VAT payable by Lithograph Ltd for the year ended 31 December 2015.** **(6 marks)**

        (ii)   **Based on your answer to part (i) above, calculate the balancing payment that would have been paid with the annual VAT return, and state the date by which this return was due for submission.** **(2 marks)**

(Total: 10 marks)

82   DENZIL DYER (ADAPTED)

Denzil Dyer has been a self-employed printer since 2007. He has recently registered for value added tax (VAT).

Denzil's sales consist of printed leaflets, some of which are standard rated and some of which are zero-rated. He sells to both VAT registered customers and to non-VAT registered customers.

Customers making an order of more than £500 are given a discount of 5% from the normal selling price. Denzil also offers a discount of 2.5% of the amount payable to those customers that pay within one month of the date of the sales invoice.

All of Denzil's printing supplies are purchased from a VAT registered supplier. He pays by credit card and receives a VAT invoice. However, Denzil also purchases various office supplies by cash without receiving any invoices.

Denzil does not use the annual accounting scheme, the cash accounting scheme or the flat rate scheme.

Required:

(a)   **Explain why it is important for Denzil to correctly identify whether a sale is standard rated or whether it is zero-rated.** **(2 marks)**

(b)   **Explain the VAT implications of the two types of discount that Denzil gives or offers to his customers.** **(2 marks)**

(c)   **Advise Denzil of the conditions that will have to be met in order for him to recover input VAT.**

        You are not expected to list those goods and services for which input VAT is non-recoverable. **(3 marks)**

(d)   **State the circumstances in which Denzil is and is not required to issue a VAT invoice, and the period during which such an invoice should be issued.** **(3 marks)**

(Total: 10 marks)

83 ANNE ATTIRE (ADAPTED) *Walk in the footsteps of a top tutor*

Anne Attire runs a retail clothing shop. She is registered for value added tax (VAT), and is in the process of completing her VAT return for the quarter ended 31 May 2015.

The following information is available (all figures are exclusive of VAT):

(1) Cash sales amounted to £42,000, of which £28,000 was in respect of standard rated sales and £14,000 was in respect of zero-rated sales.

(2) Sales invoices totalling £12,000 were issued in respect of credit sales. These sales were all standard rated. Anne offers all of her credit sale customers a 5% discount for payment within one month of the date of the sales invoice, and 90% of the customers pay within this period. The sales figure of £12,000 is stated before any deduction for the 5% discount.

(3) Purchase and expense invoices totalling £19,200 were received from VAT registered suppliers. This figure is made up as follows:

	£
Standard rated purchases and expenses	11,200
Zero rated purchases	6,000
Exempt expenses	2,000
	———
	19,200
	———

Anne pays all of her purchase and expense invoices two months after receiving the invoice.

(4) On 31 May 2015 Anne wrote off two impairment losses (bad debts) that were in respect of standard rated credit sales. The first impairment loss was for £300, and was in respect of a sales invoice due for payment on 15 April 2015. The second impairment loss was for £800, and was in respect of a sales invoice due for payment on 10 November 2014.

Anne does not use the cash accounting scheme.

Anne will soon be 60 years old and is therefore considering retirement. On the cessation of trading Anne can either sell the non-current assets of her business on a piecemeal basis to individual VAT registered purchasers, or she can sell the entire business as a going concern to a single VAT registered purchaser.

Required:

(a) **Calculate the amount of VAT payable by Anne Attire for the quarter ended 31 May 2015, and state the date by which the VAT return for this period was due for submission.** **(6 marks)**

(b) **Advise Anne Attire as to what will happen to her VAT registration, and whether output VAT will be due in respect of the non-current assets, if she ceases trading and then:**

(i) **Sells her non-current assets on a piecemeal basis to individual VAT registered purchasers;** **(2 marks)**

(ii) **Sells her entire business as a going concern to a single VAT registered purchaser.** **(2 marks)**

(Total: 10 marks)

84 ASTON MARTYN (ADAPTED) *Walk in the footsteps of a top tutor*

Aston Martyn commenced self-employment on 1 September 2014 providing consultancy services to the motor industry. His sales revenue has been as follows:

		Standard rated	Zero-rated
		£	£
2014	September	2,300	–
	October	6,400	–
	November	20,900	4,800
	December	10,700	–
2015	January	16,100	–
	February	15,800	4,200
	March	4,200	–
	April	31,500	3,300
	May	44,600	6,600

Where applicable, the above figures are stated exclusive of value added tax (VAT).

Aston only supplies services and all of his supplies are to VAT registered businesses. He does not offer any discount for prompt payment.

The following is a sample of the new sales invoice that Aston is going to issue to his customers:

SALES INVOICE

Aston Martyn **Customer:** Faster Motors plc
111 Long Road **Address:** 22 Short lane
London W1 9MG Manchester M1 8MB
Telephone 0207 123 3456

Invoice Date 6 June 2015
Tax Point 6 June 2015

Description of services
Business advice

	£
Total price (excluding VAT)	12,000.00
Total price (including VAT)	14,400.00

Aston sometimes receives supplies of standard rated services from VAT registered businesses situated elsewhere within the European Union. As business to business services these are treated as being supplied in the United Kingdom. Aston wants to know how he should account for these services for VAT purposes.

Because of the complexity of the VAT legislation, Aston is concerned that despite his best efforts he will incorrectly treat a standard rated supply as zero-rated, thus understating the amount of VAT payable. He wants to know if such an error will result in a penalty, and if so how much the penalty will be.

Required:

(a) Explain from what date Aston Martyn's business was required to be registered for VAT. **(3 marks)**

(b) State the FOUR additional pieces of information that Aston Martyn will have to show on his new sales invoices in order for them to be valid for VAT purposes. **(2 marks)**

(c) Explain when and how Aston Martyn should account for VAT in respect of the supplies of services he receives from VAT registered businesses situated elsewhere within the European Union. **(2 marks)**

(d) Assuming that Aston Martyn incorrectly treats a standard rated supply as zero-rated with the result that the amount of VAT payable is understated, advise him as to the maximum amount of penalty that is likely to be charged by HM Revenue and Customs, and by how much this penalty would be reduced as a result of a subsequent unprompted disclosure. **(3 marks)**

(Total: 10 marks)

85 SILVERSTONE LTD (ADAPTED) *Walk in the footsteps of a top tutor*

Silverstone Ltd is registered for value added tax (VAT), but currently does not use any of the special VAT schemes. The company has annual standard rated sales of £1,200,000 and annual standard rated expenses of £550,000. Both these figures are exclusive of VAT and are likely to remain the same for the foreseeable future.

Silverstone Ltd is up to date with all of its tax returns, including those for corporation tax, PAYE and VAT. It is also up to date with its corporation tax, PAYE and VAT payments. However, the company often incurs considerable overtime costs due to its employees working late in order to meet tax return filing deadlines.

Silverstone Ltd pays its expenses on a cash basis, but allows customers two months credit when paying for sales. The company does not have any impairment losses.

Silverstone Ltd is planning to purchase some new machinery at a cost of £22,000 (exclusive of VAT). The machinery can either be purchased from an overseas supplier situated outside the European Union, or from a VAT registered supplier situated in the European Union. Silverstone Ltd is not a regular importer and so is unsure of the VAT treatment for this purchase.

Required:

(a) Explain why Silverstone Ltd is entitled to use both the VAT cash accounting scheme and the VAT annual accounting scheme, and why it will probably be beneficial for the company to use both schemes; **(6 marks)**

(b) Explain when and how Silverstone Ltd will have to account for VAT in respect of the new machinery if it is purchased from:

(i) a supplier situated outside the European Union, or

(ii) a VAT registered supplier situated elsewhere within the European Union. **(4 marks)**

(Total: 10 marks)

86 THE WHITLOCK SISTERS (ADAPTED) *Walk in the footsteps of a top tutor*

 Timed question with Online tutor debrief

On 1 January 2015, sisters Beth and Amy Whitlock commenced trading as a partnership running a small hairdressing business..

(1) The partnership voluntarily registered for VAT on 1 January 2015, and immediately began using the flat rate scheme to calculate the amount of VAT payable. The relevant flat rate scheme percentage for the partnership's trade is 13%.

(2) For the quarter ended 31 March 2015 the partnership had standard rated sales of £59,700, and these were all made to members of the general public. For the same period standard rated expenses amounted to £27,300. Both figures are stated inclusive of VAT.

(3) The partnership has two private rooms in its salon that can be booked for pamper parties on a special basis by privileged customers. Such customers can book the rooms up to two months in advance, at which time they have to pay a 25% deposit.

An invoice is then given to the customer on the day of the party, with payment of the balance of 75% required within seven days. For VAT purposes, the renting out of the salon rooms is a supply of services.

Required:

(a) **Explain whether or not it was beneficial for the partnership to have used the VAT flat rate scheme for the quarter ended 31 March 2015;**

Your answer should be supported by appropriate calculations.

You should ignore the 1% reduction from the flat rate that is available during the first year of VAT registration.   **(3 marks)**

(b) **Explain whether or not it was financially beneficial for the partnership to have voluntarily registered for VAT from 1 January 2015;**

Your answer should be supported by appropriate calculations.   **(3 marks)**

(c) **Advise the partnership as to when it should account for output VAT on the renting out of its private salons to privileged customers.**   **(4 marks)**

(Total: 10 marks)

 Calculate your allowed time, allocate the time to the separate parts....................

87   KNIGHT LTD (ADAPTED) *Walk in the footsteps of a top tutor*

Knight Ltd is a UK resident trading company. The following information is available in respect of Knight Ltd's value added tax (VAT) for the quarter ended 31 March 2015:

(1)   Output VAT of £38,210 was charged in respect of sales. This figure includes output VAT of £400 on a deposit received on 29 March 2015, which is in respect of a contract that is due to commence on 20 April 2015.

(2)   In addition to the above, Knight Ltd also charged output VAT of £4,330 on sales to Are Ltd and Can Ltd. Knight Ltd owns 100% of the shares in both these UK resident companies but is not currently registered with them as a group for VAT purposes.

(3)   The managing director of Knight Ltd is provided with free fuel for private mileage driven in his company motor car. The relevant quarterly scale charge is £328. This figure is inclusive of VAT.

(4)   On 31 March 2015, Knight Ltd wrote off an impairment loss in respect of a sales invoice that was issued on 15 September 2014. This invoice was due for payment on 31 October 2014. Output VAT of £640 was originally paid in respect of the sale.

(5)   Input VAT of £12,770 was incurred in respect of expenses. This figure includes the following input VAT:

	£
Entertaining UK customers	210
Entertaining overseas customers	139
Repainting the exterior of the company's office building	1,678
Extending the office building in order to create a new reception area	3,300

For the quarters ended 31 December 2012 and 30 September 2014, Knight Ltd was two months late in submitting its VAT returns and in paying the related VAT liabilities. All of the company's other VAT returns have been submitted on time, and the related VAT liabilities have been paid on time.

Required:

(a)   Calculate the amount of value added tax (VAT) payable by Knight Ltd for the quarter ended 31 March 2015.

Your calculation should clearly refer to all of the items of input VAT listed in note (5), indicating by the use of zero (0) any items that do not require adjustment.

(6 marks)

(b)   Advise Knight Ltd of the default surcharge implications if it is two months late in submitting its VAT return for the quarter ended 31 March 2015 and in paying the related VAT liability;

(2 marks)

(c)   State the advantages if Knight Ltd, Are Ltd and Can Ltd (see note (2) above) were to register as a group for VAT purposes.

(2 marks)

(Total: 10 marks)

Section 3

ANSWERS TO PRACTICE SECTION A QUESTIONS

INCOME TAX AND NATIONAL INSURANCE

INCOME TAX BASICS AND EMPLOYMENT INCOME

1   B

Income generated from a New Individual Savings Account and a National Savings and Investments (NS&I) Certificate is exempt from income tax.

Option A, C and D are incorrect because income generated from shares (dividends) and from a NS&I Investment account (interest) is subject to income tax.

2   A

		£
Trading income		105,000
Dividend (£1,350 × 100/90)		1,500
Net income		106,500

	£	£
Basic PA		10,000
Net income	106,500	
Less: Gross Gift Aid	(2,000)	
Adjusted net income	104,500	
Less: Income limit	(100,000)	
	4,500	
Reduction of PA (50% × £4,500)		(2,250)
Adjusted PA		7,750

3   C

	£
Rental income	29,500
Dividends (£1,800 × 100/90)	2,000
Net income	31,500

	£	£
Basic PAA (born before 6 April 1938)		10,660
Net income	31,500	
Less: Gross Gift Aid	(500)	
Adjusted net income	31,000	
Less: Income limit	(27,000)	
	4,000	
Reduction of PA (50% × £4,000) = £2,000 Restricted to		**(660)**
Adjusted PAA		10,000

Tutorial note

Be careful to answer the question asked – you are asked for the reduction in the PAA, not the amount of PAA itself.

4   D

Relief is given for interest paid on loans incurred to finance expenditure for a qualifying purpose, which includes:

- The acquisition of plant and machinery by an employed person for use in his employment.

- The purchase of shares in an employee-controlled trading company by a full-time employee.

- The purchase of a share in a partnership, or the contribution to a partnership of capital or a loan. The borrower must be a partner in the partnership.

- The purchase of plant and machinery for use in the partnership, by a partner.

5 B

	£	£
Child benefit received		1,066
		————
Trading income	56,500	
Less: Gross gift aid (£400 × 100/80)	(500)	
	————	
Adjusted net income	56,000	
Less: Lower limit	(50,000)	
	————	
	6,000	
	————	

1% per £100 of £6,000 = 60%
Child benefit tax charge = 60% of £1,066 (rounded down)   639

                                                                          ————

6 D

Bao is treated as automatically non-UK resident, as he has spent less than 46 days in the UK in 2014/15 and has not been treated as UK resident in any of the three previous tax years (having spent less than 46 days in the UK each tax year).

Minh is treated as automatically resident in the UK as, although he has been here for less than 183 days, he works full time in the UK.

Tutorial note

Even though Minh is present in the UK for less than 91 days in 2014/15 he is not automatically non-UK resident as he did not work full time overseas in the tax year.

7 D

Only unquoted loan stock interest is received net. All the other forms of interest are received gross.

8 A

Interest from a NISA is always exempt from tax.

	Total	Other Income	Savings Income
	£	£	£
Rental income	12,200	12,200	
Bank interest (£8,300 × 100/80)	10,375		10,375
Gilt edged security interest	1,500		1,500
	————	————	————
Net income	24,075	12,200	11,875
Less: PA	(10,000)	(10,000)	
	————	————	————
Taxable income	14,075	2,200	11,875
	————	————	————

	£		£
Income tax liability:			
Other income – basic rate	2,200	× 20%	440
Savings income – starting rate	680	× 10%	68
	———		
	2,880		
Savings income – basic rate	11,195	× 20%	2,239
	———		
	14,075		
	———		
Income tax liability			2,747
Less: Tax deducted on interest (£10,375 × 20%)			(2,075)
			———
Income tax payable			672
			———

9   B

	Dividend income
	£
Dividends (£9,900 × 100/90)	11,000
Less: PA	(10,000)
	———
Taxable income	1,000
	———
Income tax liability (£1,000 × 10%)	100
Less: Tax credit on interest (£1,000 × 10%)	(100)
	———
Income tax payable	Nil
	———

The tax credit on the dividends in excess of the tax liability will be lost as this is not repayable.

10   C

	£	£
Rent accrued		9,600
Less: Expenses		
Council tax	900	
Replacement of broken window	300	
Insurance (£540 × 6/12) + (£480 × 6/12)	510	
Redecoration	450	
Wear and tear ((£9,600 – £900) × 10%)	870	
	———	
		(3,030)
		———
Property income		6,570
		———

Tutorial note

Property business income is assessed on the accruals basis assuming a year end of 5 April. The deduction for insurance is calculated by reference to the cost related to the year ended 5 April 2015 and the redecoration is deductible in 2014/15 as the work was completed in this year even though it was not paid for until the following tax year.

The examiner has stated that candidates are expected to know when the wear and tear allowance is applicable, and therefore they are expected to calculate the allowance for landlords of furnished property, without a prompt from the question.

11 B

	£
Premium	42,000
Less: £42,000 × 2% × (23 – 1)	(18,480)
Property business income	23,520

Alternative calculation = £42,000 × (51 – 23) / 50 = £23,520

12 D

	£
Salary ((£36,000 × 7/12) + (£36,000 × 105% × 5/12))	36,750
Bonus – received 3 April 2015	3,300
Total employment income	40,050

Tutorial note

Employment income is assessed on the receipts basis (i.e. income received in the tax year).

13 A

	£	£
Salary		55,000
Mileage allowance:		
Amount received (14,500 × 43p)	6,235	
AMAP rates:		
10,000 × 45p	(4,500)	
4,500 × 25p	(1,125)	
Excess mileage allowance		610
Employment income		55,610

14   B

The assessable benefit is the excess of the child care vouchers over the limit for a higher rate taxpayer – (£40 – £28) × 52 = £624. The other benefits are both exempt.

15   A

The original cost did not exceed £75,000, therefore it is not considered to be an 'expensive' accommodation. The only benefit is the basic charge based on the annual value of £2,600. Jo contributes more than the annual value (£250 × 12 = £3,000) and therefore the assessable benefit is nil.

16   D

CO_2 emissions = 198 g/km (rounded down to 195), available for 11 months

	%
Diesel	15
Plus: $(195 - 95) \times \frac{1}{5}$	20
	———
Appropriate percentage	35
	———

	£
Car benefit (£28,000 × 35% × 11/12)	8,983
	———

17   B

Average method	£	
Loan at start of tax year	100,000	
Loan at end of tax year	60,000	
	———	
	160,000	
	———	
Average loan (£160,000 ÷ 2)	80,000	
	———	
Assessable benefit (£80,000 × 3.25%)		£2,600
		———
Precise method		
(£100,000 × 3.25% × 4/12)	1,083	
(£60,000 × 3.25% × 8/12)	1,300	
	———	£2,383
		———

Tutorial note

Woojin will choose to use the precise method as this produces the lower taxable benefit figure.

Either the taxpayer or HMRC can decide that the precise method should be used.

---

18   D

The benefit on 6 April 2014 when Ritvik purchased the home cinema system is the higher of the market value at the time of the purchase and the market value when it was first made available less amounts previously taxed.

The amount paid, by Ritvik for the asset, of £1,500 can be deducted in computing the benefit.

	£	£
Higher of:		
(i) MV at date of transfer	2,400	
(ii) Original cost	8,500	
Less: Annual value for 2012/13 and 2013/14 for use of asset (£8,500 × 20% × 2)	(3,400)	
	5,100	5,100
Less: Employee contribution		(1,500)
Taxable benefit		3,600

INCOME TAX BASICS AND INCOME FROM SELF-EMPLOYMENT

19   A

The £450 spent on food hampers needs to be added back as gifts of food are disallowable. Costs relating to the acquisition of a short lease are disallowable so £150 must be added back. The costs of renewing a short lease would be allowable.

Employee parking fines incurred on business and amounts spent on staff entertaining (regardless of the amount) are allowable deductions from trading profits.

Tutorial note

Annual events which cost the employer more than £150 per head are a taxable benefit for the employee, but the cost is still deductible for the employer.

20   B

Haniful is treated as making a sale to himself at selling price. As no adjustment has been made in the accounts the full selling price must be added to the profits.

Tutorial note

If Haniful had made an adjustment in the accounts to remove the cost of the goods taken out of the business then only the profit element of £250 would need to be added to the trading profits for tax purposes.

21 D

Firstly the amount taxable on the landlord as property income must be calculated.

	£
Premium	25,000
Less: £25,000 × 2% × (20 – 1)	(9,500)
Property business income	15,500

Alternative calculation = £25,000 × (51 – 20) / 50 = £15,500

Fleur can then take an annual deduction spread evenly over the period of the lease:

(£15,500 ÷ 20) = £775.

As Fleur acquired the lease on 1 January 2014 the full annual amount of £775 is deductible when calculating the tax adjusted trading profits for the year ended 31 December 2014.

22 C

Any asset with private use by the owner of the business will be allocated to a private use asset column rather than the main pool.

Cars with CO_2 emissions in excess of 130 g/km are allocated to the special rate pool rather than the main pool.

23 B

A new car with CO_2 emissions up to 95 g/km qualifies for first year allowance of 100% which is never time apportioned irrespective of the length of the period of account.

The tax written down value brought forward in the main pool will be entitled to WDA at 18% time apportioned for 8 months therefore:

(£12,260 × 100%) = £12,260

(£18,000 × 18%) = £3,240 × 8/12 = £2,160

Total = (£12,260 + £2,160) = £14,420

24 D

In the final period of account only balancing adjustments arise.

		General pool £	Allowances £
TWDV b/f		15,000	
Additions		4,500	
Disposals	– pool items	(14,550)	
Disposals	– laptop retained personally	(4,150)	
		800	
Balancing allowance		(800)	800

The laptop is treated as having been disposed of at market value.

25   B

Jacinta started trading on 1 August 2014 and so 2014/15 is the first tax year of her trade.

In the first tax year, the profits taxed will be the actual profits arising from the first day of trade up to the following 5 April.

This is an eight month period and will include all the profits for the five months to 31 December 2014 and three months (1 January to 5 April 2015) from the next set of accounts.

£10,500 + 3/12 × (£24,000) = £16,500.

26   C

Lee ceases to trade on 31 January 2015 which falls into tax year 2014/15.

Up to that tax year Lee will have been taxed on the current year basis therefore in 2013/14, Lee will have been taxed on the profits of the accounting period ending in that year i.e. y/e 30 April 2013.

In the tax year in which he ceases to trade he will be taxed on any trading profits not taxed in previous years less his overlap profits that arose when he started his business, i.e.:

	£
y/e 31 April 2014	10,000
p/e 31 January 2015	14,000
Less: Overlap profits	(3,0000)
	———
Trading income assessment – 2014/15	21,000

PARTNERSHIPS

27   D

y/e 31 December 2014	*Total*	*Elizabeth*	*Henry*
	£	£	£
p/e 30 June 2014 (£80,000 × 6/12)			
Salary	5,000		5,000
Balance (70:30)	35,000	24,500	10,500
	———		
	40,000		
p/e 31 December 2014			
Salary	5,000		5,000
Balance (80:20)	35,000	28000	7,000
	———	———	———
Assessable income	80,000	52,500	27,500

TRADING LOSSES

28   B

	2012/13	2013/14	2014/15
	£	£	£
Trading income	45,000	–	1,000
Less: Losses b/f			(1,000)
Dividends (£8,100 × 100/90)	9,000	9,000	9,000
Total income	54,000	9,000	9,000

Loss memorandum:

	£
Loss arising in 2013/14	75,000
Used in 2012/13 – Prior year	(54,000)
Carried forward and used in 2014/15	(1,000)
Loss carried forward to 2015/16	20,000

Tutorial note

Brooke will make a claim against total income in 2012/13 but not in 2013/14 as her total income is covered by the personal allowance.

The loss offset in 2012/13 is not restricted to £50,000 as the restriction only applies to losses offset against other income, not income from the same trade.

The loss carried forward to 2014/15 is offset against the first available trading profits.

29   B

Tax year	Basis period	Available loss
		£
2012/13	1.11.12 – 5.4.13	
	(5/12 × £25,000)	10,417
2013/14	y/e 30.10.13	25,000
Less: Used in 2012/13		(10,417)
		14,583

The loss arising in 2012/13 of £10,417 is a loss in the first four tax years of trading and can be offset against total income in 2009/10, 2010/11 and 2011/12 in that order.

PENSIONS AND NIC

30   C

Hamid must pay Class 2 and Class 4 NICs in respect of his sole trader profits, Class 1 secondary NICs in respect of his employee's salaries and Class 1A NICs in respect of the company car benefit for employees.

Although Hamid is required to pay over the Class 1 primary NICs to HMRC, he will deduct these from the salaries paid to his employees so it is not a cost that is borne by him.

31   A

	£
(£41,865 – £7,956) × 12%	4,069
(£63,000 – £41,865) × 2%	423
	———
Class 1 Primary NICs	4,492
	———

32   B

Class 1 Secondary NICs	£
(£50,600 – £7,956) × 13.8%	5,885
	———

Working: Earnings liable to Class 1 NIC

	£
Salary	50,000
Excess mileage allowance (12,000 × (50p – 45p))	600
	———
	50,600
	———

Tutorial note

Occupational pension scheme contributions are not deductible from earnings for NIC purposes.

The excess mileage allowance above the AMAP of 45p per mile (regardless of the number of business miles) is subject to Class 1 NICs.

33   B

	£
Class 1A NIC	
£2,700 × 13.8%	373

Working: Car benefit

CO_2 emissions = 129 g/km (rounded down to 125)

	%
Petrol	12
Plus: $(125 - 95) \times \frac{1}{5}$	6
Appropriate percentage	18

	£
Car benefit (£15,000 × 18%)	2,700

34   A

Mohammed does not pay Class 2 NICs for 2014/15 as his accounting profits for the tax year are less than £5,885.

Nicole does not pay Class 2 NICs for 2014/15 as she is above the state retirement age.

35   A

	£
(£41,865 – £7,956) × 9%	3,052
(£280,000 – £41,865) × 2%	4,763
Class 1 Primary NICs	7,815

36   D

Isaac's basic rate band will be extended by the grossed up contribution as follows:

(£40,000 × 100/80) = £50,000

The contribution is lower than Isaac's relevant earnings for the year (£90,000) and therefore tax relief is available on the full amount.

37   C

2014/15

	£
2014/15 Annual allowance	40,000
Unused annual allowances b/f (W)	32,000
Maximum gross PPCs	72,000

Working: Unused annual allowances

		£
2011/12	(£50,000 – £23,000)	27,000
2012/13	(£50,000 – £40,000)	10,000
2013/14	(£50, 000 – £55,000) Used in 2013/14	(5,000)
Unused annual allowances		32,000

Tutorial note

Prior to 2014/15 the annual allowance was £50,000. This figure is given in the Tax Rates and Allowances table provided in the exam.

Unused annual allowances can be brought forward from the previous three tax years.

38   D

	£
Salary	50,000
Furnished holiday accommodation income	5,000
Relevant earnings	55,000

Tutorial note

Tax relief for both personal pension contributions and Gift Aid donations is made by extending the basic and higher rate bands by the gross contribution/donation.

There is no need to adjust relevant earnings for Gift Aid donations – this was a red herring!

ADMINISTRATION AND ETHICS

39   D

The others refer to tax avoidance.

40   B

A tax adviser must not assist a client to plan or commit any offence.

Tutorial note

A tax adviser may have a legal or professional right or duty to disclose information about a client without their authority (e.g. in the case of money laundering).

If the adviser becomes aware that a client has committed an offence they must discuss the irregularity with the client and ensure proper disclosure is made to HMRC).

A tax adviser has duties and responsibilities towards both his client and HMRC (e.g. they must ensure that all information provided to HMRC is accurate and complete).

41   A

Taxpayers who are in business, which for this purpose includes the letting of a property, must keep their records until five years after the 31 January filing date (i.e. 31 January 2021 for a 2014/15 return).

42   B

2014/15	£
Income tax liability	25,000
Income tax deducted at source	(5,400)
Income tax payable (relevant amount)	19,600
Payments on account (POA)	(18,000)
CGT liability	5,000
Balancing payment	6,600

Tutorial note

CGT is payable in full on 31 January following the tax year and must therefore be included in the balancing payment.

Although the first payment on account for 2014/15 is also due on 31 January 2016

43   B

The tax was due on 31 January 2016 and not actually paid until 10 March.

Interest on late paid tax runs from the due date until the date of payment, therefore statement (1) is true.

A 5% penalty is charged if the tax is paid more than 30 days late, therefore statement (3) is true.

44   A

	£
Daily penalties as 3 months late -maximum 90 days (£10 × 90)	900
6 months late (£6,500 × 5%)	325
Maximum penalty	1,225

Tutorial note

The 2014/15 return was due on 31 January 2016 and was therefore filed more than 6 months but less than 12 months late.

45   B

An employer must provide an employee with a P60 by 31 May following the tax year (i.e. 31 May 2015 for 2014/15).

Tutorial note

Under the RTI PAYE system information must be submitted electronically to HMRC on or before the date of payment.

Employers with more than 250 employees must pay their PAYE payments electronically. The due date for electronic payments is 17 days after the end of the tax month (i.e. by the 22nd of the month following the month of payment).

CHARGEABLE GAINS

INDIVIDUALS – CAPITAL GAINS TAX

46   C

Qualifying corporate bonds, gilt-edged securities and a main residence (which has always been lived in), are all exempt from CGT.

Assets used in the trade are still chargeable assets and will potentially realise a chargeable gain if they are sold at a profit. The wasting chattel rules do not apply to assets on which capital allowances have been claimed and vans are not treated as cars.

47   B

	£
Sale proceeds	340,000
Less: Selling costs	(2,500)
	————
Net proceeds	337,500
Less: Cost	(150,000)
	————
Chargeable gain	187,500
Less: Capital losses b/f	(80,000)
	————
	107,500
Less: AEA	(11,000)
	————
Taxable gains	96,500
	————
Capital gains tax liability (£96,500 × 28%)	27,020
	————

Tutorial note

Lexie has taxable income of £54,000 and is therefore a higher rate taxpayer. Her capital gains will therefore be subject to a tax rate of 28%.

48 B

	£
Disposal proceeds	165,000
Less: Deemed acquisition cost	(115,000)
Chargeable gain	50,000
Less: Capital losses b/f	(5,000)
	45,000
Less: AEA	(11,000)
Taxable gains	34,000
Capital gains tax payable (£34,000 × 28%)	9,520

Tutorial note

Sophia's deemed acquisition cost is equal to the deemed proceeds on the transfer from her husband. This is equal to his acquisition cost.

49 B

	£
Sale proceeds	425,000
Deemed cost of remainder (£300,000 − £112,500(W))	(187,500)
Chargeable gain	237,500
Less: AEA	(11,000)
Taxable gain	226,500
Capital gains tax liability (£226,500 × 28%)	63,420

Working: Part disposal January 2010
Deemed cost of 10 acres disposed of:
£300,000 × £150,000 / (£150,000 + £250,000) — 112,500

50 A

	£
Painting 1	
Non-wasting chattel bought and sold for < £6,000	Exempt
Painting 2	
Sale proceeds	7,200
Less: Cost	(1,000)
Chargeable gain	6,200
Gain cannot exceed:	
5/3 × (£7,200 – £6,000)	2,000
Total chargeable gain (£Nil + £2,000)	2,000

Tutorial note

The two paintings disposed of in this question are non-wasting chattels.

If non-wasting chattels are bought and sold for £6,000 or less they are exempt.

If bought for £6,000 or less but are sold for more than £6,000, the gain is restricted to:

5/3 × (gross proceeds – £6,000).

51 C

	£
Deemed sale proceeds	6,000
Less: Allowable selling costs (legal fees)	(300)
Net sale proceeds	5,700
Less: Allowable expenditure	
Cost (£22,000 + £800)	(22,000)
Incidental costs of acquisition	(800)
Allowable loss	(17,100)

Tutorial note

The vase disposed of in this question is a non-wasting chattel.

If a non-wasting chattel cost more than £6,000 but is sold for £6,000 or less, the allowable loss is calculated using deemed gross sale proceeds of £6,000.

52   D

	£
Sale proceeds	44,000
Less: Allowable element of acquisition cost (W)	(14,000)
Chargeable gain	30,000

Working: Allowable element of acquisition cost
Remaining life at disposal = 8 years
Estimated useful life = 20 years

Allowable cost = £35,000 × 8/20 = £14,000

Tutorial note

A copyright is a wasting asset which is not a chattel as it is not tangible or movable.

The allowable expenditure on these assets is deemed to waste away over the life of the asset on a straight line basis.

Consequently, on a disposal the allowable cost is restricted to take account of the asset's natural fall in value.

53   D

	£
Sale proceeds	230,000
Less: Cost (W)	(152,000)
Chargeable gain	78,000

Working: Restored asset base cost	
Original cost	142,000
Plus: Restoration expenditure	70,000
Less: Insurance proceeds	(60,000)
Revised base cost	152,000

Tutorial note

Where insurance proceeds are received in respect of an asset that has been damaged there is a part disposal.

However, if all of the insurance proceeds are used in restoring the asset the taxpayer may claim to deduct the proceeds from the cost of the asset rather than be treated as having made a part disposal of the asset.

Remember to include the amount spent restoring the asset in the revised base cost.

54   **A**

Lower of:

Quarter up method:

Lower price	120p
Add: (132p – 120p) × 1/4	3p
	123p

Average of highest and lowest recorded bargains:

(122p + 136p) ÷ 2	129p

55   **B**

	£
Exchequer Stock (gilt-edged security)	Exempt
Martin plc	
Proceeds – Market value	12,300
Less: Cost	(8,000)
Chargeable gain	4,300

Tutorial note

Where an asset is transferred to a connected party, market value is substituted for actual gross proceeds.

56   **D**

Tutorial note

The matching rules require that shares disposed of by an individual are matched against shares acquired in the following order:

1   *Shares purchased on the same day as the date of disposal; then*

2   *Shares purchased within the following 30 days; then*

3   *Shares in the share pool (made up of shares acquired before the date of disposal).*

57   A

	£	£
Shares acquired in following 30 days		
Sale proceeds (500/5,000 × £25,000)	2,500	
Less: Cost	(2,050)	
	———	450
Share pool (shares acquired pre 28 February 2015)		
Sale proceeds (4,500/5,000 × £25,000)	22,500	
Less: Cost (W)	(14,276)	
	———	8,224
		———
Chargeable gain		8,674
		———

Working: Share pool

		Number	Cost £
April 1996	Purchase	9,000	27,050
April 2010	Purchase	2,600	9,750
		———	———
		11,600	36,800
February 2015	Sale (4,500/11,600 × £36,800)	(4,500)	(14,276)
		———	———
		7,100	22,524
		———	———

58   C

The allowable cost of the shares disposed of in December 2014 is £50,000 (W)

Working: Share pool

		Number	Cost £
April 2003	Purchase	40,000	200,000
May 2006	Rights issue (1:4) @ £10 per share	10,000	40,000
		———	———
		50,000	240,000
May 2010	Bonus issue (1:5)	10,000	-
		———	———
		60,000	240,000
March 2015	Sale (12,500/60,000 × £240,000)	(12,500)	(50,000)
		———	———
		47,500	190,000
		———	———

59   C

The total consideration provided by Riley plc is:

	MV	Cost
	£	£
Cash (50,000 × £3)	150,000	50,000
Shares (50,000 × 2 × £1.20)	120,000	40,000
	270,000	90,000

Hunter has made a part disposal in relation to the cash consideration.

	£
Disposal proceeds (cash: 50,000 × £3)	150,000
Less: Original cost (£150,000/£270,000 × £90,000)	(50,000)
Chargeable gain	100,000

60   A

Zofia had periods of actual occupation before and after her absence so any period spent employed abroad would be classified as deemed occupation.

Therefore the entire eight year absence would qualify as deemed occupation.

Tutorial note

Only four years of the total eight year absence would qualify as deemed occupation if she was self-employed abroad or working elsewhere in the UK.

Only three years of the total eight year absence would qualify as deemed occupation if she was travelling, under the three years for any reason deemed occupation rule.

61   B

	£
Chargeable gain before reliefs	120,000
Less: PPR relief (£120,000 × 6/10)	(72,000)
	48,000
Less: Letting relief (W)	(40,000)
Chargeable gain	8,000

Working: Letting relief

Lowest of:

1   Maximum = £40,000

2   PPR relief = £72,000

3   Gain on letting = £48,000

Tutorial note

PPR is available on 6/10 of the gain as Masuma has always occupied six out of the ten rooms in the house. Masuma cannot benefit from the rules of deemed occupation on the remaining four rooms as she has never used them as part of her main residence.

62 B

Ben will qualify for entrepreneurs' relief as he works for the company and has owned at least 5% of the shares for at least twelve months prior to the disposal.

63 B

	£
Qualifying for ER	
Gain on sale of business	13,250,000
Less: AEA	(11,000)
Taxable gain	13,239,000
Capital gains tax:	
£10,000,000 × 10%	1,000,000
£3,239,000 × 28%	906,920
	1,906,920

64 C

Only fixed (i.e. not movable) plant and machinery qualifies for rollover relief. Shares are not qualifying assets.

65 D

	£	£
Sale of warehouse		
Sale proceeds		270,213
Less: Cost	231,211	
Less: ROR on factory (Note)	(31,083)	
		(200,128)
Chargeable gain		70,085

Tutorial note

The proceeds from the sale of the factory were fully reinvested in the warehouse.

Therefore, the gain on the factory of £31,083 can be fully rolled over against the acquisition cost of the warehouse.

66   A

Unquoted shares in a trading company are qualifying assets for gift relief irrespective of the percentage shareholding.

Quoted shares are only qualifying assets if they are in the donor's personal trading company.

A company qualifies as a donor's personal trading company for the purposes of gift relief if at least 5% of the voting rights are held by the individual. However, there is no minimum holding period and no requirement for the individual to work for the company.

Assets used by a donor's personal trading company are also qualifying assets for the purposes of gift relief but only if the company uses the asset in their trade.

COMPANIES – CHARGEABLE GAINS

67   A

	£
Sale of warehouse	
Sale proceeds	800,000
Less: Cost (£250,000 + £20,000)	(270,000)
Enhancement expenditure	(100,000)
Unindexed gain	430,000
Less: Indexation allowance (W)	
Cost (£270,000 × 0.317)	(85,590)
Enhancement expenditure (£100,000 × 0.205)	(20,500)
Chargeable gain	323,910

Working: Indexation factors

The indexation factor from December 2005 to May 2014 is:

(255.6 – 194.1)/194.1 = 0.317 (rounded to three decimal places)

The indexation factor from March 2008 to May 2014 is:

(255.6 – 212.1)/212.1 = 0.205 (rounded to three decimal places)

68   C

	£
Land	
Sale proceeds	45,000
Less: Cost	(20,000)
	————
Unindexed gain	25,000
Less: Indexation allowance (W)	
Cost (£20,000 × 1.633) – restricted (Note)	(25,000)
	————
Chargeable gain	Nil
	————
Storage unit	
Sale proceeds	75,000
Less: Cost	(80,000)
	————
Unindexed loss	(5,000)
Less: Indexation allowance (Note)	–
	————
Allowable loss	(5,000)
	————

Working: Indexation factors

The indexation factor from May 1986 to October 2014 is:

(257.6 – 97.85)/97.85 = 1.633 (rounded to three decimal places)

Tutorial note

The indexation allowance cannot increase or create a loss.

69   A

	£
Year ended 30 June 2014	
Capital loss	80,000
Offset against current year chargeable gain	(25,000)
	————
Loss carried forward	55,000
	————

Tutorial note

Capital losses can only be offset against chargeable gains arising in the same accounting period. Any remaining loss is then carried forward against future capital gains.

Capital losses cannot be carried back and offset against income or gains from previous accounting periods.

70 A

The indexed cost on the disposal of shares is £19,477 (see below).

Working: Share pool

		Number	Cost £	Indexed cost £
April 1992	*Purchase*	25,000	33,000	33,000
IA to June 2014	((256.0 – 138.8)/138.8) × £33,000			27,865
		25,000	33,000	60,865
June 2014	*Sale*			
	(8,000/25,000 × £33,000/£60,865)	(8,000)	(10,560)	(19,477)
		17,000	22,440	41,388

71 C

The election must be made within four years of the later of the end of the accounting period in which the old asset is sold and the new asset is acquired.

Tutorial note

The deferred gain of £250,000 will become chargeable 10 years after the replacement asset is acquired (i.e. on 1 November 2023).

INHERITANCE TAX

72   C

The gift to Mario's wife is exempt as the inter spouse exemption applies.

A lifetime transfer up to £5,000 given from parent to child on the occasion of the child's marriage is exempt, so the gift of £2,000 to Mario's son is exempt.

The gift into the trust is a chargeable lifetime transfer and is therefore not exempt.

The gift to Mario's daughter is more than £250 and therefore the small gifts exemption does not apply.

73   D

The gift to Shola's daughter is a potentially exempt transfer. It is not chargeable during lifetime but it does utilise the annual exemption for the current year (2014/15) and the prior year (2013/14).

The gifts to trusts are chargeable lifetime transfers (CLTs). The first CLT of £200,000 falls within the £325,000 nil rate band and therefore no inheritance tax arises.

The lifetime inheritance tax on the second CLT is £37,500 (W).

Working: CLT 29.12.2014

	£	£
Transfer of value		275,000
NRB at date of gift (2014/15)	325,000	
Less: GCTs in 7 years pre-gift (29.12.2007 – 29.12.2014)	(200,000)	
	———	(125,000)
Taxable amount		150,000
Lifetime IHT due (£150,000 × 25%) (donor pays tax)		37,500

74   C

		CLT 20.05.2014 £
Transfer of value		150,000
AE – Current year	(2014/15)	(3,000)
Previous year	(2013/14)	(3,000)
Chargeable amount		144,000
NRB at date of gift		
2012/13		
2014/15	325,000	
Less: GCTs in 7 years pre-gift		
(18.02.2006 – 18.02.2013)		
(20.05.2007 – 20.05.2014)	(274,000)	
		(51,000)
Taxable amount		93,000
Lifetime IHT due (donor pays tax)		
(£93,000 × 25%)		23,250

75   A

	£	£
CLT 1.5.2014 (2014/15)		
Nil rate band – 2014/15		325,000
GCTs in previous 7 years (1.5.2007 – 1.5.2014)		
2013/14 – To Trust	200,000	
Less: Annual exemption – 2013/14 (W)	(2,000)	
2012/13 (W)	(3,000)	
		(195,000)
Remaining nil rate band		130,000

Working: 2013/14 annual exemption available

	£
2013/14 – Gift to nephew (PET but uses AEs)	2,000
Less: Marriage exemption	(1,000)
Less: Annual exemption (2013/14)	(1,000)
	Nil

76   D

Date of death: 1.2.2015

7 years before: 1.2.2008

PET on 30 November 2007 is more than 7 years before death so no IHT payable on death.

	£	£
PET 15.6.2008		350,000
Less: Annual exemption – 2008/09		(3,000)
2007/08		(Nil)
		———
Chargeable amount		347,000
		———

Tutorial note

Although the PET made on 30 November 2007 does not become chargeable on death, it will still utilise the annual exemption for the tax year of the gift (2007/08). This annual exemption will therefore not be available to reduce the PET made in 2008/09 that becomes chargeable on death.

---

77   A

	£	£
Gross chargeable amount		586,250
NRB (2014/15)	325,000	
Less: GCTs < 7 years before gift (10.11.2002 – 10.11.2009)	(Nil)	
	———	(325,000)
		———
Taxable amount		261,250
		———
IHT payable @ 40%		104,500
Less: Taper relief		
(10.11.2009 – 16.7.2014) (4 – 5 years before death) (40%)		(41,800)
		———
		62,700
Less: IHT paid in lifetime		(52,250)
		———
IHT payable on death		10,450
		———

78   B

Date of death: 20.1.2015

7 years before: 20.1.2008

The gifts to the son and the discretionary trust are more than 7 years before death so no IHT is payable as a result of death.

The gift to the daughter is a PET which has become chargeable as a result of death. The available nil rate band is fully used by the CLT (gift to the trust) made in the 7 years before the date of the gift, so there will be an IHT liability on the gift to the daughter.

The gift to the wife is exempt under the inter spouse exemption.

79   D

	£
House (Note)	545,000
Life insurance policy (proceeds received)	350,000
	———
	895,000
Less: Exempt legacy to wife	(400,000)
	———
Gross chargeable estate	495,000
	———

Tutorial note

Endowment mortgages are not deductible as they are automatically repaid on the owner's death.

80   C

	£	£
Gross chargeable estate		
House	400,000	
Less: Repayment mortgage	(85,000)	
	———	315,000
Chattels		70,000
Cash in NISA		20,000
		———
Chargeable estate		405,000
		———

Tutorial note

Gambling debts are not incurred for valuable consideration and are not deductible from the estate.

81 D

Date of death: 20.12.2014
7 years before: 20.12.2007

Death estate	£	£
Gross chargeable estate		1,101,000
NRB at death (2014/15)	325,000	
Less: GCTs in 7 years pre-death		
(20.12.2007 – 20.12.2014)(W)	(124,000)	
		(201,000)
Taxable amount		900,000
IHT on chargeable estate (£900,000 × 40%)		360,000

Working: Lifetime gift

PET – 8.8.13 – becomes chargeable but is covered by the nil rate band of £325,000 such that no death tax is due on this gift

82 B

	£
Value of estate before transfer (7,500 × £20)	150,000
Value of estate after transfer (4,500 × £8)	(36,000)
Transfer of value	114,000

83 A

For a CLT between 6 April and 30 September the inheritance tax is due by 30 April following the end of the tax year.

The additional tax due on CLTs as a result of death is due 6 months after the end of the month of death.

84 C

Inheritance tax due on the death estate is paid by the executors but is suffered/borne by the residual legatee (i.e. the daughter).

85 C

Taper relief reduces the **IHT payable on death** provided the donor survives for more than three years following the gift, it does not reduce the chargeable amount on death..

86   D

On Willow's death the available nil rate band (NRB) was £300,000 of which £120,000 was utilised by the legacy to her son. The amount left to Stanley was exempt under the inter spouse exemption.

The unutilised proportion of the NRB is 60% ((£180,000/£300,000) × 100).

	£
Stanley: NRB on death	325,000
Proportion of Willow's unused NRB – elect to transfer to Stanley (£325,000 × 60%)	195,000
Total NRB available to Stanley	520,000

Tutorial note

The amount of NRB that can be transferred to the surviving spouse is based on the **proportion** *of the NRB unused on the first death. This proportion is applied to the NRB at the date of death of the surviving spouse.*

CORPORATION TAX

CORPORATION TAX BASICS AND ADMINISTRATION

87   C

Tutorial note

A chargeable accounting period is the period for which a charge to corporation tax is made.

A company's period of account is the period for which it prepares accounts.

The tax financial year runs from 1 April to 31 March and is identified by the year in which it begins. The rate of tax is fixed by reference to the financial year. A company may have a chargeable accounting period which straddles 31 March, for example if they prepare accounts for the year ended 31 December.

88   B

Taxable total profits – y/e 31 March 2015

	£
Trading profit before capital allowances	100,000
Less: Capital allowances	(2,000)
Tax adjusted trading profit	98,000
Interest receivable	5,000
Total profits	103,000
Less: Qualifying charitable donations	(3,200)
Taxable total profits	99,800

Tutorial note

For the purposes of the F6 exam, dividends received are not taxable and therefore are not included in taxable total profits. However, dividends received from non-associated companies are included in augmented profits which are used to determine the rate of tax paid by the company.

89   B

Taxable total profits – y/e 31 December 2014

	£
Tax adjusted trading profit	50,000
Property business profit	6,000
Interest income	2,000
Chargeable gain	12,000
Taxable total profits	70,000

Tutorial note

Interest income is taxable on an accruals basis (i.e. amount receivable for the accounting period) not on the receipts basis.

Taxable total profits should include a company's worldwide income (excluding dividends) and net chargeable gains.

Remember companies pay corporation tax on their chargeable gains and not capital gains tax.

90   D

Corporation tax liability – y/e 31 March 2015

	£
Tax adjusted trading profit	1,200,000
Property business profit	250,000
	1,450,000
Less: QCD relief	(7,000)
TTP	1,443,000
Corporation tax liability (W)(£1,443,000 × 21%)	303,030

Working: Augmented profits

	£
TTP	1,443,000
Plus: FII (£52,200 × 100/90)	58,000
Augmented profits	1,501,000

As augmented profits exceed £1,500,000 taxable total profits are taxed at the main rate.

91   A

Corporation tax liability – y/e 31 March 2015

	£
Tax adjusted trading profit	250,000
Chargeable gain	60,000
	310,000
Less: QCDs	(60,000)
Taxable total profits (TTP)	250,000
Corporation tax liability (£250,000 × 21%)	52,500
Less: Marginal relief	
1/400 × (£1,500,000 − £700,000) × £250,000/£700,000	(714)
	51,786

Working: Augmented profits

	£
TTP	250,000
Plus: FII (£405,000 × 100/90)	450,000
Augmented profits	700,000

As augmented profits are between £300,000 and £1,500,000 marginal relief applies.

92 A

Corporation tax liability – 8 m/e 31 March 2015

	£
TTP	190,000

	£
£190,000 × 21%	39,900
Less: Marginal relief	
1/400 × (£1,000,000 – £220,000) × £190,000/£220,000	(1,684)
Corporation tax liability	38,216

Working: Augmented profits

	£
TTP	190,000
Plus: FII (£27,000 × 100/90)	30,000
Augmented profits	220,000

1   Upper limit: £1,500,000 × 8/12 = £1,000,000

2   Lower limit: £300,000 × 8/12 =   £200,000

As augmented profits are between the lower limit of £200,000 and the upper limit of £1,000,000 marginal relief applies

Tutorial note

For a short accounting period the upper and lower augmented profits limits must be prorated by the length of the accounting period.

Remember to use the revised upper profits limit in the marginal relief calculation.

93 B

Corporation tax liability – y/e 31 January 2015

	£
Trading income = TTP	1,450,000
FY2013: (£1,450,000 × 2/12 × 23%)	55,583
FY2014: (£1,450,000 × 10/12 × 21%)	253,750
Corporation tax liability	309,333

Working: Augmented profits

	£
TTP	1,450,000
Plus: FII	55,000
Augmented profits	1,505,000

Upper limit: £1,500,000 × 8/12 = £1,000,000

Lower limit: £300,000 × 8/12 = £200,000

As augmented profits are above the upper limit of £1,500,000 the main rate applies.

The company's CAP straddles 31 March 2013. The first 2 months (1.2.2014 to 31.3.2014) fall into FY2013 and the second 10 months (1.04.2014 to 31.1.2015) fall into FY2014.

As the main rate of corporation tax is different in those financial years the tax must be computed separately for each financial year.

94 D

Tax adjusted trading profit – y/e 30 June 2014	£
Trading profit per the accounts	25,050
Staff entertaining	Nil
Entertaining clients	530
Leased car restriction (£2,000 × 15%)	300
Tax adjusted trading profit	25,880

Tutorial note

Where the CO_2 emissions of a leased car exceed 130 g/km 15% of the lease charges are disallowed.

Remember that there are no private use adjustments for a company. The lease payments are therefore allowed in full, irrespective of any private use, subject to the 15% restriction.

95 B

	£	Main pool £	Allowances £
y/e 31 March 2015			
TWDV b/f		35,000	
Less: WDA (18%)		(6,300)	6,300
Low emission car			
($CO_2 \leq 95$ g/km)	8,000		
Less: FYA (100%)	(8,000)		8,000
		Nil	
TWDV c/f		28,700	
Total allowances			14,300

Tutorial note

Remember that there are no private use adjustments for a company. The employee who uses the car privately will have a taxable employment benefit instead.

96   A

Property income: y/e 31 December 2014

	£
Rent receivable (£15,000 × 7/12) + (£8,000 × 2/12)	10,083
Less: Expenses	
Replacing fitted units	(500)
Property business profit	9,583

Tutorial note

The cost of replacing the damaged fitted kitchen unit is an allowable repair.

RELIEF FOR TRADING LOSSES

97   C

Loss memorandum

	£
Loss – y/e 31.3.2014	100,000
Less: Used in – y/e 31.3.14 (£12,000 + £15,000)	(27,000)
y/e 31.3.15	(20,000)
Loss carried forward	53,000

Tutorial note

If a current year loss relief claim is made, trading losses are offset against total profits before deduction of qualifying charitable donations (QCDs).

Any remaining loss is then automatically carried forward and offset against the first available trading profits from the same trade.

98   A

Year ended 31 March	*2014*	*2015*
	£	£
Trading profit	40,000	Nil
Property business profit	15,000	17,000
Chargeable gain	Nil	4,000
	————	————
Total profits	55,000	21,000
Less: Loss relief – current year		(21,000)
– carry back (£50,000 – £21,000)	(29,000)	
	————	————
	26,000	Nil
Less: QCDs	(6,000)	Wasted
	————	————
Taxable total profits	20,000	Nil
	————	————

Tutorial note

A claim to carry back losses against total profits (i.e. before QCDs) of the previous year can only be made if a claim has been made to offset the loss against current year total profits first.

99   C

Loss memorandum

	£
Loss of year ended 31.3.2015	60,000
Less: Used in current year – y/e 31.3.14	(5,000)
Less: Used in 12 month carry back	
– 9 m/e to 30.6.2014 (W)	(25,000)
– y/e 30.6.2013	
Lower of:	
(i) Total profits × 3/12 = (3/12 × 44,000) = £11,000	
(ii) Remaining loss = £30,000	(11,000)
	————
Loss carried forward	19,000
	————

Working: Loss relief

	y/e 30 June 2013 £	9 m/e 30 June 2014 £	y/e 31 March 2015 £
Trading profit	40,000	22,000	Nil
Interest income	4,000	3,000	5,000
	——————	——————	——————
Total profits	44,000	25,000	5,000
Loss relief:			
Current year			(5,000)
12 month carry back		(25,000)	
12 month carry back (£44,000 × 3/12)	(11,000)		
	——————	——————	——————
TTP	33,000	Nil	Nil
	——————	——————	——————

Tutorial note

A loss can be carried back against the total profits of the previous 12 months (provided a current year claim has been made first).

Where an accounting period falls partly into the 12 month carry back period the total profits must be time apportioned and only those falling in the 12 month carry back period can be relieved.

100 D

Loss memorandum

	£
Loss of year ended 31.3.2015	100,000
Less: Loss relief	(14,000)
Current year	
Terminal loss relief (Previous 3 years on LIFO basis):	
y/e 31.3.2014	(19,000)
y/e. 31.3.2013	(32,000)
y/e. 31.3.2012 (balance)	(35,000)
	——————
Loss not utilised	Nil
	——————

Working – Loss relief

Year ended 31 March	2012	2013	2014	2015
	£	£	£	£
Trading profit	45,000	32,000	10,000	Nil
Chargeable gain	5,000	Nil	9,000	14,000
Total profits	50,000	32,000	19,000	14,000
Less: Loss relief				
Current year				(14,000)
Terminal loss relief LIFO):				
First			(19,000)	
Second		(32,000)		
Third	(35,000)			
Taxable total profits	15,000	Nil	Nil	Nil

Tutorial note

A loss in the final 12 months of trading can be set against the total profits of the three preceding years on a LIFO basis, provided a claim has been made against current year total profits first.

101 B

Loss memorandum

	£
Loss of year ended 31.3.2014	65,000
Less: Loss relief	
Used in current year claim – y/e 31.3.2014 (W)	(20,000)
Carried forward – y/e 31.3.15 (W)	(35,000)
Loss not utilised as at 31.3.2015	10,000

Working – Loss relief

Year ended 31 March	2013	2014	2015
	£	£	£
Trading profit	16,000	20,000	25,000
Property business profit	5,000	Nil	10,000
	————	————	————
Total profits	21,000	20,000	35,000
Less: Loss relief			
Current year		(20,000)	
Brought forward			(35,000)
	————	————	————
	21,000	Nil	Nil
Less: QCDs	(800)	wasted	wasted
	————	————	————
Taxable total profits	Nil	Nil	Nil
	————	————	————

Tutorial note

A property business loss is automatically (no choice available) set against the total profits (before QCDs) of the current year. Any unused loss is automatically carried forward against the first available future total profits (before QCDs).

Property business losses cannot be carried back.

WITH GROUP ASPECTS

102   D

There are 5 associated companies (Telephone, Desk, Chair, Window and Curtain).

Associated companies are companies under common control (Control = > 50% of the ordinary share capital).

Overseas companies are included but dormant companies are excluded.

A company acquired during an accounting period is treated as associated for the whole of the accounting period.

103   D

There are 3 associated companies (Novak, Roger and Rafael), and there is a 7 month CAP.

Lower limit: (£300,000 ÷ 3 × 7/12) = £58,333

Upper limit: (£1,500,000 ÷ 3 × 7/12) = £291,667

Andy Ltd is not included as an associated company as it is dormant.

104   C

A loss group consists of a company and directly/indirectly owned companies where there is a shareholding of at least 75%.

An overseas company can be part of the loss group structure but it cannot itself claim or surrender losses.

Computer Ltd has a direct holding of 75% in Chair Ltd and 100% in Paper Inc and an indirect 75% holding, through Paper Inc, in Cardboard Ltd (100% × 75%).

So the loss can be surrendered to Chair Ltd and Cardboard Ltd but not to Paper Inc as it is resident overseas.

105   B

Where the companies in a loss group have non-coterminous accounting periods, the available profits and losses must be time apportioned, to find the relevant amounts falling within the corresponding accounting period.

In this situation, the maximum loss that can be surrendered

= Lower of:

- Allowable loss in the surrendering (loss making) company for the corresponding accounting period = (3/12 × £100,000) = £25,000
- Taxable total profits in the claimant company for the corresponding accounting period = (3/6 × £80,000) = £40,000

106   C

A capital gains group comprises the parent company and its 75% (direct or indirect) subsidiaries and also, the 75% subsidiaries of the first subsidiaries and so on. However the parent company must have an effective interest of over 50% in all group companies

Brazil Ltd has a direct 100% holding in Germany Ltd and a direct 75% holding in Holland Ltd. Russia also forms part of the group as Brazil Ltd has an overall effective interest of over 50% (75% × 75% = 56.25%).

Belgium does not form part of the group as it is not a 75% subsidiary of Germany.

107   A

The deemed acquisition cost is £150,000.

This is made up of the original cost of the asset to Apple (£100,000) plus indexation allowance up to the date of the transfer (£50,000).

Tutorial note

When an asset is transferred between companies in a gains group the asset is deemed to be transferred at a price that gives rise to neither a gain or loss to the company transferring the asset.

The deemed transfer price becomes the deemed acquisition cost for the transferee.

108   B

> **Tutorial note**
>
> *If a period of account is split into two chargeable accounting periods, the related corporation tax return must be submitted within 12 months of the end of the period of account, not the end of the chargeable accounting periods.*

109   A

Companies which are not large (i.e. do not pay tax at the main rate), are required to pay their corporation tax 9 months and 1 day after the end of the chargeable accounting period.

W Ltd and Z Ltd both have a chargeable accounting period ending on 30 June 2014 so the due date for payment of corporation tax is 1 April 2015.

X Ltd's 15 month period of account contains two chargeable accounting periods for tax purposes, the year ended 30 June 2014 and the 3 months ended 30 September 2014. Therefore it also has a due date for payment of corporation tax of 1 April 2015.

Y Ltd's due payment date in respect of the year ended 31 March 2014 is 1 January 2015.

110   B

> **Tutorial note**
>
> *A large company is required to pay its final instalment of corporation tax by the 14th day of the 4th month after the end of the chargeable accounting period (CAP). Note that for a 12 month AP this is 16 months after the start of the AP.*
>
> *Where a CAP is less than 12 months, the first instalment is due by the 14th day of the 7th month after the start of the CAP. Subsequent instalments are due at 3 monthly intervals thereafter, until the date of the final instalment is reached.*
>
> *For an eight month CAP instalments of 3/8 × corporation tax liability are payable on 14 November 2014 (14th day of month 7 of the AP) and 14 February (3 months later). The final instalment of 2/8 × corporation tax liability is due on 14 April 2015 (the 14th day of the 4th month after the end of the CAP.*

VALUE ADDED TAX

111   A

Under the future prospects test, Fred is required to register for VAT when taxable supplies in the next 30 days in isolation are expected to exceed £81,000.

Fred had grounds for expecting this to be the case on 1 June 2015 when he received an order to supply £90,000 of goods by 30 June 2015. Registration is effective from the start of the 30 day period so Fred must start charging VAT from 1 June 2015.

112   B

Taxable supplies for 7 m/e 31 July 2014 are £66,000 and for 8 m/e 31 August 2014 taxable supplies are £96,000. Wilma therefore exceeds the registration limit of £81,000 in August 2014.

Wilma must notify HM Revenue & Customs by 30 September 2014 and she will be registered from 1 October 2014.

113   C

VAT cannot be reclaimed on cars which are used for private purposes.

VAT can be reclaimed on fuel used partially for private purposes (although output VAT will be due based on the fuel scale charge).

Pre-registration input VAT can only be reclaimed on services if they were supplied within six months of registration.

114   D

Companies that are under common control (≥50%) can be in a VAT group provided they all have a place of business in the UK.

115   B

A VAT registered trader must notify HM Revenue and Customs within 30 days of ceasing to make taxable supplies.

116   B

The basic tax point is the date the handbag is delivered. This is only overridden if a tax invoice is issued or payment is made before the basic tax point or an invoice is issued within 14 days after the basic tax point.

117 A

	£
Brochure price	2,000
Less: Trade discount (£2,000 × 10%)	(200)
	———
Discounted price	1,800
Less: Settlement discount (£1,800 × 5%)	(90)
	———
	1,710
	———
VAT (£1,710 × 20%)	342
	———

Tutorial note

If a cash discount is offered, then VAT must be calculated as if the maximum discount available was taken.

118 B

Recoverable input VAT

	£
Entertaining new suppliers	Nil
Car leasing (£3,000 × 1/6 × 50%)	250
	———
	250
	———

Tutorial note

VAT can only be recovered on entertaining staff and overseas customers.

Where any car, which has some private use, is leased only 50% of the input VAT can be recovered. The level of the car's CO_2 emissions is irrelevant.

119 D

Quarter ended 31 March 2015

	£	£
Output tax:		
Sales (£30,000 × 1/6)	5,000	
Samples	Nil	
	———	5,000
Input tax:		
Purchases (£15,000 × 1/6)	2,500	
Relief for impairment losses (£800 × 1/6)	133	
	———	(2,633)
VAT payable		2,367

Tutorial note

Relief for impairment losses is only available where at least six months has elapsed since the debt was due for payment and the seller has written the debt off in their VAT account.

The VAT on the £1,000 debt (net of any recovery from the liquidator) can be recovered in the quarter to 30 June 2015.

Business samples are not treated as taxable supplies and therefore no output VAT is payable in respect of them.

120 C

Quarter ended 31 March 2015

	£	£
Output tax:		
Standard rated supplies (£40,000 × 95% × 20%)	7,600	
Fuel scale charge (£485 × 1/6)	81	
	———	7,681
Input tax:		
Purchases and expenses (£22,000 × 1/6)		(3,667)
VAT payable		4,014

121 C

122 D

123 B

This is the second time the return is late. On the first offence a surcharge liability period (SLP) would start, which would end on 31 October 2015 (the 12- month anniversary of the VAT period to which the default relates.

The second offence is the first default in the SLP, the SLP is extended to 31 January 2016 and a 2% penalty of £520 (£26,000 × 2%) is charged.

124 A

The error is smaller than the greater of £10,000 or 1% of turnover (£3,800) and can therefore be corrected on the next quarter's VAT return. Any error that can be corrected on the next return will not attract an interest charge.

125 D

To join the scheme a trader's taxable turnover (excluding VAT and sales of capital assets) for the next twelve months must not exceed £1,350,000.

126 A

There will have been nine payments at 10% of last year's liability in months 4 to 12 totalling £3,240 (9 × 10% × £3,600).

This year's liability is £4,115 leaving a balance left to pay of £875 (£4,115 – £3,240).

127 D

The flat rate scheme applies a percentage to the VAT inclusive total turnover including zero rated and exempt sales. Expenses are not deductible.

Standard rated sales = (£80,000 + 20% VAT) = £96,000.

Total VAT inclusive turnover = (£96,000 + £15,000 + £10,000) = £121,000

This is multiplied by the flat rate percentage to calculate the VAT due to HMRC

(£121,000 × 13%) = £15,730

128 A

The UK trader accounts for output VAT of £2,000 as the goods would be standard rated if supplied in the UK. The UK trader can claim back input VAT of £2,000 on the same return as the goods are used in a taxable supply business.

Section 4

ANSWERS TO PRACTICE SECTION B QUESTIONS

INCOME TAX AND NATIONAL INSURANCE

INCOME TAX BASICS AND EMPLOYMENT INCOME

1   **SALLY BURTON (ADAPTED)** *Online question assistance*

Key answer tips

This question requires calculation of income tax for a taxpayer entitled to a personal age allowance. However, due to the level of income, abatement of the allowance is necessary.

Always watch out for exempt income and consider whether income is received gross or net.

(a)   **Sally Burton**

Income tax computation – 2014/15

	Total £	Other income £	Savings income £
Salary	12,000		
Car benefit (W1)	3,402		
Living accommodation (W2)	2,194		
	———		
Employment income	17,596	17,596	
Property business income (W3)	7,690	7,690	
NS&I Savings Certificate interest	Exempt		
Building society interest (£1,800 × 100/80)	2,250		2,250
	———	———	———
Total income	27,536	25,286	2,250
Less: PAA (W4)	(10,232)	(10,232)	
	———	———	———
Taxable income	17,304	15,054	2,250
	———	———	———

Income tax

£		£
15,054 × 20% (Other income)		3,011
2,250 × 20% (Savings income)		450
17,304		

	£
Income tax liability	3,461
Less: Tax suffered at source	
PAYE	(2,400)
Building society interest (£2,250 × 20%)	(450)
Income tax payable	611

Tutorial note

NS&I Savings Certificate income is exempt from income tax.

Workings

(W1) Car benefit

CO_2 emissions = 172 g/km (rounded down to 170), available for 10 months

	%
Petrol	12
Plus: $(170 - 95) \times \frac{1}{5}$	15
Appropriate percentage	27

	£
List price of car	17,118
Less: Capital contribution	(2,000)
	15,118
Car benefit (£15,118 × 27% × 10/12)	3,402

Tutorial note

The maintenance costs are ignored as the car benefit covers all of the running expenses of the car. The car parking cost is an exempt benefit

(W2) Living accommodation

	£
Annual value	1,632
Additional benefit for expensive accommodation	
(£120,000 (Note) – £75,000) × 3.25%	1,462
	———
	3,094
Less: Contributions to employer (£75 × 12 months)	(900)
	———
	2,194
	———

Tutorial note

The property was bought in 2006, which is more than 6 years before it was made available to Sally. Therefore in the calculation of the additional benefit, the cost must be replaced with the market value of the accommodation when the property was first made available.

(W3) Property business income

	£
Premium	10,680
Less: £10,680 × 2% × (15 – 1)	(2,990)
	———
Property business income	7,690
	———

Tutorial note

An alternative calculation of the assessment of the premium received on the granting of a short lease is as follows:

$P \times (51 - D) / 50$

$= £10,680 \times (51 - 15) / 50 = £7,690$

(W4) Personal age allowance

	£		£
PAA (born between 6.4.1938 and 5.4.1948)			10,500
Less: Abatement			
Total income	27,536		
Income limit	(27,000)		
	———		
Excess	536	× 50%	(268)
	———		———
Reduced PAA			10,232
			———

2 VIGOROUS PLC (ADAPTED)

Key answer tips

This question required the calculation of three benefit packages for three P11D (i.e. higher paid) employees. All of the key benefits that you need to be able to deal with in the F6 examination appear in this question!

Easy marks were available in part (b) for explaining how benefits are assessed.

However, careful calculation is required for the benefits as there are many places where calculations can go wrong. Remember to time apportion the calculation where the benefit is not available all year, and don't forget to deduct any employee contributions paid.

(a) **Assessable benefits – 2014/15**

Andrea Lean

	£
Car benefit (W1)	4,990
Fuel benefit (W1)	7,595
Living accommodation	
– Annual value	7,000
– Additional benefit (W2)	2,242
– Furniture (£6,000 at 20%)	1,200

Tutorial note

1   *The living accommodation cost in excess of £75,000 so there will be an additional benefit.*

    Since the property was purchased within six years of first being provided, the benefit is based on the cost of the property plus improvements prior to 6 April 2014 (see W2).

2   *The annual running costs are personally borne by Andrea and therefore are not included as a benefit. Had her employer paid the costs, a £4,000 benefit would arise which she would have reduced to £Nil if she reimbursed the company directly.*

Workings

(W1) Car and fuel benefits

CO_2 emissions = 250 g/km, available all year

	%	
Petrol	12	
Plus: $(250 - 95) \times \frac{1}{5}$	31	
	——	
Appropriate percentage	43	Restricted to 35%
	——	

	£
Car benefit (£19,400 × 35%)	6,790
Less: Contributions (£150 × 12)	(1,800)
	4,990
Fuel benefit (£21,700 × 35%)	7,595

(W2) Additional benefit for expensive accommodation

	£
Cost of property (January 2010)	130,000
Improvements before 6 April 2014	14,000
	144,000
Less: Limit	(75,000)
	69,000
Additional benefit	× 3.25% £2,242

Tutorial note

Improvements in May 2014 are not taken into account in calculating the benefit for 2014/15, as only improvements up to the start of the tax year are included.

However, they will be taken into account next year in calculating the benefit for 2015/16.

Ben Slim

	£
Beneficial loan (W1)	2,681
Relocation costs (£9,300 − £8,000) (Note 1)	1,300
Childcare vouchers ((£60 − £28) × 36) (Note 2)	1,152

Tutorial note

1   *Only £8,000 of relocation costs is exempt.*

2   *For a higher rate taxpayer the payment of up to £28 per week for approved childcare is an exempt benefit.*

Workings

(W1) Beneficial loan

	£
Average method	
Loan at start of year	120,000
Loan at end of year	100,000
	220,000
Average loan (£220,000 ÷ 2)	110,000

	£
Assessable benefit (£110,000 × 3.25% × 9/12)	£2,681

	£
Precise method	
(£120,000 × 3.25% × 5/12)	1,625
(£100,000 × 3.25% × 4/12)	1,083
	£2,708

Ben will not elect for the precise method and in view of the small difference it is unlikely that HMRC will make the election so the benefit will therefore be £2,681.

Chai Trim

	£
Van benefit (£3,090 × 10/12) (Note 1)	2,575
Television (W)	330
Health club membership (Note 2)	150

Tutorial note

1   *The van was only available for ten months of 2014/15 so the fixed annual £3,090 benefit is time apportioned.*

2   *In-house benefits are valued at the marginal cost to the employer of providing the benefit. The taxable benefit in relation to the health club membership is therefore the direct costs of £150.*

Working: Benefit for the sale of the television

Greater of

		£	£
(i)	MV at date of transfer	250	
	Less: Amount paid	(150)	
			100
(ii)	Original cost	800	
	Less: Annual value for 2012/13 and 2013/14		
	(20% × £800 × 2 years)	(320)	
		480	
	Less: Amount paid	(150)	
			330

Therefore the taxable benefit is £330.

(b)   **Income tax liability in respect of assessable benefits**

- The income tax on recurring benefits, such as company motor cars, will normally be collected through the PAYE system by a reduction in the employee's tax coding.

- Tax not collected on this basis will be due under the self-assessment system.

- However, tax of less than £3,000 can be collected by an adjustment to an employee's tax coding for a subsequent tax year, whilst tax on minor benefits may be paid under an employer's PAYE settlement agreement.

3   ALI PATEL (ADAPTED) *Walk in the footsteps of a top tutor*

Key answer tips

A common style question requiring the comparison of two remuneration packages and the impact on the income tax computation and national insurance liabilities.

Part (b) requires a decision to be made based on the net cash flow position after taking account of all costs including income tax and national insurance.

Tutor's top tips

Part (a) of this question involves some fairly straightforward income tax computations.

Don't forget that there is no car benefit if Ali uses his own car for business purposes!

You also need to calculate Class 1 NICs. Remember that for the employee, only cash earnings are subject to national insurance.

(a)   **Income tax and Class 1 NICs**

(i)   **First remuneration package**

Ali's income tax liability – 2014/15

	£
Salary (£29,000 + (£500 × 12))	35,000
Mileage allowance (W)	496
	———
Employment income	35,496
Less: Personal allowance	(10,000)
	———
Taxable income	25,496
	———
Income tax liability (£25,496 × 20%)	5,099
	———
Class 1 primary NIC – 2014/15	
(£35,000 – £7,956) × 12%	3,245
	———

Working: Mileage allowance

The relocation is not expected to last for more than 24 months, so the branch office will be treated as a temporary workplace.

Mileage for the year = (1,600 × 12) = 19,200 miles

Ali will therefore be taxed on the mileage allowance paid by Box plc as follows:

	£	£
Mileage allowance received (19,200 at 38p)		7,296
Authorised mileage allowance:		
10,000 miles at 45p	4,500	
9,200 miles at 25p	2,300	
	———	(6,800)
		———
Taxable benefit		496
		———

Tutorial note

For NIC purposes only the excess mileage allowance above 45p per mile is subject to NIC. As Ali will be paid 38p per mile, none of the mileage allowance is charged to NIC.

(ii) **Second remuneration package**

Ali's income tax liability – 2014/15

	£
Salary	29,000
Living accommodation (W)	9,600
Property business profit	6,000
	———
Total income	44,600
Less: Personal allowance	(10,000)
	———
Taxable income	34,600
	———

Income tax

£		
31,865 × 20%		6,373
2,735 × 40%		1,094
———		
34,600		
———		———
Income tax liability		7,467
		———

Class 1 primary NIC – 2014/15

(£29,000 – £7,956) × 12%	2,525
	———

Working: Living accommodation

The benefit of living accommodation will be the greater of:

(i)	Annual value	£4,600
(ii)	Rent paid by the employer (£800 × 12)	£9,600

(b) **Most beneficial remuneration package**

Tutor's top tips

When calculating the net disposable income think just in terms of cash and identify all cash coming in and all cash payments going out. Cash payments obviously include the tax liabilities calculated in part (a), but also include other expenses such as commuting costs.

Even if you made some mistakes in part (a), as long as you include your tax figures here in this part you will be awarded full marks.

The question specifically asks you to advise Ali as to which remuneration package is most beneficial, so make sure that you do this. A statement of which package should be accepted is therefore needed.

You will be given full marks here if your advice is consistent with your analysis, even if it is the wrong advice!

	Package (1) £	Package (2) £
Salary	35,000	29,000
Property business income	Nil	6,000
Mileage allowance received	7,296	Nil
Commuting costs	(1,800)	Nil
Class 1 NIC	(3,245)	(2,525)
Income tax	(5,099)	(7,467)
	———	———
Net disposable income	32,152	25,008
	———	———

Ali should choose the first remuneration package as he will be £7,144 (£32,152 − £25,008) better off.

4   FLICK PICK (ADAPTED) *Walk in the footsteps of a top tutor*

Key answer tips

Part (a) required the computation of taxable income for an individual with several sources of income.

Straight forward marks were available for dealing with the employment income aspects and rental income. The profits for the partnership were a little trickier and a strict order of processing the calculations needed.

Part (b) was more involved in that it required an understanding of the timing of payments of tax liabilities and planning opportunities in choosing the accounting date of a business.

Tutor's top tips

Read the requirements carefully. Part (a) requires the taxable income only, therefore do not waste time calculating the income tax liability or income tax payable as they will earn no marks in the exam.

When calculating the tax adjusted trading profits for the partnership, remember that the period of account is 4 months and therefore you must time apportion the capital allowances and, when allocating the profits between the partners, the salary received by the partner Art.

In calculating the trading income assessment for the first tax year of trading, apply the opening year basis of assessment rules and tax only 3 months of the 4 month accounting period (i.e. from the date of commencement to the following 5 April).

(a)   **Taxable income – 2014/15**

		£
Salary		23,700
Living accommodation	– Annual value	4,600
	– Additional benefit (W1)	2,242
	– Furniture (£9,400 × 20%)	1,880
		———
Employment income		32,422
Trading profit (W2)		8,238
Property business profit (W4)		5,940
		———
Total income		46,600
Less: PA		(10,000)
		———
Taxable income		36,600
		———

Workings

(W1) Living accommodation additional benefit

The benefit is based on the market value when first provided.

	£
Market value	144,000
Less: Limit	(75,000)
Excess	69,000

The additional benefit is therefore £2,242 (£69,000 at 3.25%).

Tutorial note

As the property was purchased by the company more than six years before it was first provided to Flick Pick, the benefit is based on the market value of the property when first provided rather than the original purchase price.

(W2) Trading profit

Flick's share of the partnership's trading profit – period ended 30 April 2015:

	£
Trading profit	29,700
Less: Capital allowances (W3)	(240)
Adjusted profit after capital allowances	29,460
Salary paid to Art (£6,000 × 4/12)	(2,000)
Balance to be divided in PSR	27,460
Profit share (£27,460 × 40%)	10,984

Flick's trading income assessment for 2014/15:

(£10,984 × 3/4) = £8,238

Tutorial note

Both the capital allowances and salary paid to Art must be time apportioned.

Flick's trading income assessment for her opening year assessment in 2014/15 is the actual profits in the period 1 January 2015 to 5 April 2015.

(W3) Capital allowances

	Special rate pool £		Allowances £
Addition	15,000		
Less: WDA (8% × 4/12)	(400)	× 60%	240
TWDV c/f	14,600		

Tutorial note

The partnership's motor car has CO_2 emissions over 130 grams per kilometre and therefore qualifies for writing down allowances at the rate of 8%.

However, the WDA needs to be time apportioned for a four month accounting period, and only the business percentage of the allowances can be claimed.

(W4) Property business profit

	£	£
Rent receivable (£660 × 12)		7,920
Council tax	1,320	
Wear and tear allowance (W5)	660	
Furniture (Note)	0	
		(1,980)
Property business profit		5,940

Tutorial note

No deduction is available for replacement furniture as the expenditure is capital in nature and the wear and tear allowance gives relief for the deterioration of the assets whilst in use.

(W5) Wear and tear allowance

(Rents received less council tax) × 10%

= (£7,920 − £1,320) = £6,600 × 10% = £660

(b) Advantages and disadvantages of a 30 April accounting date

Tutor's top tips

Remember that there are always advantages in delaying tax liabilities in terms of cash flows and planning.

Advantages

- The interval between earning profits and paying the related tax liability will be 11 months longer. This can be particularly beneficial where profits are rising.

- It will be possible to calculate taxable profits well in advance of the end of the tax year, making it much easier to implement tax planning such as making pension contributions and Gift Aid donations.

Disadvantages

- The application of the basis period rules is more complicated.

- The amount of profit assessed in the tax year of cessation could potentially be quite high as the basis period will be up to 23 months in length.

- Although overlap profits are deductible, these might be insignificant if the opening years' profits are low.

5   JOE JONES (ADAPTED) *Walk in the footsteps of a top tutor*

Key answer tips

This question covered various aspects of employment income in quite a lot of detail. It is important to be familiar with both how to calculate taxable benefits and which benefits are exempt.

There were many aspects of part (a) which should not have caused concern and on which easy marks could be obtained. However, some aspects were more peripheral to the syllabus and some students may not have been confident in the treatment of some of the benefits.

Part (b) covered administration in relation to certain PAYE forms in some detail, which was quite demanding and this area is difficult to answer if the rules have not been learnt. There were still some easy marks for common sense comments here though, and all students should be familiar with the contents of a P11D form. This part of the question has been added to following the introduction of PAYE real time reporting, and now tests the new rules.

(a)   **Taxable income – 2014/15**

Tutor's top tips

Remember to read the requirement carefully. You have not been asked to calculate the income tax payable, only the taxable income – do not go further than you have been asked to do as there are no additional marks available.

Although you may find part (a) easier than part (b), don't overrun on time and lose the ability to score some easy marks on part (b).

> *There are some aspects of part (a) about which you may not be confident, but it is important to make a quick decision and move on. You can't afford to waste time debating whether a benefit is taxable and miss out on marks elsewhere. You should just make an assumption, state it and then forget about it! Remember if you make a mistake you will still get follow through marks for the remainder of your answer.*
>
> *You also need to be careful when thinking about the personal allowance as Joe has income in excess of £100,000. You need to consider the adjusted net income and compare it with the income limit for the reduction of the personal allowance.*

	£
Employment income – Firstly plc	
Salary (£12,400 × 9)	111,600
Bonus (Note 1)	Nil
Less: Pension contributions (£111,600 × 6%) (Note 2)	(6,696)
	————
	104,904
Gym membership (Note 3)	1,050
	————
	105,954
Employment income – Secondly plc	
Salary (£16,200 × 3)	48,600
Company gym (Note 4)	Nil
Mobile telephone (Note 5)	Nil
	————
	154,554
Less: PA (W1)	Nil
	————
Taxable income	154,554
	————

Workings

(W1) Personal allowance (Note 6)

As Joe's income exceeds £100,000, it is necessary to calculate adjusted net income (ANI) and compare this with the income limit for the reduction of the personal allowance.

	£
Net income	154,554
Less: Personal pension contributions	(3,000)
	————
ANI	151,554
Less: Income limit	(100,000)
	————
Excess	51,554
	————

As the ANI exceeds the income limit by more than twice the personal allowance, it will be reduced to £Nil.

Tutorial notes

1   *Salaries and bonuses are taxable on the earlier of the date of receipt and the date the employee becomes entitled to the payment. The £12,000 bonus was therefore taxable in 2013/14 as Joe became entitled to it on 22 March 2014.*

2   *Occupational pension contributions are deducted from the salary in calculating taxable employment income. Personal pension contributions extend the basic and higher rate bands when calculating the tax liability (see below) and are deducted in the calculation of ANI when calculating the reduction of the personal allowance as in working 1 above.*

3   *All benefits for which there is no specific rule to calculate the benefit will be taxable based on the cost to the employer. Therefore the taxable benefit in respect of the gym membership is simply £1,050.*

4   *The use of a company gym is exempt provided that it is available for use by all employees and it is not available to the general public.*

5   *The provision of one mobile telephone is exempt even if the employer pays for private calls.*

6   *The answer above includes a working (working 1) to establish that Joe's personal allowance is reduced to nil. In a situation such as this, where it is obvious that this will be the case given the level of ANI, it is acceptable to not show a working, but instead to state 'Personal allowance will be reduced to nil on the basis that ANI exceeds £100,000 by more than twice the personal allowance of £10,000.' The working is shown here for completeness and to demonstrate the effect of personal pension contributions on ANI.*

7   *Although you were not asked to calculate the income tax liability, and you therefore should not do so in the exam, you may find it good practice to attempt the calculation as Joe is an additional rate taxpayer and has made personal pension contributions. You need to remember that the basic rate and higher rate bands will be extended by the gross personal pension contributions, therefore the basic rate band will be £34,865 (£31,865 + £3,000) and the upper limit of the higher rate band will be £153,000 (£150,000 + £3,000).*

The calculation should therefore be as follows:

	£
£34,865 × 20%	*6,973*
£118,135 × 40%	*47,254*
£1,554 × 45%	*699*
Income tax liability	*54,926*

(b)   (i)   **PAYE forms**

Tutor's top tips

Part (b)(i) tests some of the rules regarding the PAYE system in quite a lot of detail. If you don't know these rules many parts of this question will be hard to answer, and there is no point wasting time dwelling on something you simply don't know!

It is likely that you at least know the circumstances in which someone is given a P45 however, and you should certainly know what form P11D is used to report. You can also probably make a sensible guess at who is supposed to provide these forms, and you may be able to state something about what should be included on them. If you don't know the dates the forms should be provided then you have little hope at guessing them.

Form P45

- Form P45 should be completed by Firstly plc when Joe leaves the company's employment. It will show his taxable earnings, income tax deducted in the tax year, and his tax code at the date of leaving.

- Firstly plc should have provided this form to Joe immediately after he left employment with the company.

Form P60

- Form P60 is a year-end summary which should be prepared by Secondly plc. It will show Secondly plc's name and address, Joe's taxable earnings for the tax year, income tax and NICs deducted, and his final PAYE code.

- Secondly plc should have provided this form to Joe by 31 May 2015.

Form P11D

- A form P11D should have been prepared by Firstly plc including details of the cash equivalents of the taxable benefits provided to Joe. The benefits provided by Secondly plc were both exempt benefits and therefore the company was not required to complete a P11D for Joe.

- Firstly plc should have provided a form to Joe by 6 July 2015.

(ii)   **Real time reporting**

Tutor's top tips

Part (b)(ii) tests the administration of PAYE for an employer. Although the term is not mentioned in the question, you should recognise that the system being tested is real time reporting. A basic awareness of the system should achieve the mark for the monthly reporting, however, the second mark cannot be achieved unless you have learnt the date for the final submission of the year.

- Secondly plc must submit income tax and NIC information to HMRC electronically on or before the date that Joe is paid each month.

- Income tax and NIC deducted under PAYE must be paid to HMRC electronically by the 22nd of the month following the end of the tax month.

Examiner's report

Part (a) of this question was reasonably well answered, but part (b) caused problems for virtually all candidates.

In part (a) there were no areas that consistently caused difficulty, although a surprising number of candidates did not appreciate that a bonus would have been assessed in the previous tax year as the taxpayer was entitled to it in that year.

Candidates should try not to repeat their answers. For example, exempt benefits were often shown as such in the computation of taxable income, but were then shown again in subsequent notes. There is no need to do this.

It was surprising in part (b) that very few candidates knew much about the PAYE forms. This just seems to be an area of the syllabus that was not revised. A bit of common sense together with the knowledge that form P45 is given when employment ceases, form P60 is given at the end of the tax year, and form P11D is in respect of the benefits provided to a taxpayer, would have meant that most of the marks were easily obtainable.

Note: The examiner's report has been edited to remove comments on elements of the question that have been deleted due to changes to the exam format.

ACCA marking scheme			Marks
(a)		Salary – Firstly plc	0.5
		Bonus	0.5
		Occupational pension scheme contributions	1.0
		Gym membership	1.0
		Salary – Secondly plc	0.5
		Company gym	0.5
		Mobile telephone	1.0
		Personal pension contributions – deducted from ANI	0.5
		Personal allowance	1.5
			7.0
(b)	(i)	**Form P45**	
		By Firstly plc when employment ceases	0.5
		Details	1.0
		Date provided	0.5
		Form P60	
		By Secondly plc at end of tax year	0.5
		Details	1.0
		Date provided	0.5
		Form P11D	
		Firstly plc only	0.5
		Details	1.0
		Date provided	0.5
			6.0
	(ii)	Monthly real time reporting	1.0
		Deadline for payment of PAYE	1.0
			2.0
Total			**15.0**

6   SAMMI SMITH (ADAPTED) *Walk in the footsteps of a top tutor*

Key answer tips

This was a very unusual style of question for the F6 exam, which would probably challenge many students. However, we can expect more questions like this in the future.

The question required the comparison of two remuneration options, and consideration of the tax consequences from both the employee and the employer's perspective.

It therefore required four separate calculations (each option from each party's perspective), covering income tax, corporation tax and NICs.

The requirements here were very clear and easy marks could be gained from some very basic tax calculations, provided students were not scared off by the style of the question.

The final part of the question, which required the calculation of 'after tax net costs' of both options, may have thrown some students. It is helpful to sit back and think through all the tax and other cash consequences of both options before attempting to answer this part.

Tutor's top tips

The key when you are challenged by a style of question you have not seen before is not to panic!

In the more challenging questions the F6 examiner will often help you through the order in which he sets out the requirements and by providing guidance within the requirements themselves. That is the case here, and if you consider the requirements carefully and work through them systematically you will find that the tax calculations themselves are actually very straightforward and it is possible to score very highly on parts (a) and (b).

A comparison of the choices of the provision of a car or remuneration to fund a car is a classic exam scenario. Bear in mind that you already know how to calculate the taxable benefit on a car, you know how to tax employee remuneration and you know the tax consequences for a company of providing a car to an employee or of paying salary to an employee. This question simply combines those calculations.

Ensure that you use clear headings, showing which calculation you are doing, so that the marker can more easily give you credit.

Part (c) may cause more difficulty as it is unfamiliar, but again not technically demanding. Ensure you pick up your figures from parts (a) and (b) as well as any other costs mentioned in the question.

(a) **Sammi Smith – Company car**

CO_2 emissions = 305 g/km, available all year

	%
Petrol	12
Plus: (305 − 95) × 1/5	42
Appropriate percentage	54
Percentage restricted to	35

	£
List price of car	81,858
Car benefit (£81,858 × 35%)	28,650
Income tax at marginal rate (£28,650 × 40%)	11,460

There are no NIC implications for an employee in receipt of a non-cash benefit, such as a company car.

Sammi Smith – Additional remuneration

	£
Income tax at marginal rate (£26,000 × 40%)	10,400
NICs at marginal rate (£26,000 × 2%)	520
Total tax cost	10,920

Tutorial notes

1   *The maximum amount for the car benefit percentage (35%) is not listed in the tax tables and must be learnt.*

2   *The list price of the car is £81,858 and this is used to calculate the car benefit.*

3   *There is no fuel benefit to calculate here as Sammi has not been provided with any private fuel.*

4   *It is not necessary to do a full income tax computation in order to calculate the income tax implications of either option. Instead you need to establish Sammi's marginal rate of tax, which is the rate at which additional income will be taxed. As Sammi already receives director's remuneration in excess of £45,000, she is already a higher rate taxpayer, and neither option will take her near the threshold for the reduction in the PA or for tax at the additional rate. Therefore her marginal rate of income tax is 40%.*

5   *Benefits are not subject to NICs for the employee unless they are readily convertible into cash (in which case they form part of earnings and are subject to Class 1 NICs).*

6   *Sammi's marginal rate for NICs can be established in the same way as for income tax. As Sammi's remuneration is in excess of £45,000 she has already exceeded the upper earnings limit and any further income will be taxable at 2%.*

(b)   **Smark Ltd – Company car**

Tutor's top tips

This part is slightly more challenging than the previous part as the NICs payable by the company have an impact on the corporation tax payable. It is therefore important that you calculate the NICs before the corporation tax in both cases.

You should also be careful when considering whether all of the lease costs are an allowable deduction for corporation tax purposes.

	£
Annual lease cost	26,540
Disallowance – high emission car (£26,540 × 15%)	(3,981)
	22,559
Class 1A NICs payable (£28,650 × 13.8%)	3,954
Total tax allowable costs	26,513
Corporation tax reduction (£26,513 × 21%)	5,568

Smark Ltd – Additional remuneration

	£
Additional remuneration	26,000
Class 1 secondary NICs (£26,000 × 13.8%)	3,588
Total costs	29,588
Corporation tax reduction (£29,588 × 21%)	6,213

Tutorial notes

1   *Cars with CO_2 emissions in excess of 130 g/km are considered 'high emission' cars and 15% of the lease cost will be disallowed.*

2   *Class 1A NICs are payable on the taxable benefit. You therefore need to use the figure you have calculated in part (a).*

3   *Once you have calculated the relevant allowable costs for tax purposes (including the Class 1A NICs) you can calculate the reduction in the corporation tax liability at the company's marginal rate, which is 21% as you are told in the question that the company pays tax at the main rate of 21%.*

(c)   **Most beneficial choice for Sammi Smith**

Tutor's top tips

This is the part of the question you may find most difficult, as rather than involving a tax calculation, you need to pull together the tax figures you have already calculated as well as the costs per the question to recommend which option Sammi and Smark Ltd will prefer.

You need to remember to include all the relevant costs in your calculations – the cost of providing the car or the remuneration, the IT costs, the NIC costs (for both Sammi and Smark Ltd) and the CT saving.

If you have made an error in your calculations earlier in the question, you will still get follow through marks provided you use your own figures correctly in this part.

- If Sammi is provided with a company car the only cost will be the additional income tax of £11,460.

- If Sammi chooses the director's remuneration the net after tax cost will be:

	£
Cost of leasing car	26,540
Additional tax cost	10,920
Additional remuneration	(26,000)
Net after tax cost	11,460

- The net costs are exactly the same; it therefore shouldn't matter to Sammi which option is chosen.

Most beneficial choice for Smark Ltd

- If Smark Ltd provide Sammi with a company car, the net after tax cost will be:

	£
Cost of leasing car	26,540
Additional NIC cost	3,954
Corporation tax saving	(5,568)
Net after tax cost	24,926

- If Smark Ltd provide Sammi with additional director's remuneration, the net after tax cost will be:

	£
Remuneration cost	26,000
Additional NIC cost	3,588
Corporation tax saving	(6,213)
Net after tax cost	23,375

- Smark Ltd would therefore prefer to provide Sammi with additional remuneration, as this option costs less overall.

Examiner's report

This question was generally answered quite badly, with the main problem being that candidates simply did not spend enough time thinking and planning their answers, but just plunged straight in performing every calculation that they could think of.

In part (a) the answer was in fact very straightforward, with a fairly simple car benefit calculation and then income tax and NIC calculations at the director's marginal rates of 40% and 2% respectively.

Far too many candidates calculated a fuel benefit despite being told that fuel was not provided for private journeys.

In part (b) many candidates stated that capital allowances would be available despite the motor car being leased.

Candidates often stated that the company's corporation tax liability would be increased rather than reduced as a result of the additional expenditure, and very few candidates appreciated that NIC was a deductible expense.

Part (c) was more difficult, although credit was given for any sensible approach such as comparing the tax liabilities under each alternative.

	ACCA marking scheme	Marks
(a)	Company car	
	Car benefit	2.0
	Income tax	1.0
	NIC implications	0.5
	Additional director's remuneration	
	Income tax	0.5
	Class 1 NIC	1.0
		5.0
(b)	Company car	
	Class 1A NIC	1.0
	Allowable leasing costs	1.0
	Corporation tax saving	1.0
	Additional director's remuneration	
	Class 1 NIC	1.0
	Corporation tax saving	1.0
		5.0
(c)	Sammi	
	Director's remuneration – net cost	1.0
	Conclusion	1.0
	Smark Ltd	
	Director's remuneration – net cost	1.0
	Company car – net costs	1.0
	Conclusion	1.0
		5.0
Total		**15.0**

7 PHILIP & CHARLES (ADAPTED) *Walk in the footsteps of a top tutor*

Key answer tips

This question involved preparing two separate income tax computations which covered different income tax topics, tested knowledge of NIC and some basic tax planning.

The requirements and mark allocation are very clear and all the topics are covered at a basic level and should therefore have been manageable.

The first individual is an elderly taxpayer eligible for the personal age allowance (PAA), but this needs abatement due to the level of his net income.

The second individual is a high earner requiring abatement to his standard personal allowance due to the level of his net income.

Tutor's top tips

Always ensure that you read the question carefully.

In part (a) the requirement is to calculate income tax liability. Therefore do not waste time calculating income tax payable as this will not gain you any additional marks.

Make the marker your friend, if you keep your calculations clear and easy to read you will score much higher marks. Always ensure your workings are clearly labelled.

(a) (i) **Philip Wind**

Income tax computation – 2014/15

	Total income £	Other income £	Savings income £
Pensions	13,500	13,500	
Building society interest (£11,680 × 100/80)	14,600		14,600
Total income/Net income	28,100	13,500	14,600
Less: PAA (W)	(10,110)	(10,110)	
Taxable income	17,990	3,390	14,600

Income tax		£
£		
3,390 × 20%		678
14,600 × 20%		2,920
17,990		
Income tax liability		3,598

Working: Personal age allowance

	£		£
PAA (born before 6.4.1938)			10,660
Less: Abatement			
Net income	28,100		
Less: Income limit	(27,000)		
Excess	1,100	× 50%	(550)
			10,110

Tutorial note

Taxable other income (£3,390) exceeds £2,880, so the starting rate of 10% does not apply to the savings income.

Tutor's top tips

Whenever you are given the date of birth of a taxpayer you need to consider whether this will impact on certain calculations. The two areas where date of birth will have an impact are the personal age allowance and NIC. Philip was born before 6 April 1938 so is entitled to the higher age allowance (subject to abatement for his income) and he is over the state pension age so pays no NIC.

(ii) **Charles Wind**

Income tax computation – 2014/15

	£
Trading profit/total income/net income	109,400
Less: Adjusted PA (W1)	(5,700)
Taxable income	103,700

Income tax

£		£
32,665 × 20% (W2)		6,533
71,035 × 40%		28,414
103,700		
Income tax liability		34,947

Workings

(W1) Adjusted personal allowance

	£	£
Personal allowance		10,000
Total income = net income	109,400	
Less: Gross Gift Aid	(800)	
	———	
ANI	108,600	
Less: Limit	(100,000)	
	———	
	8,600	× 50%	(4,300)
	———	———
Adjusted PA		5,700
		———

Tutorial note

1 *Charitable donations under Gift Aid are grossed up before being used in the adjusted personal allowance computation and to extend the basic rate band. The gross figure is given in the question; therefore there is no need to gross up the figure given.*

2 *As the adjusted net income exceeds £100,000 the allowance is reduced by £1 for every £2 it exceeds the limit. Net income for these purposes is adjusted (i.e. reduced) for both gross Gift Aid and gross Personal Pension Contributions (PPCs) made in the year.*

(W2) Extension of basic rate band

	£
Basic rate band threshold	31,865
Plus: Gross Gift Aid	800
	———
Extended basic rate band	32,665
	———

Tutor's top tips

Always check carefully whether you have been given income or payments gross or net.

(b) **National Insurance Contributions – 2014/15**

Philip Wind

- No National Insurance contributions (NIC) are payable by Philip.

- This is because NICs are not payable on pension income or building society income, and he is over the state pension age so would not pay NIC in any case.

Charles Wind

- As Charles is self-employed; Class 2 and Class 4 NICs are payable.

- Class 2 NICs payable:
  (£2.75 × 52 weeks)   £143
  _____

- Class 4 NICs payable:

                                                                £
  (£41,865 – £7,956) = £33,909 × 9%   3,052
  (£109,400 – £41,865) = £67,535 × 2%   1,351
                                                            _____
                                                              4,403
                                                            _____

(c)   **Reduction in income tax liabilities**

Key answer tips

This part of the question will require some thought and planning before answering.

It is important to consider **all** the implications of personal pension contributions – remember that they are taken into account in the ANI calculation in relation to the reduction of the basic personal allowance as well as extending the basic rate band.

If Charles had contributed £8,600 into a personal pension scheme

- Charles' adjusted net income will now be reduced to £100,000 (£108,600 – £8,600). He will therefore be entitled to the full personal allowance, and it will not be restricted by £4,300 as shown above.

- The personal pension scheme contribution will also further extend the basic rate tax band by £8,600.

- Charles' income tax liability for 2014/15 would therefore have been reduced as follows:

                                                                £
  Extra personal allowance (as no restriction)
  (£4,300 at 40%)   1,720
  Extension of the basic rate band (Note)
  (£8,600 at (40% – 20%))   1,720
                                                            _____
                                                              3,440
                                                            _____

Tutorial note

The extension of the basic rate band ensures that income formerly taxable at the higher rate of 40% is now taxable at the basic rate of 20%, and therefore saves income tax at 20%.

Examiner's report

Part (a) was very well answered, particularly for the second taxpayer.

There were few problems in part (b) as regards the calculation of the national insurance contributions.

Part (c) was the most difficult aspect on the paper, and it was pleasing to see several good attempts.

For the second taxpayer most candidates appreciated that the basic rate tax band would be extended by the amount of the pension contribution, and several candidates realised that the amount of contribution was the exact amount required so that the personal allowance was not restricted.

Note: *The examiner's report has been edited to remove comments on elements of the question that have been deleted due to changes to the exam format.*

ACCA marking scheme				Marks
(a)	(i)	**Philip Wind**		
		Pensions		0.5
		Building society interest		0.5
		Personal allowance		2.0
		Income tax		1.0
				4.0
	(ii)	**Charles Wind**		
		Trading profit		0.5
		Personal allowance		2.0
		Extension of basic rate band		0.5
		Income tax		1.0
				4.0
(b)		**Philip Wind**		
		No NIC		1.0
		Charles Wind		
		Class 2 NIC		1.0
		Class 4 NIC		2.0
				4.0
(c)		**Charles Wind**		
		Personal allowance		1.0
		Basic rate band		1.0
		Income tax liability		1.0
				3.0
Total				**15.0**

8   LETICIA STONE *Walk in the footsteps of a top tutor*

Key answer tips

This question required the calculation of property losses – one for a furnished holiday letting property and one for the other let properties.

The calculations are not difficult provided you remember the following:

1   Property income is assessed on an accruals basis as if the individual had a trade with a 5 April year end.

2   Separate calculations are required for furnished holiday lettings, but all other property income and expenses are pooled into one calculation

3   One of the advantages of furnished holiday lettings is that they are entitled to capital allowances rather than the wear and tear allowance.

Two easy marks were available in part (b) for explaining what an individual can do with property losses.

(a)   **Furnished holiday letting loss – 2014/15**

	£	£
Rent receivable (£425 × 22)		9,350
Loan interest	12,700	
Repairs (£12,200 – £10,900)	1,300	
Mileage allowance (W)	455	
Other expenses	3,770	
Capital allowances (£4,600 × 100%)	4,600	
	———	(22,825)
Furnished holiday letting loss		(13,475)

Working: Mileage allowance

The mileage that Leticia drove in respect of the property purchase is capital in nature, and therefore does not qualify.

Her mileage allowance is therefore:

(880 + 130) = 1,010 at 45p = £455

Tutor's top tips:

You are told in the question that property one qualifies as a trade under the furnished holiday letting rules. Hence you will not receive any marks for writing out the conditions for a property to be a furnished holiday let and trying to apply them to any of the properties.

Property business loss – 2014/15

	Notes	£	£
Premium received for sub-lease			45,000
Less: £45,000 × 2% × (5 – 1)			(3,600)
	1		41,400
Rent receivable	2		
– Property 2 (£2,160 × 4 × 11/12)	3		7,920
– Property 3 (£580 × 10)	4		5,800
– Security deposit	5		Nil
			55,120
Rent payable (£1,360 × 11)		14,960	
Impairment loss		580	
Loan interest		9,100	
Other expenses		36,240	
			(60,880)
			(5,760)
Furnished room (£3,170 – £4,840)	6		(1,670)
Property business loss			(7,430)

Tutorial note

1   *An alternative calculation of the assessment of the premium received on the granting of a short lease is as follows:*

   P × (51 – D) / 50

   = £45,000 × (51 – 5) / 50 = £41,400

2   *Rents are assessed on an accruals basis. Therefore the rents receivable between 6 April 2014 and 5 April 2015 are required.*

3   *Property 2 is rented out for 11 months of the tax year, but the rents are quoted in the question on a quarterly basis. Therefore the annual rents needs to be calculated and 11/12ths of the annual rents are assessed in 2014/15.*

4   *Property 3 is only rented out for 10 months of the tax year, but the information is given in monthly terms, so the calculation is straightforward.*

5   *The security deposit relating to Property 3 is received in the tax year, but it relates to the tenancy of the property in 2015/16 (commencing 15 April 2015). Therefore it will not be assessed in 2014/15.*

6   *Leticia would use the normal basis of assessment in respect of the furnished room since this allows a loss to be generated.*

(b)   **Relief for property losses**

- The furnished holiday letting loss will be carried forward and relieved against Leticia's future profits from furnished holiday lettings only.
- The property business loss will be carried forward and relieved against the first available future property business profits only.

Examiner's report

Part (a) of this question was very well answered, with no aspect causing significant problems.

However, several candidates claimed the wear and tear allowance for the furnished holiday letting rather than capital allowances.

Although candidates were not penalised if they combined the property losses into just one calculation, not separating out the furnished holiday letting loss invariably meant that marks were then lost in part (b) as marks were not awarded for vague details on loss relief if it was not clearly stated as to which reliefs were available for which type of loss.

ACCA marking scheme		Marks
(a)	**Furnished holiday letting loss**	
	Rent receivable	0.5
	Loan interest	1.0
	Repairs	1.0
	Mileage allowance	1.5
	Other expenses	0.5
	Capital allowances	1.0
	Business property loss	
	Lease premium received	1.0
	Rent receivable – Property 2	1.0
	– Property 3	1.0
	– Security deposit	0.5
	Rent payable	1.0
	Impairment loss	1.0
	Loan interest	0.5
	Other expenses	0.5
	Furnished room	1.0
		13.0
(b)	Furnished holiday letting loss	1.0
	Property business loss	1.0
		2.0
Total		**15.0**

9   KIM BAXTER (ADAPTED) *Walk in the footsteps of a top tutor*

(a)   **Income tax computation – 2014/15**

Tutor's top tips

A straightforward income tax computation, but watch the dates very carefully here!

Where a benefit has only been available for part of the tax year, it must be time apportioned.

However, if you forget to do this, you will only be penalised once and could still score full marks for the calculation of tax.

	Total	Other income	Savings income
	£	£	£
Salary	21,689		
Beneficial loan (£14,250 × 3.25% × 10/12)	386		
Less: Expense claim (W)	(5,125)		
Employment income	16,950	16,950	
Interest (£600 × 100/80)	750		750
Total income	17,700	16,950	750
Less: Relief for interest paid (Note)	(140)	(140)	
Net income	17,560	16,810	750
Less: PA	(10,000)	(10,000)	
Taxable income	7,560	6,810	750
Income tax:			
On Other income	6,810	@ 20%	1,362
On Savings income	750	@ 20%	150
	7,560		
Income tax liability			1,512

Tutorial note

The loan interest paid of £140 is eligible for relief since the loan was used by Kim to finance expenditure for a relevant purpose. The interest is quoted gross and is paid gross.

Working: Expense claim

Ordinary commuting (i.e. travel between home and the permanent workplace) does not qualify for relief. The travel to a temporary workplace qualifies as it is for a period lasting less than 24 months.

Business mileage is therefore 12,500 miles (11,200 + 1,300)

Expense claim is therefore:

	£
10,000 miles at 45p	4,500
2,500 miles at 25p	625
	———
	5,125
	———

(b)   Tax planning suggestions

Tutor's top tips

It should be clear from your answer to part (a) that Kim is a basic rate taxpayer and from the information in part (b) that Richard pays no tax at all.

Make sure you set out the rates of tax that each will be subject to, taking into account the availability of Richard's personal allowance, and have a go at calculating the tax saving that could be achieved here.

The highlighted *words are key phrases that markers are looking for.*

New individual savings accounts

• Kim can invest up to a maximum of £15,000 each tax year into a cash NISA.

• Interest received from NISAs is exempt from income tax, so Kim will save tax at the rate of 20%.

• She received £600 interest in 2014/15 which is net of basic rate tax. Kim will therefore save tax on gross interest of £750 (£600 × 100/80) if she invested in a NISA (i.e. £750 × 20%).

   This is assuming that the interest that will be received on the NISA will be the same rate of interest as her existing investment.

Transfer to Richard's sole name

• Kim pays income tax at the rate of 20%, whilst Richard's personal allowance and basic rate tax band are not utilised.

• Transferring the building society deposit account into Richard's name would therefore save tax of £150 (£750 × 20%).

Examiner's report

This question was very well answered by the majority of candidates.

Part (a) was well answered, with only the expense claim for the business mileage causing any difficulty. This was often treated as a benefit rather than as an expense.

Part (b) was answered reasonably well. Many candidates correctly calculated the amount of income tax saving.

Note: *The examiner's report has been edited to remove comments on elements of the question that have been deleted due to changes to the exam format.*

ACCA marking scheme		Marks
(a)	Income tax computation	
	Salary	0.5
	Beneficial loan	1.0
	Expense claim	1.5
	Building society interest	0.5
	Loan interest	1.0
	Personal allowance	0.5
	Income tax	1.0
		———
		6.0
		———
(b)	New individual savings accounts	
	Limit	1.0
	Tax saving	1.0
		———
		2.0
		———
	Transfer to Richard	
	Tax rates	1.0
	Tax saving	1.0
		———
		2.0
		———
Total		**10.0**
		———

INCOME TAX BASICS AND INCOME FROM SELF-EMPLOYMENT

10   CAROL COURIER (ADAPTED)

Key answer tips

A straight forward purely computational question dealing with the income tax and National Insurance consequences of being employed and self-employed.

Part (c) requires a comparison of the net disposable income arising from the two options.

(a) **Carol continues to be employed**

Carol's income tax liability – 2014/15

	£
Salary	37,500
Less: Pension contributions (£37,500 × 5%)	(1,875)
Employment income	35,625
Less: PA	(10,000)
Taxable income	25,625
Income tax liability (£25,625 × 20%)	5,125

Class 1 NICs – Primary contributions

	£
(£37,500 – £7,956) × 12%	3,545

(b) **Carol accepts self-employed contract**

Carol's income tax liability – 2014/15

	£
Income (£43,500 + £8,000)	51,500
Less: Expenses (£4,400 + £2,800)	(7,200)
Trading income	44,300
Less: PA	(10,000)
Taxable income	34,300
Income tax liability (£34,300 × 20%) (Working)	6,860

Class 4 NICs

	£
(£41,865 – £7,956) × 9%	3,052
(£44,300 – £41,865) × 2%	49
	3,101

Class 2 NICs

	£
(£2.75 for 52 weeks)	143

Working: Extension of the basic rate band

	£
Basic rate band	31,865
Plus: Gross pension contributions	3,000
Extended basic rate band	34,865

All of Carol's taxable income of £34,300 falls into this extended basic rate band and is therefore taxed at 20%.

(c)   **Benefit of accepting self-employed contract**

	Employed £	Self employed £
Salary	37,500	Nil
Trading income	Nil	44,300
Pension contributions paid (Note)	(1,875)	(2,400)
NIC – Class 1 and Class 4	(3,545)	(3,101)
NIC – Class 2	Nil	(143)
Income tax	(5,125)	(6,860)
Net disposable income	26,955	31,796

It is therefore beneficial for Carol to accept the offer to provide delivery services on a self-employed basis as her net income will increase by £4,841 (£31,796 – £26,955).

Tutorial note

Carol will pay personal pension contributions net of basic rate tax. If self-employed she will therefore pay £2,400 (£3,000 × 80%).

Key answer tips

When calculating the net disposable income think just in terms of cash and identify all cash coming in and all cash payments going out.

Cash payments obviously include the tax liabilities but also include other expenses such as pension contributions.

11   IDRIS WILLIAMS *Walk in the footsteps of a top tutor*

Key answer tips

This question has been written to test the new rules introduced in Finance Act 2013 on the cash basis as well as the choice of accounting date.

Students should be familiar with the factors that influence the choice of accounting date and the advantages and disadvantages of choosing an accounting date early or late in the tax year.

The new cash basis rules are examinable in F6 to a limited extent. This question tests all the rules which could be examined.

Tutor's top tips

There are four marks available for part (a), therefore four clear points should be made.

(a)   **Advantages of a 5 April accounting date**

- If Idris chooses to prepare his accounts to 5 April, the application of the basis period rules will be simplified.

- Idris will not have any overlap profits on the commencement of trade. If he prepares his accounts to 30 June, nine months of overlap profits will arise and these would not be relieved until the cessation of trading.

Advantages of a 30 June accounting date

- If Idris prepares his accounts to 30 June the interval between earning profits and paying the related tax liability will be 9 months longer than with an accounting date of 5 April.

- An accounting date of 30 June would make it easier to implement tax planning measures as there is a longer period over which to plan.

(b)   (i)   **Tax adjusted trading profit – accruals basis – year ended 5 April 2015**

Tutor's top tips

This question does not specifically request that you start with the net profit figure and adjust for any disallowable items, but this was the most obvious approach to take.

Always show your workings if the figure you are adjusting for is not clear from the question.

When using the normal accruals basis no adjustment should be made for any receivables or payables.

	£	£
Net profit	20,175	
Food, utilities, etc. (personal use)	4,500	
Depreciation	1,250	
Motor expenses (£9,340 × 7,000/20,000)	3,269	
Capital allowances (W)		4,553
	―――	―――
	29,194	4,553
	(4,553)	―――
	―――	
Tax adjusted trading profit	24,641	

Tutorial note

The usual presentation of an adjustment of profits is produced above. However, an alternative method of calculating the same taxable trading profit figure is to reproduce the accounts just deducting the expenses which are allowable, as opposed to adding back those that are not allowable to the net profit. This alternative presentation is given below as it provides a more direct comparison of the difference in the treatment when the cash basis is used.

	£	£
Revenue		49,910
Food, utilities and other household goods (£17,660 – £4,500)		(13,160)
		36,750
Depreciation	Nil	
Motor expenses (£9,340 × 13,000/20,000)	6,071	
Other expenses	1,485	
Capital allowances (W)	4,553	
		(12,109)
		24,641

Working: Capital allowances

	General pool £	Private use car £		Allowances £
Additions (no AIA)				
Car (96 – 130 g/km)		9,000		
Additions (with AIA)				
Furniture	3,500			
Less: AIA	(3,500)			3,500
	Nil			
WDA (18%) (Note)		(1,620)	× 65%	1,053
TWDV c/f	Nil	7,380		
Total allowances				4,553

Tutorial note

Capital allowances on new car purchases are calculated based on the CO_2 emissions.

As the car purchased in this question has CO_2 emissions of between 96 – 130 g/km, it is eligible for a WDA at 18%. The WDA then needs to be adjusted for the private use by Idris, as only the business use proportion of the allowance can be claimed.

The business mileage is 13,000 out of 20,000 miles (i.e. 65%).

(ii) **Cash basis**

Idris is entitled to use the cash basis as his revenue is below the VAT registration threshold of £81,000.

Tutor's top tips

When operating the cash basis adjustments need to be made for any receivables and payables.

The examiner has stated that where the cash basis is used you should assume that flat rate expenses are claimed for motor expenses and private use of business premises.

The motor expenses deduction should be calculated on the basis of the approved mileage allowances. The private use of business premises flat rate adjustment covers the private use of food, utilities and other household goods and services.

Capital purchases are deductible in full in the year of purchase; however, no deduction is available for the purchase of a motor car as this is covered by the approved mileage allowance.

		£	£
Revenue (£49,910 – £10,275)			39,635
Less: Food, utilities, etc. (£17,660 × 95%)			(16,777)
			22,858
Plus:	Flat rate private use adjustment		4,200
Less:	Depreciation	Nil	
	Capital expenditure	3,500	
	Motor expenses (W)	5,250	
	Other expenses (£1,485 – £400)	1,085	
			(9,835)
Tax adjusted trading profit			17,223

Working: Motor expenses

Idris is entitled to claim a deduction for his business mileage of 13,000 miles at the approved mileage rates.

	£
10,000 miles at 45p	4,500
3,000 miles at 25p	750
	5,250

(iii) **More beneficial basis**

Using the cash basis will result in Idris being taxed on a lower amount in 2014/15, and is therefore preferable. The difference is £7,418 (£24,641 – £17,223).

12 FOO DEE (ADAPTED)

Key answer tips

Part (a) requires you to calculate an individual's employment income. This includes a tricky element in the business mileage claim allowance to be deducted. Knowledge of the ordinary commuting rules and temporary workplace rules are tested.

Part (b) requires a simple adjustment of profit and capital allowances computation which should not have caused any problems if you remembered that it is a 9 month accounting period and therefore the maximum AIA and WDAs are time apportioned.

This style of question is often examined, so you need to make sure you know the approach and techniques required.

(a)   **Employment income computation – 2014/15**

	Total £
Salary	38,000
Less: Pension contributions (6%)	(2,280)
	————
	35,720
Employer contribution to childcare costs (W1)	2,145
Expense claim (W2)	(2,048)
	————
Employment income	35,817
	————

Workings

(W1) Childcare costs

Gastronomic-Food plc's contribution towards Foo's mother looking after her two children is taxable in full as employment income assuming that her mother is not an approved childcare provider. The exemption of £55 per week (for a basic rate taxpayer) only applies where childcare vouchers are provided to employees for use with approved childcare providers.

The taxable amount is calculated as follows:

(£55 × 39 weeks) = £2,145

(W2) Expense claim

Ordinary commuting (i.e. travel between home and the permanent workplace, including journeys to turn off the fire alarm) and private travel do not qualify for relief.

The travel to a temporary workplace qualifies as business mileage as it is for a period lasting less than 24 months.

Therefore, business mileage = (750 + 3,800) = 4,550 miles

As the company does not reimburse Foo Dee for any mileage, she is allowed to claim an allowable deduction based on the HMRC AMAPs.

Expenses claim = (4,550 miles × 45p) = £2,048

(b)   **Trading profit – period ended 30 September 2015**

	£	£
Net profit	130,854	
Depreciation	3,500	
Motor expenses (£4,200 × 2,000/6,000)	1,400	
Private accommodation (£12,800 × 1/4)	3,200	
Capital allowances (W)		82,514
	138,954	82,514
	(82,514)	
Trading profit	56,440	

Working: Capital allowances – nine months ended 30 September 2015

	General pool £	Private use car £	Allowances £
Additions (no AIA)			
Car (96 – 130 g/km)		14,600	
Additions (with AIA)			
Equipment	81,200		
Less: AIA (Note 1)	(81,200)		81,200
	——	Nil	
WDA (18% × 9/12)			
(Note 2)		(1,971) × 4/6	1,314
TWDV c/f	Nil	12,629	
Total allowances			82,514

Tutorial note

1   *Both the WDA and the AIA available are time apportioned by 9/12 as the accounting period is only 9 months long. The maximum AIA available is therefore £375,000 (£500,000 × 9/12).*

2   *Capital allowances on new car purchases are calculated based on the CO_2 emissions.*

As the car purchased in this question has CO_2 emissions of between 96 – 130 g/km, it is eligible for a WDA at 18%. The WDA then needs to be adjusted for the short accounting period and for the private use by Foo Dee, as only the business use proportion of the allowance can be claimed.

The business mileage is 4,000 out of 6,000 miles.

13   SAM WHITE (ADAPTED) *Walk in the footsteps of a top tutor*

Key answer tips

A classic self-employed scenario. The adjustment of profits was straightforward, except that some may not have known what to do with the patent royalties. In fact, if you did nothing, that was the right thing to do!

Be careful with the calculation of the private use/business use proportion of the car and remember the impact private use has on both the adjustment of profits computation and capital allowances.

Tutor's top tips

The key to success when you are doing an adjustment of profits is to think about what, if anything, has already been included in the statement of profit or loss.

If an expense is disallowable and has been deducted, you need to add it back. If it hasn't been deducted you do nothing. Conversely, if an expense is allowable and has been deducted, you include it with a zero adjustment. If it hasn't been deducted, you need to deduct it.

Read the question carefully here! As the question just asks you to 'calculate', you do not need to explain why you are making adjustments, although you do need to make sure you label your answers so that the marker can see which expenses you are adding back or deducting. It is also important to include all the major items of expenditure in the question, showing a zero for the adjustment figure where the expenditure is allowable.

Always show your workings if the adjustment figure is not clear from the question.

Sam White – Trading profit for the year ended 5 April 2015

	£	£
Net profit	100,000	
Depreciation	7,600	
Motor expenses (£8,800 × 20%) (W1)	1,760	
Patent royalties (Note 1)	0	
Breach of contract fees (Note 2)	0	
Accountancy fees (Note 2)	0	
Personal capital gains tax advice	320	
Gifts to customers (£560 + £420) (Note 3)	980	
Use of office (£5,120 × 1/8)		640
Private telephone (£1,600 × 25%)		400
Own consumption (Note 4)	1,480	
Capital allowances (W2)		3,957
	–––––––	–––––
	112,140	4,997
	(4,997)	–––––
	–––––––	
Trading profit	107,143	
	–––––––	

Tutorial note

1   Patent royalties are allowed as a deduction when calculating the trading profit, because they are for the purposes of the trade. As they have already been deducted in arriving at the profit, no adjustment is required.

2   The fees incurred for accountancy and the breach of contract defence are allowable as incurred wholly and exclusively for the purposes of the trade.

3   Gifts to customers are an allowable deduction if they cost less than £50 per recipient per year, are not of food, drink, tobacco or vouchers exchangeable for goods and carry a conspicuous advertisement for the company making the gift.

4   Goods for own consumption must be treated as a sale at full market value. As no entries have been made in the accounts, the full sale proceeds are adjusted for. Had the cost of the goods been accounted for already, only the profit element would need to be adjusted for.

Workings

(W1) Private/business mileage

	Total	Private	Business
Total miles	25,000		
Visiting suppliers	(5,000)		5,000
	———		
Allocate (25:75)	20,000	5,000	15,000
	———	———	———
		5,000	20,000
		———	———
(5,000/25,000)		20%	
(20,000/25,000)			80%

Tutor's top tips

A familiar full blown capital allowances computation is given in the workings to this answer to show clearly how the allowances are calculated.

However, where there are not many transactions it is perfectly acceptable to do one or two lines and just calculate the allowances available on each asset acquired rather than a full computation.

If you do this however, be careful and make sure you explain your calculations clearly.

(W2) Capital allowances

	General pool £	Private use car £	Allowances £
TWDV b/f	14,800	20,200	
WDA (18%)	(2,664)		2,664
WDA (8%)(W1)		(1,616) × 80%	1,293
TWDV c/f	12,136	18,584	
Total allowances			3,957

Tutorial note

The motor car is a high emission car (CO$_2$ emissions exceed 130 g/km) and is eligible for a WDA at 8%.

Examiner's report

This question was very well answered by the majority of candidates.

The adjustments for use of office, business use of a private telephone and own consumption caused the most problems, with a number of candidates being unsure as to whether adjustments should be added or subtracted in order to arrive at the tax adjusted trading profit.

Note: *The examiner's report has been edited to remove comments on elements of the question that have been deleted due to changes to the exam format.*

ACCA marking scheme		
		Marks
(a)	Net profit	0.5
	Depreciation	0.5
	Motor expenses	1.5
	Patent royalties	0.5
	Professional fees	1.5
	Gifts to customers	1.0
	Use of office	1.0
	Private telephone	1.0
	Own consumption	0.5
	Capital allowances — Pool	1.0
	— Motor car	1.0
Total		**10.0**

14 ANDREW ZOOM *Walk in the footsteps of a top tutor*

Key answer tips

A classic tax exam question on self-employed versus employed which was not difficult, but presented in a scenario requiring the application of knowledge to the particular situation given.

This is a newer style of question for F6 students, requiring the calculation of income tax and NIC on the same amount of income for both an employee and a sole trader. This is useful preparation for those planning to move on to P6.

Tutor's top tips

It is important to learn the rules for determining whether an individual is self-employed.

However, it is not enough here to simply state those rules; instead they must be applied to the situation given.

The question requirement specifically asks only for those factors that indicate employment rather than self-employment.

The answer must therefore focus on those factors, not any factors you can remember and not those that would clearly suggest self-employment rather than employment.

Even without detailed knowledge of the rules here, common sense suggestions should enable students to pick up some marks.

(a) **Factors indicating employment**

- Andrew is under the control of Slick-Productions Ltd.
- Andrew is not taking any financial risk.
- Andrew works a set number of hours, is paid by the hour and is paid for overtime.
- Andrew cannot profit from sound management, i.e. he cannot make a profit if he does the agreed amount of work in a shorter period of time.
- Andrew is required to do the work personally.
- There is an obligation to accept work that is offered.
- Andrew does not provide his own equipment.

(b)　(i)　**Treated as an employee**

Tutor's top tips

Part (b) involves straightforward income tax and NIC calculations, which you should be able to score well on, regardless of your answer to part (a).

Don't miss the opportunity to gain these easy marks by being put off by the first part of the question, or by running out of time.

Andrew's income tax liability for 2014/15 will be:

	£	£
Employment income		50,000
Less: PA		(10,000)
Taxable income		40,000

Income tax

£		£
31,865 × 20%		6,373
8,135 × 40%		3,254
40,000		
Income tax liability		9,627

Class 1 NIC for 2014/15 will be:

(£41,865 – £7,956) × 12%	4,069	
(£50,000 – £41,865) × 2%	163	
		4,232
Total income tax and NICs		13,859

(ii)　**Treated as self-employed**

	£	£
Andrew's trading profit for 2014/15 will be £50,000, so his income tax liability will be unchanged (as above)		9,627
Class 2 NIC for 2014/15 (52 weeks × £2.75)		140

Class 4 NIC for 2014/15:

(£41,865 – £7,956) × 9%	3,052	
(£50,000 – £41,865) × 2%	163	
		3,215
Total income tax and NICs		12,982

Examiner's report

This question was very well answered by the majority of candidates.

However, in part (a) only a few candidates pointed out that the taxpayer did not take any financial risk or profit from sound management.

The only common mistake in part (b) was that candidates often based their NIC calculations on the taxable income figure rather than on employment income or trading profit.

ACCA marking scheme		
		Marks
(a) Control		0.5
Financial risk		0.5
Basis of remuneration		1.0
Sound management		0.5
Required to do the work personally		0.5
Obligation to accept work offered		0.5
Equipment		0.5
		———
		4.0
		———
(b) (i) **Treated as an employee**		
Employment income		0.5
Personal allowance		0.5
Income tax liability		0.5
Class 1 NIC		1.5
		———
		3.0
		———
(ii) **Treated as self employed**		
Income tax liability		0.5
Class 2 NIC		1.0
Class 4 NIC		1.5
		———
		3.0
		———
Total		**10.0**
		———

15 SOPHIA WONG (ADAPTED) *Walk in the footsteps of a top tutor*

Key answer tips

Part (a) is a relatively straightforward comparison of the tax cost of trading as either a sole trader or through a company.

The cost of trading as a sole trader is given in the question so detailed calculations are in fact only required for the cost of extracting profits from a company as either remuneration or dividends. The examiner provides a lot of guidance in the question; giving figures for the amount of salary and dividends to use in the calculations and telling you the calculations that are required in the notes to the requirement. So if you follow the instructions carefully the calculations are relatively easy.

Part (b) covered a topic that is no longer in the syllabus and has therefore been replaced with a new topic.

Tutor's top tips

Make sure you set out your answer clearly and logically, using headings so it is clear which calculations relate to each scenario.

In part (i) consider the implications, for both Sophia of receiving employment income and for the company of paying remuneration. Likewise in part (ii) consider the implications for both parties of paying a dividend. Consider what tax consequences there may be, such as:

Is the payment tax deductible for the company?

Is it subject to NIC?

For each part work through the calculations specified in the notes to the requirements. And don't forget to summarise the total costs for each alternative and conclude on whether it is more or less than the cost of being self-employed – there are easy marks to be gained here.

(a)   (i)   **Profits withdrawn as director's remuneration**

- Employer's Class 1 NIC will be = (£80,000 – £73,021) = £6,979

Tutorial note

If all of the profits of £80,000 are withdrawn as director's remuneration (including the employer's Class 1 NIC) and the gross remuneration is £73,021 (per the question) then the employer's Class 1 NIC must be the difference of £6,979.

The examiner has taken this 'short cut' approach, however if you were unsure of this approach you could prepare the usual NIC calculation as follows:

(£73,021 – £7,956) × 13.8% = £8,979 -£2,000 =£6,979

The deduction of £2,000 is the NIC employment allowance. As Sophia will be the only employee of the company it will be deducted from the company's Class 1 NIC due on her salary.

- Sophia's income tax liability for 2014/15 will be:

	£
Director's remuneration	73,021
Less: PA	(10,000)
Taxable income	63,021
Income tax	
£	
31,865 × 20%	6,373
31,156 × 40%	12,462
63,021	
Income tax liability	18,835

- Sophia's employee Class 1 NIC for 2014/15 will be as follows:

	£
(£41,865 − £7,956) × 12%	4,069
(£73,021 − £41,865) × 2%	623
	4,692

- There is no corporation tax liability for the new company as the profits are entirely withdrawn as director's remuneration.

- The total tax and NIC cost if all of the new company's profits are withdrawn as director's remuneration is as follows:

	£
Employer's NIC	6,979
Sophia's income tax	18,835
Sophia's employee NIC	4,692
	30,506

This is more than the cost on a self-employed basis of £25,585.

(ii) **Profits withdrawn as dividends**

- There will be no Class 1 NIC.
- The corporation tax liability of the new company for the year ended 5 April 2015 will be £16,000 (£80,000 − £64,000).

Tutorial note

If all of the profits of £80,000 are withdrawn as dividends (after allowing for corporation tax) and the net dividends are £64,000 (per the question) then the corporation tax liability must be the difference of £16,000.

The examiner has taken this 'short cut' approach, however if you were unsure of this approach you could prepare the usual corporation tax calculation as follows:

(£80,000 × 20%) = £16,000.

Remember that dividends are not tax deductible.

- The income tax payable by Sophia for 2014/15 will be:

	£
Dividends (£64,000 × 100/90)	71,111
Less: PA	(10,000)
Taxable income	61,111

Income tax

£	£
31,865 × 10%	3,186
29,246 × 32.5%	9,505
———	
61,111	
———	———
Income tax liability	12,691
Less: Tax suffered at source	
Dividend tax credit	
(Restricted to £61,111 × 10%)	(6,111)
	———
Income tax payable	6,580
	———

Tutorial note

The personal allowance has reduced the amount of the dividend which is taxed. The 10% dividend tax credit is restricted to 10% of the taxable dividend.

The examiner stated that credit would also be given if the full dividend tax credit of £7,111 was incorrectly offset.

- The total tax and NIC cost if all of the new company's profits are withdrawn as dividends is as follows:

	£
Corporation tax	16,000
Sophia's income tax	6,580
	———
	22,580
	———

This is £3,005 (£25,585 − £22,580) less than the cost on a self-employed basis.

(b) **Sophia Wong**

Capital gains tax liability – 2014/15

	Not qualifying for ER	Qualifying for ER
	£	£
Qualifying for Entrepreneurs' relief		
Sale of business: Goodwill (£150,000 − £Nil)		150,000
Not qualifying for Entrepreneurs' relief		
Necklace	11,053	
	———	
Chargeable gains	11,053	150,000
Less: Annual exempt amount (Note 2)	(11,000)	(Nil)
	———	———
Taxable gains	53	150,000
	———	———

	£
Capital gains tax liability	
Qualifying for ER (£150,000 × 10%)	15,000
Not qualifying for ER (£53 × 28%)	15
	15,015

Election

An election for Entrepreneurs' relief must be submitted by 31 January 2017. (i.e. within 12 months of the 31 January following the tax year in which the disposal is made).

Tutorial note

1   *Where an individual sells the whole or part of a business which they have owned for at least 12 months they can elect for Entrepreneurs' relief to apply such that the net chargeable gains (up to a lifetime maximum of £10 million) arising on the disposal are taxed at a lower rate of 10%.*

2   *The annual exempt amount is set against the chargeable gain from the sale of the necklace as it does not qualify for Entrepreneurs' relief and therefore this saves CGT at the higher rate of 28% rather than 10%.*

3   *The gains qualifying for Entrepreneurs' relief have to be taxed first and they utilise the remaining BR band of £11,865 (£31,865 − £20,000). Therefore the gain on the necklace is taxed at 28%.*

Examiner's report

Part (a) as a whole was very badly answered, often as a result of being attempted last with inadequate time remaining. Many students did not seem to notice that they had been given some of the information (employer's NIC when withdrawing profits as director's remuneration, and corporation tax when withdrawing profits as dividends) and wasted time trying to calculate the figures themselves.

As regards withdrawing profits as director's remuneration, very few candidates appreciated that there would be no taxable profit and hence no corporation tax liability. As regards withdrawing profits as dividends, far too many candidates did not appreciate that no NIC would be payable. Some candidates even attempted to answer this section with just one calculation combining the director's remuneration and dividend, and very few marks were available with this approach.

Part (b) has been replaced with a new question as the original topic is no longer in the syllabus. So the examiner's comments for this part are not relevant.

ACCA marking scheme			
			Marks
(a)	(i)	Profits withdrawn as director's remuneration	
		Employer's Class 1 NIC	1.0
		Sophia's income tax liability	
		Personal allowance	0.5
		Tax at 20%	0.5
		Tax at 40%	0.5
		Sophia's employee class 1 NIC	1.5
		No corporation tax liability	1.0
		Summary of cost and conclusion	1.0
			6.0
	(ii)	Profits withdrawn as dividends	
		No class 1 NIC	0.5
		Corporation tax liability	1.0
		Sophia's income tax payable	
		Dividends grossed up	0.5
		Personal allowance	0.5
		Tax at 20%	0.5
		Tax at 40%	0.5
		Tax suffered at source	0.5
		Summary of cost and conclusion	1.0
			5.0
(b)		Gain on goodwill	0.5
		Annual exempt amount offset against gain on necklace	0.5
		CGT calculation	1.0
		Necklace	
		Normal CGT calculation	1.0
		Chattels gain restriction	0.5
		Date of Entrepreneurs' relief election	0.5
			4.0
Total			**15.0**

16   JOHN AND LIAN (ADAPTED)   *Walk in the footsteps of a top tutor*

Key answer tips

Part (a) of the original question tested a topic which is no longer examinable. It has been replaced with a tax administration question covering the opening years of a business.

Part (b) also included a topic which is no longer examinable and this part has therefore been amended. This part now tests knowledge of the basis of assessment rules for a sole trader both on commencement and cessation of trade, including the related capital allowance rules.

(a) **John Higgins – New business**

Tutor's top tips

For written parts, write short succinct sentences in bullet point form. Use precise language especially when explaining deadlines and time limits etc.

Bear in mind the mark allocation. In general, there is usually one mark allocated for each valid point made. Do not therefore dwell on any one point too much and keep an eye on the clock.

(i) John must notify HM Revenue & Customs that he is chargeable to income tax in respect of his trading income by 5 October 2015 (i.e. 6 months from the end of the tax year in which the income tax liability arises).

(ii) John must keep all of the records (not just his business records) which support his 2014/15 tax return until 31 January 2021 (i.e. 5 years after the filing date for the return).

(iii) John will be required to make the first payment of tax in respect of his trading profits by 31 January 2016 (i.e. 31 January following the end of the tax year).

Tutorial note

1   *The first tax year that John will be assessed to tax in respect of his business profits will be 2014/15 (i.e. the tax year in which trade commences).*

2   *John will not be required to make payments on account of his income tax liability for his first tax year (2014/15) as he did not have an income tax liability in the previous tax year which exceeded the tax deducted at source. He therefore makes just one payment for 2014/15 on the balancing payment due date.*

(b) **Lian Zhang – Assessable profits for the years 2012/13 to 2015/16**

Tutor's top tips

Deal with the information in strict date order, starting with the opening year rules, then CYB and finally the closing year rules.

Remember that all basis of assessment periods, other than in the first and final tax years must be of 12 months duration.

However, before you can calculate the closing year rules, you need to calculate the capital allowances for the 14 month closing period of account.

		£
2012/13	1 May 2012 to 5 April 2013	
	(£50,400 (W1) × 11/12)	46,200
2013/14	CYB	
	Year ended 30 April 2013 (W1)	50,400
2014/15	CYB	
	Year ended 30 April 2014 (W1)	37,200
2015/16	Period of cessation	
	Period ended 30 June 2015	
	Trading profit	61,500
	Less: Capital allowances (W2)	(4,400)
		57,100
	Less: Relief for overlap profits (W3)	(46,200)
		10,900

Tutorial note

1   2012/13 is the first tax year of trading. Using the opening year rules the basis of assessment is the period from the date of commencement to the following 5 April.

2   There is a 12 month period of accounts ending in the second tax year (2013/14) and these are therefore taxed under the current year basis in that tax year.

3   In 2014/15 the current basis applies.

4   2015/16 is the tax year of cessation. The basis period for 2015/16 runs from the end of the basis period for the previous tax year to the date of cessation (i.e. the 14-months to 30 June 2015). Overlap profits arising on commencement are relieved in the final tax year.

5   Over the life of a business the total profits of the business are taxed. Therefore you can check:

Total profits: (£50,400 + £37,200 + £61,500 − £4,400) = £144,700

Assessments: (£46,200 + £50,400 + £37,200 + £10,900) = £144,700

Workings

(W1) Taxable trading profits

Year ended 30 April	2013	2014
	£	£
Trading profit	62,300	75,400
Less: Capital allowances	(11,900)	(38,200)
Taxable trading profit	50,400	37,200

(W2) Capital allowances

	Main pool	Allowances
	£	£
14 months ended 30 June 2015		
TWDV b/f	14,400	
Addition: Machine	12,000	
Disposal	(22,000)	
	4,400	
Balancing allowance	(4,400)	4,400
Total allowances		4,400

Tutorial note

1   For an unincorporated trader (unlike companies), capital allowances are computed for the long period of account (i.e. in this case for the 14 months to 30 June 2015).

A long period of account for sole traders is not split into the first 12 months and the balance period as it is for companies.

2   In the period of account in which business is permanently ceased the AIA, WDAs and FYAs are not available. Additions and disposals are added to the relevant pool and a balancing charge or allowance is calculated.

(W3) Relief for overlap profits

In 2013/14, there are overlap profits of £46,200 in respect of the 11-month period 1 May 2012 to 5 April 2013.

These are relieved in the final tax year of trade.

ACCA marking scheme		
		Marks
(a)	Date re notification of chargeability	1.0
	Retention of records date	1.0
	First payment of tax date in opening year	1.0
		3.0
(b)	2012/13 assessment	1.0
	2013/14 assessment	0.5
	2014/15 assessment	0.5
	2015/16 assessment – Period of account 14 months long	1.5
	Taxable trading profits	1.0
	Capital allowances	2.0
	Overlap relief	0.5
		7.0
Total		**10.0**

17   FANG, HONG AND KANG *Walk in the footsteps of a top tutor*

Key answer tips

A question covering three different scenarios all concerned with self-employed individuals.

Part (a) is a straight forward question involving the opening year basis of assessment rules and the deductibility of pre-trading expenditure for an individual starting a business.

Part (b) involves an established trader who has incurred trading losses. This is not a difficult question but involves a number of loss offsets and therefore needs to be approached in a methodical manner.

Part (c) involves a partnership where one of the partners is retiring. This is a commonly tested scenario and should not have caused any difficulties.

(a)   **Fang**

   (i)   **Assessments**

		£
2012/13	Actual	
	(1 August 2012 to 5 April 2013)	
	(£45,960 × 8/12)	30,640
2013/14	CYB (Year ended 31 July 2013)	45,960
2014/15	CYB (Year ended 31 July 2014)	39,360

In 2013/14 there are overlap profits of £30,640 (i.e. the eight-month period 1 August 2012 to 5 April 2013).

(ii) **Pre-trading expenditure**

- The trading expenditure will be treated as incurred on 1 August 2012 provided it was incurred within the previous seven years and would have been allowable if the trade had already commenced.
- The computer equipment which Fang already owned will be an addition for capital allowances purposes based on its market value at 1 August 2012.

(b) **Hong**

Tutor's top tips

There is a lot of information in this relatively short question which can appear daunting so it is important to approach the question in a methodical manner.

You are asked to calculate taxable income, taxable gains and the amount of trading loss carried forward – so layout your pro formas and start by filling in the easy numbers.

Then consider the trading losses – dealing with the earliest loss first. You are told how to offset the loss for the year ended 5 April 2015 in the question so you do not need to decide how best to use the loss – just follow the instructions!

Taxable income – 2013/14

	£
Trading profit	29,700
Less: Loss relief b/f	(2,600)
	27,100
Property business profit	3,900
	31,000
Total income	31,000
Less: Loss relief – Current year	(31,000)
Net income	Nil
Less: Personal allowance	(wasted)
Taxable income	Nil

Taxable gain – 2013/14

	£
Chargeable gain	17,800
Less: Trading loss relief (W1)	(11,600)
	6,200
Less: Capital loss b/f (Note)	(Nil)
	6,200
Less: Annual exempt amount (part wasted)	(6,200)
Taxable gain	Nil

The trading loss carried forward is £3,200 (W2).

Tutorial note

Relief for trading losses against total income and net chargeable gains is 'all or nothing' (i.e. the relief cannot be restricted to preserve the PA for income tax or the AEA for CGT).

Capital losses brought forward however do not have to be offset if they would result in wasting the AEA. Therefore, in this case, capital losses brought forward would not be utilised and would be carried forward to set against future net chargeable gains.

Workings

(W1) Trading loss relief

The trading loss relief claim against the chargeable gain = Lower of:

- Chargeable gain less capital loss brought forward

  = (£17,800 – £6,200) = £11,600, and

- Trading loss remaining = (£45,800 – £31,000) = £14,800

Therefore, can only offset £11,600 against gains

(W2) Loss memorandum

	£
Loss – 2012/13	2,600
Less: Set off against trading profits – 2013/14	(2,600)
Loss – 2014/15	45,800
Less: Carry back against 2013/14 income	(31,000)
Loss relief extended to capital gains in 2013/14 (W1)	(11,600)
Loss carried forward	3,200

Tutorial note

The loss brought forward from 2012/13 must be set against the first available trading profits in subsequent years (i.e. 2013/14). The loss is offset before losses arising in later years.

The loss arising in 2014/15 can be offset against total income in 2014/15 and/or 2013/14. Once a claim has been made to offset the loss against the total income of a particular tax year (e.g. 2013/14) a claim can also be made to offset any remaining trading losses against chargeable gains of the same tax year.

(c)   **Kang, Ling and Ming**

Allocation of profits

	Total £	Kang £	Ling £	Ming £
Year ended 30 June 2013				
(£148,800 × 1/3)	148,800	49,600	49,600	49,600
Year ended 30 June 2014				
1 July 2013 to 31 October 2013				
(£136,800 × 4/12 × 1/3)	45,600	15,200	15,200	15,200
1 November 2013 to 30 June 2014				
(£136,800 × 8/12 × ½)	91,200	45,600	45,600	0
	136,800	60,800	60,800	15,200

Trading income assessments

	Kang £	Ling £	Ming £
2013/14			
Year ended 30 June 2013 – CYB	49,600	49,600	
Cessation rules:			
Year ended 30 June 2013			49,600
Period ended 31 October 2013			15,200
			64,800
Less: Relief for overlap profits			(29,400)
			35,400
2014/15			
Year ended 30 June 2014 – CYB	60,800	60,800	Nil

Tutorial note

The cessation rules apply to Ming for 2013/14 since she ceased to be a partner on 31 October 2013. Her basis period for 2013/14 runs from the end of the basis period for 2012/13 to the date of cessation (i.e. 1 July 2012 to 31 October 2013).

				Marks
ACCA marking scheme				
(a)	(i)	2012/13 assessment		1.0
		2013/14 assessment		0.5
		2014/15 assessment		0.5
		Overlap profits		1.0
				——
				3.0
				——
	(ii)	Pre-trading revenue expenditure		1.0
		Addition for capital allowance purposes at MV		1.0
				——
				2.0
				——
(b)		Taxable income		
		Trading profit		0.5
		Less trading losses b/f		0.5
		Property business profit		0.5
		Less loss of 2014/15 against total income		0.5
		PA = £Nil		0.5
		Taxable gain		
		Chargeable gain		0.5
		AEA		0.5
		Trading loss c/f		0.5
		Maximum loss relief against chargeable gain		1.0
				——
				5.0
				——
(c)		Allocation of profits		
		Year ended 30.6.13		0.5
		Year ended 30.6.14		1.5
		Assessments		
		2013/14 – year ended 30.6.13		0.5
		2013/14 – plus period ended 31.10.13 for Ming		1.0
		Ming overlap relief		1.0
		2014/15		0.5
				——
				5.0
				——
Total				**15.0**
				——

18   NA STYLE (ADAPTED)   *Walk in the footsteps of a top tutor*

Key answer tips

This question is a classic self-employed individual scenario, testing opening year's basis of assessment and the compilation of an income tax computation. There is also an element of self-assessment at the end.

The first part is relatively easy to score highly on.

Part (b) was straightforward provided the self-assessment rules had been learnt and applied to the information given.

Tutor's top tips

Remember to read the requirement carefully.

This question has clear mark allocations, which should be used to allocate the time spent on each section. You need to adopt a logical approach, using the requirements to break down the information and plan your answer.

The first part just requires the application of the opening year rules to figures given in the question. It is possible to score very well on this sort of question, which is not technically difficult, as long as you do not panic.

Be sure to explain your answer; clearly showing the tax year, basis of assessment and calculation so that method marks can be given even if the maths goes awry!

Don't forget to highlight the overlap profits as they are specifically asked for and will therefore be mark earning.

(a) **Assessable trading profits – first three tax years**

Tax year	Basis of assessment	£
2011/12	Actual basis (1 January 2012 to 5 April 2012) (£25,200 × 3/6)	12,600
2012/13	First 12 months trading (1 January 2012 to 31 December 2012) £25,200 + (£21,600 × 6/12)	36,000
2013/14	Current year basis (Year ended 30 June 2013)	21,600
2014/15	Current year basis (Year ended 30 June 2014)	30,665

Overlap profits

Tax year	Profits taxed twice	£
2012/13	(1 January 2012 to 5 April 2012) (£25,200 × 3/6)	12,600
2013/14	(1 July 2012 to 31 December 2012) (£21,600 × 6/12)	10,800
		23,400

Tutorial note

The assessment for 2012/13 is the first 12 months of trading as the accounting period ending in that year is less than 12 months from the commencement of trading.

(b) (i) **Income tax computation – 2014/15**

Tutor's top tips

For part (b) a systematic approach is needed.

Remember not to ignore exempt income, as credit is given for stating that it is exempt, even though you do NOT include the figure in your computation.

Always ensure that you read the question carefully – make sure you understand whether you have to compute income tax liability or payable.

The requirement for part (b)(i) is to calculate income tax payable; therefore you need to calculate the liability and deduct the tax credits for tax already suffered at source.

Part (b)(ii) goes on to require the balancing payment after taking account of payments on account (POAs) already paid, and then requires the POAs to be paid in the following year.

	£
Trading profit	30,665
Building society interest (£560 × 100/80)	700
Interest from New Individual Savings Account (exempt)	Nil
Interest from NS&I savings certificate (exempt)	Nil
Interest from government stocks (received gross)	370
Dividends (£1,080 × 100/90)	1,200
Total income	32,935
Less: PA	(10,000)
Taxable income	22,935

Analysis of income (Note)

Dividends = £1,200;
Savings (£700 + £370) = £1,070;
Other income (£22,935 – £1,200 – £1,070) = £20,665

Income tax	£
£	
20,665 × 20% (other income)	4,133
1,070 × 20% (savings income)	214
1,200 × 10% (dividend income)	120
22,935	
Income tax liability	4,467
Less: Tax suffered at source	
Dividends (£1,200 × 10%)	(120)
Building society interest (£700 × 20%)	(140)
Income tax payable	4,207

Tutorial note

There is nothing wrong in presenting your computation in columnar form if you prefer to, however there is also no need to do so if you do not want to.

However, you do need to be able to break down the taxable income into the different types of income, namely: dividends, savings and other income, in order to apply the correct rates of tax to each type of income.

    (ii)   **Tax payments**

- Na's balancing payment for 2014/15 due on 31 January 2016 is £1,007 (£4,207 – £3,200).

- Her payments on account for 2015/16 will be £2,104 and £2,103 (£4,207 × 50%). These will be due on 31 January 2016 and 31 July 2016.

Examiner's report

This question was very well answered, and there were many high scoring answers.

In part (a) some candidates lost marks because they did not show the relevant tax years in which profits were assessable.

There were few problems as regards the income tax payable, although many candidates did not appreciate that interest from government stocks is received gross and is taxable.

As regards the balancing payment and payments on account, candidates were often not aware of the relevant dates.

Note: *The examiner's report has been edited to remove comments on elements of the question that have been deleted due to changes to the exam format.*

ACCA marking scheme				Marks
(a)	2011/12			1.0
	2012/13	– Assessment		1.0
		– Overlap profits		1.0
	2013/14	– Assessment		1.0
		– Overlap profits		1.0
	2014/15	– Assessment		1.0
				6.0
(b)	(i)	Income tax computation		
		Trading profit		0.5
		Building society interest		0.5
		New Individual Savings Account		0.5
		Interest from NS&I savings certificate		0.5
		Interest from government stocks		1.0
		Dividends		0.5
		Personal allowance		0.5
		Income tax		1.0
		Tax suffered at source		1.0
				6.0

ACCA marking scheme		
		Marks
(ii) Tax payments		
Balancing payment		1.5
Payments on account		1.5
		———
		3.0
		———
Total		**15.0**
		———

19 SIMON HOUSE (ADAPTED) *Walk in the footsteps of a top tutor*

Key answer tips

A very familiar style question covering the badges of trade and requiring the calculation of the tax consequences of a transaction being deemed to be a trading transaction or a capital event.

Easy marks should have been picked up in this question.

Tutor's top tips

*Usually these questions start with the requirement for you to list and then apply the badges of trade. However, this question is unusual in that it kindly gives you the badges of trade that it requires you to consider and asks you to explain the **meaning** of each for only 3 marks.*

It is fairly certain that half a mark will be allocated to each explanation and so therefore it is not possible, or necessary, to write huge amounts on any one explanation. Note also that it only requires an explanation of the badges of trade listed. Do not waste time explaining other badges of trade that are used by HM Revenue & Customs as you will not gain any extra marks.

Try to be clear, succinct and to the point and then move on!

(a) **Badges of trade**

- Trading is indicated where the property (subject matter) does not yield an ongoing income or give personal enjoyment to its owner.
- The sale of property within a short time of its acquisition is an indication of trading.
- Trading is indicated by repeated transactions in the same subject matter.
- A trading motive is indicated where work is carried out to the property to make it more marketable, or where steps are taken to find purchasers.
- A forced sale to raise cash for an emergency is an indication that the transaction is not of a trading nature.
- If a transaction is undertaken with the motive of realising a profit, this is a strong indication of trading.

(b) **Treated as carrying on a trade**

Tutor's top tips

If the transaction is treated as a trade transaction, a straightforward trading profit computation is required.

Simon is then liable to income tax and Class 4 NICs on the trading profit and Class 2 NICs as he will be self-employed.

Make sure you show your calculations for each liability clearly.

Income tax – 2014/15

	£	£
Income		260,000
Cost of property	127,000	
Renovation costs	50,600	
Loan interest (£150,000 × 6% × 4/12)(Note)	3,000	
Legal fees (£1,800 + £2,600)	4,400	
		(185,000)
Trading profit		75,000
Less: PA		(10,000)
Taxable income		65,000

£		
31,865 × 20%		6,373
33,135 × 40%		13,254
65,000		
Income tax liability		19,627

Tutorial note

If treated as a trade, all costs incurred wholly and exclusively for the purposes of the trade are allowable deductions – including interest on the loan to purchase the house.

National Insurance – 2014/15

	£
Class 2 NIC (18 weeks × £2.75)	49
Class 4 NIC	
(£41,865 − £7,956) × 9%	3,052
(£75,000 − £41,865) × 2%	663
	3,715

(c)   **Treated as a capital transaction**

Tutor's top tips

You should know that the consequences of applying the badges of trade are to determine whether or not the transaction is a trading one, or a capital event.

However, you did not necessarily need to remember that in this question as the examiner has kindly told you to what to do (i.e. calculate the capital gains tax liability).

Capital gains tax liability – 2014/15

	£	£
Proceeds		260,000
Less: Incidental costs – legal fees		(2,600)
		257,400
Less: Cost	127,000	
Enhancement expenditure	50,600	
Loan interest (Note)	Nil	
Incidental costs	1,800	
		(179,400)
Chargeable gain		78,000
Less: AEA		(11,000)
Taxable gain		67,000

£		
31,865 × 18%		5,736
35,135 × 28%		9,838
67,000		
Capital gains tax liability		15,574

Tutorial note

If it is treated as a capital transaction, no relief is available for the interest on the loan used to finance the transaction.

PPR and letting relief are not available as the property has never been his principal private residence.

Entrepreneurs' relief is not available as the house is an investment property, not a business.

The gain is taxed at 18% to the extent that it falls in the basic rate band and 28% on the excess. As Simon has no other income or gains, the first £31,865 is taxed at 18%.

Examiner's report

This question was very well answered, and often helped marginal candidates to achieve a pass mark.

In part (a) a number of candidates failed to score any marks because they did not state what did or did not indicate trading. For example, stating that the 'length of ownership' means how long an item has been owned did not score any marks. It was necessary to explain that the sale of property within a short time of its acquisition is an indication of trading.

Part (b) presented no problems for most candidates. In this type of question it is always best to produce full computations for each option. This will maximise marks if any mistakes are made.

It was pleasing to see that many candidates correctly restricted the Class 2 NIC to 18 weeks' contributions.

	ACCA marking scheme		
			Marks
(a)		The subject matter	0.5
		Length of ownership	0.5
		Frequency	0.5
		Work done	0.5
		Circumstances responsible for realisation	0.5
		Motive	0.5
			───
			3.0
			───
(b)		Income	0.5
		Cost of property	0.5
		Renovation costs	0.5
		Loan interest	1.0
		Legal fees	1.0
		Personal allowance	0.5
		Income tax liability	1.0
		Class 2 NIC	1.5
		Class 4 NIC	1.5
			───
			8.0
			───
(c)		Proceeds	0.5
		Cost	0.5
		Enhancement expenditure	0.5
		Incidental costs	0.5
		Loan interest	0.5
		Annual exempt amount	0.5
		Capital gains tax	1.0
			───
			4.0
			───
Total			**15.0**
			═══

20 **BAYLE DEFENDER (ADAPTED)** *Walk in the footsteps of a top tutor*

Key answer tips

A time pressured question on self-employment, employment and calculation of income tax.

Part (a) firstly requires a straightforward adjustment of profits computation which should not have caused problems.

The subsequent income tax computation in part (b) tests the reduction of the personal allowance for high earners and the additional rates of tax.

Part (b) requires figures brought forward from previous parts. However it is important to remember that full credit will still be given for subsequent parts even if the earlier part is calculated incorrectly.

(a) **Trading profit – year ended 30 September 2014**

	£
Net profit	172,400
Impairment loss (Note 1)	0
Gifts to customers – Clocks (Note 2)	3,300
– Bottles of champagne (Note 2)	2,480
Donations to political parties	2,900
Lease of motor car (£10,360 × 15%) (Note 3)	1,554
Personal tax advice (Note 4)	600
Property expenses (£46,240 × 2/5)	18,496
Parking fines (Note 4)	220
Speeding fine (Note 4)	300
Professional subscription	0
Golf club membership fee (Note 4)	960
	———
Tax adjusted trading profit	203,210
	———

Tutorial note

1   *The recovered impairment loss will have been allowed as a deduction when originally written off, so the recovery is now taxable. As it is already included in the revenue figure given, there is no adjustment required.*

2   *Gifts to customers are only an allowable deduction if they cost less than £50 per recipient per year, are not of food, drink, tobacco or vouchers exchangeable for goods and carry a conspicuous advertisement for the company making the gift.*

Therefore the clocks are not allowable as they cost in excess of £50, and the champagne is drink and not allowable.

> 3 The leased motor car has a CO_2 emission rate in excess of 130 grams per kilometre, therefore 15% of the leasing costs are not allowed.
>
> 4 Personal expenditure is not allowable. Therefore the tax advice, the golf membership, the parking fines and the speeding fine of Bayle are not allowable and need to be adjusted for. Note that parking fines incurred by employees whilst on business activity would be allowable, but not fines incurred by the owner of the business, and speeding fines are never allowed, regardless of who incurs them.

(b) **Income tax computation – 2014/15**

	Total £	Other £	Savings £	Dividends £
Trading profit (part (a)) (Note 1)	203,210	203,210		
Employment income				
Director's remuneration	42,000	42,000		
Bonus payment (Note 2)	6,000	6,000		
NS&I certificates interest (Note 3)	Exempt			
Government stock interest (Note 4)	3,600		3,600	
Dividends (£9,900 × 100/90)	11,000			11,000
Total income	265,810	251,210	3,600	11,000
Less: PA (Note 5)	(Nil)			
Taxable income	265,810	251,210	3,600	11,000

Income tax

	£		£
31,865 × 20% (other)			6,373
118,135 × 40% (other)			47,254
150,000			
101,210 × 45% (other)			45,544
251,210			
3,600 × 45% (savings)			1,620
11,000 × 37.5% (dividends)			4,125
265,810			
Income tax liability			104,916
Less: Tax suffered at source			
Dividends (£11,000 × 10%)			(1,100)
PAYE ((£42,000 + £6,000) = £48,000 × 45%)			(21,600)
Income tax payable			82,216

Tutorial note

1   The trading income figure comes from part (a). However, full credit would be given for this part, even if the previous part was calculated incorrectly, provided you calculate the income tax correctly based on your figure.

2   The bonus payment of £6,000 that Bayle became entitled to on 10 March 2014 will have been taxed already as it would have been treated as received during 2013/14.

3   Interest received on the maturity of savings certificates issued by National Savings & Investments is exempt income. Note that in the examination, do not ignore exempt income. Instead, make sure you clearly show that you know it is exempt income.

4   Interest received on government stocks (gilts) is received gross.

5   Bayle's total income = net income = adjusted net income (ANI) as she has no reliefs and has not made any Gift Aid donations or personal pension contributions in the tax year. Accordingly, there is no personal allowance available to Bayle as her ANI of £265,810 exceeds £120,000.

Examiner's report

This question was generally well answered.

In part (a) the only consistent problem was the revenue received in respect of a previously written off impairment loss. Most candidates did not appreciate that no adjustment was necessary.

In part (b) it was often not appreciated that one of the bonuses was treated as being received in the previous tax year, and often bonuses were included or excluded without any explanation as to why. It should have been obvious that with income of over £250,000 no personal allowance was available, yet many candidates wasted time by showing a calculation for this.

Note: The examiner's report has been edited to remove comments on elements of the question that have been deleted due to changes to the exam format.

ACCA marking scheme		
		Marks
(a)	Impairment loss	1.0
	Gifts to customers	1.0
	Donations to political parties	0.5
	Lease of motor car	1.0
	Personal tax advice	0.5
	Property expenses	1.0
	Parking fines	0.5
	Speeding fines	0.5
	Professional subscription	0.5
	Golf club membership fee	0.5
		7.0

ACCA marking scheme		
		Marks
(b)	Trading profit	0.5
	Director's remuneration	0.5
	Bonus payments	1.0
	Interest from government stocks	0.5
	Interest from savings certificate	0.5
	Dividends	0.5
	Personal allowance	1.0
	Income tax	2.0
	Tax suffered at source	1.5
		————
		8.0
		————
Total		**15.0**
		————

21 TIM BURR (ADAPTED) *Walk in the footsteps of a top tutor*

Key answer tips

A short but complex question involving a new person joining a sole trade business part way through the accounting period and tax year, either as an employee or partner.

The employment NIC calculations were not straightforward as the annual thresholds need to be apportioned before they can be applied to the 4 months of earnings. In addition, the trading income assessments need to be very carefully calculated by allocating the partnership profits first, then applying the opening year rules.

The self-employment NIC calculations are however straightforward and should not cause difficulties.

Part (b)(ii) requires figures brought forward from the previous part. However it is important to remember that full credit will still be given in this part even if the earlier part is calculated incorrectly.

(a) **National insurance – if Hazel is employed**

Class 1 – primary employee contributions – paid by Hazel

(£3,300 – £663 (W)) × 12% × 4 months = £1,266

Class 1 – secondary employer contributions – paid by Tim

(£3,300 – £663) × 13.8% × 4 months = £1,456

As Hazel is the only employee the Class 1 secondary liability will be fully covered by the £2,000 employment allowance.

Working: Monthly earnings thresholds

Employee Class 1 NIC

Primary earnings threshold (PET) = (£7,956 × 1/12) = £663

Upper earnings limit = (£41,865 × 1/12) = £3,489

Hazel's monthly earnings are £3,300 which falls in between these limits.

For each month that Hazel is employed, she is therefore liable to Class 1 NICs at 12% on the excess over the PET of £663.

Employer Class 1 NIC

Secondary earnings threshold (SET) = (£7,956 × 1/12) = £663

Tim, as Hazel's employer, is liable to Class 1 NICs at 13.8% on the excess over the SET of £663.

Hazel will be employed for 4 months of the tax year (December to March inclusive).

Tutor's top tips

Usually at F6, for simplicity, NICs are calculated on an annual basis using the annual limits. In this question however the individual has only been employed for four months in the tax year. Accordingly, the annual limits need to be time apportioned.

This is because NICs are actually calculated on a payment period basis. This means that if an individual is paid monthly, the monthly limits are used (e.g. for primary Class 1 NICs, £663 and £3,489). If they are paid on a weekly basis, the weekly limits are used. For primary Class 1 NICs these are £153 (£7,956 × 1/52) and £805 (£41,865 × 1/52).

The examiner has confirmed that the alternative approach of using the annual earnings threshold and then taking 4/12ths of an annual NIC figure was acceptable in the exam.

(b) (i) **Trading income assessments**

Allocation of partnership profits

	Total £	Tim £	Hazel £
y/e 30.9.15			
1.10.14 to 30.11.14 (2 months)			
All profits to Tim	36,000	36,000	
1.12.14 to 30.09.15 (10 months)			
PSR (80%:20%)	180,000	144,000	36,000
	216,000	180,000	36,000
y/e 30.9.16			
PSR (80%:20%)	240,000	192,000	48,000

Applying basis of assessment rules

If Hazel joins the partnership on 1 December 2014, the opening year rules will apply to her profit share as follows:

Tax year	Basis of assessment	£	£
2014/15	Actual basis		
	(1.12.14 to 5.4.15)		
	(£36,000 × 4/10) (Note)		14,400

Tax year	Basis of assessment	£	£
2015/16	First 12 months trading (1.12.14 to 30.11.15)		
	10 m/e 30.9.15	36,000	
	y/e 30.9.16 × 2/12 (£48,000 × 2/12)	8,000	
		————	44,000

Tutorial note

The partnership profits should be allocated to the partners according to the partnership agreement in the accounting period.

The basis of assessment rules are then applied to each partner's share of profits separately.

Tim was a sole trader and becomes a partner. However he will continue to be assessed on a current year basis (CYB).

The commencement rules will apply to Hazel's share of profits from 2014/15 since she will join as a partner on 1 December 2014.

(ii) **NICs – 2014/15**

Paid by Hazel – self employed

Class 2 NICs (Note 1) = (18 weeks × £2.75) = £49

Class 4 NICs (Note 2) = (£14,400 – £7,956) × 9% = £580

Paid by Tim

There are no NIC implications for Tim in relation to Hazel's trading income assessments (Note 3).

Tutorial note

1   *Class 2 NICs are £2.75 per week. If Hazel joins the partnership on 1 December 2014, she will be a partner for the period 1 December 2014 to 5 April 2015 which is 126 days (31 + 31 + 28 + 31 + 5), which is 18 weeks (126 days ÷ 7).*

2   *Class 4 NICs are calculated using the full annual lower profits limit (£7,956 in 2014/15), they are not time apportioned, as the opening year rules produce an assessment for the full tax year 2014/15.*

   This trading income assessment figure comes from the previous part. However, full credit would be given for this part even if the assessment was calculated incorrectly provided you calculated the NICs correctly based on your figure.

3   *The question asks for the NICs to be paid by Tim, but only in relation to Hazel's trading income assessment. The question specifically states that his own NICs are not to be calculated.*

Examiner's report

In part (a) it was pleasing to see several candidates correctly restricted NIC contributions to the four months of employment.

Although there were also many good answers to part (b), there were also a lot of candidates who wasted time by doing NIC calculations for both the taxpayer and the new person, or NIC calculations for both years, instead of just the one required.

Note: *The examiner's report has been edited to remove comments on elements of the question that have been deleted due to changes to the exam format.*

	ACCA marking scheme	
		Marks
(a)	Monthly earnings threshold	1.0
	Employee Class 1 NIC	1.0
	Employer Class 1 NIC	1.0
	Employment allowance reduces Class 1 secondary to £nil	1.0
		———
		4.0
		———
(b)	Trading income assessments	
	2014/15	1.5
	2015/16	2.5
		———
		4.0
		———
	NIC re Hazel	
	Class 2 NIC	0.5
	Class 4 NIC	1.0
	Tim	0.5
		———
		2.0
		———
	Total	10.0
		———

22   RICHARD FEAST (ADAPTED) *Walk in the footsteps of a top tutor*

Key answer tips

Part (a) is a fairly straightforward adjustment of trading profit computation, which should not have caused any problems.

Part (b) requires employer's NIC calculations for an employee. It was important to limit your answer to just the classes of NIC required.

Part (c) requires knowledge of basic self-assessment administration issues and should not have caused any problems.

(a)   **Trading profit – year ended 5 April 2015**

Tutor's top tips

This straightforward adjustment of profit computation is presented in a familiar format, with a statement of profit or loss followed by a number of notes.

As is common with this type of question you are instructed to start your computation with the net profit figure and list all items in the question, using a zero if no adjustment is necessary. Note that marks are available for correctly showing zero for a non-adjusting item, so do not lose easy marks by ignoring these items. Work methodically through the statement, referring to the notes where appropriate, and entering each item in your computation as you go.

Remember to adjust for private use by the proprietor, but not an employee.

	£
Net profit	32,200
Motor expenses – Richard (£4,710 × 70%)	3,297
Motor expenses – Chef	0
Parking fines	280
Property expenses (£16,200 × 1/5)	3,240
Decorating – Restaurant	0
– Apartment	1,320
Other expenses – Legal fees (capital)	2,590
	42,927
Less: Capital allowances (W)	(3,780)
Trading profit	39,147

Working – Capital allowances

	General pool £	Private use car £	Business use %	Allowances £
Additions not qualifying for AIA:				
Private use car (96 – 130 g/km)		14,000		
Car (96 – 130 g/km)	16,800			
WDA (18%)		(2,520)	× 30%	756
WDA (18%)	(3,024)			3,024
TWDV c/f	13,776	11,480		
				3,780

Tutorial note

Both motor cars have CO_2 emissions between 96 and 130 grams per kilometre and therefore qualify for writing down allowances at the rate of 18%.

The private use of a motor car by an employee is irrelevant, since such usage will be assessed on the employee as a benefit.

(b)   **Employer National Insurance contributions**

Tutor's top tips

This question only requires the calculation of the employer's NIC liabilities, so do not waste time calculating employee's NICs.

Make sure that you clearly identify the different classes of NIC payable (i.e. Class 1 and Class 1A) and the different income on which they are charged.

	£	£
Employer's Class 1 NIC		
(£46,000 – £7,956) × 13.8%	5,250	
Less: NIC employment allowance (Note)	(2,000)	
	———	3,250
Employer's Class 1A NIC		
£2,856 (W1) × 13.8%		394
		———
Total NICs		3,644
		———

Tutorial note

As the chef is the only employee the employment allowance will be offset against the employer's Class 1 NIC liability on his salary.

Workings:

(W1) Car benefit

CO$_2$ emissions = 123 g/km (rounded down to 120g/km) available for the full tax year

	%
Petrol	12
Plus: (120 – 95) × 1/5	5
	——
Appropriate percentage	17
	——
List price (same as cost)	£16,800
	———
Car benefit (£16,800 × 17%)	£2,856
	———

(c)   **Self-assessment**

- Unless the notice to file a return is issued late, the latest date that Richard can file a paper self-assessment tax return for 2014/15 is 31 October 2015.

- However, he has until 31 January 2016 to file his self-assessment tax return for 2014/15 online.

Compliance checks

- If HM Revenue and Customs intend to carry out a compliance check into Richard's 2014/15 tax return, they will have to notify him within 12 months of the date that they receive the return.

- HM Revenue and Customs have the right to carry out a compliance check as regards the completeness and accuracy of any return, and such a check may be made on a completely random basis.

- However, compliance checks are generally carried out because of a suspicion that income has been undeclared or because deductions have been incorrectly claimed. For example, where accounting ratios are out of line with industry norms.

ACCA marking scheme			
			Marks
(a)		Motor expenses – Richard	1.0
		Motor expenses – Chef	0.5
		Parking fines	0.5
		Property expenses	1.0
		Decorating – Restaurant	0.5
		Decorating – Apartment	0.5
		Legal fees – Purchase of property	0.5
		Working – Capital allowances	
		– Private use (PU) car – in own column	0.5
		– Car 2 – in general pool	0.5
		WDA on PU car	1.0
		WDA on Car 2	0.5
			7.0
(b)		Employer's Class 1 calculation	1.0
		Deducting employment allowance	0.5
		Class 1A calculation	0.5
		Car benefit calculation	1.0
			3.0
(c)	(i)	Paper return date	1.0
		Online return date	1.0
			2.0
	(ii)	Notify within 12 months of date received return	1.0
		Right to carry out compliance check on any return	1.0
		Generally carried out if suspicion of errors in return	1.0
			3.0
Total			**15.0**

TRADING LOSSES

23 NORMA (ADAPTED)

> **Key answer tips**
>
> The first part required the computation of taxable income for five tax years before considering loss relief. Marks should have been gained here in laying out pro forma computations and filling in the easy numbers before applying the opening and closing year rules to establish the trading income assessments. A loss arises in the final tax year and so the trading income assessment in that year will be £Nil.
>
> The second part involved consideration of the options available for loss relief, including a terminal loss.
>
> It is important to communicate to the examiner that you know the loss relief rules; however you must apply the knowledge to the specific facts of the question.

(a) **Taxable income and gains before loss relief**

	2010/11	2011/12	2012/13	2013/14	2014/15
	£	£	£	£	£
Trading income (W)	25,250	17,000	15,500	8,835	Nil
Employment income					
(£11,400 × 10/12)					9,500
Interest income	2,000	2,000	2,000	2,000	2,000
	——	——	——	——	——
Total income	27,250	19,000	17,500	10,835	11,500
Less: PA	(10,000)	(10,000)	(10,000)	(10,000)	(10,000)
	——	——	——	——	——
Taxable income	17,250	9,000	7,500	835	1,500
	——	——	——	——	——
Taxable gain				35,000	
				——	

Working: Trading income

Tax year	Basis of assessment	£	£
2010/11	Actual basis (1.5.10 – 5.4.11)		
	Period to 31.12.10	21,000	
	1.1.11 – 5.4.11 (£17,000 × 3/12)	4,250	
		——	25,250
2011/12	Year ended 31.12.11		17,000
2012/13	Year ended 31.12.12		15,500
2013/14	Year ended 31.12.13		8,835
2014/15	Year of cessation		
	Period to 31 May 2014	(11,000)	
	Less: Overlap profits (1.1.11 – 5.4.11)		
	(£17,000 × 3/12)	(4,250)	
		——	
	Trading loss/Trading assessment	(15,250)	Nil
		——	

Tutorial note

If the trader does not have a 31 March (or 5 April) year end you should be looking for overlap relief.

The overlap relief increases the loss of the final year and is included in the calculation of the terminal loss.

(b)   **Options available to utilise loss arising in period ended 31 May 2014**

(1)   **Relief against total income**

The loss arising in 2014/15 can be set against total income in 2014/15 and/or 2013/14, in either order.

(i)   Setting the loss against total income of 2014/15 first (i.e. employment income and bank interest) would reduce total income to £Nil, would waste the personal allowance and save tax at 10% on £1,500 (see Tutorial Note).

The remaining loss of £3,750 (£15,250 – £11,500) could be offset against total income of 2013/14, wasting part of the personal allowance and saving tax at 10% on £835 (see Tutorial Note).

(ii)   Setting the loss against total income of 2013/14 first would reduce total income to £Nil, would waste the personal allowance and save tax at 10% on £835.

The remaining loss of £4,415 (£15,250 – £10,835) could be offset against total income of 2014/15, which would waste part of the personal allowance and save tax at 10% on £1,500.

Tutorial note

The rate of tax saving in 2013/14 on £835 and in 2014/15 on £1,500 is 10% because Norma's taxable income includes savings income which will fall into the first £2,880 of taxable income in those years.

(2)   **Relief against chargeable gains**

Alternatively, once a claim has been made to offset trading losses against total income in 2013/14, a claim can be made to offset any remaining losses against chargeable gains in 2013/14 instead of total income in 2014/15.

Accordingly, the £4,415 loss remaining after the offset against total income in 2013/14 could be set against the chargeable gain arising in that year.

Assuming that the current tax rates apply throughout this question, this will save tax at 18% on some of the gain and 28% on the remaining gain (see note).

Tutorial note

Currently, before loss relief, there is £31,030 (£31,865 – £835) of gain in the basic rate band and £3,970 (£35,000 – £31,030) in the higher rate band.

So using £4,415 of loss against the gain would save 28% on the top £3,970 of the gain, and 18% on £445 (£4,415 – £3,970).

(3) **Terminal loss relief**

The loss arising in the final 12 months of trading can be set against:

- available trading profits
- in the year of cessation, and
- the three preceding tax years
- on a last-in-first-out (LIFO) basis.

Calculation of terminal loss

				£
(1)	6 April before cessation to date of cessation (6.4.14 – 31.5.14) (£11,000 loss × 2/5)			4,400
(2)	12 months before cessation to 5 April before cessation			

		£		
1.6.13 – 31.12.13 (£8,835 profit × 7/12)		5,154	Profit	
1.1.14 – 5.4.14 (£11,000 loss × 3/5)		(6,600)	Loss	
		(1,446)	Net Loss	1,446

				£
(3)	Overlap relief 1.1.11 – 5.4.11 (£17,000 × 3/12)			4,250
	Terminal loss			10,096

Utilisation of terminal loss

Norma has no trading profits in 2014/15, the year of cessation.

The terminal loss can therefore be carried back against the trading profits arising in the preceding three years, on a LIFO basis, as follows:

	2011/12 £	2012/13 £	2013/14 £
Trading income	17,000	15,500	8,835
Less: Terminal loss relief	(Nil)	(1,261)	(8,835)
	17,000	14,239	Nil
Interest income	2,000	2,000	2,000
Net income	19,000	16,239	2,000
Less: PA	(10,000)	(10,000)	(10,000)
Taxable income	9,000	6,239	Nil

The terminal loss reduces taxable income in 2013/14 to £Nil, wasting the personal allowance and saving tax at 10% on £835.

The remaining loss of £1,261 (£10,096 – £8,835) is then offset against the taxable income in 2012/13, saving tax at 20% on £1,261.

Tutorial note

Taxable income before loss relief in 2012/13 of £7,500 comprises other income of £5,500 (£15,500 – £10,000 PA) and savings income of £2,000. Tax on the loss of £1,261 is therefore saved at 20% on other income.

24 LEONARDO

Key answer tips

An opening year loss relief question, requiring a calculation of the assessments for the first few tax years and consideration of loss claims available.

Part (b) should have provided easy marks in stating due dates for making elections.

(a) **Assessments**

Tax year	Basis period		£
2011/12	Actual basis		
	(1.9.11 – 5.4.12)	7/9 × £40,500	31,500
2012/13	First 12 months		
	(1.9.11 – 31.8.12)	£40,500 – (3/12 × £54,000)	27,000
2013/14	CYB (y/e 31.5.13)	Loss	Nil
2014/15	CYB (y/e 31.5.14)	Loss	Nil
2015/16	CYB (y/e 31.5.15)		11,000

Key answer tips

As Leonardo will not be making any significant profits in the foreseeable future there is no point in carrying losses forward, therefore offset the losses as soon as possible.

Note the question does not require any calculation of tax savings, just computations to show how the loss would be utilised.

Loss memoranda

Loss in 2013/14

	£
Loss in y/e 31.5.2013	54,000
Less: Relief given in 2012/13 when applying the opening year rules (£54,000 × 3/12)	(13,500)
	40,500
Less: Special opening year loss relief – in 2011/12	(31,500)
– in 2012/13	(9,000)
	Nil

Loss in 2014/15

	£
Loss in y/e 31.5.2014	27,000
Less: Special opening year loss relief in 2012/13 (£27,000 – £9,000)	(18,000)
Loss carried forward to 2015/16	9,000

Assessments after loss relief claims

	2011/12 £	2012/13 £	2013/14 £	2014/15 £	2015/16 £
Trading income	31,500	27,000	Nil	Nil	11,000
Less: Loss relief b/f	–	–	–	–	(9,000)
	31,500	27,000	Nil	Nil	2,000
Less: Special opening year loss relief					
– 2013/14 Loss	(31,500)	(9,000)			
– 2014/15 Loss		(18,000)			
Net income	Nil	Nil	Nil	Nil	2,000

> ***Tutorial note***
>
> *Under special opening year loss provisions, losses that arise in the **first four tax years** of a trade may be set off against:*
>
> - *the total income*
> - *of the three years preceding the tax year of loss*
> - *on a first-in-first-out (FIFO) basis.*
>
> *Losses should be dealt with in **chronological** order. Therefore the loss arising in 2013/14 is utilised before the loss arising in 2014/15.*

(b) **Loss relief time limits**

    (i) **Special opening year loss relief and 'normal' loss relief against total income**

        For claims to carry back losses in the first four years of a trade against income of the three preceding years, and claims to set-off losses against income of the year of the loss and income of the preceding year, the claim must be made:

        - within 12 months from 31 January next following the tax year in which the loss was sustained.

        In the case of the loss sustained in the year ended 31 May 2013 (i.e. the loss in 2013/14), the claim must be made:

        - by 31 January 2016.

        In the case of the loss sustained in the year ended 31 May 2014 (i.e. the loss in 2014/15), the claim must be made:

        - by 31 January 2017.

    (ii) **Carry forward of losses**

        There is no specific statutory time limit on claims to carry forward losses against future trading income.

        However, a claim to establish the amount of the loss to be carried forward must be made:

        - within four years from the end of the tax year in which the loss was sustained

        In the case of the loss sustained in the year ended 31 May 2014 (i.e. the loss in 2014/15)

        - by 5 April 2019.

25   DEE ZYNE (ADAPTED) *Walk in the footsteps of a top tutor*

Key answer tips

An individual that is employed for part of the year, then sets up a business which is initially loss-making, is a common scenario in examination questions.

The calculation of the adjusted loss was straight forward provided you remembered to time apportion WDAs in the opening period of account.

Part (b) required consideration of alternative claims for Dee's trading loss, which is a common requirement in loss relief questions and you should therefore make sure that you are well prepared for this. The highlighted words in the written sections are key phrases that markers are looking for.

Tutor's top tips

In this question, Dee has 5 April as her year end, so the capital allowances are calculated for the period ended 5 April 2015.

However, where a sole trader chooses a different year end, remember that the capital allowances are always calculated for the period of account before matching profits or losses to tax years.

(a)   **Tax adjusted trading loss – 2014/15**

	£
Trading loss	(11,440)
Patent royalties (Note)	(500)
Capital allowances (W)	(5,690)
	(17,630)

Tutorial note

The patent royalties were incurred for trade purposes and are therefore deductible in computing the tax adjusted trading loss. As the question says they have not been accounted for in arriving at the loss of £11,440, they must be adjusted for and will increase the loss.

Working – Capital allowances

	General Pool £	Car £	Allowances £
Additions (no AIA)			
Car (between 96 – 130 g/km)	10,400		
Car (> 130 g/km) (Note 1)		17,800	
Additions (with AIA)			
Computer	1,257		
Office furniture	2,175		
	———		
	3,432		
Less: AIA (Note 2)	(3,432)		3,432
	———		
		Nil	
Less: WDA (18% × 9/12)	(1,404)		1,404
Less: WDA (8% × 9/12) (Note 3)		(1,068) × 80%	854
		———	
TWDV c/f	8,996	16,732	
	———	———	———
Total allowances			5,690
			———

Tutorial note

1   *Capital allowances on purchases of cars are calculated based on their CO_2 emissions.*

     The car with CO_2 emissions of between 96 – 130 g/km is put in the main pool and is eligible for a writing down allowance at 18%.

     The car with CO_2 emissions of > 130 g/km is a private use car, has its own column and is eligible for a writing down allowance at 8%.

2   *The maximum AIA and the WDAs are time apportioned because Dee's period of account is only nine months' in length.*

     However, the maximum AIA of £375,000 (£500,000 × 9/12) exceeds the total qualifying expenditure and therefore all of the expenditure is eligible for relief.

3   *Only private use by the owner restricts capital allowances. Private use of the employee's motor car therefore does not affect the capital allowance claim, but will instead result in an assessable employment benefit for that employee.*

(b)   **Alternative uses of trading loss**

Tutor's top tips

When you are describing use of losses, you must be very specific about exactly what the loss can be set against, and when. For example, don't just say 'the loss can be set off in the current year'. Specify in which tax year that is, and state that the loss can be set against total income.

The examiner has said that the use of section numbers is not required and is not encouraged at the expense of explaining the relief.

- The loss could have been claimed against total income for 2013/14 and/or 2014/15.

- By claiming loss relief against her total income for 2014/15, Dee has relieved the loss entirely at the basic rate of 20% and reduced her income tax liability by £3,526 (£17,630 × 20%).

- If the loss is carried back to 2013/14 when Dee's total income was £80,000, Dee could relieve the loss entirely at the higher rate of 40% and reduced her income tax liability by £7,052 (£17,630 × 40%).

- The loss is incurred within the first four years of trading, so a claim for special opening year loss relief could have been made against total income for the three years 2011/12 to 2013/14, earliest first.

- As Dee's total income in the years 2011/12 to 2013/14 was £80,000, this would also have relieved the loss at the higher rate of 40%, and resulted in an income tax refund of £7,052 (£17,630 × 40%).

26 SAMANTHA FABRIQUE (ADAPTED)

Key answer tips

This is a losses question that requires you to choose the best use of the loss.

Given the information about gains it should be fairly obvious that you need to consider a claim against capital gains. However, remember that this only saves tax at 18% or 28% (for a higher rate taxpayer) and can only happen after a claim against total income has been made first in the same tax year.

Be careful to consider the loss relief restriction which applies to loss claims against total income other than the profits of the same trade. This restriction did not apply in the question as originally set, as these rules did not exist then.

Part (a) should have provided easy marks listing the factors a taxpayer takes into account when deciding what to do with a loss.

(a) **Factors influencing choice of loss relief claims**

- The rate of income tax or capital gains tax at which relief will be obtained, with preference being given to income charged at the higher rate of 40% or additional rate of 45%.

- The timing of the relief obtained, with a claim against total income/chargeable gains of the current year or preceding year resulting in earlier relief than a claim against future trading profits.

- The extent to which personal allowances and the capital gains annual exempt amount may be wasted.

Key answer tips

As long as you addressed the factors influencing the choice of relief, not what the relief options are, you should have scored well here.

(b) **Taxable income**

	2013/14 £	2014/15 £	2015/16 £
Trading income	21,600	Nil	10,500
Interest	52,100	3,800	1,500
	73,700	3,800	12,000
Less: Loss relief		(Nil)	
– against trade profits (no restriction)	(21,600)		
– against other income (restricted)	(50,000)		
	2,100	3,800	12,000
Less: PA	(10,000)	(10,000)	(10,000)
Taxable income	Nil	Nil	2,000

Taxable gains

	2013/14 £	2014/15 £	2015/16 £
Capital gains	53,300	Nil	11,300
Less: Trading loss relief	(10,300)		
	43,000	Nil	11,300
Less: Capital loss b/f	–	–	(300)
	43,000	Nil	11,000
Less: AEA	(11,000)	(wasted)	(11,000)
Taxable gains	32,000	Nil	Nil

Tutorial note

The loss relief in 2013/14 against total income is restricted due to the cap on income tax reliefs. The losses offset against profits from the same trade are not restricted; therefore £21,600 of loss can be set against trading income. A further £50,000 of loss relief is available as this is the higher of £50,000 and 25% of total income (£73,700 × 25% = £18,425).

Although these two claims are both set off against total income in the computation, you may find it helpful to separate them out to ensure you relieve the correct amount of loss.

Key answer tips

Where loss questions require you to set off a loss against income and gains, make sure that you keep your income tax computation and CGT computation **separate**.

This is not only technically correct, but will also make it easier for you to see where best to set off the losses and apply your PA and AEA, and much easier for the marker to mark your answer!

Loss memorandum

	£
Loss in 2014/15	81,900
Less: Relief against total income	
2014/15 (no claim as income covered by PA)	(Nil)
2013/14 – total claim	(71,600)
	———
Loss remaining	10,300
Less: Relief against chargeable gains	
2013/14	(10,300)
	———
Loss carried forward	Nil
	———

Utilisation of losses

Trading loss

Loss relief has been claimed:

- against total income for 2013/14,
- then against the chargeable gains of 2013/14.

This gives relief at the earliest date and at the highest rates of tax.

Capital loss

The capital loss for 2014/15 is carried forward and set against the chargeable gains for 2015/16.

The use of brought forward capital losses is restricted to the level that reduces gains down to equal the annual exempt amount (£11,300 – £300 = £11,000).

The balance of the loss £3,100 (£3,400 – £300) is carried forward against future gains.

Tutorial note

For 2013/14, if relief is claimed, the personal allowance is partially wasted in that year and the tax saving will be at 40% and 20% for income tax and 28% for capital gains.

Offsetting losses in 2014/15 however would utilise £3,800 of the loss, would waste the personal allowance and would not save any tax.

A claim against total income must be made before relief against chargeable gains can be considered.

Carrying all of the loss forward would use £10,500 of the loss in 2015/16 (as could only carry forward against future trading profits from the same trade), would waste most of the personal allowance and would only save tax partly at 20% and partly at 10%.

The taxable income (before loss relief) of £2,000 represents other income of £500 (£10,500 – £10,000) and savings income of £1,500. Tax of £100 (20% × £500) would be saved on the other income.

All of the savings income falls in the starting rate band of £2,880 and tax of £150 (10% × £1,500) would therefore be saved. The remaining loss would not be relieved until subsequent years.

The optimum relief is therefore to claim against total income for 2013/14, then against the chargeable gains of 2013/14, since this gives relief at the earliest date and at the highest rates of tax.

Examiner's report

This question was generally not answered well.

Although it was technically the most demanding question on the paper, requiring a bit more thought than the other four questions, it was quite short and should not have presented too many difficulties for reasonably well prepared candidates.

In part (a) many candidates explained the loss reliefs that were available rather than the factors that must be taken into account when deciding which loss reliefs to actually claim.

In part (b) it was extremely disappointing to see the vast majority of candidates include the capital gains in their computation of taxable income. The capital gains annual exempt amount was often then deducted against the combined figure of taxable income and taxable gains.

Many candidates claimed loss relief against the total income for the year of the loss despite this income clearly being covered by the personal allowance.

Very few candidates, even if they showed the capital gains separately, claimed loss relief against capital gains.

ACCA marking scheme		
		Marks
(a)	Rate of tax	1.0
	Timing of relief	1.0
	Personal allowance and annual exempt amount	1.0
		3.0
(b)	Trading income	0.5
	Building society interest	0.5
	Loss relief against total income	2.0
	Personal allowance	0.5
	Capital gains	1.5
	Loss relief against capital gains	1.0
	Capital loss carried forward	1.0
	Explanation of most beneficial route	5.0
		12.0
Total		**15.0**

27 MICHAEL AND SEAN *Walk in the footsteps of a top tutor*

Key answer tips

Part (a) offered four easy marks to identify the reliefs available for New Individual Savings Accounts, pensions, Gift Aid, Entrepreneurs' relief and capital allowances.

Part (b) was tricky and the hardest part of the whole examination. It involved opening and closing year losses.

Consideration of the optimum use of the losses was required together with the identification of the rates at which tax would be saved. A good knowledge of the loss relief rules and a lot of practice at application prior to sitting the exam was needed to score well on this part in the time given.

In order to score well in part (b) computations alone showing the different loss reliefs were not enough; explanations of how the reliefs work and advice on the most beneficial course of action were also needed.

Tutor's top tips

When you need to explain how tax policies can encourage individuals to take certain actions, always think about how those actions can save tax for the individual.

By opening a NISA, individuals can save income tax on the interest.

By saving money in a pension fund, individuals can save income tax by either reducing their employment income or extending their basic and higher rate bands.

By donating money to a charity, the individual can save income tax by either reducing their employment income (payroll deduction scheme) or extending their basic and higher rate bands (Gift Aid donations).

When the sole trader buys plant and machinery he gets capital allowances that reduce trading profits saving income tax.

(a) **Government tax policies**

(i) **Individuals to save**

Saving is encouraged by offering individuals tax incentives such as tax-free New Individual Savings Accounts (NISAs) and tax relief on pension contributions.

(ii) **Individuals to support charities**

Charitable support is encouraged by giving individuals tax relief on donations made through the Gift Aid scheme or the Payroll Deduction Scheme.

(iii) **Entrepreneurs to build businesses and invest in plant and machinery**

Entrepreneurs are encouraged to build their own businesses through various capital gains tax reliefs such as Entrepreneurs' relief.

Investment in plant and machinery is encouraged through capital allowances.

(b)   **Michael**

Tutor's top tips

It is difficult to comment on loss relief by just reading the scenario. Set up the income tax computations for each tax year involved, bringing in the figures given in the question.

This will give a clear picture of the position and will help to decide on the appropriate reliefs for the loss. It will also make it easier to comment on the tax savings and possible wastage of the personal allowance.

Loss relief available

1   **Special opening year loss relief**

The loss of £24,600 for 2013/14 can be claimed against total income for the three preceding years, earliest first, since it is incurred in the first four years of trading.

Amount of loss claim

The loss relief claim will therefore be £16,800 in 2010/11 and £7,800 (£24,600 – £16,800) in 2011/12.

Tax saving

For 2010/11 this will waste Michael's personal allowance, with the balance of the claim of £6,800 (£16,800 – £10,000) (W2) saving income tax at the basic rate of 20%.

For 2011/12 Michael has income of £8,735 (£50,600 – £10,000 – £31,865) subject to income tax at the higher rate of 40%, so the claim of £7,800 will save tax at the higher rate.

2   **Carry loss forward**

Alternatively, Michael could have carried the trading loss forward against future trading profits, but the trading profit of £7,100 for 2014/15 is less than the personal allowance, and therefore no tax is saved in that year. There is no information available regarding future trading profits.

Most beneficial

Claim special opening year loss relief.

Tutorial note

A standard loss relief claim against total income in the year of the loss (2013/14) and/or the preceding year (2012/13) is not possible since Michael does not have any income for either of these years.

Special opening year loss relief is one claim for all three years (if there is sufficient loss) on a FIFO basis, it is not possible to only claim in one year, and it is an 'all or nothing relief' (i.e. cannot restrict the offset to preserve the personal allowance).

Note that the limit on the amount of loss relief that can be deducted from other income in any tax year does not need to be considered in this question, as the loss is not sufficiently high for it to be an issue.

Workings

(W1) Opening year assessments

	£
2013/14 – Actual basis	
1.7.2013 – 5.4.2014 Loss of £24,600	Nil
2014/15 – Current year basis	
Year ended 5.4.2015	7,100

(W2) Taxable income for 2010/11 to 2014/15 (ignoring loss relief)

	2010/11	2011/12	2012/13	2013/14	2014/15
	£	£	£	£	£
Employment income	16,800	50,600	Nil	Nil	Nil
Trading income				Nil	7,100
Less: PA	(10,000)	(10,000)	Nil	Nil	(10,000)
Taxable income	6,800	40,600	Nil	Nil	Nil
Basic rate band		(31,865)			
Taxed at higher rate		8,735			

The loss carried back is offset against income before the personal allowance is deducted. This means that £10,000 of the loss each year does not actually save tax as it merely replaces the personal allowance. This working enables you to see how much of the loss actually saves tax and at what rate.

Sean

Amount of the loss

The unused overlap profits brought forward are added to the loss for the year ended 31 December 2014, so the total loss for 2014/15 is £26,700 (£23,100 + £3,600).

Loss relief available

1   Terminal loss relief

The whole of the loss can be claimed as a terminal loss since it is for the final 12 months of trading.

The claim is against trading income for the tax year of the loss and the three preceding tax years, latest first.

Amount of loss claim

The terminal loss claim will therefore be £3,700 in 2013/14, £18,900 in 2012/13 and £4,100 (£26,700 – £3,700 – £18,900) in 2011/12.

Tax saving

The property business profits are sufficient to utilise Sean's personal allowance for each year, so the loss relief claims will save income tax at the basic rate of 20%.

2   Standard loss relief against total income

Alternatively, Sean could have initially claimed loss relief against his total income for 2014/15 and/or 2013/14, but this would have wasted his personal allowance for either or both of those years.

Most beneficial

Claim terminal loss relief.

Tutorial note

A claim against future trading profits is not available since the business is ceasing and a trading loss can only be carried forward against future trading profits of the same trade.

A terminal loss claim is against trading profits only, on a LIFO basis, and is an 'all or nothing' relief (i.e. cannot restrict the offset to preserve the personal allowance).

The terminal is the loss of the last 12 months of trading. It is normally calculated as follows:

	£
6 April before cessation to the date of cessation	
Actual trading loss in this period (£23,100 × 9/12)	*17,325*
Overlap profits not yet relieved	*3,600*
12 months before cessation to 5 April before cessation	
Actual trading loss in this period (£23,100 × 3/12)	*5,775*
	―――
Terminal loss	*26,700*
	―――

However when the final period of account is 12 months long it is unnecessary to prepare this detailed working and it is acceptable to take the examiner's approach of simply adding the unused overlap profits to the trading loss for the final 12 month period.

Examiner's report

Part (a) was generally well answered, although candidates should note that where just one or two marks are available for a requirement then just a short sentence is required – not a detailed explanation.

Not surprisingly, part (b) was the section of the paper that caused the most problems.

For Michael, the claims should have been fairly straightforward given that he only had one source of income for each year. However, some candidates were not even aware that a claim could be made against total income.

For Sean, a few candidates suggested that the loss be carried forward despite the trade ceasing. In both cases, it was generally not appreciated that the most advantageous choice of loss relief claims would generally preserve the benefit of personal allowances.

ACCA marking scheme				
				Marks
(a)	(i)	Saving		1.0
	(ii)	Charitable support		1.0
	(iii)	Businesses		1.0
		Plant and machinery		1.0
				4.0
(b)	**Michael**			
	Relief against total income – opening year loss relief			1.0
	Amount of loss claims			1.0
	Rate of tax saved – 2010/11			1.0
	– 2011/12			1.0
	Carry forward			1.0
	Sean			
	Available loss			1.0
	Terminal loss relief			1.0
	Amount of loss claim			1.0
	Rate of tax saved			1.5
	Relief against total income			1.5
				11.0
Total				**15.0**

PARTNERSHIPS

28 PETER, QUINTON AND ROGER (ADAPTED)

Key answer tips

A loss making partnership presents a tricky problem and it is important to approach the computation in part (b) with care.

Firstly, profits/(losses) need to be allocated to each partner and then the opening year rules applied for each partner according to the date they joined the firm.

There are many loss relief options available. A brief mention of each is all you have time for in the exam. Be careful not to go into too much detail and there is no need to discuss the relative merits of each option in this question.

It is much better to mention all the reliefs available and applicable to the question succinctly than to talk about any one relief in great detail.

(a) **Basis of assessment – Joining partners**

- Each partner is treated as a sole trader running a business.
- The commencement rules therefore apply when a partner joins the partnership, with the first year of assessment being on an actual basis (i.e. date of commencement to the following 5 April).

(b)   **Trading income assessments**

	Peter £	Quinton £	Roger £
2011/12 Peter and Quinton Actual basis (1 January 2012 to 5 April 2012) (£40,000 × 1/2 × 3/12)	5,000	5,000	
2012/13 Peter and Quinton CYB (y/e 31 December 2012) (£40,000 × 1/2)	20,000	20,000	
Roger Actual basis (1 January 2013 to 5 April 2013) (£90,000 × 1/3 × 3/12)			7,500
2013/14 All partners – CYB (y/e 31 December 2013) (£90,000 × 1/3)	30,000	30,000	30,000

Tutorial note

The commencement rules apply to:

*   *Peter and Quinton from 2011/12, as the partnership started on 1 January 2012.*

*   *Roger from 2012/13, since he joined as a partner on 1 January 2013.*

(c)   **Possible methods of relieving trading loss for 2014/15**

*   Peter, Quinton and Roger each have a tax adjusted trading loss of £10,000 (£30,000 × 1/3) for 2014/15.

*   Peter resigned as a partner on 31 December 2014. His unrelieved overlap profits of £5,000 (1 January 2012 to 5 April 2012) will therefore increase his loss to £15,000 (£10,000 + £5,000).

*   *Carry forward relief:*

    Quinton and Roger can carry their share of the loss forward against their first available future trading profits arising in the same trade.

*   *Relief against total income:*

    Peter, Quinton and Roger can claim relief against their total income for 2014/15 and/or 2013/14.

*   *Special opening year loss relief:*

    Peter, Quinton and Roger can carry back their share of the loss against their total income for 2011/12 to 2013/14, earliest year first.

- *Terminal loss relief:*

  Peter can carry back his share of the loss of the last 12 months trading against his trading profits for 2013/14.

  He has insufficient losses to carry back the loss any further. If he had more losses, he could carry back the loss and make a claim in respect of 2012/13 and 2011/12, in that order.

Key answer tips

The requirement is to 'State the possible ways to relieve the losses'. Therefore there will be no marks for discussing in detail the relative merits of each claim and which would be the most beneficial.

Remember that it is much better to mention all the reliefs available and applicable to the question succinctly than to talk about any one relief in great detail.

29 AE, BEE, CAE, AND DEE (ADAPTED) *Walk in the footsteps of a top tutor*

Key answer tips

This question tests the basis of assessment rules, but with the application of the rules to partnerships, and includes the opening year rules and overlap profits.

A well prepared student should have been able to secure good marks on this question and each part is independent.

Part (b) of this question has been amended due to syllabus changes.

Tutor's top tips

Part (a) deals with both the partnership profit sharing rules together with straightforward opening year rules. Opening year rules can be tricky, but are commonly tested so you should make sure that you are prepared for a question on this topic.

(a) **Ae, Bee & Cae**

Tax year	Basis of assessment	Ae £	Bee £	Cae £
2012/13	Actual basis 1 July 2012 to 5 April 2013 £54,000 × 9/12 × 1/2	20,250	20,250	
2013/14	CYB (y/e 30 June 2013) £54,000 × 1/2	27,000	27,000	
2014/15	CYB (y/e 30 June 2014) £66,000 × 1/2	33,000	33,000	
	Actual basis 1 July 2014 to 5 April 2015 £87,000 × 9/12 × 1/3			21,750

Tutorial note

The commencement rules apply for Ae & Bee in the tax year 2012/13 and for Cae in the tax year 2014/15, as this is the tax year in which each partner started to trade.

In the case of Cae, the fact that the partnership had been trading in the years before is not relevant.

(b) (i) **Dee – Relief for losses**

Key answer tips

Part (b) has been rewritten due to syllabus changes since the question was originally set. It now tests the new cap on loss reliefs against total income and loss reliefs in a partnership.

Dee can claim relief against her total income in 2014/15 (the year of the loss), and/or 2013/14 (the previous tax year). As she has no trading profits in either year, any loss relief will be claimed against other income and the cap on income tax reliefs will apply. The maximum claim is therefore £50,000 in each year as this is greater than 25% of Dee's adjusted total income of £85,000 (i.e. 25% × £85,000 = £21,250). The remaining loss must then be carried forward for relief against her share of any future trading profits from the partnership.

It is likely that she will obtain relief for some of the carried forward loss in 2016/17 when she anticipates that the business will become profitable again. The fact that the business will then be a partnership does not prevent the future loss relief.

Loss memorandum

	£
Loss in 2014/15	165,000
Less: Relief against total income	
2014/15 (maximum)	(50,000)
2013/14 (maximum)	(50,000)
Carried forward against future trading profits	65,000

Tutorial note

It is assumed that the £5,000 loss for 2013/14 has been carried back to 2012/13 and set off against the savings income in that year.

Tutor's top tips

Since the question asked you to 'explain' the loss reliefs available, it is important to write narrative describing the loss reliefs as well as calculating the amount of loss relief that will be claimed.

(ii) **Eae – relief for losses**

Eae will be entitled to claim relief for her share of the partnership's trading loss in the year ended 5 April 2016 as follows.

- The loss could be claimed against total income for 2015/16 (the year of the loss) and/or 2014/15 (the previous tax year).

- Since Eae has just joined the partnership, the loss is incurred within the first four years of trading from her perspective; therefore a claim for special opening year loss relief could be made against total income for the three years 2012/13 to 2014/15, starting with the earliest first.

Tutorial note

Since the question refers to a 'small' loss, it can be assumed that the cap on income tax reliefs is not relevant in this part.

Examiner's report

This question was extremely well answered by the majority of candidates, many of whom scored maximum marks.

One of the main problems in the answers of poorer candidates was not showing the appropriate tax years, thus losing a lot of marks throughout.

Note: *The final part of the examiner's report referred to the original part (b) which is no longer examinable following syllabus changes.*

ACCA marking scheme				
				Marks
(a)		Ae, Bee & Cae – 2012/13		1.5
		– 2013/14		1.0
		– 2014/15 Ae & Bee		1.0
		– 2014/15 Cae		1.5
				5.0
(b)	(i)	Dee	– 2014/15 claim	1.0
			– 2013/14 claim	1.0
			– loss carried forward	1.0
	(ii)	Eae	– total income claim	1.0
			– opening years relief	1.0
				5.0
Total				**10.0**

30   AUY MAN AND BIM MEN (ADAPTED)   *Walk in the footsteps of a top tutor*

Key answer tips

This question was unusual in that the scenario was a partnership. However, this should not have caused concern as there were many easy marks to be gained.

Part (a) may have caused some problems if the definition of residence status had not been learnt, however it was only worth 2 marks. The rules regarding the definition of residence have been amended since this question was set and are now more complicated.

Parts (b) and (c) involved preparing familiar adjustment of profits and capital allowances computations, followed by a straightforward allocation of profits between the partners and Class 4 NIC calculations.

Tutor's top tips

Remember to read the requirement carefully.

This question has clear mark allocations, which should be used to allocate the time spent on each section. Don't overrun on parts which carry only a few marks.

The first part required the application of the residence status rules. Note that just stating the rules would not have gained full marks. You must apply the knowledge to the facts of the specific individuals.

(a)   **Residence status**

- Auy will be treated as resident in the United Kingdom (UK) for 2014/15 as she was present in the UK for 190 days and therefore she meets the first automatic UK residency test (i.e. in the UK for at least 183 days in the tax year) .

- Bim will be treated as resident in the UK for 2014/15 as she was previously resident In the UK, was present here for between 91 and 120 days and she meets two of the sufficient ties tests.

  She has a home in the UK which she makes use of for 100 days during the tax year (the 'accommodation' test) and she has spent 90 days or more in the UK during both of the previous tax years (the 'days in UK' test).

Tutorial note

When considering residence it is important to approach a question systematically.

*You should firstly consider whether the individual meets one of the automatic non-residence tests. However, it is clear that these are not relevant here as the examiner has told you in the question that both individuals **are** resident in the UK.*

Secondly, you should consider whether the individual meets one of the automatic residence tests. This is the case for Auy in this question.

Finally, if neither of the automatic tests are applicable, you should consider how many days the individual has spent in the UK, whether they were resident in the UK within the previous three tax years, and how many of the sufficient ties tests are met. The table showing the number of ties which must be met is provided in the examination.

These rules are now more complex than they were when this question was originally set.

(b)   **Tax adjusted trading profit – year ended 5 April 2015**

Tutor's top tips

Part (b) gives you clear guidance on the approach that is needed for an adjustment of profits, and you should follow this – starting with the net profit and then making the necessary adjustments.

Work through the notes and the plant and machinery information in order. Ensure you have dealt with every single item, and shown, as stated in the requirement, nil in the profits adjustment where an adjustment is not necessary, as marks are given for this.

If you are not sure of how to deal with an item, make a sensible assumption and move on, but do not ignore it, or waste unnecessary time.

Note that as the question has asked you to 'calculate' the adjusted profits you do not need to explain each adjustment that you make, but you should show any workings.

	£	£
Net profit	87,780	
Depreciation	3,400	
Entertaining employees (Note 1)	0	
Appropriation of profit (Note 2)	4,000	
Capital allowances (W1)		12,938
	95,180	12,938
	(12,938)	
Tax adjusted trading profit	82,242	

Tutorial note

1   The only exception to the non-deductibility of entertainment expenditure is when it is in respect of employees.

2   Salaries paid to a partner are not allowable. They merely represent an agreed form of allocation of the partnership profits in the partnership agreement. Appropriations of profit (i.e. drawings such as partner's salaries) need to be added back to profit.

Allocation of profits – 2014/15

Tutor's top tips

Once the net profit of the partnership has been calculated, it must be allocated between the partners in accordance with the partnership agreement in force in the accounting period.

Note that full marks can be obtained for this part in showing clearly how you have allocated the amounts; even if your tax adjusted trading profit figure is incorrect.

	Total	Auy Man	Bim Men
	£	£	£
Salary	4,000		4,000
Interest (£56,000/£34,000 at 5%)	4,500	2,800	1,700
Balance (80%/20%)	73,742	58,994	14,748
	82,242	61,794	20,448

Trading income assessments – 2014/15

	£
Auy Man	61,794
Bim Man	20,448

Tutorial note

The profit share for each partner must now be assessed in the correct tax year. The basis of assessment rules need to be applied to determine in which tax year the profits are assessed.

However, in this question the partnership has a 5 April year end and therefore the rule is simple: the actual profits for the year ended 5 April 2015 will be assessed in 2014/15.

Working – Capital allowances

Tutor's top tips

A standard capital allowances computation is required; however it is slightly unusual in that the only transactions in the year involve cars. There are no other additions and therefore there is no AIA.

The rules for cars need to be known in detail and applied carefully here. Each of the cars has a different CO_2 emissions rate so these need to be considered carefully to determine the correct available capital allowances. Also watch out for 'private use' adjustments.

	£	Main pool £	Motor car (1) £	Special rate pool £	Allowances £
TWDV b/f		3,100	18,000		
Additions (no AIA)					
Motor car (3)		14,200			
Motor car (4)				8,700	
		17,300	18,000	8,700	
WDA (18%)		(3,114)			3,114
WDA (8%)			(1,440) × 70%		1,008
WDA (8%)				(696)	696
Addition (with FYA)					
Motor car (2)	11,600				
FYA (100%)	(11,600) × 70%				8,120
		Nil			
TWDV c/f		14,186	16,560	8,004	
Total allowances					12,938

Tutorial note

1   *Capital allowances on car purchases are calculated based on the CO_2 emissions of the car as follows:*

      –   *New car with CO_2 emissions of ≤ 95 g/km:*
          eligible for a FYA of 100% (i.e. Motor Car (2))

      –   *CO_2 emissions of between 96 – 130 g/km:*
          put in main pool and eligible for a WDA at 18% (i.e. Motor Car (3))

      –   *CO_2 emissions of > 130 g/km:*
          put in special rate pool and eligible for a WDA at 8% (i.e. Motor Car (4))

     However, cars with an element of private use by a partner (i.e. owner of the business) are given a separate column and only the business use percentage of the allowances can be claimed.

     Note that motor car (2) is a de-pooled asset and in practice should be given a separate column and carried forward at a tax written down value of Nil. When it is sold it will result in a balancing charge, but only the business proportion will be taxed.

2   *Motor car (1), which was owned at the beginning of the year, has CO_2 emissions of > 130 g/km and is therefore eligible for a WDA at 8%. This must then be adjusted for private use.*

(c)   **Class 4 National Insurance Contributions – 2014/15**

Tutor's top tips

Straightforward computations are required for this part.

Remember that full marks can be obtained for this part, even if your allocation of profit to the partners is incorrect, provided that you use the partners' profit allocations which you have calculated in part (b) as the basis of your national insurance calculations. Just make sure that you clearly show the method of calculation.

        Auy Man

	£
(£41,865 – £7,956) × 9%	3,052
(£61,794 – £41,865) × 2%	399
	3,451

        Bim Men

(£20,448 – £7,956) × 9%	1,124

ACCA marking scheme		
		Marks
(a)	Auy Man	1.0
	Bim Men	1.0
		2.0
(b)	**Trading profit**	
	Depreciation	0.5
	Entertaining employees	0.5
	Appropriation of profit	0.5
	Deduction of capital allowances	0.5
	Capital allowances – Main pool	1.0
	– Motor car (1)	1.5
	– Special rate pool	1.5
	– FYA	1.5
	Trading income assessments	
	Salary	0.5
	Interest on capital	1.0
	Balance of profits	1.0
		10.0
(c)	Auy Man	2.0
	Bim Men	1.0
		3.0
Total		**15.0**

PENSIONS AND NIC

31   JOHN BEACH (ADAPTED) *Walk in the footsteps of a top tutor*

Key answer tips

Part (a) required the computation of the income tax liability of an employed individual with several employment benefits and both an occupational and personal pension scheme.

Straight forward marks were available for calculating the employment benefits. The pension scheme contributions were a little trickier and required knowledge of how tax relief is obtained for both types of contribution and the operation of the annual allowance.

The NIC computations in part (b) were relatively straightforward provided the key facts about National Insurance contributions had been learnt.

Tutor's top tips

For part (a) a systematic approach is needed, taking one note at a time, and therefore breaking up the information given into smaller, manageable chunks.

Make the marker your friend, if you keep your calculations clear and easy to read you will score much higher marks. Always ensure your workings are clearly labelled.

(a) **Income tax computation – 2014/15**

	£	£
Director's remuneration		184,000
Mileage allowance (W1)		1,425
		———
		185,425
Occupational pension contributions (Note 1)		(28,000)
		———
		157,425
Beneficial loan (W2)		1,070
Long service award (gold watch) – exempt		nil
		———
Total income		158,495
Less: PA (W3,W4)		(Nil)
		———
Taxable income		158,495
		———

Income tax
£		
69,865 × 20% (W5)		13,973
88,630 × 40%		35,452
———		
158,495		
———		
Income tax liability		49,425
		———

Tutorial notes

1   Tax relief for contributions to occupational pension schemes is given by deduction from employment income. Contributions made by an employer are an exempt employment benefit.

2   Long service awards are exempt where there has been at least 20 years of service by the employee and where the cost is £50 or less for each year of service.

3   No personal allowance is available as John's adjusted net income is too high (see W4).

Workings

(W1) Mileage allowance

	£
Amount received by John (5,960 miles × 60p)	3,576
Less: Approved mileage allowance	
(4,270 + 510) = 4,780 miles × 45p	(2,151)
	———
Taxable benefit	1,425
	———

Tutorial note

Travel between home and office is ordinary commuting which does not qualify for tax relief.

(W2) Beneficial loan

Tutor's top tips

The question states that the average method is used to calculate the taxable benefit, so do not waste time also preparing calculations using the precise (or accurate) method which will score no marks.

John repaid £24,000 (£12,000 + £12,000) of the loan during 2014/15, so the outstanding balance at 5 April 2015 is £60,000 (£84,000 – £24,000).

The benefit calculated using the average method is:

	£
((£84,000 + £60,000) ÷ 2) × 3.25%	2,340
Less: Interest paid	(1,270)
Taxable benefit	1,070

(W3) Personal pension contributions

Tutor's top tips

You must calculate the amount of personal pension contributions paid by John in 2014/15 by reference to the available annual allowance. Read the question carefully as this provides some hints on how to approach the calculation.

Remember that ALL contributions count towards the available annual allowance. Once you have calculated the available annual allowance for 2014/15, you will need to consider the unused allowances from the three prior tax years. Although John's contributions will be the same in these prior years, you need to factor in that the annual allowance was £50,000 per annum prior to the 2014/15 tax year.

	£
Annual allowance – 2014/15	40,000
Less: Employee occupational scheme contributions	(28,000)
Employer occupational scheme contributions	(10,000)
Unused annual allowance – 2014/15	2,000
Available annual allowance for previous three tax years ((£50,000-£38,000) × 3)	36,000
Maximum available annual allowance in 2014/15 (£2,000 + £36,000)	£38,000

John would therefore have made gross personal pension contributions (PPCs) of £38,000 in 2014/15.

Tutorial note

1 *Both employee and employer pension contributions count towards the annual allowance.*

2 *Unused annual allowances can be carried forward for three years.*

3 *The annual allowance is the maximum gross amount that can be contributed into pension schemes in a tax year without incurring an annual allowance charge. The £38,000 is therefore the gross amount of contributions made by John into the personal pension scheme.*

4 *Higher and additional rate tax relief for personal pension scheme contributions is given by the extension of the basic and higher rate tax bands (W5).*

5 *Remember that the PPCs also affect John's adjusted net income (ANI) for the purposes of calculating the PA available.*

(W4) Personal allowance

	£
Total income = net income	158,495
Less: Gross PPCs	(38,000)
ANI	120,495

As John's ANI exceeds £120,000 (i.e. £100,000 + (2 × £10,000)) there is no PA available to John in 2014/15.

(W5) **Extension of basic and additional rate bands**

	Basic rate £	Additional rate £
Basic rate band threshold	31,865	150,000
Plus: Gross PPCs	38,000	38,000
	———	———
Extended basic and additional rate bands	69,865	188,000
	———	———

(b)   **National Insurance contributions – 2014/15**

Tutor's top tips

You are asked to calculate the Class 1 and Class 1A National Insurance contributions payable by both John Beach and Surf plc. Make sure you present your answer so that it is clear which contributions are paid by whom.

John Beach

- Class 1 primary NICs payable:

    Cash earnings = (£184,000 salary + £1,425 mileage allowance) = £185,425

	£
(£41,865 – £7,956) × 12%	4,069
(£185,425 – £41,865) × 2%	2,871
	———
	6,940
	———

Tutorial note

Class 1 NICs are assessed on cash earnings without any allowable deductions. Accordingly pension contributions are ignored, and non-cash benefits are not subject to Class 1 NICs.

Note that the taxable mileage allowance paid in respect of home to office travel is cash earnings and is subject to Class 1 NIC.

Surf plc

- Class 1 secondary NICs payable:

    Also payable on cash earnings of £185,425.

	£
(£185,425 – £7,956) × 13.8%	24,491
	———

- Class 1A NICs payable:

    Payable on non-cash benefits of £1,070 (Part (a)).

	£
(£1,070 × 13.8%)	148
	———

Tutorial note

Class 1A NIC is payable on non-cash employment benefits by the employer only.

Examiner's report

Part (a) was generally very well answered, and the only aspect that caused problems was the calculation of the personal pension contributions. A common mistake was to gross up the contributions.

Part (b) was well answered by the majority of candidates.

Note: *The examiner's report has been edited to remove comments on elements of the question that have been deleted due to changes to the exam format.*

ACCA marking scheme		Marks
(a)	Director's remuneration	0.5
	Mileage allowance received	0.5
	Authorised mileage allowance	1.0
	Taxable benefit on mileage	0.5
	Occupational pension contributions	1.0
	Outstanding balance on loan	1.0
	Loan interest at official rate	1.0
	Interest paid	0.5
	Long service award	0.5
	Personal allowance	1.0
	Income tax liability	1.0
	Unused annual allowance for 2014/15	0.5
	Total available annual allowance	1.0
	Extension of basic and higher rate bands	1.0
		11.0
(b)	Employee Class 1 NIC	2.0
	Employer Class 1 NIC	1.0
	Employer Class 1A NIC	1.0
		4.0
Total		**15.0**

32   DUKE AND EARL UPPER-CRUST (ADAPTED)

Key answer tips

Part (a) involves a couple of income tax computations:

*   one for an additional rate taxpayer with reduced personal allowances requiring the extension of the basic rate band for personal pension contributions;

*   the other is a basic rate taxpayer requiring no entries in the income tax computation in respect of pension contributions.

Parts (b) and (c) are wholly written, covering the rules on the pension contributions annual allowance.

(a)   **Duke Upper-Crust – Income tax computation – 2014/15**

	£
Employment income (£114,000 + £40,000)	154,000
Less: Adjusted PA (W1)	(500)
Taxable income	153,500

£		
66,865 × 20% (W2)	13,373
86,635 × 40%	34,654
153,500	
Income tax liability	48,027

Net amount paid to pension company

All of Duke's pension contribution of £35,000 qualifies for tax relief as it is less than 100% of his earnings (£154,000).

He will therefore have paid £28,000 (£35,000 less 20%) to his personal pension company.

Workings

(W1) Adjusted personal allowance

	£	£
Personal allowance		10,000
Employment income = Total income		
= Net income	154,000	
Less: Gross PPC	(35,000)	
	119,000	
Less: Limit	(100,000)	
	19,000 × 50%	(9,500)
Adjusted PA		500

(W2) Extension of basic rate and additional rate band

	£	£
Basic rate band threshold	31,865	150,000
Plus: Gross PPC	35,000	35,000
Extended basic rate band	66,865	185,000

As taxable income of £153,500, is all employment income, and falls below £185,000, all of the income in excess of £66,865 will be taxed at 40%.

Earl Upper-Crust – Income tax computation – 2014/15

	£
Trading profit	34,000
Less: PA	(10,000)
Taxable income	24,000
Income tax liability (£24,000 × 20%)	4,800

Tutorial note

As Earl is a basic rate taxpayer there is no need to extend his basic rate band for the pension contribution. Relief for allowable contributions is given at source.

Net amount paid to pension company

Only £34,000 (gross) of Earl's pension contribution of £40,000 qualifies for tax relief, since relief is only available up to 100% of his earnings.

The amount of tax relief is therefore £6,800 (£34,000 at 20%), which is given at source, and so Earl will have paid £33,200 (£40,000 – £6,800) to his personal pension company.

(b) **Effect of annual allowance**

- Although tax relief is available on pension contributions up to the amount of earnings for a particular tax year, there is no limit as to the amount of earnings that can qualify for tax relief. However, the annual allowance limit of £40,000 acts as an effective annual limit.

- Any tax relieved contributions paid in excess of the annual allowance are subjected to an additional tax charge for the tax year in which the contributions are paid. The tax charge is calculated at the taxpayer's marginal rate of tax.

- The annual allowance limit (£40,000) is increased by any unused annual allowance from the previous three tax years.

- Prior to 2014/15, the annual allowance was £50,000, and therefore this is the amount that can be carried forward from 2011/12, 2012/13, and 2013/14, subject to any reduction for contributions in these years.

(c)   **Maximum additional contributions**

- There is no restriction regarding the amounts that Duke and Earl could have contributed into a personal pension scheme for 2014/15.
- However, tax relief is available on the lower of:
  (i)   Gross contributions paid
  (ii)   Higher of:
  - £3,600
  - 100% of relevant earnings

Duke

- Duke could therefore receive tax relief on additional contributions of up to £119,000 (£154,000 relevant earnings – £35,000 gross contributions paid).
- However, if his gross contributions exceed £55,000 (£40,000 plus unused AA limit of £5,000 (£50,000 – £45,000) in each of the last three years) an annual allowance charge will arise.

Earl

- Earl has already made a pension contribution in excess of his earnings for 2014/15, and so any additional pension contribution would not have qualified for any tax relief.

Due date

- Pension contributions for 2014/15 would have had to have been paid between 6 April 2014 and 5 April 2015, as it is not possible to carry back contributions.

Key answer tips

Remember to state the due date of payment; an easy mark to gain, but easily lost if you are not efficient in making sure you address all parts of a question or run out of time.

This could have been answered early in the answer before getting involved with the computations, to make sure you gain the easy marks as quickly as possible.

---

33   VANESSA AND SERENE (ADAPTED) *Walk in the footsteps of a top tutor*

Key answer tips

This question is fairly straightforward, and asks for income tax and national insurance computations for a sole trader and an employee. It should be a good test of whether you have learnt the basics well.

Tutor's top tips

You should be able to score highly on part (a), although there were a few tricky points.

Where a sole trader has just purchased a single asset, there is no need to do a full capital allowances computation, as long as you show your workings. Remember that only the business proportion of the allowances can be claimed.

The car provided to Serene has CO_2 emissions between 76 g/km and 94 g/km and therefore a special rate applies. Note also that the question specifically says that the company did not provide Serene with any fuel for private journeys, so don't waste time calculating a fuel benefit! (See examiner's comments).

Watch out for the pension contributions:

- *the contribution to the personal pension is paid net, and extra relief is given by extending the basic rate band by the gross amount*

- *the occupational pension is paid gross, and is simply deducted from employment income.*

Try not to get these confused.

Remember that you will score full marks for the calculation of tax if you use the correct rates, even if your taxable income figure is wrong.

(a) **Vanessa Serve**

Income tax computation – 2014/15

	Total	Other income	Savings income
	£	£	£
Trading income	52,400		
Less: Capital allowances (W1)	(1,310)		
	51,090	51,090	
Interest received (Note)	1,100		1,100
Total income	52,190	51,090	1,100
Less: PA	(10,000)	(10,000)	
Taxable income	42,190	41,090	1,100
Income tax:			
On Other income (W2)	38,265	× 20%	7,653
On Other income	2,825	× 40%	1,130
	41,090		
On Savings income	1,100	× 40%	440
	42,190		
Income tax liability and payable			9,223

Tutorial note

Interest from NS&I investment accounts is taxable and is received gross.

Vanessa's income tax payable is the same as her income tax liability as all of her income was received gross.

Workings

(W1) Capital allowances

The car has CO_2 emissions of between 96 g/km and 130 g/km and is therefore eligible for a WDA at 18%.

Only the business proportion of the allowance can be claimed.

WDA = (£10,400 × 18%) × 14,000/20,000 = £1,310

(W2) Extension of basic rate band

	£
Basic rate band threshold	31,865
Plus: Personal pension contribution (gross)	6,400
Extended basic rate band	38,265

Serene Volley

Income tax computation – 2014/15

	£
Salary	26,400
Less: Pension contributions (£26,400 × 5%)	(1,320)
	25,080
Car benefit (W)	3,458
Employment income	28,538
Interest from NS&I Savings Certificate (exempt)	Nil
Total income	28,538
Less: Personal allowance	(10,000)
Taxable income	18,538
Income tax liability (£18,538 × 20%)	3,708
Less: Tax suffered at source – PAYE	(3,016)
Income tax payable	692

Working: Car benefit

CO_2 emissions = 87 g/km, available all year

As the CO_2 emissions are between 76 – 94 g/km, the basic percentage of 11% is used.

However, as it is a diesel car, the appropriate percentage is 14%.

Car benefit (£24,700 × 14%) = £3,458

There is no fuel benefit as private petrol is not provided by the company.

(b) **National Insurance**

Tutor's top tips

Remember that sole traders pay Class 2 and 4 national insurance, whereas employees pay Class 1 primary contributions.

As long as you calculate Vanessa's Class 4 contributions correctly based on your adjusted trading income figure from part (a), you will be awarded full marks.

Vanessa Serve

	£
Class 2 NICs	
(£2.75 for 52 weeks)	143
	———
Class 4 NICs	
(£41,865 – £7,956) × 9%	3,052
(£51,090 – £41,865) × 2%	184
	———
	3,236
	———
Serene Volley	
Class 1 NICs	
(£26,400 – £7,956) × 12%	2,213
	———

Tutorial note

Class 1 NICs are based on cash earnings, without any allowable deductions. Therefore, pension contributions are ignored, and benefits are not subject to employee Class 1 NIC.

Benefits are assessed to Class 1A NICs which are payable by the employer only, not the employee. However, the requirement is to calculate the NICs payable by the employee only, not the employer.

Examiner's comments

This question was generally very well answered.

In part (a) many candidates did not appreciate that it was not necessary to gross up the interest received from an NS&I investment account, or that interest from savings certificates is exempt from tax.

The contribution to the occupational pension scheme was often used to extend the basic rate tax band rather than being deducted in calculating employment income.

Many candidates wasted time in calculating a fuel benefit despite the question clearly stating that no fuel was provided for private journeys.

Note: *The examiner's report has been edited to remove comments on elements of the question that have been deleted due to changes to the exam format.*

ACCA marking scheme		
		Marks
(a)	**Vanessa Serve**	
	Trading profit	0.5
	Capital allowances	1.5
	Interest from NS&I	1.0
	Personal allowance	0.5
	Extension of basic rate band	1.0
	Income tax	1.0
	Serene Volley	
	Salary	0.5
	Pension contributions	1.0
	Car benefit	1.5
	Interest from savings certificate	0.5
	Personal allowance	0.5
	Income tax	1.0
	Tax suffered at source – PAYE	0.5
		──
		11.0
		──
(b)	**Vanessa Serve**	
	Class 2 NIC	1.0
	Class 4 NIC	1.5
	Serene Volley	
	Class 1 NIC	1.5
		──
		4.0
		──
Total		**15.0**
		──

34   ANN, BASIL AND CHLOE (ADAPTED) *Walk in the footsteps of a top tutor*

Key answer tips

This question covers the pension relief available to three different individuals. This should be a straightforward question provided the rules had been learnt.

Relief for pension contributions is a key area of the syllabus that is tested regularly.

Note that this question has been adapted in light of the new syllabus and part (b) is a new addition to the question to test new rules introduced in the pension legislation.

Tutor's top tips

This question is classic in style with individuals in different situations contributing to a personal pension scheme.

The key is to:

- *Remember the definition of 'relevant earnings'*

- *Compare the gross contributions paid with the 'relevant earnings' (or £3,600 if this is higher) to decide the maximum tax allowable amount*

- *Consider the annual allowance limit charge.*

Note that the maximum contribution allowable for a person without any relevant earnings in the tax year (£3,600) and the annual allowance limit are given in the exam.

(b) (i) **Ann Peach**

Amount of pension contributions qualifying for relief

Ann can obtain relief for the lower of:

(1) Gross contributions of £42,000

(2) Higher of:

    (i) £3,600

    (ii) Relevant earnings of £38,000

Therefore, £38,000 will qualify for tax relief and her basic rate band is extended to £69,865 (W).

Her taxable income falls into the extended basic rate band and is therefore taxed at 20%.

Income tax liability

	£
Trading profit	38,000
Less: PA	(10,000)
Taxable income	28,000
Income tax liability (£28,000 × 20%) (W)	5,600

Working: Extension of basic rate band

	£
Basic rate band	31,865
Plus: Gross allowable pension contributions	38,000
Extended basic rate band	69,865

Tutorial note

The annual allowance charge is not applicable to Ann, as although she has made pension contributions in excess of £40,000, she has only received tax relief for contributions of £38,000. The annual allowance charge is intended to claw back tax relief for contributions in excess of the limit, which is not applicable here.

(ii) **Basil Plum**

Amount of pension contributions qualifying for relief

Basil can obtain relief for the lower of:

(1) Gross contributions of £40,000

(2) Higher of:

    (i) £3,600

    (ii) Relevant earnings of £120,000

Therefore, £40,000 will qualify for tax relief and his basic rate band is extended to £71,865 (W2).

Tutorial note

Note that this scenario differs from the treatment for Ann (above) as Ann had contributed more than 100% of her relevant earnings into a scheme, whereas Basil has contributed less than 100% of his relevant earnings into the scheme.

Income tax liability

	£
Employment income	120,000
Less: PA (W1)	(10,000)
Taxable income	110,000

Income tax:	£
£	
71,865 × 20% (W2)	14,373
38,135 × 40%	15,254
110,000	
Income tax liability	29,627

Workings

(W1) Personal allowance

Although Basil's income is in excess of £100,000, there is no restriction of his personal allowance and he will be entitled to the full personal allowance as his adjusted net income (ANI) is £80,000.
His ANI is calculated as follows:

	£
Employment income = Total income = Net income	120,000
Less: Gross PPC	(40,000)
ANI	80,000

(W2) Extension of basic rate band

	£
Basic rate band	31,865
Plus: Gross PPC	40,000
Extended basic rate band	71,865

(iii) Chloe Pear

Amount of pension contributions qualifying for relief

Property income does not qualify as relevant earnings (unless it relates to qualifying furnished holiday accommodation).

Therefore, as Chloe has no relevant earnings, she will only receive tax relief on £3,600 of her pension contributions.

Her taxable income falls below the basic rate band even before extension due to pension contributions; therefore her income is taxed at 20%.

Income tax liability

	£
Property income	23,900
Less: PA	(10,000)
Taxable income	13,900
Income tax (£13,900 × 20%)	2,780

(b) Consequences of Banana Bank plc contributing into Basil's pension fund

There is no limit on the amount that can be put into a personal pension fund by an individual and his employer.

However, there is a maximum amount of tax relief

- that the individual can obtain on their contributions into the scheme (i.e. the maximum contribution each year), and
- on the total contributions paid into a scheme by the individual and others on their behalf (i.e. the annual allowance).

If Basil's employer contributes into his personal pension scheme, the employer contributions are:

- a tax free benefit
- a tax allowable deduction in Banana Bank plc's corporation tax computation
- combined with Basil's contributions and compared to the annual allowance of £40,000 (£50,000 in 2013/14 and prior years).

Where the annual allowance is exceeded (as is the case if Banana Bank plc pays £100,000 into the scheme):

- a tax charge is levied on the individual.

Unused allowances from the previous three tax years can be carried forward.

In Basil's case the maximum contributions that can be made in 2014/15 without incurring the annual allowance charge is £70,000 (£40,000 + (£50,000 − £40,000) × 3).

Basil will therefore pay the annual allowance charge in 2014/15 on contributions of £70,000 (£40,000 + £100,000 − £70,000).

The tax charge is calculated at the taxpayer's marginal rate of tax. In Basil's case this is 40%, as the higher rate band is extended by his gross contribution in 2014/15 to £190,000 (£150,000 + £40,000).

Examiner's report

This question was reasonably well answered, although there were few first-rate answers.

For the first taxpayer the most common mistake was to extend the basic rate tax band by the amount of contributions rather than earnings.

For the second taxpayer the basic rate band was often extended by the amount of annual allowance rather than the contributions.

Very few candidates stated that the third taxpayer would have received tax relief up to £3,600 of her contributions.

Note: *This question has been adapted in light of the new syllabus and part (b) is a new addition to the question.*

ACCA marking scheme		
		Marks
(a)	**Ann Peach**	
	Taxable income	0.5
	Extension of basic rate band	1.0
	Income tax	0.5
	Amount qualifying for tax relief	1.0
		3.0
	Basil Plum	
	Taxable income	0.5
	Personal allowance	1.0
	Extension of basic rate band	1.5
	Income tax	1.0
	Amount qualifying for tax relief	1.0
		5.0

ACCA marking scheme		
		Marks
Chloe Pear		
Taxable income		0.5
Income tax		0.5
Amount qualifying for tax relief		1.0
		————
		2.0
		————
(b)	Employer contributions	
	No limit to contributions	0.5
	Limit to relief for individual	0.5
	Tax free benefit	0.5
	Tax allowable deduction for corporation tax	0.5
	Exceeding annual allowance	0.5
	Unused annual allowance for previous 3 years brought forward	0.5
	Basil's maximum contributions	1.0
	Charged at marginal rate	0.5
	Charged at 40% for Basil	0.5
		————
		5.0
		————
Total		**15.0**
		————

SELF-ASSESSMENT

35   PI CASSO

Key answer tips

The first part of this question involves detailed calculations to work out the income tax, Class 4 NICs and CGT payable under self-assessment and when the payments are due.

The remaining three parts require wholly written answers on three common self-assessment topics.

These are marks which are easy to gain if you have done your work, but easy to lose if you do not invest the time in learning the self-assessment rules.

(a)   **Due dates of payment of tax under self-assessment**

Due date	Tax year	Payment	£
31 July 2014	2013/14	Second payment on account (W1)	2,240
31 January 2015	2013/14	Balancing payment (W2)	5,980
31 January 2015	2014/15	First payment on account (W3)	1,860
31 July 2015	2014/15	Second payment on account (W3)	1,860
31 January 2016	2014/15	Balancing payment (W4)	Nil
31 January 2016	2015/16	First payment on account (W5)	1,860

Workings

(W1) Second payment on account – 2013/14

The second payment on account for 2013/14 is based on Pi's income tax and Class 4 NIC liability for 2012/13 as follows:

	£
Income tax	3,240
Class 4 NICs	1,240
	4,480
Payments on account (50%)	2,240

(W2) Balancing payment – 2013/14

	£
Income tax	4,100
Class 4 NICs	1,480
Capital gains tax (see Tutorial Note)	4,880
	10,460
Less: POAs (£2,240 × 2)	(4,480)
Balancing payment	5,980

(W3) Payments on account – 2014/15

Pi will make a claim to reduce her total payments on account for 2014/15 as follows:

	£
Income tax	2,730
Class 4 NICs	990
	3,720
Payments on account (50%)	1,860

(W4) Balancing payment – 2014/15

	£
Income tax and Class 4 NICs	3,720
Capital gains tax	Nil
	3,720
Less: POAs (£1,860 × 2)	(3,720)
Balancing payment	Nil

(W5) First payments on account – 2015/16

The first payment on account for 2015/16 is based on Pi's income tax and Class 4 NIC liability for 2014/15.

	£
Income tax	2,730
Class 4 NICs	990
	3,720
Payments on account (50%)	1,860

Tutorial note

Class 2 NICs are payable twice a year on 31 January in the tax year and 31 July after the end of the tax year. Payments can be made in a number of ways, including six monthly direct debits or following payment requests by HMRC. Note that they are not paid via the self-assessment system.

Capital gains tax is collected via self-assessment and is payable all in one payment on 31 January following the end of the tax year along with the balancing payment for income tax and Class 4 NICs.

Payments on account are not required for CGT.

(b) Reduction of payments on account to £Nil

- If Pi's payments on account for 2014/15 were reduced to £Nil, then she would be charged late payment interest on the payments due of £1,860 from the relevant due date to the date of payment.

- A penalty will be charged if the claim to reduce the payments on account to £Nil was made fraudulently or negligently.

(c) Latest submission date

- Unless the return is issued late, the latest date that Pi can submit a paper based self-assessment tax return for 2014/15 is 31 October 2015.

- If Pi completes a paper based tax return by 31 October 2015 then HMRC will prepare a self-assessment tax computation on her behalf.

- Alternatively, Pi has until 31 January 2016 to file her self-assessment tax return for 2014/15 online.

- A self-assessment tax computation is then automatically provided as part of the filing process.

(d) HMRC enquiry

- If HMRC intend to enquire into Pi's 2014/15 tax return they will have to notify her within twelve months of the date that they receive the return.

- HMRC has the right to enquire into the completeness and accuracy of any return and such an enquiry may be made on a completely random basis.

- However, enquiries are generally made because of a suspicion that income has been undeclared or because deductions have been incorrectly claimed.

Examiner's report

This question was generally not well answered, and the impression given was that candidates had struggled with time management and had a lack of time remaining for this question.

Part (a) caused the most problems, with the vast majority of candidates not being able to demonstrate how payments are calculated and paid under the self-assessment system.

Class 2 national insurance contributions were often incorrectly included, whilst few candidates appreciated that a claim to reduce payments on account was possible.

In part (b) most candidates appreciated that interest would be due, but very few mentioned the potential penalty that could be charged.

It was disappointing that the self-assessment tax return submission dates were often not know in part (c), despite these being covered in the Finance Act article.

The same comment applies to part (d). Candidates often gave a long list of reasons why HMRC could enquire into a return, but failed to mention that an enquiry might be on a completely random basis.

	ACCA marking scheme	
		Marks
(a)	Second payment on account for 2013/14	1.5
	Balancing payment for 2013/14	2.0
	Claim to reduce payments on account	1.0
	Payments on account for 2014/15	1.0
	Balancing payment for 2014/15	0.5
	First payment on account for 2015/16	1.0
		7.0
(b)	Interest	1.0
	Penalty	1.0
		2.0
(c)	Paper based return	2.0
	Return filed online	1.0
		3.0
(d)	Notification date	1.0
	Random basis	1.0
	Income/Deductions	1.0
		3.0
Total		**15.0**

36   ERNEST VADER (ADAPTED) *Walk in the footsteps of a top tutor*

Key answer tips

This is an unusual and tricky question requiring substantial written explanations and statements about ethical issues and self-assessment.

Detailed knowledge is required to score highly on this question; however the application of some basic common sense would also gain quite a few marks.

No calculations are required except for part (d) (i) which accounts for 2 of the 15 marks.

The highlighted words are key words or phrases that markers are looking for.

The legislation regarding the general anti-abuse rule and dishonest conduct by tax agents did not exist when this question was first written, and have been added since to test these areas. The original part (c) tested HMRC's information powers, which are no longer in the syllabus and this part has therefore been removed.

Tutor's top tips

Remember to read the requirement carefully and allocate the time spent on each section.

Part (a) covers the classic topic of tax evasion and tax avoidance, but care must be taken to apply your knowledge to Ernest's particular problem. This part also tests awareness of the new general anti-abuse rule.

Part (b) requires the application of common sense if the specific guidelines have not been learnt.

Parts (c) and (d) are straightforward if the self-assessment rules have been learnt, difficult if not learnt.

(a)   **Tax evasion and tax avoidance**

- Tax evasion is illegal and involves the reduction of tax liabilities by not providing information to which HMRC is entitled, or providing HMRC with deliberately false information.

- In contrast, tax avoidance involves the minimisation of tax liabilities by the use of any lawful means. However, certain tax avoidance schemes must be disclosed to HMRC.

- The general anti-abuse rule is a rule to counter artificial and abusive schemes where arrangements (which cannot be regarded as a reasonable course of action) are put in place deliberately to avoid tax.

- If Ernest makes no disclosure of the capital gain then this will be viewed as tax evasion as his tax liability for 2014/15 will be understated by £18,000.

(b)   **Failure to disclose information to HMRC**

- How to deal with the failure to disclose is a matter of professional judgement, and a trainee Chartered Certified Accountant would be expected to act honestly and with integrity.

- Ernest should therefore be advised to disclose details of the capital gain to HMRC.

- If such disclosure is not made by Ernest, you would be obliged to report under the money laundering regulations, and you should also consider ceasing to act for Ernest.

   In these circumstances you would be advised to notify HMRC that you no longer act for him although you should not provide any reason for this.

(c)   **Penalties for tax agent**

- A civil penalty may be payable by the firm if they have engaged in dishonest conduct, which may be the case if they have failed to supply the information HMRC have requested.

- The potential penalty is up to £50,000.

(d)   **Interest and penalties**

   (i)   **Interest payable**

- Late payment interest will run from the due date of 31 January 2016 to the payment date of 31 July 2016.

- The interest charge will therefore be £270 (£18,000 × 3% × 6/12).

   (ii)   **Penalties**

- Ernest has made an error on his 2014/15 tax return as he did not disclose the capital gain.

- The amount of penalty for an incorrect return is based on the tax due but unpaid as a result of the error (i.e. the CGT liability of £18,000).

- However, the actual penalty payable is also based on Ernest's behaviour (i.e. whether it was a genuine mistake or a careless or deliberate error).

- Since Ernest is now aware that he should have reported the capital gain and has now chosen not to do so he would appear to have made a deliberate error. The penalty is therefore likely to be 70% of the tax unpaid which is £12,600 (£18,000 × 70%). This assumes that there is no attempt at concealment.

- The penalty would have been substantially reduced if Ernest had disclosed the capital gain, especially if the disclosure had been unprompted by HMRC prior to discovery. The maximum reduction would be to 20% of the tax unpaid.

Examiner's report

This question was not well answered, with many candidates attempting it as their final question or omitting it altogether. This was disappointing given that several sections covered recent tax management changes which have been covered in my Finance Act articles.

In part (a) most candidates knew the difference between tax evasion and tax avoidance, but many failed to score an easy mark by not stating that the taxpayer's actions would be viewed as tax evasion.

Part (b) caused problems for most candidates but a common sense approach would have gained most of the available marks. Unfortunately, far too many candidates instead just incorrectly explained that it would be necessary to inform HMRC themselves.

The examiner's comments on the original part (c) have been deleted as this related to HMRC's information powers which are no longer in the syllabus.

There was little excuse for getting the interest calculation wrong in part (d) as candidates were given the tax liability, the due date, the payment date and the rate of interest.

There was little awareness of the penalty regime.

ACCA marking scheme			Marks
(a)		Tax evasion	1.0
		Tax avoidance	1.0
		General anti-abuse rule	1.0
		Non-disclosure of disposal	1.0
			4.0
(b)		Professional judgement	1.0
		Advise disclosure	1.0
		Obligation to report	1.0
			3.0
(c)		Civil penalty for dishonest conduct	1.0
		£50,000 penalty	1.0
			2.0
(d)	(i)	Interest period	1.0
		Calculation	1.0
			2.0
	(ii)	Based on tax lost	1.0
		Link to behaviour	1.0
		Deliberate error so penalty 70%	1.0
		Disclosure – potential reduction to 20%	1.0
			4.0
Total			**15.0**

CHARGEABLE GAINS

INDIVIDUALS – CAPITAL GAINS TAX

37   MICHAEL CHIN (ADAPTED)   *Online question assistance*

Key answer tips

A typical exam question on capital gains tax with a series of disposals covering a variety of topics. All the disposals are gifts and so you must use the market value as the proceeds in the computation of the gains.

Be careful to distinguish disposals (1) and (2), which do qualify for gift relief, from the remaining disposals which do not.

Capital gains tax liability – 2014/15

	£	£
Disposal of business (Note 1)		
Goodwill		
Deemed proceeds = MV	60,000	
Less: Cost	(Nil)	
	————	
	60,000	
Less: Gift relief	(60,000)	
	————	Nil
Freehold property		
Deemed proceeds = MV	150,000	
Less: Cost	(86,000)	
	————	
	64,000	
Less: Gift relief (W1)	(48,000)	
	————	16,000
Net current assets		Nil
		————
Total chargeable gains on the disposal of the business		16,000
Ordinary shares in Minnow Ltd (Note 2)		
Deemed proceeds = MV	180,000	
Less: Cost	(87,500)	
	————	
	92,500	
Less: Gift relief (W2)	(74,000)	
	————	18,500
		————
Chargeable gains c/f		34,500

	£	£
Chargeable gains b/f		34,500
Painting (Notes 3 and 4)		
Deemed proceeds = MV	7,500	
Less: Cost	(4,000)	
Gain	3,500	
Chargeable gain restricted to maximum of:		
5/3 × (£7,500 – £6,000)	2,500	2,500
Necklace (Note 5)		
Non-wasting chattel bought and sold for < £6,000 = exempt		Nil
Total chargeable gains		37,000
Less: Capital loss b/f (W3)		(15,700)
Net chargeable gains		21,300
Less: AEA		(11,000)
Taxable gain		10,300
Capital gains tax (£10,300 × 28%)		2,884

Tutorial note

1   *Disposal of the business*

The disposal of a business is treated as separate disposals of each chargeable asset in the business. A gain must be calculated on each chargeable asset.

However, the net current assets (e.g. inventory, receivables and payables) are not chargeable assets for capital gains tax purposes.

Gift relief is available on any gain relating to qualifying business assets disposed of, but not on the portion of the building that had never been used for his business.

Per the question, Entrepreneurs' relief is to be ignored.

However, for tutorial purposes, where the full gain is not covered by gift relief, Entrepreneurs' relief may be available. It will be available on the gift of a qualifying business provided the business has been owned for at least 12 months. If this is the case, the remaining gain would be taxed at 10%.

2   *Minnow Ltd shares*

Gift relief is available as ordinary shares in an unquoted trading company are qualifying assets for gift relief purposes. However full relief is not available as the company holds investments.

Per the question, Entrepreneurs' relief is to be ignored. However, for tutorial purposes, where the full gain is not covered by gift relief, Entrepreneurs' relief may be available.

> *It will be available on the gift of shares in a personal trading company (i.e. donor owns at least 5% interest), provided the donor works for the company and has owned the shares for at least one year. If this is the case, the remaining gain would be taxed at 10%.*
>
> 3 Painting
>
> *A painting is not a qualifying asset for gift relief purposes.*
>
> 4 Chattels
>
> *It is important to be able to recognise when an asset is a chattel (i.e. tangible and moveable) and therefore that the disposal is subject to special rules. The painting and antique necklace are both chattels.*

Workings

(W1) Freehold property

The proportion of the freehold property gain relating to non-business use is £16,000 (£64,000 × 25%), and this amount does not qualify for gift relief.

The remaining gain of £48,000 (£64,000 − £16,000) can be held over (i.e. deferred) with a gift relief claim.

(W2) Minnow Ltd

The gift relief in respect of the ordinary shares in Minnow Ltd is restricted because the shares are in Michael's personal trading company (i.e. he owns > 5%) and the company has investment assets.

The proportion of gain eligible for gift relief is the proportion of chargeable business assets to chargeable assets, calculated as follows:

Gift relief = (£92,500 × £200,000/£250,000) = £74,000

(W3) Capital loss brought forward

	£
Chargeable gain – 2013/14	12,100
Less: Capital loss b/f from 2012/13 – Used (Note)	(1,100)
	————
Net chargeable gains	11,000
Less: AEA	(11,000)
	————
Taxable gain	Nil
	————

Tutorial note

The capital loss brought forward is used in 2013/14 but the offset is restricted to preserve the annual exempt amount.

Loss left to c/f to 2014/15

	£
Capital loss	16,800
Less: Used in 2013/14 (above)	(1,100)
Loss c/f to 2014/15	15,700

38 DAVID AND ANGELA BROOK (ADAPTED) *Walk in the footsteps of a top tutor*

Key answer tips

A classic question involving the calculation of capital gains tax liabilities of both a husband and his wife, with joint assets and assets held personally.

Tutor's top tips

Be careful to spot the exempt asset. You don't need to do any calculations for this asset; just say that it is exempt!

Predictably a husband and wife nil gain/nil loss transfer is included, with the subsequent disposal by the recipient spouse.

Remember also to consider Entrepreneurs' relief on the disposal of shares.

David Brook

Capital gains tax liability – 2014/15

	£
Motor car (exempt)	Nil
House (W1)	31,439
Shares in Bend Ltd (W3)	Nil
Total chargeable gains	31,439
Less: AEA	(11,000)
Taxable gain	20,439
Capital gains tax (£20,439 at 18%)	3,679

Tutorial note

David has no taxable income. All of his gains therefore fall into his basic rate band and are taxed at 18%. Entrepreneurs' relief is not available on any of his gains.

Angela Brook

Capital gains tax liability – 2014/15

	£
House (W1)	31,439
Ordinary shares in Bend Ltd (W4)	26,400
	————
Total chargeable gains	57,839
Less: AEA	(11,000)
	————
Taxable gain	46,839
	————

£		
555 × 18% (W5)		100
46,284 × 28%		12,960
————		
46,839		
————		————
Capital gains tax liability		13,060
		————

Tutorial note

Angela has taxable income that uses some of, but not all of, her basic rate band. Therefore part of her taxable gain is taxed at 18% and the majority is taxed at 28%.

There is no Entrepreneurs' relief available on any of her gains therefore the 10% rate does not apply.

Workings

(W1) House

Tutor's top tips

If an asset is jointly owned by husband and wife, all you need to do is calculate the gain as usual and then split it 50:50.

Make sure you show your working for the calculation of principal private residence relief. Even if you can't count months, you will still be given marks for applying the correct principles!

	£
Disposal proceeds	381,900
Less: Cost	(86,000)
	————
	295,900
Less: Principal private residence exemption (W2)	(233,021)
	————
Chargeable gain	62,879
	————

David and Angela will each be assessed on 50% of the chargeable gain:

Chargeable gain each = (£62,879 × 50%) = £31,439

(W2) Occupation of the house

The total period of ownership of the house is 240 months (189 + 51), of which 189 months qualify for exemption as follows:

		Total months	Exempt months	Chargeable months
1.10.94 to 31.3.98	(occupied)	42	42	
1.4.98 to 31.12.01	(working in UK)	45	45	
1.1.02 to 31.12.08	(occupied)	84	84	
1.1.09 to 31.03.13	(unoccupied)	51		51
1.04.13 to 30.9.14	(final 18 months)	18	18	
		240	189	51

PPR relief = (189/240 × £295,900) = £233,021

Tutor's top tips

Make sure that you include a brief explanation for the periods you allow as exempt due to the deemed occupation rules – as the examiner has said that such explanations are required to obtain maximum marks in these questions.

(W3) Shares in Bend Ltd – gift by David

Tutor's top tips

Remember that the market value at the time of the inter-spouse gift is a red herring and irrelevant. The transfer will be at no gain/no loss.

Transfers between husband and wife are no gain/no loss transfers.

David makes no gain and Angela takes over David's cost of £48,000.

(W4) Shares in Bend Ltd – Sale by Angela

	£
Disposal proceeds	62,400
Less: Cost (£48,000 × 15,000/20,000)	(36,000)
Chargeable gain	26,400

Tutorial note

It is not clear what percentage interest Angela has in Bend Ltd and whether it is her personal trading company (i.e. she holds 5% interest or more). However, even if she does hold at least 5%, Entrepreneurs' relief is not available as Angela does not work for the company.

(W5) Remaining basic rate band

	£
Basic rate band	31,865
Less: Taxable income	(31,310)
Remaining basic rate band	555

Examiner's report

Although there were some very good answers to this question from well prepared candidates, it caused problems for many and was often the reason that they failed to achieve a pass mark.

One particular problem was that a lot of time was often spent performing unnecessary calculations for the exempt asset, and then not having sufficient time to deal with the chargeable assets.

Many candidates therefore did a lot of work for this question but scored few marks.

The jointly owned property caused particular difficulty. Only a few candidates correctly calculated the principal private residence exemption.

Some candidates did not allocate the resulting chargeable gain between the couple but instead deducted an annual exempt amount and calculated a separate tax liability.

Note: *The examiner's report has been edited to remove comments on elements of the question that have been deleted due to changes to the exam format.*

ACCA marking scheme		Marks
Jointly owned property – Motor car		0.5
– House – Proceeds		0.5
– Cost		0.5
– Period of exemption		2.5
– Exemption		1.0
– Division of gain		1.0
David Brook – Bend Ltd		0.5
– Annual exempt amount		0.5
– Capital gains tax		0.5
Angela Brook– Bend Ltd – Proceeds		0.5
– Cost		1.0
– Annual exempt amount		0.5
– Capital gains tax		0.5
Total		**10.0**

39 WILSON BIAZMA (ADAPTED)

Key answer tips

Part (a) relates to the test for residence. This question was originally written before the residence rules changed, and the test became more complex. Don't forget to read all the requirements and state the consequences of the residence on the liability of an individual to capital gains tax. Do not discuss the automatic non-UK residency tests or the sufficient ties tests as the question only asks for the automatic UK residence tests.

Part (b) involved two disposals testing entrepreneurs' relief, which is a regular feature in the F6 exam.

(a) **Automatic residence tests**

A person will be treated as automatically UK residence if they meet one of the following tests:

- They are in the UK for at least 183 days in the tax year.
- Their only home is in the UK.
- They work full time in the UK.

Liability to capital gains tax

- A person is liable to capital gains tax (CGT) on the disposal of assets during any tax year in which they are resident in the UK.

(b) **Chargeable gains – 2014/15**

	£	£
Gains not qualifying for Entrepreneurs' relief:		
Office building (W1)	110,000	
Gains qualifying for Entrepreneurs' relief:		
Goodwill (W3)		120,000
	———	———
Total chargeable gains	110,000	120,000
Less: AEA	(11,000)	
	———	———
Taxable gains	99,000	120,000
	———	———
Capital gains tax:		
Qualifying gains (£120,000 × 10%)		12,000
Not qualifying gains (£99,000 × 28%)		27,720
		———
CGT payable		39,720
		———

Tutorial note

Wilson is a higher rate taxpayer. Therefore he will pay capital gains tax at 28% on his gains that do not qualify for Entrepreneurs' relief.

Those gains that qualify for Entrepreneurs' relief will be taxed at 10% regardless of whether they fall into the basic rate or higher rate band. If applicable, these qualifying gains are deemed to utilise any remaining basic rate band first before the gains not qualifying for the relief.

Workings

(W1) Office building

	£
Disposal proceeds	246,000
Less: Cost	(104,000)
	———
Capital gain before reliefs	142,000
Less: Rollover relief (W2)	(32,000)
	———
Chargeable gain	110,000
	———

Tutorial note

Entrepreneurs' relief is not available as this is the disposal of a single asset, not the whole or part of a business.

(W2) Rollover relief

Rollover relief is not available in full because not all the proceeds are reinvested.

The gain remaining chargeable is the lower of:

(i)   Total gain of £142,000, or

(ii)   Proceeds not reinvested (£246,000 – £136,000) = £110,000

Rollover relief is therefore £32,000 (£142,000 – £110,000).

(W3) Goodwill

	£
Disposal proceeds	120,000
Less: Cost	Nil
	———
Chargeable gain qualifying for Entrepreneurs' relief	120,000
	———

Tutorial note

Entrepreneurs' relief is available as Wilson has disposed of a complete business which he has owned for at least one year.

ACCA marking scheme		
		Marks
(a)	Present in the UK 183 days	1.0
	Only home in the UK	1.0
	Work full time in the UK	1.0
	Liability to CGT	1.0
		────
		4.0
		────
(b)	**Office building**	
	Gain	1.0
	Rollover relief	1.5
	No Entrepreneurs' relief	0.5
	Goodwill	
	Gain	1.0
	Entrepreneurs' relief – need to keep gain separate	0.5
	Calculation of CGT payable	
	Annual exempt amount	0.5
	Entrepreneurs' relief rate	0.5
	Rate for remainder of gains	0.5
		────
		6.0
		────
Total		**10.0**
		────

40   BILL DING *Walk in the footsteps of a top tutor*

Key answer tips

This is a tricky question, examining the interaction between gift relief and Entrepreneurs' relief. A good knowledge of the conditions for both reliefs and the way that they are applied is needed to score well here, and this should be a good test of whether you are well prepared for these topics!

In section (a) a father gifts shares qualifying for Entrepreneurs' relief to his daughter, and they make a joint claim for gift relief. The daughter then sells the shares before 12 months have elapsed, meaning her disposal does not qualify.

In section (b) you are asked to not apply gift relief, in order for the father to benefit from Entrepreneurs' relief on the full gain.

In section (c) you are asked to compare sections (a) and (b). This style of requirement has become a frequent feature of the F6 exam, so you should make sure that you are prepared for it.

(a)   **Bill and Belle make a joint claim for gift relief**

Bill

Capital gains tax liability – 2014/15

	£
Deemed proceeds (Market value)	260,000
Less: Cost	(112,000)
	148,000
Less: Gift relief (W)	(123,333)
Chargeable gain	24,667
Less: AEA	(11,000)
Taxable gain	13,667
Capital gains tax (£13,667 × 10%) (Note)	1,367

Working: Gift relief on shares in High Rise Ltd

Gift relief is available on these shares as Bill owns 100% of the shares.

However, the gift relief in respect of the shares in High Rise Ltd is restricted because the shares are in Bill's personal trading company (i.e. he owns > 5%) and the company has investment assets.

The proportion of gain eligible for gift relief is the proportion of chargeable business assets to chargeable assets, calculated as follows:

Gift relief = (£148,000 × £150,000/£180,000) = £123,333

Belle

Capital gains tax liability – 2014/15

	£
Proceeds	265,000
Less: Cost (£260,000 – £123,333)	(136,667)
Chargeable gain	128,333
Less: AEA	(11,000)
Taxable gain	117,333
Capital gains tax (£117,333 × 28%)	32,853

Tutorial note

1   *High Rise Ltd qualifies as Bill's personal company, as he holds at least 5% of the shares, and he works for the company. He has also held the shares for at least 12 months and therefore Entrepreneurs' relief is available.*

2   *High Rise Ltd also qualifies as Belle's personal company. However, she has not held the shares for 12 months and therefore does not qualify for Entrepreneurs' relief.*

3   *As a joint claim for gift relief has been made, the cost for Belle is reduced by the amount of relief claimed.*

(a)   **Bill and Belle do not make a joint claim for gift relief**

Bill

Capital gains tax liability – 2014/15

	£
Deemed proceeds (Market value)	260,000
Less: Cost	(112,000)
Chargeable gain	148,000
Less AEA	(11,000)
Taxable gain	137,000
Capital gains tax (£137,000 × 10%)	13,700

Belle

Capital gains tax liability 2014/15

	£
Proceeds	265,000
Less: Cost	(260,000)
Chargeable gain	5,000
Less AEA	(5,000)
Taxable gain	Nil

(b)   **Comparison capital gains tax payable under options (a) and (b)**

	Option (a) £	Option (b) £
Bill	1,367	13,700
Belle	32,853	Nil
Total	34,220	13,700

Conclusion of best option

- Total capital gains tax payable is £20,520 lower under option (b) (£34,220 – £13,700) as more of the gain is taxable on Bill, who pays tax at 10% as the disposal qualifies for Entrepreneurs' relief.

- Bill however, may prefer option (a) as his own capital gains tax payable is £12,333 (£1,367 – £13,700) lower due to the claim for gift relief.

Tutor's top tips

In part (c) you are asked to summarise the capital gains tax liabilities that you have calculated in parts (a) and (b) and conclude on the most favourable option.

Provided that you use the capital gains tax figures that you have calculated in the earlier parts of the question, and come to a sensible conclusion, you will score marks here, even if your answers to parts (a) and (b) are incorrect.

41   BO AND CHARLES (ADAPTED)   *Walk in the footsteps of a top tutor*

Key answer tips

A capital gains tax question requiring the calculation of chargeable gains for two different individuals.

Each scenario covers a different capital gains tax relief: gift relief and principal private residence relief.

In part (a) the question requires the application of gift relief to a gift of shares.

The requirement specifically asked for the chargeable gain, not the capital gains tax liability. Therefore, Entrepreneurs' relief is not relevant, but to make sure the examiner clearly indicated in the notes to the question that you should ignore Entrepreneurs' relief.

In part (b) you are required to calculate PPR relief and then to consider the impact of letting the property out on the chargeable gain. This type of requirement, asking you to consider two alternatives, has become very common in the F6 exam, so you should make sure that you are prepared for it.

(a)   (i)   **Bo Neptune**

Chargeable gain – 2014/15

Tutor's top tips

Part (a) involves the gift of shares in an unquoted trading company. You should be aware that these shares qualify for gift relief. However even if you couldn't remember the definition of a qualifying asset for gift relief purposes, the question clearly states that an election has been made to holdover (i.e. defer) the gain arising as a gift of a business asset.

Remember that full relief is available for outright gifts of qualifying assets, but there may only be partial gift relief for sales at an undervalue (i.e. where the actual sale proceeds received are less than the market value of the asset at the time of the gift).

Full relief is not available where the actual sale proceeds received exceed the original cost of the asset. This is because, despite selling the asset for less than it is worth now, an actual capital profit has still been made by the owner on the disposal.

- This is a gift, and therefore the market value of the shares sold is used. Bo therefore has a chargeable gain of £116,000 (MV £210,000 – Cost of £94,000).

- Since no consideration has been paid for the shares, all of Bo's chargeable gain can be held over (i.e. deferred) with a gift relief claim.

- The base cost of the son's 50,000 £1 ordinary shares in Botune Ltd is:

	£
MV of shares acquired	210,000
Less: Gift relief	(116,000)
Base cost of shares	94,000

(ii)   **Sale at undervaluation**

- The consideration paid for the shares is less than the market value, but exceeds the allowable cost by £66,000 (£160,000 – £94,000). This amount will be immediately chargeable to capital gains tax.

- The remaining gain of £50,000 (£116,000 – £66,000) can be deferred with a gift relief claim.

- The base cost of the son's 50,000 £1 ordinary shares in Botune Ltd will be:

	£
MV of shares acquired	210,000
Less: Gift relief	(50,000)
Base cost of shares	160,000

Tutorial note

With a sale at undervalue, the chargeable gain will still be calculated using the full market value of the asset, as before.

However, any actual capital profit made by the owner at the time of the sale will be immediately chargeable.

(b)   (i)   **Charles Orion**

            Chargeable gain – 2014/15

Tutor's top tips

Part (c) involves the disposal of Charles' house. It tests the application of the deemed occupation rules and in the second part, letting relief.

This is a classic PPR question which is fairly straightforward but be careful with the dates and identifying the impact of the last 18 months rule.

Charles' chargeable gain on the house is calculated as follows:

	£
Chargeable gain before reliefs	172,000
Less: PPR relief (W)	(43,000)
Chargeable gain	129,000

Working: PPR relief

	Total months	Exempt months	Note	Chargeable months
1.10.02 to 31.3.04 (occupied)	18	18		
1.4.04 to 31.03.13 (unoccupied)	108	0	1	108
1.04.13 to 30.09.14 (last 18 months)	18	18		
	144	36		108

PPR exemption = (£172,000 ×36/144) = £43,000

Tutor's top tips

Make sure that you include a brief explanation for the periods you allow as exempt due to the deemed occupation rules – as the examiner has said that such explanations are required to obtain maximum marks in these questions.

Tutorial note

1   The first 36 months of the 'unoccupied' period is a **not** a period of 'deemed occupation' because 36 months are allowed for no reason provided:

–   the property is actually occupied at some time before and at some time after the period of absence, and

–   there was no other PPR at that time.

Charles did not reoccupy the property and therefore the exemption is not available.

2   The last 18 months are always allowable provided the property was the taxpayer's PPR at some time.

(ii)   **If the property is rented**

- The letting relief exemption will be available if the property is let during periods that are not covered by the PPR exemption.

- The letting relief exemption is the lowest of:

   (i)   PPR exemption = £43,000

   (ii) the amount of the gain not covered by PPR that is attributable to the period of letting = £129,000 (£172,000 × 108/144) (Note)

   (iii) Maximum = £40,000.

- Charles' chargeable gain will therefore be:

	£
Gain after PPR relief	129,000
Less: Letting relief	(40,000)
	———
Chargeable gain	89,000
	———

Tutorial note

In this part the house is let for the whole period of Charles' absence.

Therefore, the 'amount of the gain not covered by PPR that is attributable to the period of letting' will be the whole of the remaining gain after PPR, as it is let throughout the whole period.

If the property had only been let for a portion of that chargeable period, letting relief would be restricted accordingly.

Examiner's report

This question was not as well answered as would have been expected given that it was effectively two short separate questions on reasonably straightforward areas of capital gains tax. On an overall note, the question clearly stated that Entrepreneurs' relief was to be ignored, yet some candidates still showed this relief as being claimed.

Base costs were often not shown despite these being required in part (a). Part (a) was reasonably well answered, although few candidates could correctly calculate the revised base cost following the restriction of holdover relief in the second section.

Although there were some very good answers to part (b), far too many candidates had problems calculating the principal private residence exemption, and often lost marks by not showing detailed workings.

Even when the correct exemption was calculated this was often shown as the amount chargeable rather than the exempt amount. In the second section it was not always appreciated that letting relief was available.

Note: *The examiner's report has been edited to remove comments on elements of the question that have been deleted due to changes to the exam format.*

		ACCA marking scheme	
			Marks
(a)	(i)	Chargeable gain	1.0
		Gain held over	1.0
		Base cost of shares	1.0
			3.0
	(ii)	Gain chargeable	1.0
		Base cost of shares	1.0
			2.0
(b)	(i)	Period of exemption	1.0
		Principal private residence relief	1.0
			2.0
	(ii)	Letting relief	2.0
		Revised chargeable gain	1.0
			3.0
Total			**10.0**

42 ALPHABET LTD (ADAPTED) *Walk in the footsteps of a top tutor*

Key answer tips

This is a familiar style capital gains tax question involving three individuals making disposals. All of them had shares in a company which is taken over.

Takeovers can be complicated where there is mixed consideration and many students may have been put off by the opening paragraph. However, in this question, there is no mixed consideration and it is quite straightforward.

They are disposing of their existing shares and have a choice of either cash or shares, but not a mixture of the two.

Of the three individuals, one chooses cash and therefore they just have a straightforward disposal of shares for cash.

The other two choose shares, which is just a share for share exchange with no capital gains tax consequences at that time. The new shares just 'stand in the shoes' of the old shares and are deemed to have been acquired at the same cost and at the same time as the original shares. They then dispose of some of the new shares.

For the first part, detailed knowledge of the Entrepreneurs' relief conditions is required. However, the requirement of part (a) indicates that only Aloi's disposal is eligible for Entrepreneurs' relief. Therefore, even if you could not remember the detailed conditions for part (a), you should have realised that in calculating the capital gains tax liabilities in part (b) the gains for two of the individuals cannot be taxed at 10% whilst some of Aloi's gains would be taxed at 10%.

(a) **Entrepreneurs' relief**

Bon

Bon acquired her shareholding and became a director on 1 February 2014, so the qualifying conditions were not met for the 12 months prior to the date of disposal.

Cherry

Cherry owned 3,000 shares out of the 100,000 shares in the company, which is a 3% shareholding.

This is less than the minimum required holding of 5% to qualify for the relief.

Tutorial note

To qualify for Entrepreneurs' relief, the company must be trading and the individual must:

- *Own 5% or more of the shares, and*
- *Work for the company, and*
- *Must satisfy both of these conditions for 12 months prior to the date of disposal.*

(b)   **Aloi**

Capital gains tax liability – 2014/15

	Not qualifying for ER £	Qualifying for ER £
Qualifying for Entrepreneurs' relief		
Ordinary shares in Alphabet Ltd		
Disposal proceeds (60,000 × £6)		360,000
Cost (£50,000 + £18,600)		(68,600)
Not qualifying for Entrepreneurs' relief		
Investment property	22,600	
Chargeable gains	22,600	291,400
Less: Annual exempt amount (Note 1)	(11,000)	(Nil)
	11,600	291,400
Capital gains tax liability		
Qualifying for ER (£291,400 × 10%) (Note 2)		29,140
Not qualifying for ER (£11,600 × 28%) (Note 3)		3,248
		32,388

Tutorial note

1   *The annual exempt amount is set against the chargeable gain from the sale of the investment property as it does not qualify for Entrepreneurs' relief and therefore this saves CGT at the higher rate of 28% rather than 10%.*

2   *The gains qualifying for Entrepreneurs' relief have to be taxed first and, if applicable, they utilise any remaining BR band before non-qualifying gains are considered.*

3   *Gains not qualifying for Entrepreneurs' relief are then taxed based on the level of taxable income. As Aloi's taxable income is £60,000 the basic rate band has been utilised and therefore the non-qualifying gains will be taxed at 28%.*

Bon

Capital gains tax liability – 2014/15

	£
Ordinary shares in XYZ plc	
Deemed proceeds (10,000 × £7·12) (W1)	71,200
Less: Cost (W2) (Note 1)	(36,880)
Chargeable gain	34,320
Less: Annual exempt amount	(11,000)
Taxable gain	23,320
Capital gains tax liability	
(£23,320 × 28%) (Note 2)	6,530

Tutorial note

1   *Following the takeover Bon received 25,000 ordinary shares in XYZ plc.*

Where there is a share for share exchange, the cost of the original shareholding is treated as the cost of the new shareholding acquired on the takeover.

The cost of the new shares disposed of is therefore a proportion of the original cost of the Alphabet shares.

2   *As Entrepreneurs' relief is not available, the gain is taxed according to the level of Bon's taxable income. As she has taxable income of £55,000 she is a higher rate taxpayer and the gain will be taxed at 28%.*

Workings

(W1) Value of XYZ plc shares

The shares in XYZ plc are valued using the quarter up method:

(£7.10 + (£7.18 – £7.10) × 1/4) = £7.12

There is no comparison to an average value as there were no recorded bargains for the date of the gift.

(W2) Cost of shares

The cost attributable to the 10,000 shares sold is:

(£92,200 × 10,000/25,000) = £36,880

Cherry

Capital gains tax liability – 2014/15

Disposal of ordinary shares in XYZ plc (Note):

There is no CGT liability on the sale of the XYZ plc shares as

* the sale proceeds were only £6,600, and
* Cherry had no other disposals

therefore, even if the shares had £Nil cost, the gain is below the annual exempt amount of £11,000.

Transfer of XYZ plc on Cherry's death:

Transfers on death are exempt disposals.

Tutor's top tips

The gain on the disposal of the XYZ plc shares is:

	£
Proceeds	*6,600*
Less: Cost (£4,800 × 1,000/3,000)	*(1,600)*
Chargeable gain	*5,000*

However, there is no need to do any calculation in this part to conclude that there is no capital gains tax liability (see examiner's report).

Examiner's report

Answers to this question either tended to be very good or quite poor, with many candidates making the calculations far more complicated than they actually were.

In part (a) many candidates simply reproduced the qualifying conditions for Entrepreneurs' relief, without relating them to the information given for each of the two shareholders.

In part (b) a number of candidates included taxable income as part of their calculations, and the annual exempt amount was often omitted.

For the third shareholder, it should have been obvious that with sales proceeds of just £6,600 there would be no capital gains tax liability, yet the vast majority of candidates wasted time attempting to calculate a liability.

Similarly, there was little awareness that the transfer on death was an exempt disposal.

Note: *The examiner's report has been edited to remove comments on elements of the question that have been deleted due to changes to the exam format.*

ACCA marking scheme				Marks
(a)	Bon			1.0
	Dinah			1.0
				2.0
(b)	**Aloi**	Alphabet Ltd – Disposal proceeds		0.5
		– Cost		1.0
		Investment property		0.5
		Annual exempt amount		0.5
		Capital gains tax		1.0
	Bon	Deemed proceeds		1.0
		Cost		1.0
		Annual exempt amount		0.5
		Capital gains tax		0.5
	Cherry	Sale of shares		1.0
		Exempt disposal on death		0.5
				8.0
Total				**10.0**

43   JORGE JUNG (ADAPTED) *Walk in the footsteps of a top tutor*

Key answer tips

A fairly involved capital gains question requiring the calculation of the total taxable gains of an individual, but not the capital gains tax liability. There are some easy marks to be gained but also some tricky aspects to watch out for.

Copyrights appear in the question, which has become a more popular disposal and, as always, there are a couple of exempt assets disposed of which need to be identified.

The classic part disposal should not give cause for concern, although the seller had not purchased the asset; he had acquired it via an inter-spouse transfer and his wife had inherited it from her father. Identification of the correct base cost to use is important.

Finally a sale at undervaluation of a qualifying asset tests the gift relief rules.

A lot to deal with in a short space of time.

Tutor's top tips

Make sure you quickly identify the exempt assets so that you do not waste time trying to calculate gains on those assets.

Note that you only have to calculate taxable gains which are the net chargeable gains less the annual exempt amount. Make sure you get the mark for deducting the annual exempt amount and do not waste time trying to calculate the capital gains tax liability.

Taxable gains computation – 2014/15

	Notes	£	£
Copyright			
Disposal proceeds		8,200	
Less: Depreciated cost (£7,000 × 8/10)	1	(5,600)	
		———	2,600
Painting	2		Exempt
Motor car	3		Exempt
Land – part disposal	4		
Disposal proceeds		92,000	
Less: Cost			
£28,600 × (£92,000/(£92,000 + £38,000))		(20,240)	
Less: Legal fees		(354)	
£500 × (£92,000/(£92,000+£38,000))			
		———	71,406
			———
Total chargeable gains c/f			74,006

	Notes	£	£
Total chargeable gains b/f			74,006
Ordinary shares in Futuristic Ltd			
Deemed proceeds	5	64,800	
Less: Cost		(26,300)	
		38,500	
Less: Gift relief (W)		(24,800)	
			13,700
Total chargeable gains			87,706
Less: Annual exempt amount			(11,000)
Taxable gains			76,706

Tutorial note

1   The copyright is a wasting asset. The cost of £7,000 must therefore be depreciated based on an unexpired life of ten years at the date of acquisition and an unexpired life of eight years at the date of disposal.

2   The painting is a non-wasting chattel, but is exempt from CGT because the gross sale proceeds and the acquisition cost were less than £6,000.

3   Motor cars are exempt from CGT, so the loss of £3,900 (£14,600 – £10,700) is not allowable.

4   The cost of the land for Jorge's wife is £28,600 which is the value when Jorge's father-in-law died. Remember that where an individual inherits an asset the cost of acquisition is the market value at the date of death (i.e. probate value). In addition she incurred £500 on legal fees defending her title to the land, which is an allowable cost of acquisition. Her total base cost is therefore £29,100 (£28,600 + £500). Jorge would have taken over his wife's base cost when she transferred the land to him as transfers between spouses take place at no gain/no loss.

The proportion of the acquisition cost and the allowable cost of acquisition that can be deducted on the part disposal by Jorge are shown as separate calculations in the computation. It would be equally correct to show this as one calculation based on the total base cost of £29,100 as follows:

£29,100 × (£92,000/(£92,000 + £38,000)) = £20,594

5   Jorge and his sister are connected persons, and therefore the market value of the ordinary shares in Futuristic Ltd is used.

Working: Gift relief

The sale of the Futuristic Ltd shares is a sale at undervaluation (i.e. for less than the full market value).

Gift relief is available, but not for the full gain as the actual proceeds received exceed the original cost.

Gain chargeable immediately = (Actual sale proceeds received − Original cost)

= £40,000 − £26,300 = £13,700

Gift relief = gain less amount chargeable immediately

= (£38,500 − £13,700) = £24,800

Examiner's report

This question was well answered. However, quite a few candidates wasted time by calculating the taxpayer's tax liability when the requirement was to just calculate the taxable gains.

The easy half-mark for deducting the annual exempt amount was often missed.

ACCA marking scheme		Marks
Copyright	– Proceeds	0.5
	– Cost	1.5
Painting		0.5
Motor car		0.5
Land	– Proceeds	0.5
	– Relevant cost	1.0
	– Apportionment of cost	1.0
	– Incidental cost of acquisition (legal fees)	1.0
Ordinary shares	– Deemed proceeds	1.0
	– Cost	0.5
	– Gift relief	1.5
Annual exempt amount		0.5
		—
Total		**10.0**

---

44 WINSTON KING (ADAPTED) *Walk in the footsteps of a top tutor*

Key answer tips

This question tests basic capital gains tax computations for individuals, along with a key relief: Entrepreneurs' relief.

Easy marks were available in part (b)(i) for the computation of the capital gains tax liability on the disposal of the painting. Do not forget that the taxable income reduces the basic rate band available which needs to be considered when determining the rate of capital gains tax.

Part (b) (ii) involved calculating the total CGT liability again for 2014/15, but including the disposal of a business eligible for Entrepreneurs' relief.

Tutor's top tips

In the written parts, write short succinct bullet points, but write each bullet in full sentences.

(a)   **Individuals subject to capital gains tax on the disposal of UK assets**

An individual is subject to capital gains tax (CGT) on the disposal of chargeable assets during any tax year in which they are resident in the UK.

Companies subject to corporation tax on gains on the disposal of UK assets

A company is subject to corporation tax on gains from the disposal of chargeable assets if it is resident in the UK (see tutorial note).

Tutorial note

*Note that the requirement specifically wants to know which individuals/companies will be taxed on gains arising on the disposal of **UK assets** only here.*

There is no mention of overseas assets and only two marks available and therefore there is no need to give a long answer. Note that for individuals, if an individual is not resident in the UK, they are not liable to CGT on the disposal of any assets, not even UK assets. However, if the individual is resident in the UK, they will be liable on their UK assets, and possibly on all of their overseas gains.

For companies, if resident in the UK, they are assessed to corporation tax on their worldwide chargeable gains. If not resident in the UK, they are liable on their UK chargeable gains only, but not overseas assets. Mention of this would be correct. However, since this question was written, the overseas aspects of corporation tax has been removed from the syllabus and so it would no longer be part of the marking guide as students are not expected to know this.

(b)   **Winston King**

Capital gains tax liability – 2014/15

Tutor's top tips

Don't forget to take into consideration the taxable income using part of the basic rate band when calculating the CGT liability arising on the disposal of the painting. Part of the gain is therefore taxed at 18% and part at 28%.

In part (b) (ii) remember that Entrepreneurs' relief applies only on disposals of assets used in the business. Also note that the qualifying gains are taxed before the non-qualifying ones and hence use up the basic rate band.

The capital loss arising from the disposal of the freehold warehouse, the capital losses brought forward and the annual exempt amount should be deducted from the gain arising from the disposal of the painting.

(i) **Assuming that Winston King does not sell his sole trader business**

	£
Chargeable gain on painting	45,860
Less: Capital loss brought forward	(1,500)
Less: Annual exempt amount	(11,000)
Taxable gains	33,360

	£		
Basic rate	9,465 (W)	× 18%	1,704
Higher rate	23,895	× 28%	6,691
	33,360		
CGT liability			8,395

Working: Basic rate band remaining

	£
Basic rate band	31,865
Less: Taxable income	(22,400)
Basic rate band remaining	9,465

(ii) **Assuming that Winston King does sell his sole trader business**

	Qualifying for ER £	Not qualifying for ER £
Freehold shop (£140,000 – £80,000)	60,000	
Painting		45,860
Freehold warehouse (£88,000 – £102,000)		(14,000)
Net chargeable gains	60,000	31,860
Less: Capital loss brought forward		(1,500)
Less: Annual exempt amount	(Nil)	(11,000)
Taxable gains	60,000	19,360
(£60,000 × 10%)		6,000
(£19,360 × 28%)		5,421
CGT liability		11,421

Tutorial note

The capital loss on the sale of the freehold warehouse, the annual exempt amount, and the brought forward loss are set against the chargeable gain from the sale of the painting as this saves CGT at the higher rate of 28%.

For the purposes of determining the rate of CGT payable the remaining basic rate tax band of £9,465 is set against the gain qualifying for Entrepreneurs' relief of £60,000 even though this has no effect on the 10% tax rate. So CGT is payable at 28% on the full amount of the gains not qualifying for Entrepreneurs' relief.

Examiner's report

There were many correct answers to part (a). However, candidates should appreciate that for just two marks a detailed explanation of the residence rules was not required.

Part (b) was very well answered, with many candidates achieving maximum marks. However, it was sometimes not appreciated that the disposal of the business would fully utilise the available basic rate band – resulting in the painting being charged at the higher rate of 28%.

Note: *The examiner's report has been edited to remove comments on elements of the question that have been deleted due to changes to the exam format.*

ACCA marking scheme			
			Marks
(a)	(i)	Resident in the UK – individuals	1.0
	(ii)	Resident in the UK – companies	1.0
(b)	(i)	Annual exempt amount	1.0
		Capital loss brought forward	1.0
		Unused basic rate tax band	0.5
		Capital gains tax	1.5
			4.0
	(ii)	Freehold shop	0.5
		Painting	0.5
		Current year capital loss	0.5
		Brought forward capital loss	0.5
		Annual exempt amount	0.5
		Capital gains tax	1.5
			4.0
Total			**10.0**

45 GINGER AND NIGEL (ADAPTED) *Walk in the footsteps of a top tutor*

Key answer tips

This question tests two important capital gains tax reliefs: gift relief and Entrepreneurs' relief.

Part (a) tested gift relief but in a slightly unusual way which required the application of the modified gift relief rules for sales at an undervaluation, and a calculation of the maximum number of shares that can be gifted without a capital gains tax liability arising.

If you are ever unsure of how to deal with part of a question it is important to make a sensible attempt and move on, rather than waste time, or potentially miss easy marks by not attempting to answer the part.

Part (b) compares the CGT payable by a husband or wife on the disposal of shares. Again easy marks were available for the basic gains computation in each case and the calculation of the difference in tax payable by the two individuals.

(a) **Ginger**

Tutor's top tips

Remember that where there is a disposal at an undervalue (as opposed to an outright gift) then part of the gain may be chargeable now and cannot be held over (deferred).

The examiner has given you a hint in the question as to how to approach the answer by stating that Ginger has not utilised the annual exempt amount for 2014/15.

- The disposal is at an undervalue, so only the 'gift' element of the gain can be held over.
- The consideration paid for each share will be immediately chargeable to capital gains tax to the extent that it exceeds the allowable cost.
- The chargeable amount is therefore £1·60 (£4·00 – £2·40) per share.
- Ginger's annual exempt amount for 2014/15 is £11,000.
- She can therefore sell 6,875 shares (£11,000/£1·60) to her daughter without this resulting in any capital gains tax liability for 2014/15.

Tutorial note

This method may have proved quite challenging to some students. If you are unsure how to tackle the question, then make sure you write down what you do know.

One mark was available for simply stating how to calculate the gain on a transfer at an undervalue and another half mark for stating the amount of the annual exempt amount!

Proof of the calculation:	
	£
MV of shares (6,875 × £6.40)	*44,000*
Less: Cost (6,875 × £2.40)	*(16,500)*
Capital gain	*27,500*
Less: Gift relief (6,875 × (£6.40 – £4.00))	*(16,500)*
Chargeable gain (6,875 × (4.00 – £2.40)) (excess actual proceeds received)	*11,000*
Less: Annual exempt amount	*(11,000)*
Taxable gain	*Nil*

(b)   **Innocent and Nigel**

Tutor's top tips

Clearly, the CGT is not going to be the same for both Innocent and Nigel, so you need to look out for the differences in their circumstances. You are given a lot of information concerning their total shareholdings and employment position. As this is different for each of them this should give you a hint that you should consider how this is relevant for determining their CGT liability.

- If Innocent makes the disposal, then her CGT liability for 2014/15 will be:

	£
Disposal proceeds	65,000
Less: Cost (2,000 × £1)	(2,000)
Chargeable gain	63,000
Capital gains tax (£63,000 × 10%)	6,300

Innocent pays CGT at 10% as the disposal qualifies for Entrepreneurs' relief.

- If Nigel makes the disposal, then his CGT liability for 2014/15 will be:

	£
Disposal proceeds	65,000
Less: Cost (£46,200 × 2,000/3,000)	(30,800)
Chargeable gain	34,200
Capital gains tax (£34,200 × 28%)	9,576

Nigel pays CGT at 28% because he is a higher rate taxpayer and the disposal does not qualify for Entrepreneurs' relief.

- The capital gains tax saving if Innocent makes the disposal rather than Nigel is therefore £3,276 (£9,576 – £6,300).

Tutorial notes

1   A disposal by Innocent will qualify for Entrepreneurs' relief as she is the managing director of Cinnamon Ltd, the company is a trading company, her shareholding of 20% (20,000/100,000) is more than the minimum required holding of 5% and she has held the shares for more than 12 months. The gain is therefore taxed at 10%.

2   A disposal by Nigel will not qualify for Entrepreneurs' relief as he is not an officer or an employee of Cinnamon Ltd and his shareholding is only 3% (3,000/100,000). As Nigel is a higher rate taxpayer (taxable income £80,000) the gain is taxed at the higher rate.

Examiner's report

Although there were a number of correct answers to part (a), it caused difficulty for many candidates. The main problem was not appreciating that the annual exempt amount should be used, despite a fairly heavy hint to this effect being given in the question.

Part (b) was another well answered section, with many candidates achieving maximum marks.

Note: The examiner's report has been edited to remove comments on elements of the question that have been deleted due to changes to the exam format.

ACCA marking scheme			Marks
(a)		Consideration paid in excess of cost is chargeable	1.0
		Chargeable amount per share	1.0
		Identifying available annual exempt amount	0.5
		Maximum number of shares that can be sold	1.5
			———
			4.0
			———
(b)	**Innocent**		
	Disposal proceeds		0.5
	Cost		1.0
	Capital gains tax		1.5
	Nigel		
	Disposal proceeds		0.5
	Cost		1.0
	Capital gains tax		1.0
	CGT saving		0.5
			———
			6.0
			———
Total			**10.0**
			———

46   MARLON AND LEROY (ADAPTED) *Walk in the footsteps of a top tutor*

Key answer tips

A typical capital gains question with two parts.

The first part tests the rules for PPR relief and husband and wife transfers.

The second part involves the disposal of shares and tests the valuation of a gift, the share matching rules and the composition of the share pool.

Each part involves a fairly straightforward disposal followed by an alternative scenario involving an element of tax planning. The alternative scenarios are however quite simple and should not have caused well prepared students any problems.

(a)   **Marlon and Alvita**

(i)   **Marlon – Chargeable gain – 2014/15**

	£
Disposal proceeds	497,000
Less: Costs of disposal	(3,700)
Net proceeds	493,300
Less: Cost	(146,000)
Incidental costs of acquisition	(2,900)
Capital gain	344,400
Less: Principal private residence relief (W)	(229,600)
Chargeable gain	114,800

Working: PPR relief

One-third of Marlon's house was always used exclusively for business purposes, so the principal private residence relief is restricted to £229,600 (£344,400 × 2/3).

Tutorial note

*The last 18 months exemption does not apply to the whole house as one third has **always** been used for business purposes. If the business use had only been for part of the period of ownership the last 18 months would have applied to the whole house.*

(ii) **Transfer of 50% ownership to Alvita**

The capital gains tax saving if 50% ownership of the house had been transferred to Alvita prior to its disposal would have been calculated as:

	£
Additional AEA available for Alvita	
– exempts part of gain (£11,000 × 28%)	3,080
Gains falling into the BRB for Alvita	
– lower rate of CGT applied (£31,865 × 10% (28% – 18%))	3,187
	─────
Total tax saving	6,267
	─────

Tutorial note

Transferring 50% ownership of the house to Alvita prior to its disposal would have enabled her annual exempt amount and lower rate tax band of 18% for 2014/15 to be utilised.

Note that the tax saving could be calculated by computing the tax payable by Marlon at 28%, and then compute the tax payable by Marlon and Alvita sharing the gain equally.

However, with only 2 marks available, there is insufficient time to perform all of these calculations. Therefore, the examiner expects you to be able to see the effect of the planning on the computations and perform a two line short cut calculation.

(b) **Leroy**

(i) **Chargeable gains – 2014/15**

	£
Gift of ordinary shares in Jerk-Chic plc – October 2014	
Deemed proceeds = MV of shares (4,000 × £7.90) (W1)	31,600
Less: Cost (W2)	(6,800)
	─────
Chargeable gain	24,800
	─────
Sale of ordinary shares in Jerk-Chic plc – April 2015	
Disposal proceeds	83,400
Less: Cost (W2)	(20,400)
	─────
Chargeable gain	63,000
	─────

Workings

(W1) Market value of shares

The shares in Jerk-Chic plc are valued using the quarter up method as there are no recorded bargains on the date of disposal.

(£7.80 + 1/4 × (£8.20 – £7.80)) = £7.90 per share

(W2) Share pool

	Number	Cost £
Purchase 1 March 2006	20,000	19,800
Purchase 20 July 2010	8,000	27,800
	28,000	47,600
Disposal 23 October 2014 (£47,600 × 4,000/28,000)	(4,000)	(6,800)
	24,000	40,800
Disposal 2 April 2015 (£40,800 × 12,000/24,000)	(12,000)	(20,400)
Balance c/f	12,000	20,400

(ii)   **Delaying sale to 6 April 2015**

Delaying the sale of the 12,000 shares in Jerk-Chic plc until 6 April 2015 would have deferred the due date for the related capital gains tax liability from 31 January 2016 to 31 January 2017.

Tutorial note

CGT is always due on 31 January following the end of the tax year of disposal.

Delaying the sale from 2 April 2015 (tax year 2014/15) until 6 April 2015 (tax year 2015/16) would therefore delay the payment of tax by 12 months.

Usually the key advantage of delaying a disposal is that the following year's AEA is available, as well as the cash flow advantage of paying the tax later. However, in this question the AEA is already utilised in 2015/16, therefore the only advantage is moving the payday.

Note also that with only one mark available, you should not be expecting to write more than one key advantage.

ACCA marking scheme			
			Marks
(a)	(i)	Disposal proceeds	0.5
		Less costs of disposal	0.5
		Cost	0.5
		Costs of acquisition allowable cost	0.5
		PPR relief	1.0
			3.0
	(ii)	AEA at 28%	1.0
		Lower rate tax band at 10%	1.0
			2.0

ACCA marking scheme			
			Marks
(b)	(i)	Gift: Deemed proceeds	1.0
		Sale: Proceeds	0.5
		Share pool	
		Balance after additions in March 2006 and July 2010	0.5
		Disposal cost 23.10.14	1.0
		Disposal cost 2.4.15	1.0
			───
			4.0
			───
	(ii)	Deferred due date for tax by one year	1.0
Total			───
			10.0
			───

COMPANIES – CHARGEABLE GAINS

47 FORWARD LTD (ADAPTED)

Key answer tips

This question requires the calculation of the corporation tax liability of a company, however before that can be calculated two chargeable gains need to be calculated.

Remember that companies are entitled to an indexation allowance and that rollover relief for replacement of business assets is a key relief available for companies. No other reliefs are available. Note that the effect of reinvesting in a depreciating asset as in part (b) must be understood as this is an area that is often tested.

(a) **Corporation tax liability – year ended 31 March 2015**

	£
Trading profit	78,000
Net chargeable gains	
(£30,000 (W1) + £37,695 (W3))	67,695
	──────
Taxable total profits	145,695
	──────
Corporation tax liability	
FY 2014 (£145,695 × 20%)	29,139
	──────
Due date	1 January 2016

Workings

(W1) Freehold office building

	£
Disposal proceeds	290,000
Less: Cost	(148,000)
Unindexed gain	142,000
Less: Indexation allowance	
(255.6 – 149.1)/149.1 = 0.714 × £148,000	(105,672)
Chargeable gain before reliefs	36,328
Less: Roll over relief (W2)	(6,328)
Chargeable gain	30,000

(W2) Rollover relief

The sale proceeds of the office building are not fully reinvested.

The chargeable gain which cannot be rolled over is calculated as follows:

	£
Disposal proceeds	290,000
Less: Reinvested in qualifying business asset	(260,000)
Sale proceeds not reinvested = chargeable now	30,000

The remaining gain of £6,328 (£36,328 – £30,000) can be deferred with a rollover relief claim.

(W3) Ordinary shares in Backward plc

	£
Disposal proceeds	62,500
Less: Cost (W4)	(12,895)
Unindexed gain	49,605
Less: Indexation allowance (£24,805 – £12,895) (W4)	(11,910)
Chargeable gain	37,695

Tutorial note

The gain cannot be rolled over into the acquisition of the shares in Sideways plc as shares are not qualifying assets for the purpose of rollover relief.

(W4) Share pool – Backward plc

			Number	Cost £	Indexed cost £
April 1989	Purchase		9,000	18,000	18,000
Indexation to November 2014					
£18,000 × (258.0 – 114.3)/114.3					22,630
(do not round indexation factor)					
					40,630
November 2014	Purchase		500	6,500	6,500
			9,500	24,500	47,130
November 2014	Disposal				
Cost × (5,000 / 9,500)			(5,000)	(12,895)	(24,805)
Balance c/f			4,500	11,605	22,325

(b)   Reinvestment in leasehold office building

- The freehold office building's sale proceeds of £290,000 will be fully reinvested, and so the whole of the gain of £36,328 is eligible for rollover relief.

- The leasehold office building is a depreciating asset, so its base cost will not be adjusted.

- The base cost of the 15 year lease will therefore be its actual cost of £300,000.

- The gain will be deferred until the earliest of:

  - ten years from the date of acquisition of the leasehold building,

  - the date that it is disposed of, or

  - the date that it ceases to be used for trading purposes.

48   HAWK LTD (ADAPTED) *Walk in the footsteps of a top tutor*

Key answer tips

This question requires the computation of a corporation tax liability for a company; however a chargeable gain needs to be calculated before the corporation tax liability computation can be performed.

You need to remember that disposals made by a company will usually include an indexation allowance, so you need to be aware of the rules regarding the rounding of the indexation factor.

The only capital gains relief available to companies is rollover relief and therefore it is not surprising to see it in this question and it is often tested in corporation tax questions.

Tutor's top tips

Part (a) consisted of a reasonably straightforward disposal made by a company and should be a good opportunity to score marks.

Part (b) covers rollover relief and requires you to apply your knowledge of the relief, so is trickier than part (a).

(a)   **Hawk Ltd**

Corporation tax computation – year ended 31 March 2015

	£
Trading profit	250,000
Net chargeable gain (W)	51,445
	———
Taxable total profits	301,445
	———
FY 2014 (£301,445 × 21%)	63,303
Less: MR	
1/400 × (£1,500,000 – £301,445)	(2,996)
	———
Corporation tax liability	60,307
	———

Tutorial note

Hawk Ltd has no associated companies. Its taxable total profits of £301,445, which fall entirely in FY2014, fall between the lower profits limit of £300,000 and the upper limit of £1,500,000. It therefore pays tax at the main rate of 21% but is entitled to marginal relief.

Working: Chargeable gain on office building

	£
Proceeds (April 2014)	260,000
Less: Costs of disposal	(3,840)
	———
Net disposal proceeds	256,160
Less: Cost and legal fees (July 1994)	
(£81,000 + £3,200)	(84,200)
Enhancement (May 2006)	(43,000)
	———
Unindexed gain	128,960
Less: Indexation allowance	
On cost (July 1994 to April 2014)	
(255.2 – 144.0)/144.0 = 0.772 × £84,200	(65,002)
On enhancement (May 2006 to April 2014)	
(255.2 – 197.7)/197.7 = 0.291 × £43,000	(12,513)
	———
	51,445
	———

(b)   **Rollover relief**

(i)   **Minimum amount of reinvestment**

- The office building was sold for £256,160 (net of disposal expenses) and this is therefore the amount that Hawk Ltd will have to reinvest in order to claim the maximum possible amount of rollover relief.

Tutorial note

HMRC allow full rollover relief provided the net sale proceeds are reinvested in qualifying assets within the qualifying time period. It is not necessary to reinvest the gross sale proceeds.

(ii)   **Period of reinvestment**

- The reinvestment will have to take place between 1 May 2013 and 30 April 2017 (i.e. one year before and three years after the date of sale).

(iii) **Amount of corporation tax deferred**

- If the maximum possible amount of rollover relief is claimed the company's taxable total profits will be reduced to £250,000. The company will now pay tax at the small profits rate of 20% as profits are below the lower limit of £300,000.

- The revised corporation tax liability is £50,000 (£250,000 × 20%). The amount of corporation tax that will be deferred is £10,307 (£60,307 − £50,000).

Examiner's report

Part (a) was reasonably well answered.

As regards the freehold office building, many candidates did not appreciate that indexation would also be available for the incidental costs of acquisition.

Part (b) was also reasonably well answered, with a number of candidates providing perfect answers.

Note: *The examiner's report has been edited to remove comments on elements of the question that have been deleted due to changes to the exam format.*

ACCA marking scheme		
		Marks
(a)	**Office building**	
	Disposal proceeds	0.5
	Costs of disposal	0.5
	Cost	0.5
	Costs of acquisition	0.5
	Enhancement expenditure	0.5
	Indexation – Cost	1.0
	– Enhancement	1.0
	Corporation tax liability	
	Calculation	1.5
		–––
		6.0
		–––
(b)	Amount of reinvestment	1.0
	Period of reinvestment	1.0
	Corporation tax saving	2.0
		–––
		4.0
		–––
Total		**10.0**
		–––

49 ACEBOOK LTD (ADAPTED) *Walk in the footsteps of a top tutor*

Key answer tips

This is a standard chargeable gains question, based on a company making three disposals. The question covers the disposal of shares, a part disposal of land and the receipt and partial reinvestment of insurance proceeds on the destruction of an asset.

The third disposal may be difficult for students, who are perhaps less familiar with the rules regarding damage or destruction of an asset. However, the examiner has given a hint in the question, in saying that the company has made a claim to defer the gain, and this information could be used to make a sensible assumption about the treatment of the insurance proceeds.

If you are ever unsure of how to deal with part of a question it is important to make a sensible guess and move on, rather than waste time, or potentially miss easy marks by not attempting to answer the part.

Acebook Ltd – Chargeable gains for the year ended 31 December 2014

Tutor's top tips

There are three disposals to deal with here, some more complicated than others. There is no need for you to calculate the gains in order if you prefer to do the easier computations first – as long as you clearly label each disposal as you attempt it.

Remember that disposals by a company are entitled to an indexation allowance.

The disposal of shares by a company requires the construction of a share pool and the calculation of the indexation allowance before recording each operative event. The calculation of the gain is then straightforward.

Part disposals are regularly examined, and it is important to learn the formula for calculating the cost and to know how to apply it. You should not be misled by the size or number of the parts bought and sold; it is the values which are used in the calculation.

The receipt of insurance proceeds is treated as a disposal of a destroyed asset. Note that the company has reinvested part of the insurance proceeds in a new asset and claimed to defer the gain arising on the disposal.

	£	£
Oogle plc		
Disposal proceeds (28,800 × £3·20)	92,160	
Less: Cost (W)	(45,840)	
	———	
Unindexed gain	46,320	
Less: Indexation allowance (£55,098 – £45,840) (W)	(9,258)	
	———	
Chargeable gain		37,062
Land		
Disposal proceeds	192,000	
Less: Indexed cost (Note 1)		
(£192,000/(£192,000 + £53,000)) × £196,000	(153,600)	
Less: Enhancement expenditure		
(£192,000/(£192,000 + £53,000)) × £29,400	(23,040)	
	———	
Chargeable gain		15,360
Investment property (Note 2)		
Insurance proceeds	189,000	
Less: Indexed cost	(138,400)	
	———	
	50,600	
Less: Gain deferred (balancing figure)	(34,000)	
	———	
Chargeable gain (proceeds not reinvested) = (£189,000 – £172,400)		16,600
		———
Total chargeable gains		69,022
		———

Tutorial note

1   This standard part disposal computation requires the appropriate proportion of the indexed cost to be calculated using the A / (A + B) formula. The cost of clearing and levelling the land is enhancement expenditure. The cost relates to all four acres so again the standard part disposal computation requires the appropriate proportion of the indexed cost to be calculated using the A / (A + B) formula.

2   Where an asset is destroyed and the insurance proceeds are reinvested in a replacement asset within 12 months then the gain may be deferred against the cost of the replacement asset. Where the insurance proceeds are not fully reinvested then the amount which is not reinvested is chargeable immediately.

Working: Oogle plc

Share pool	Number	Cost £	Indexed cost £
Purchase June 2006	8,000	25,200	25,200
Bonus issue October 2009			
(8,000 × 2/1)	16,000		
	24,000		
Indexation to February 2011			
(£25,200 × 0·165)			4,158
Rights issue February 2011			
(24,000 × 1/5) = 4,800 × £4·30	4,800	20,640	20,640
	28,800	45,840	49,998
Indexation to March 2014			
(£49,998 × 0·102)			5,100
			55,098
Disposal – March 2014	(28,800)	(45,840)	(55,098)

Tutorial note

1   As a bonus issue involves no cost it is not an operative event and there is no indexation to be calculated.

2   A rights issue is simply a purchase of shares (usually at a price below the market rate) and is therefore an operative event (i.e. index up to the date of the rights issue, and then add in the number and cost of the shares).

Examiner's report

This question was generally very well answered, and there were many high scoring answers. One common mistake with the ordinary shares was to index the share pool prior to the bonus issue. Despite being told that the entire shareholding was disposed of, some candidates complicated the calculation by making a part disposal.

Many candidates wasted time by calculating the CGT liability (often for an individual rather than a company) despite being instructed to just calculate chargeable gains.

Note: The examiner's report has been edited to remove comments on elements of the question that have been deleted due to changes to the exam format.

ACCA marking scheme	
	Marks
Oogle plc	
Proceeds	0.5
Less cost and indexation allowance	1.0
Land	
Proceeds	0.5
Less indexed cost	1.0
Less enhancement expenditure	0.5
Investment property	
Gain before deferral	1.0
Chargeable gain (proceeds not reinvested)	1.0
Share pool	
Purchase June 2006	0.5
Bonus issue October 2009	1.0
Indexation to February 2011	1.0
Rights issue February 2011	1.0
Indexation to March 2014	1.0
	────
Total	**10.0**
	────

INHERITANCE TAX

50   JIMMY (ADAPTED) *Walk in the footsteps of a top tutor*

Key answer tips

This is a straightforward IHT question with two lifetime gifts, (one PET and one CLT) and a simple estate. This question should have provided an opportunity to score highly.

(a)   **The importance of the distinction between PETs and CLTs**

PETs

*   A PET only becomes chargeable to IHT if the donor dies within seven years of making the gift.

CLTs

*   A CLT is immediately charged to IHT.

*   Additional IHT may arise if the donor dies within seven years of making the gift.

Tutor's top tips

There are only 2 marks for this part therefore you need to be efficient with time and not take too long on this part. Short, succinct points need to be made.

(b) **Jimmy**

Lifetime tax on lifetime gifts

	PET 2 August 2013	CLT 14 November 2013	
	£	£	£
Transfer of value	50,000		800,000
Less: Marriage exemption	(2,500)		
AE – 2013/14	(3,000)		(Nil)
– 2012/13 b/f	(3,000)		(Nil)
	———		———
Chargeable amount	41,500		800,000
	———		———
NRB at time of gift – 2013/14		325,000	
Less: GCTs in 7 years pre-gift			
(14.11.06 to 14.11.13) Ignore PET		(Nil)	
		———	(325,000)
			———
Taxable amount in lifetime	Nil		475,000
	———		———
Lifetime IHT payable (£475,000 × 25%)			
(Net gift)	Nil		118,750
	———		———
GCT c/f (£800,000 + £118,750)	41,500		918,750
	———		———

Tutorial note

1   *For lifetime IHT calculations, never cumulate PETs in calculating the gross chargeable transfers (GCTs) in the 7 years before the gift, as at that stage they are 'potentially' exempt and not chargeable.*

2   *Jimmy paid the IHT on the gift into the trust. It is therefore a net gift and the lifetime IHT is calculated at 25%.*

Death tax on lifetime gifts

	PET 2 August 2013		CLT 14 November 2013	
	£	£	£	£
Chargeable amount		41,500		918,750
NRB at death – 2014/15	325,000		325,000	
Less: GCTs in 7 years pre-gift				
(2.8.06 to 2.8.13)	(Nil)			
(14.11.06 to 14.11.13) Include PET			(41,500)	
	——	(325,000)	——	(283,500)
Taxable amount on death		Nil		635,250
		£		£
Death IHT payable (£635,250 × 40%)		Nil		254,100
Less: Taper relief (< 3 years)				(Nil)
				254,100
Less: Lifetime IHT payable				(118,750)
IHT payable		Nil		135,350

Tutorial note

1   *For death IHT calculations on lifetime gifts, cumulate PETs in calculating the gross chargeable transfers (GCTs) in the 7 years before the gift if they have become chargeable on death, but not if they have become completely exempt.*

2   *Taper relief Is not available as there are less than three years between the date of both gifts and the date of death.*

Death estate

	£	£
Property		260,000
Proceeds of life assurance policy		210,000
Gross chargeable estate		470,000
NRB at death – 2014/15	325,000	
Less: GCTs in 7 years pre death		
(£41,500 + £918,750)	(960,250)	
	——	(Nil)
Taxable amount		470,000
IHT liability (£470,000 × 40%)		188,000

Examiner's report

This question was extremely well answered, with a high number of perfect answers.

In part (a) a number of candidates wrote far too much for what should have been a short answer.

In part (b) the only consistent problem was that the gross figure for the chargeable lifetime transfer was often taken as the tax plus the chargeable portion of the transfer, rather than the tax plus the total net transfer.

Note: *The examiner's report has been edited to remove comments on elements of the question that have been deleted due to changes to the exam format.*

ACCA marking scheme			Marks
(a)	PET		1.0
	CLT		1.0
			———
			2.0
			———
(b)	**Lifetime transfers**		
	PET	– Recognition as a PET	0.5
		– Marriage exemption	0.5
		– Annual exemptions	1.0
	CLT	– Recognition as a CLT	0.5
		– IHT liability	2.0
	Additional liabilities arising on death		
	PET		0.5
	CL	– IHT liability	1.0
		– IHT already paid	0.5
	Death estate		
	Property		0.5
	Life assurance policy		0.5
	IHT liability		0.5
			———
			8.0
			———
Total			**10.0**
			———

51   ETHEL AND BLU (ADAPTED) *Walk in the footsteps of a top tutor*

Key answer tips

This question has two distinct parts covering quite different topics. A multi-part question covering different topics is possible in the examination. It is unlikely that IHT will be combined with the cash basis in the real exam; however this question provides useful revision of some elements of these topics.

Part (a) tested a topic which is no longer in the syllabus and has therefore been replaced with a question testing the cash accounting and flat rate basis rules introduced in FA2014.

Part (b) was a very straightforward IHT question requiring the calculation of the lifetime and death tax on one CLT.

Tutor's top tips

You do not have to answer this question in the order set. Provided you start each part on a separate page and clearly indicate which part you are answering, you can answer in any order. Hence you might prefer to start with part (b) on IHT as this may be more familiar.

However, do take care when attempting a question out of order, as sometimes the answer to part (a) is required in part (b), and so on. This is clearly not the case in this question as each part involves a different individual.

(a)   **Ethel Brown – Notes on cash accounting and flat rate expense adjustments**

  (1)   **Business premises used partly for private purposes**

   - The total payments of £25,000 can be deducted from the trading profit but the flat rate private use adjustment of £7,800 must be added to the trading profit for tax purposes.

   - A net deduction from trading profits of £17,200 can therefore be claimed for tax purposes.

  (2)   **Car used for private and business purposes**

   - The cash payments in respect of the purchase and running costs of the car totalling £17,000 (£14,000 + £3,000) are not deductible from the trading profit and capital allowances are not available.

   - Instead a tax deduction for the car is allowed using the approved mileage allowances for the business mileage as follows:

	£
First 10,000 miles at 45p/mile	4,500
1,000 miles at 25p/mile	250
Allowable deduction	4,750

  (3)   **Kitchen equipment**

   - A tax deduction can be claimed from the trading profits for the full cost of the kitchen equipment when the invoice is paid.

   - No tax deduction is therefore allowed in the accounts for the year to 5 April 2015 but Ethel will obtain a tax deduction of £350 from trading profits in the following year to 5 April 2016.

Tutorial note

1   The question states that Ethel opts to use the cash basis and the flat rate expense adjustments. Note that the examiner has stated that whilst the use of flat rate expenses is optional it should be assumed in any question involving the cash basis that flat rate expenses are claimed.

2   Where a business premises is used partly for private purposes (e.g. a bed and breakfast or small care home), a private use adjustment must be made for tax purposes if the full cost of food, utilities and other household goods have been included in the accounts. The HMRC flat rate private use adjustments are based on the number of occupants and will be provided as part of the question in the exam. Any information regarding actual private expenses is irrelevant.

3   The flat rate expense adjustment in respect of cars is based on the HMRC approved mileage allowances. These are the same rates that are used to calculate the taxable benefit/allowable deduction where employees use their own cars for business purposes. The rates are given in the tax tables provided in the exam.

4   Under the cash basis a 100% trading deduction is given for the acquisition cost of items of plant and machinery rather than capital allowances.

(b)   **Blue Reddy**

Inheritance tax computation

Lifetime tax on lifetime gift – 15 January 2015

	£	£
Value of shares held before the transfer (300,000 × £4)		1,200,000
Value of shares held after the transfer (100,000 × £2)		(200,000)
Transfer of value (Note 1)		1,000,000
Less: AE (ignore per question)		(Nil)
Chargeable transfer (Net)		1,000,000
NRB at time of gift	325,000	
GCTs in 7 years pre gift (15.1.2008 – 15.1.2015)	(Nil)	
		(325,000)
Taxable amount		675,000
IHT liability (£675,000 × 25%) (Note 2)		168,750
Gross chargeable transfer c/f (£1,000,000 + £168,750)		1,168,750

**Additional death tax due on lifetime gift – 15 January 2015
(assuming death occurs 31 May 2019)**

	£	£
Gross chargeable transfer		1,168,750
NRB at time of death	325,000	
GCTs in 7 years pre death (31.5.2012 – 31.5.2019)	(Nil)	
	————	(325,000)
		————
Taxable amount		843,750
		————
IHT liability (£843,750 × 40%)		337,500
Less: Taper relief		
(15.1.2015 – 31.5.2019) (4 – 5 years) (40%)		(135,000)
		————
		202,500
Less: Lifetime IHT paid		(168,750)
		————
Additional IHT payable on death		33,750
		————

Tutorial note

1   *The transfer of value is calculated by reference to the diminution in the value of the donor's estate. The value of the 40% shareholding transferred (i.e. 200,000 shares at £3 for a 40% shareholding) is irrelevant for IHT purposes. This is particularly relevant in this situation, where company shares are involved, where the diminution in value of Blu's estate from reducing his interest in the company from 60% to 20% (i.e. £1,000,000) is far greater than valuing a 40% shareholding in isolation (£600,000).*

2   *Remember that where the donor pays the tax the appropriate tax rate is 25% as their estate has been diminished not just by the gift but also by the IHT paid. The gross chargeable transfer is the value of the gift plus the tax paid.*

Examiner's report

This was the least well answered of the three 15 mark questions, although it was often the last one to be answered with time pressure being an issue.

Candidates were helped in part (b) by being told to ignore annual exemptions, but many also ignored these instructions.

They were not penalised for this, but it made the calculations a bit more complicated than was necessary.

When calculating the additional liability arising on death many candidates had problems computing the amount of brought forward gross chargeable transfer, and taper relief was often calculated and deducted at the wrong point in the computation.

Candidates should also appreciate that examinations are not quite the same as real life.

With a six mark section it should be obvious that the value of the transfer was more than the nil rate band of £325,000 – many candidates calculating the transfer as (200,000 × £1) = £200,000. Using any of the other values would have enabled some marks to be obtained.

However, there were many perfect answers to part (b), with the six marks obtained often being the difference between a pass and a fail.

Note: *The examiner's report has been edited to remove comments on elements of the question that have been deleted due to changes to the exam format.*

	ACCA marking scheme	
		Marks
(a)	Business premises used for private purposes	
	Food etc. payments deductible	0.5
	Less £7,800 flat rate private use adjustment	0.5
	Car	
	Payments re purchase and running costs not deductible	0.5
	No capital allowances available	0.5
	Calculation of deductible amount	1.0
	Equipment	
	Cost of acquisition 100% trading deduction	0.5
	Deductible when payment made i.e. following accounting period	0.5
		───
		4.0
		───
(b)	Lifetime transfer	
	Value transferred	2.0
	IHT liability	1.5
	Additional liability arising on death	
	Gross chargeable transfer	0.5
	IHT liability	0.5
	Taper relief	1.0
	IHT already paid	0.5
		───
		6.0
		───
Total		**10.0**
		───

52   NING GAO (ADAPTED) *Walk in the footsteps of a top tutor*

Key answer tips

Part (a) required advice on how much nil rate band was available for the computation of inheritance tax on the death estate.

To secure the three marks, both supporting calculations as well as narrative explanations were required.

The first part of part (b) was a straight forward death estate computation with easy marks available for presenting the figures given in the question in a standard layout/pro forma.

The second part required consideration of alternative dates of death – and even without reading the question it should have been fairly obvious that the examiner is testing the 'seven year rule' and it is likely that a gift will 'drop out' of cumulation and have a knock on effect for the tax calculations.

Tutor's top tips

Whenever the examiner asks for the amount of NRB available for a death estate, consider two things:

1   *Whether the individual is a widow or widower and therefore whether there is any unused nil rate band available to be transferred from the former spouse.*

2   *Whether the deceased made any lifetime gifts in the seven years before their death as these will utilise some of the nil rate band available for the death estate.*

(a)   **Nil rate band available on death**

- Ning's personal representatives could claim her deceased husband's unused nil rate band of £227,500 (£325,000 × 70%).

- The total amount of nil rate band is therefore £552,500 (£325,000 + £227,500).

- The potentially exempt transfer on 7 November 2014 will utilise £220,000 of the nil rate band, so only £332,500 (£552,500 − £220,000) is available against the death estate.

(b)   **Inheritance tax payable on Ning's death estate**

Tutor's top tips

The death estate usually just involves listing the assets given in the question and adding them up. Remember that there are no exempt assets for IHT. Therefore, whilst cars, NISAs and NS&I Savings Certificates may be exempt for income tax and/or capital gains tax purposes, they are taxable for IHT purposes and must be brought into the estate computation.

For the second part, be careful to read the dates carefully.

If Ning dies six years from 20 March 2015 the new date of death will be 20 March 2021 and seven years before that will be 20 March 2014. Therefore the PET on 7 November 2014 remains chargeable and there will be no change in the tax on the estate.

However, if the death is one year later, seven years before death is 20 March 2015 and the PET will become completely exempt. There will therefore be more nil rate band available to match against the estate and the IHT on the estate will be less.

(i)   **Assuming death on 20 March 2015**

	£	£
First property	674,000	
Less: Repayment mortgage	(160,000)	
	———	514,000
Second property	442,000	
Less: Endowment mortgage (Note 1)	(Nil)	
	———	442,000
Motor cars		194,400
		———
		1,150,400
Less: Bank loan		(22,400)
Legal fees (Note 2)		(Nil)
		———
Chargeable estate		1,128,000
Nil rate band at death (part (a))	552,500	
Less: GCTs in previous 7 years	(220,000)	
	———	
Nil rate band available		(332,500)
		———
Taxable amount		795,500
		———
IHT liability (£795,500 × 40%)		318,200
		———

Responsible for paying the inheritance tax:

The personal representatives of Ning's estate.

Tutorial note

1   *There is no deduction in respect of the endowment mortgage as this will be repaid upon death by the life assurance element of the mortgage.*

2   *The promise to pay the nephew's legal fees is not deductible as it is purely gratuitous (not made for valuable consideration). Only legally enforceable debts can be deducted.*

(ii)   **Assuming death six or seven years later**

If Ning were to live for another six years until 20 March 2021:

The IHT payable in respect of her estate would not alter, as the PET on 7 November 2014 will still be made within the previous seven years.

If Ning were to live for another seven years until 20 March 2022:

The PET will become completely exempt, and the IHT payable in respect of her estate would therefore decrease by £88,000 (£220,000 at 40%).

Examiner's report

Part (a) was well answered, with candidates being given credit for their treatment of the PET even if this was included in part (b).

In part (b) candidates needed to appreciate the different treatment of repayment mortgages (deductible) and endowment mortgages (not deductible), and the type of debts which can be deducted from the value of an estate. This part was also well answered, although a number of candidates deducted the endowment mortgage (it would have been repaid upon death by the life assurance element of the mortgage) and the promise to pay a nephew's legal fees (not deductible being purely gratuitous).

Somewhat surprisingly, there was often little knowledge of who was responsible for paying the tax – many candidates stated that it was the beneficiaries (or even the deceased!), rather than the personal representatives.

The effect of living for another six years or another seven years was often not understood – the difference being that after seven years the PET would become exempt, thus increasing the available nil rate band.

Too many candidates discussed taper relief despite this having no impact on the tax payable in respect of the estate.

Note: *The examiner's report has been edited to remove comments on elements of the question that have been deleted due to changes to the exam format.*

ACCA marking scheme			
			Marks
(a)		Husband's nil rate band	1.0
		Total nil rate band	1.0
		PET on 7 November 2014	1.0
			3.0
(b)	(i)	Property	1.0
		Repayment mortgage	0.5
		Endowment mortgage	0.5
		Motor cars	0.5
		Bank loan	0.5
		Legal fees	0.5
		IHT liability	0.5
		Payment responsibility	1.0
			5.0
	(ii)	Live for six more years	1.0
		Live for seven more years	1.0
			2.0
Total			**10.0**

53   ROSIE AND TOM (ADAPTED) *Walk in the footsteps of a top tutor*

Key answer tips

This question involves two separate topics. The requirements and mark allocation are very clear. Make sure that you allocate your time in relation to the mark allocation. A multi-part question covering different topics is possible in the examination. It is unlikely that IHT will be combined with pensions in the real exam; however this question provides useful revision of some elements of these topics.

Part (a) tests the income tax implications personal pension contributions. Relief for pension contributions is a key area of the syllabus that is tested regularly.

Part (b) is a straightforward IHT question testing the fundamentals of IHT. It deals with the lifetime tax payable on a chargeable lifetime gift.

(a)   **Rosie Rohan – Personal pension contributions**

Tutor's top tips

Read the question carefully – there are three parts to this requirement. You must deal with the amount of annual allowance available, how tax relief is given for contributions and the tax implications of making excess contributions. Make sure you address them all and do not spend too long on one part at the expense of another.

*Note that the question is concerned with **personal pension scheme** contributions and this will affect your answer on how tax relief is given for contributions.*

Also note that the amount of the annual allowance is given in the table of Tax Rates and Allowances provided in the exam.

Annual allowances

- Rosie was a member of a pension scheme for 2013/14, so the full annual allowance of £50,000 for that year is available.
- She has unused allowances of:

		£
2011/12	(£50,000 – £41,000)	9,000
2012/13	(£50,000 – £26,000)	24,000
2013/14		50,000
2014/15		40,000
		——————
		123,000
		——————

Tax relief

- Personal pension contributions will be made net of basic rate tax.

- Higher and additional rate tax relief will be given by extending Rosie's basic and higher rate tax bands for 2014/15 by the gross amount of the pension contributions.

Excess contributions

- If pension contributions are made in excess of the available annual allowances, then there will be an annual allowance charge.

- This charge will be subject to income tax at Rosie's marginal rate(s) of income tax.

(b) **Tom Tirith**

Tutor's top tips

The only difference between the two computations in this part will be the rate of tax paid on the gift. Remember that if Tom pays the tax his estate will be reduced by the value of the gift and the associated tax – this is reflected in the rate of tax paid on the gift.

(i) **Inheritance tax (IHT) paid by donee (the trust)**

	£	£
Value transferred		450,000
Annual exemption – 2014/15		(3,000)
– 2013/14		Nil
		————
Gross chargeable transfer		447,000
NRB at date of gift	325,000	
Less: GCTs < 7 years before gift	(Nil)	
	————	
NRB available		(325,000)
		————
Taxable amount		122,000
		————
IHT payable × 20%		24,400
		————

IHT paid by donor (Tom)

	£
Taxable amount (as above)	122,000
	————
IHT payable × 25%	30,500
	————
Gross chargeable transfer (£447,000 + £30,500)	477,500
	————

Tutorial note

The potentially exempt transfer made on 20 December 2013 utilises the annual exemption for 2013/14 but does not use any of the nil rate band as Tom is still alive.

(ii)   **Effect of gift on 20 December 2013 being to a trust**

- If Tom had made a gift to a trust rather than to his daughter, it would have been a chargeable lifetime transfer rather than a potentially exempt transfer.

- No inheritance tax would be payable on the gift on 20 December 2013, as it is below the nil rate band for 2013/14.

- It would therefore reduce the nil rate band available for the chargeable lifetime transfer on 20 February 2015, resulting in more of the second gift being chargeable to inheritance tax in Tom's lifetime.

Examiner's report

Part (a) was generally well answered, with many candidates correctly calculating the amount of available annual allowances. However, it was often not appreciated that basic rate tax relief is given by contributions being made net, and also that an annual allowance charge is subject to tax at the taxpayer's marginal rate.

Most candidates answered part (b)(i) extremely well, often gaining all of the available marks. However, the PET was sometimes incorrectly included in the workings for the first requirement – not only losing marks, but also complicating the otherwise straightforward calculations.

Note: *The examiner's report has been edited to remove comments on elements of the question that have been deleted due to changes to the exam format.*

ACCA marking scheme		Marks
(a)	Rosie Rohan	
	Annual allowances	
	Full allowance for 2013/14 as member of pension scheme	0.5
	Calculation of total unused allowances	2.0
	Tax relief	
	Paid net of basic rate tax	0.5
	Higher/additional rate relief – extend tax bands by gross contributions	0.5
	Excess contributions	
	Annual allowance charge	0.5
	Taxed at marginal rate of income tax	1.0
		———
		5.0
		———

ACCA marking scheme		Marks
(b) Tom Tirith		
(i) Inheritance tax (IHT) paid by donee (the trust)		
Annual exemption		0.5
IHT liability		1.0
IHT paid by donor (Tom)		
IHT liability		0.5
Gross chargeable transfer		1.0
		———
		3.0
		———
(ii) Gift would be a CLT rather than a PET		0.5
No IHT due as bellow NRB		0.5
Reduces NRB available for second CLT and increases IHT		1.0
		———
		2.0
Total		———
		10.0
		———

54 PERE JONES (ADAPTED) *Walk in the footsteps of a top tutor*

Key answer tips

This 10-mark question involved knowledge of two taxes: inheritance tax (IHT) and capital gains tax.

Part (a) required a calculation of the IHT that would be payable on a PET and the estate, as a result of death. This involved a straightforward IHT computation with the only trickier points being remembering to include taper relief and including it in the correct place in the computation.

Part (b) required a calculation of an individual's capital gains tax liability. The key skill was in distinguishing between capital and revenue income/expenditure.

(a) **Pere Jones**

Inheritance tax (IHT) arising on death

Lifetime transfer – 23 August 2009

	£	£
Value transferred		420,000
Less: Marriage exemption		(5,000)
Annual exemptions – 2009/10		(3,000)
– 2008/09		(3,000)
		———
Potentially exempt transfer		409,000
NRB at death	325,000	
Less: GCTs in previous 7 years	(Nil)	
	———	
NRB available		(325,000)
		———
Taxable amount		84,000
		———
IHT × 40%		33,600
Less: Taper relief (23.8.2009 to 20.3.2015) (5 – 6 years) (60%)		(20,160)
Less: Lifetime IHT paid (£Nil – as it is a PET)		Nil
		———
IHT payable		13,440
		———

Tutorial note

The gift is a potentially exempt transfer that becomes chargeable as a result of Pere dying within seven years of making it.

Pere died more than five but less than six years after the date of the gift so taper relief of 60% is available. The taper relief table is given in the Tax Rates and Allowances provided in the exam.

Death estate

	£
Value of estate	880,000
Less: Inter spouse exemption (£880,000 ÷ 2)	(440,000)
	———
Chargeable estate	440,000
	———
IHT liability at 40% (Note)	176,000
	———

Tutorial note

There is no nil rate band available to set against the death estate as it has been fully utilised against the lifetime gift to Phil, which was within seven years of Pere's death.

(b)   **Phil Jones**

Capital gains tax computation – 2014/15

	£
House	
Disposal proceeds	504,000
Less: Incidental costs of disposal	(8,600)
	————
Net disposal proceeds	495,400
Less: Cost	(420,000)
Enhancement expenditure (boundary wall)	(5,300)
	————
Chargeable gain	70,100
Less: Annual exempt amount	(11,000)
	————
Taxable gain	59,100
	————
Capital gains tax liability	
(£59,100 × 28%) (note 2)	16,548
	————

Tutorial note

1   *The cost of replacing the property's chimney is revenue expenditure as the chimney is a subsidiary part of the house. The cost of the new boundary wall is capital expenditure as the wall is a separate, distinct, entity.*

2   *Phil is a higher rate taxpayer as he has earnings from employment of £80,000 in 2014/15. He therefore has no basic rate band remaining and all of his chargeable gain is taxable at 28%.*

Examiner's report

Part (a) was generally very well answered, with many candidates achieving maximum marks. The only aspect that consistently caused problems was taper relief, with either the incorrect rate being used or relief being given at the wrong point in the computation.

Note: *The examiner's report has been edited to remove comments on elements of the question that have been deleted due to changes to the exam format.*

ACCA marking scheme		
		Marks
(a) Lifetime transfer – 23 August 2009		
Marriage exemption		1.0
Annual exemptions 2009/10		0.5
2008/09		0.5
Potentially exempt transfer		0.5
Nil rate band		0.5
IHT liability at 40%		0.5
Taper relief		1.0
Death estate		
Spouse exemption		1.0
IHT liability at 40%		0.5
		———
		6.0
		———
(b) **Capital gains tax**		
Disposal proceeds		0.5
Cost		1.0
Enhancement expenditure		1.0
Incidental costs of disposal		0.5
Annual exempt amount		0.5
CGT at 28%		0.5
		———
		4.0
		———
Total		**10.0**
		———

55 AFIYA (ADAPTED) *Walk in the footsteps of a top tutor*

Key answer tips

This is a typical IHT question, dealing with lifetime gifts and a death estate.

The IHT calculations should be straightforward involving a chargeable lifetime transfer, a PET which becomes chargeable on death and then the tax on the death estate.

The question should not pose too much difficulty to a well-prepared and well-practised student.

(a) **Inheritance tax on death**

Lifetime transfers – lifetime IHT

Tutor's top tips

Remember that the loss to the donor (or diminution in value) principle applies when calculating the transfer of value for IHT purposes. This is particularly relevant when valuing shares where a majority shareholding has a higher value per share than a minority shareholding in a company.

	PET 14.9.13	CLT 27.1.14	
	£	£	£
Transfer of value (W)	59,500		400,000
Less: AE – 2013/14	(3,000)		
– 2012/13	(3,000)		(Nil)
Chargeable amount	53,500	(Net gift)	400,000
NRB at date of gift		325,000	
Less: GCTs in last 7 years		(Nil)	
			(325,000)
Taxable amount			75,000
Lifetime IHT	Nil	(x 25%)	18,750
Gross chargeable amount c/f (£400,000 + £18,750)			418,750

Working: PET – 14 September 2013

	£
Value of shares held before the transfer (8,000 × £8)	64,000
Less: Value of shares held after the transfer (1,500 × £3)	(4,500)
Transfer of value	59,500

Tutorial note

Prior to the transfer Afiya had 8,000 shares (an 80% (8,000/10,000) shareholding) in the company and the shares are valued at £8 per share.

After the transfer Afiya owns 1,500 shares (a 15% shareholding) and the shares are valued at £3 per share.

The transfer of value is the amount by which Afiya's estate has diminished and not the market value of the asset gifted.

IHT on CLTs and PETs becoming chargeable on death

14 September 2013

	£
Potentially exempt transfer	
– covered by nil rate band on death of £325,000	53,500

27 January 2014

	£	£
Gross chargeable transfer		418,750
NRB at death	325,000	
Less: GCTs in 7 yrs pre gift		
(include PETs which become chargeable on death)		
(27.1.07 – 27.1.14)	(53,500)	
NRB available		(271,500)
Taxable amount		147,250
IHT due on death (£147,250 × 40%)		58,900
Less: Taper relief (27.1.14 to 29.11.14) (< 3 years)		(Nil)
Less: IHT paid in lifetime		(18,750)
IHT payable on death		40,150

Death estate

	£	£
Value of estate		620,000
Less: Spouse exemption		(150,000)
Chargeable estate		470,000
NRB at death	325,000	
Less: GCTs in 7 yrs pre death		
(29.11.07 – 29.11.14) (£53,500 + £418,750)	(472,250)	
NRB available		(Nil)
Taxable amount		470,000
IHT liability × 40%		188,000

(b)   **Due dates**

- The due date for the IHT liability of £18,750 payable by Afiya was 31 July 2014, being six months from the end of the month in which the gift was made.

- The due date for the additional liability on death of £40,150 is 31 May 2015, being six months after the end of the month in which Afiya (the donor) died.

(c) **Amount of inheritance**

Afiya's children will inherit the residue of £242,000 calculated as follows:

	£
Value of estate	620,000
Less: Legacy to husband	(150,000)
Specific legacy to sister	(40,000)
IHT on estate	(188,000)
	———
Residue	242,000
	———

ACCA marking scheme		Marks
(a)	Lifetime transfers – lifetime IHT	
	14.9.13	
	Value before transfer	0.5
	Value after transfer	0.5
	2013/14 AE	0.5
	2012/13 AE	0.5
	27.1.14	
	NRB at gift	0.5
	£75,000 at 20/80	0.5
	Lifetime transfers – tax on death	
	27.1.14 – GCT £418,750	0.5
	Remaining NRB	1.0
	IHT at 40%	0.5
	Less lifetime tax paid	0.5
	Death estate	
	Value of estate	0.5
	Spouse exemption	0.5
	No NRB remaining and IHT at 40%	0.5
		———
		7.0
		———
(b)	Due date lifetime tax	1.0
	Due date tax on death	1.0
		———
		2.0
		———
(c)	Residue	1.0
		———
Total		**10.0**
		———

CORPORATION TAX

CORPORATION TAX BASICS AND ADMINISTRATION

56   ARABLE LTD (ADAPTED)

Key answer tips

This question deals with the calculation of corporation tax for a short accounting period. You should remember that the length of the period affects the calculation of the maximum AIA and the WDA for capital allowances, and the limits for determining the rate of corporation tax to apply.

Other things to watch out for in this question are the effect of the short period on the lease premium deduction and the fact that the company has associated companies, which affects the small profits limits for calculating corporation tax.

Corporation tax computation – 9 months ended 31 December 2014

	£	£
Trading profit		601,611
Deduction for lease premium (W1)	2,700	
Capital allowances – Plant and machinery (W2)	396,240	
	———	(398,940)
		202,671
Property business income (W3)		49,700
Interest income – Loan interest (£6,000 + £3,000)		9,000
		———
Taxable total profits		261,371
Plus: Franked investment income (£18,000 × 100/90)		20,000
		———
Augmented profits		281,371
		———
Corporation tax (W4)		
FY2014		
£261,371 × 21%		54,888
Less: Marginal relief		
1/400 × (£375,000 – £281,371) × £261,371/£281,371		(217)
		———
Corporation tax liability		54,671
		———

Workings

(W1) Deduction for lease premium

The first office building has been used for business purposes, and so a proportion of the lease premium assessed on the landlord can be deducted.

Assessment on landlord:

	£
Premium received	75,000
Less: 2% × £75,000 × (15 − 1)	(21,000)
Assessment on landlord (Note)	54,000
Allowable deduction for 9 month period (£54,000 ÷ 15 × 9/12)	2,700

Tutorial note

Alternative calculation of the assessment on the landlord:

£75,000 × (51 − 15)/50 = £54,000

(W2) Plant and machinery

	General pool	Special rate pool	Allowances
	£	£	£	£
Additions (no AIA or FYA) (Note 1)				
Car (CO$_2$ between 96 − 130 g/km)		11,200		
Car (CO$_2$ > 130 g/km)			14,600	
Additions (with AIA) (Note 2)				
Delivery lorries	418,350			
Less: AIA (£500,000 × 9/12) (Note 2)	(375,000)			375,000
	———			
Transfer to pool		43,350		
		———		
		54,550		
WDA (18% × 9/12) (Note 2)		(7,364)		7,364
WDA (8% × 9/12) (Note 2)			(876)	876
Additions (with FYA) (Note 1)				
Car (CO$_2$ < 96 g/km)	13,000			
Less: FYA (100%)	(13,000)			13,000
	———	Nil		
TWDV c/f		47,186	13,724	
		———	———	
Total allowances				396,240

Tutorial note

1   *Capital allowances on car purchases are calculated based on the CO_2 emissions of the car as follows:*

New cars with CO_2 emissions of < 96 g/km:
eligible for a FYA of 100%.

CO_2 emissions of between 96 – 130 g/km:
put in general pool, eligible for a WDA at 18%.

CO_2 emissions of > 130 g/km:
put in special rate pool, eligible for a WDA at 8%.

The appropriate rates are given in the tax rates and allowances.

2   *The maximum AIA and WDAs are time apportioned because Arable Ltd's accounting period is nine months long. The maximum AIA is £375,000 (£500,000 × 9/12).*

(W3) Property business income

	£
Premium received for lease	50,000
Less: 2% × £50,000 × (5 – 1)	(4,000)
	———
Assessment on premium received (Note)	46,000
Plus: Rent receivable (£14,800 × 3/12)	3,700
	———
Property business income	49,700
	———

Tutorial note

Alternative calculation of the assessment on the lease:

£50,000 × (51 – 5)/50 = £46,000

(W4) Corporation tax rates

		£
Upper limit	(£1,500,000 × 1/3 × 9/12)	375,000
Lower limit	(£300,000 × 1/3 × 9/12)	75,000
Augmented profits		281,371
		Marginal relief
		applies

The limits are reduced for a nine month period and there are three associated companies in the group.

57 ZOOM PLC (ADAPTED) *Online question assistance*

Key answer tips

This question has many of the usual features of corporation tax questions with marks for computing capital allowances and taxable total profits.

One unusual aspect however is part (b) where the examiner gives you the figure of taxable total profits and asks for a reconciliation between that and the profit before tax figure.

Do not waste time trying to make your reconciliation agree if it doesn't on your first attempt.

(a) **Capital allowances for plant and machinery**

y/e 31 March 2015	General Pool	Short life asset	Special rate pool	Allow -ances
	£	£	£	£
TWDV b/f	19,600	20,200		
Additions (no AIA or FYA) (Note 1)				
Car (CO_2 > 130 g/km)			16,600	
Additions (with AIA)				
Computer (Note 2)	12,300			
Less: AIA (Note 3)	(12,300)			12,300
	———	Nil		
Disposal proceeds (Note 4)		(19,200)		
(£9,800 + £1,000)	(10,800)			
	———	———		
	8,800	1,000		
Balancing allowance		(1,000)		1,000
		———		
WDA (18%)	(1,584)			1,584
WDA (8%)			(1,328)	1,328
	———		———	
TWDV c/f	7,216		15,272	
	———		———	
Total allowances				16,212
				———

Tutorial note

Capital allowances on car purchases are calculated based on the CO_2 emissions of the car as follows:

1 New cars with CO_2 emissions of < 96 g/km: eligible for a FYA of 100%.

CO_2 emissions of between 96 – 130 g/km:
put in general pool, eligible for a WDA at 18%.

CO_2 emissions of > 130 g/km:
put in special rate pool, eligible for a WDA at 8%.

The appropriate rates are given in the tax rates and allowances.

2   It is assumed that the election to treat the computer as a short life asset has not been made.

If it had been made, a separate column would be set up, but the allowances in this year would be identical whether or not the election is made.

3   *The sale proceeds for all of the assets disposed of are less than the original cost. The proceeds are therefore deducted from the short life asset column and the general pool (for the lorry and equipment).*

(b)   **Reconciliation of profits – year ended 31 March 2015**

Key answer tips

In the reconciliation it is important to list all the major items in the question, showing a zero (0) for items which require no adjustment. This is because credit will be given for showing no adjustment where none is needed. List the adjustments in the order they appear in the question.

If required, also add notes to show why you have not adjusted for an item, or why you have added it back. However, lengthy explanations are not required where the requirement is just to 'prepare a computation', rather than to explain the reconciliation.

Always show your workings if the figure you are adjusting for is not clear from the question.

	£	£
Profit before taxation	865,320	
Depreciation	59,227	
Capital allowances (part (a))		16,212
Income from investments		82,420
Interest payable (Note)	0	
	───────	───────
	924,547	98,632
	(98,632)	───────
	───────	
Trading profit	825,915	
Interest income – Bank interest	10,420	
– Loan interest	22,500	
	───────	
Taxable total profits	858,835	
	───────	

Tutorial note

The interest on a loan used for trading purposes is deductible in calculating the trading profit and has already been deducted, so no adjustment is required.

58   DO-NOT-PANIC LTD (ADAPTED)

Key answer tips

This 10 mark question involves a long period of account requiring knowledge of the rules of how to split income and gains between two chargeable accounting periods.

When the question was set, the capital allowance rules were different and more was involved in the calculation than under the current rules.

Corporation tax liabilities – Fifteen-month period ended 31 March 2015

	y/e 31.12.2014 £	p/e 31.3.2015 £
Trading profit (12/15 : 3/15) (Note 1)	350,000	87,500
Less: Capital allowances (W1)	(Nil)	(24,000)
	350,000	63,500
Net chargeable gains (£42,000 – £4,250) (Note 2)	Nil	37,750
Taxable total profits	350,000	101,250
Plus: Franked investment income (Note 3)	Nil	25,000
Augmented profits	350,000	126,250

Corporation tax (W2)		
FY2013: (£350,000 × 23% × 3/12)	20,125	
Less: Marginal relief		
3/400 × (£1,500,000 – £350,000) × 3/12	(2,156)	
FY2014: (£350,000 × 21% × 9/12)	55,125	
Less: Marginal relief		
1/400 × (£1,500,000 – £350,000) × 9/12	(2,156)	
FY2014: (£101,250 × 21%)		21,262
Less: Marginal relief		
1/400 × (£375,000 – £126,250) × £101,250/£126,250		(499)
Corporation tax liability	70,938	20,763
Due dates	1 Oct 2015	1 Jan 2016
Total liability		£91,701

Tutorial note

Trading profits are allocated on a time basis: 12/15 to the year ended 31 December 2014 and 3/15 to the period ended 31 March 2015.

The capital loss of £4,250 for the year ended 31 December 2014 is carried forward and set against the first available future gains in the 3 months ended 31 March 2015.

The figure provided in the question was franked investment income rather than the dividend received, therefore grossing up by 100/90 is not necessary.

Workings

(W1) Capital allowances

		General pool	Allowances
	£	£	£
Year ended 31 December 2014			
No additions in the period			
Period ended 31 March 2015			
Additions (with AIA)			
Equipment	24,000		
Less: AIA (Max £500,000 × 3/12)	(24,000)		24,000
	———	Nil	
		———	
TWDV c/f		Nil	
		———	
Total allowances			24,000
			———

Tutorial note

The maximum AIA is time apportioned because the company's accounting period is three months long.

(W2) Corporation tax rate

		y/e 31.12.14	*p/e 31.3.15*
		£	£
Upper limit	(Full / 3/12)	1,500,000	375,000
Lower limit	(Full / 3/12)	300,000	75,000
Augmented profits		350,000	126,250
		Marginal relief applies	*Marginal relief applies*

The accounting period ended 31 December 2014 falls partly into FY2013 (3 months) and partly into FY2014 (9 months).

As the tax rates are different in these financial years the liability must be calculated separately for each year.

Examiner's report

Depending on whether candidates appreciated that the period of account needed to be split into a twelve-month period and a three-month period, this question was either answered very well or quite badly.

Invariably many of the less well prepared candidates calculated corporation tax based on a fifteen-month period.

Even when the correct approach was taken, many candidates did not appreciate that the first twelve month period spanned two financial years.

The due dates were often omitted or incorrect.

ACCA marking scheme		Marks
Trading profit		1.0
Capital allowances	– Year ended 31 December 2014	0.5
	– Period ended 31 March 2015	1.5
Capital gains		1.0
Franked investment income		1.0
Corporation tax	– Year ended 31 December 2014	2.5
	– Period ended 31 March 2015	1.5
Due dates		1.0
Total		**10.0**

---

59 CRASH BASH LTD (ADAPTED) *Walk in the footsteps of a top tutor*

Key answer tips

A standard corporation tax question requiring a capital allowances computation for plant and machinery followed by a corporation tax computation.

These areas are often tested and should not have caused many difficulties.

The original question also tested various overseas aspects of corporation tax, which are no longer examinable. This part has been replaced by a question on corporation tax administration, which is an area which is frequently tested and must be learnt.

Tutor's top tips

Be sure to read the requirement carefully and pay attention to the mark allocation.

Part (a) only requires two bullet points to be made, but remember to relate your answer to the specific information given in the question.

Part (b) is where the time should be spent, however, don't run out of time to attempt part (c) by spending too long here.

Part (c) deals with the implications of missing filing deadlines, and is a straightforward test of knowledge retention.

(a)   **Residence status**

- Companies that are incorporated overseas are only treated as being resident in the UK if their central management and control is exercised in the UK.

- Since the directors are UK based and hold their board meetings in the UK, this would indicate that Crash-Bash Ltd is managed and controlled from the UK, and therefore it is resident in the UK.

(b)   **Corporation tax liability – period ended 31 January 2015**

Tutor's top tips

Remember to use your time effectively for this part.

Computations for capital allowances are required in workings before the corporation tax computation can be drawn up. Remember to reference your workings clearly to your main answer to the question.

Note that this question is now simpler than the original question set as there are no longer any overseas aspects.

The mark allocation in this answer has been adjusted accordingly.

	£	£
Trading profit per question		1,002,924
Advertising expenditure (Note 1)	12,840	
Capital allowances – Plant and machinery (W1)	389,044	
		(401,884)
Tax adjusted trading profit		601,040
Taxable total profits		601,040
Plus: FII (£36,000 × 100/90) (Note 2)		40,000
Augmented profits		641,040
Corporation tax (W2)		
FY2014 (£601,040 × 21%)		126,218

Tutorial note

1   The advertising expenditure incurred during April 2014 is pre-trading revenue expenditure. Accordingly it is treated as incurred on the first day of trading (i.e. 1 May 2014) and is therefore an allowable deduction for corporation tax purposes.

As no adjustment has been made for this expenditure yet, an adjustment is required.

2   If the dividends are received from a non-associated company, they must be grossed up at 100/90 and included in FII. However, dividends from an associated company are excluded from the definition of FII. Safety Ltd is a 100% subsidiary and therefore it is an associated company and any dividends received are not FII.

Workings

(W1) Plant and machinery

	£	General pool £	Allowances £
Additions (with AIA):			
Machinery	381,250		
Less: AIA (Maximum) (Note 2)	(375,000)		375,000
	———	6,250	
Less: WDA (Note 2)			
(£6,250 × 18% × 9/12)		(844)	844
Additions (with FYA):			
Car (CO_2 < 96 g/km)	13,200		
Less: FYA (100%)	(13,200)		13,200
	———	Nil	
TWDV c/f		5,406	
Total allowances			389,044

Tutorial note

1   Capital allowances on car purchases are calculated based on the CO_2 emissions of the car. A new car with CO_2 emissions of < 96 g/km is eligible for a FYA of 100%.

2   The maximum Annual Investment Allowance is £375,000 (£500,000 × 9/12) because Crash-Bash Ltd's accounting period is nine months long.

The writing down allowance is similarly restricted to 9/12, however first year allowances are never restricted according to the length of the accounting period.

(W2) Corporation tax rate

- The accounting period is nine months long and falls entirely in FY2014.
- Crash-Bash Ltd has one associated company.

- The upper and lower limits for corporation tax purposes are:

Upper limit	(£1,500,000 × 9/12 × ½)	£562,500
Lower limit	(£300,000 × 9/12 × ½)	£112,500

- The augmented profits of £641,040 exceed the upper limit and therefore Crash-Bash Ltd is a main rate company.

(c) **Implications of late filing and payment**

- Crash-Bash Ltd's self-assessment tax return for the period ended 31 January 2015 must be submitted by 31 January 2016.

- If the company submits its self-assessment tax return eight months late, then there will be an automatic fixed penalty of £200, since the return is more than three months late.

- There will also be an additional corporation tax related penalty of £12,622 (£126,218 × 10%) being 10% of the tax unpaid, since the self-assessment tax return is more than six months late.

Tutorial note

The tax geared penalty starts when 18 months or more have passed after the end of the return period (i.e. this is the same as saying 6 months or more after the filing date).

Examiner's report

Although the numerical aspects of this question were well answered, most candidates achieved lower marks for this question than for question one, despite this question being five marks longer.

In the first section of part (a) most candidates were not aware that the essential point regarding residence is where a company's central management and control is exercised.

Most candidates had little difficulty with the corporation tax computation, and there were many perfect answers to this part of the question.

Note: *The examiner's report has been edited to remove comments on elements of the question that have been deleted due to changes to the exam format.*

ACCA marking scheme		
		Marks
(a)	Central management and control	1.0
	Board meetings held in the UK	1.0
		2.0
(b)	Trading profit	0.5
	Advertising expenditure	1.0
	P & M – AIA	1.5
	– WDA	1.5
	– FYA (100%)	1.5
	Dividend from associate – not included in FII	0.5
	Franked investment income	0.5
	Adjustment of profits limits	1.0
	Corporation tax calculation	1.0
		9.0

ACCA marking scheme			Marks
(c)	Due date		1.0
	Fixed penalty		1.5
	Corporation tax related penalty		1.5
			4.0
Total			**15.0**

60 QUAGMIRE LTD *Walk in the footsteps of a top tutor*

Key answer tips

This question covers the quarterly instalment system of payment for large companies. It is not difficult provided the self-assessment rules for companies have been learnt.

In particular you need to know the conditions for determining whether or not a company is large for this purpose, and the key due dates of payment.

Tutor's top tips

Part (a) requires an explanation of why the company has to pay by instalments. The clue that the company is large is therefore in the requirement.

The question itself gives taxable total profits and FII which should trigger alarm bells that the level of 'augmented profits' is an important consideration.

The fact that both this year and last year's information is given should also be a clue that they are both important to determine the status of the company.

(a) **Quarterly instalment payments**

- Large companies have to make quarterly instalment payments in respect of their corporation tax liability. A large company is one paying corporation tax at the main rate.

- Quagmire plc has one associated company, so the upper limit is reduced to £750,000 (£1,500,000 × 1/2). Corporation tax will therefore be at the main rate for the year ended 31 January 2015.

- There is an exception for the first year that a company is large, provided profits do not exceed £10 million (divided by the number of associated companies).

 However, no exception applies in this case because Quagmire plc was also a large company for the year ended 31 January 2014.

Tutorial note

The instalment payment system is not applied if:

1　*The corporation tax liability is less than £10,000, or*

2　*The company is 'large' for the first time and the profits do not exceed £10 million (divided by number of associates if applicable)*

(b)　**Corporation tax liability and due dates for payment**

Corporation tax – year ended 31 January 2015

	£
FY2013 (£1,200,000 × 23% × 2/12)	46,000
FY2014 (£1,200,000 × 21% × 10/12)	210,000
Corporation tax liability	256,000

The accounting period falls partly within FY2013 (2 months) and partly within FY2014 (10 months).

The tax rates are different in each financial year so the corporation tax liability must be calculated separately for each financial year.

- Quagmire plc's corporation tax liability for the year ended 31 January 2015 is £256,000.

- The company will have paid this in four quarterly instalments of £64,000 (£256,000/4).

- The instalments will have been due on the 14th of August 2014, November 2014, February 2015 and May 2015.

Tutorial note

Remember that the corporation tax liability is calculated on taxable total profits, not 'augmented profits'.

The instalments are due on the 14th day of the 7th, 10th, 13th and 16th month after the start of the chargeable accounting period.

(c)　**Revised position assuming Quagmire did not have an associated company**

Tutor's top tips

The requirement asks for an explanation of the effect if there is no associate – so make sure that you explain in words and do not just do a calculation.

The revised calculation is worth only 1.5 of the 4 marks available.

- Quagmire plc's augmented profits for the year ended 31 January 2015 are £1,400,000 (£1,200,000 plus franked investment income of £200,000).

- Quagmire plc is no longer a large company since its profits are below the upper limit of £1,500,000. The corporation tax liability will therefore be due in one amount on 1 November 2015.

- The corporation tax liability will be:

	£
FY2013	
(£1,200,000 at 23% × 2/12)	46,000
Less: Marginal relief	
3/400 × (£1,500,000 − £1,400,000) × £1,200,000/£1,400,000 × 2/12	(107)
FY2014	
(£1,200,000 at 21% × 10/12)	210,000
Less: Marginal relief	
1/400 × (£1,500,000 − £1,400,000) × £1,200,000/£1,400,000 × 10/12	(179)
Corporation tax	255,714

Tutorial note

The normal due date for corporation tax is 9 months and 1 day after the end of the chargeable accounting period.

Examiner's report

This question was reasonably well answered.

In part (a) very few candidates appreciated that there was a possible exception and that the exception did not apply. This was the reason why figures were given for the previous year, and less well prepared candidates created a lot of problems for themselves by trying to use these figures as part of their calculations.

Candidates had little difficulty in calculating the corporation tax liability in part (b), but they often struggled with the quarterly due dates.

There was a similar problem in part (c) where many candidates failed to score an easy mark by omitting the due date.

ACCA marking scheme		Marks
(a)	Large companies	1.0
	Associated company	1.0
	No exception	1.0
		3.0
(b)	Corporation tax liability	1.0
	Instalments	1.0
	Due dates	1.0
		3.0

ACCA marking scheme		Marks
(c)	Augmented profits	1.0
	No longer a large company	0.5
	Due date	1.0
	Corporation tax	1.5
		4.0
Total		**10.0**

61 MOLTEN METAL PLC (ADAPTED) *Walk in the footsteps of a top tutor*

Key answer tips

Part (a) requires a corporation tax computation including a partial adjustment of profits, an involved capital allowances computation and interest income.

Detailed knowledge of capital versus revenue expenditure, capital allowances and the treatment of interest is needed.

Part (b) tests the quarterly instalment system and is straightforward.

(a) **Corporation tax computation – year ended 31 March 2015**

	£	£
Trading profit per question		2,090,086
Loan stock interest payable (W1) (Note 1)	22,000	
Repairs to office building (Note 2)	0	
Capital allowance – P & M (W2)	524,354	
		(546,354)
Tax adjusted trading profit		1,543,732
Interest income (W3)		8,700
TTP		1,552,432
Corporation tax (£1,552,432 × 21%)		326,011

Tutorial note

1. *Interest paid in respect of a loan used for trading purposes is deductible in calculating the trading profit.*

2. *The repairs to the office building are not deductible as revenue expenditure. They are treated as capital in nature, as the building was not in a usable state when purchased and this fact was reflected in the reduced purchase price.*

Workings

(W1) Interest payable

	£
Accrual b/f at 1 April 2014	(4,200)
Loan stock interest paid	22,500
Accrual c/f at 31 March 2015	3,700
	22,000

Tutorial note

The loan stock was issued to raise funds for a trading purpose; therefore the interest is an allowable deduction against trading profit, calculated on an accruals basis.

(W2) Plant and machinery

	£	General pool £	Special rate pool £	Allowances £
TWDV b/f		87,800		
Additions not qualifying for AIA				
Motor cars (£17,300 × 2) (Note 1)		34,600		
Additions qualifying for AIA				
Integral features (Note 2)				
Ventilation system	83,000			
Lift	10,000			
	93,000			
Less: AIA (Note 3)	(93,000)			93,000
			Nil	
Other plant and machinery				
Machinery	390,000			
Building alterations (Note 4)	7,000			
Wall (Note 5)	Nil			
Partition walls (Note 5)	22,900			
	419,900			
Less: AIA (Note 3)	(407,000)			407,000
		12,900		
		135,300		
Less: WDA (18%)		(24,354)		24,354
TWDV c/f		110,946	Nil	
Total allowances				524,354

Tutorial note

1   The motor cars have CO_2 emissions between 96 and 130 grams per kilometre, and therefore go in the general pool. They do not qualify for the AIA but do qualify for writing down allowances at the rate of 18%.

   The private use of a motor car is irrelevant for company capital allowances computations, since such usage will be assessed on the employee as an employment benefit.

2   The purchase of an office building itself is not eligible for plant and machinery allowances.

   However, the ventilation system and lift are both integral to a building and are eligible for plant and machinery allowances as special rate pool items.

3   It is beneficial to claim the AIA of £500,000 initially against the special rate pool expenditure, as it would otherwise only qualify for writing down allowance at the rate of 8%.

   Any remaining AIA, up to a maximum of £500,000 in total, is set against the plant and machinery expenditure and the balance is put in the general pool.

4   The building alterations were necessary for the installation of the machinery, and therefore qualify for capital allowances.

5   Walls are specifically excluded as qualifying for capital allowances, with the exception of partition walls which are movable and intended to be so moved. The partition walls perform a 'function' (enabling the office space to be changed and used efficiently) unlike the wall which is just decorative and is the 'setting' for the business.

(W3) Interest income

	£
Loan interest receivable (£9,800 + £3,100)	12,900
Bank interest receivable	2,600
	15,500
Less: Loan interest expense	(6,800)
Interest income	8,700

(b) Final quarterly instalment payment

	£
Corporation tax liability	326,011
Less: Quarterly instalments paid	(298,200)
Final instalment payment	27,811
Due date:	14 July 2015

Examiner's report

This question was generally well answered, and there were many very good answers.

In part (a) there was no need to have separate computations for the trading profit and for taxable total profits, since it was quite straightforward to combine everything into one computation.

The accruals for the interest payable and interest income often caused problems, and many candidates did not appreciate that no adjustment to the trading profit was necessary in respect of any of the items debited to the capital expenditure account. The writing down allowance for a motor car with private use was often restricted, despite such an adjustment only being relevant for an unincorporated business.

Although most candidates correctly calculated the final quarterly instalment in part (b), the due date was generally not known.

Note: The examiner's report has been edited to remove comments on elements of the question that have been deleted due to changes to the exam format.

ACCA marking scheme		Marks
(a)	Trading profit	0.5
	Loan stock interest payable	1.5
	Repairs to office building	1.0
	P & M – Office building	0.5
	– Ventilation system and lift	1.0
	– AIA	1.0
	– Machinery	0.5
	– Building alterations	0.5
	– Wall	0.5
	– Partition walls	1.0
	– AIA	1.0
	– General pool transfer	1.0
	– General pool WDA	0.5
	Interest income	2.0
	Corporation tax liability	0.5
		13.0
(b)	Instalment payment	1.0
	Due date	1.0
		2.0
Total		15.0

62   STRETCHED LTD (ADAPTED)

Key answer tips

This question deals with the rules for a 15 month period of account which must be split into two accounting periods of 12 months and 3 months.

For ease, use a columnar layout to do the corporation tax computations side by side. Don't forget to pick up the easy marks for stating the due dates of payment.

(a)   **Corporation tax computations**

	y/e 31.12.14 £	p/e 31.3.15 £
Trading profit (12/15 : 3/15) (Note 1)	514,000	128,500
Less: Capital allowances (W1)	Nil	(125,338)
	514,000	3,162
Less: Loss relief b/f	(273,000)	Nil
	241,000	3,162
Property business profit (12/15 : 3/15) (Note 1)	36,000	9,000
Chargeable gains (£44,000 – £3,000) (Note 2)	41,000	Nil
	318,000	12,162
Less: QCD relief	Nil	(5,000)
Taxable total profits	318,000	7,162
Plus: Franked investment income	30,000	Nil
Augmented profits	348,000	7,162
Corporation tax (W2)		
FY2013		
(£318,000 × 23% × 3/12)	18,285	
Less: Marginal relief		
3/400 × (£1,500,000 – £348,000) × £318,000/£348,000 × 3/12	(1,974)	
FY2014		
(£318,000 × 21% × 9/12)	50,085	
Less: Marginal relief		
1/400 × (£1,500,000 – £348,000) × £318,000/£348,000 × 9/12	(1,974)	
FY2014: (£7,162 × 20%)		1,432
	64,422	1,432
Due dates	1 Oct 2015	1 Jan 2016

Tutorial note

1   Trading profits and property business profits are allocated on a time basis: 12/15 to the year ended 31 December 2014 and 3/15 to the period ended 31 March 2015.

2   The capital loss of £6,700 for the period ended 31 March 2015 is carried forward, it cannot be carried back and set off against previous gains.

Workings

(W1) Capital allowances

	£	General pool £	Allowances £
3 months ended 31 March 2015			
Additions (with AIA)			
Office equipment	132,500		
Less: AIA (Max £500,000 × 3/12)	(125,000)		125,000
		7,500	
Less: WDA (18%) × 3/12		(338)	338
TWDV c/f		7,162	
Total allowances			125,338

Tutorial note

The AIA and WDA must be time apportioned as the chargeable accounting period is only three months in length.

(W2) Corporation tax rates

		y/e 31.12.14 £	p/e 31.3.15 £
Upper limit	(Full / × 3/12)	1,500,000	375,000
Lower limit	(Full / × 3/12)	300,000	75,000
Augmented profits		348,000	7,162
		Marginal relief	Small profits

The accounting period ended 31 December 2014 falls partly into FY2013 (3 months) and partly into FY2014 (9 months).

As there has been a change in rate of tax the corporation tax liability must be calculated separately for each financial year.

(b)   **Advantages of 31 March year end**

- Being aligned with the financial year will make it easier for a company to calculate its corporation tax liability, since the same rates, reliefs and legislation will apply throughout the accounting period.

- For owner-managed companies, alignment with the income tax year (the odd five days can be ignored) will make it easier as regards calculating the most tax efficient method of extracting profits from the company.

63   STARFISH LTD (ADAPTED) *Walk in the footsteps of a top tutor*

Key answer tips

This question covers corporation tax aspects of a loss making company.

Part (a) involved a basic adjustment of profits computation with the standard requirement to calculate capital allowances. However, the period is loss-making and is the period of cessation. Particular care is therefore needed in the calculation of the capital allowances, especially as you are required to deal with the impact of VAT on the additions and disposals.

Part (b) was a little trickier as it involved the need to deal with two trading losses; an opening period loss and a terminal loss in the period of cessation. However, it is a company making the losses, not an individual and the loss relief rules for companies are much more straightforward. There are no special opening year and closing year rules to apply. The terminal loss can just be carried back 36 months rather than 12 months. Make sure you deal with the losses in strict date order.

It is therefore a fairly standard loss question which is largely computational and should not have been too difficult provided the approach to losses questions had been practised. For ease, a columnar format should be used to present the loss offset and remember to show your record of the losses and how they have been relieved in a working.

Tutor's top tips

This is a long time pressured question and you need to work through it methodically. The requirements are broken down into small parts which help you to structure your answer.

(a) **Starfish Ltd**

Tax adjusted trading loss – period ended 31 March 2015

	Notes	£	£
Loss before taxation			190,000
Depreciation		34,400	
Donation to political party		300	
Qualifying charitable donation	1	1,350	
Impairment loss		0	
Entertaining customers	2	3,600	
Entertaining employees	2	0	
Counselling services	3	0	
Capital allowances (W)			2,300
		———	———
		39,650	192,300
		(192,300)	———
		———	
Trading loss		(152,650)	
		———	

Tutorial note

1   *Qualifying charitable donations (QCDs) made by a company to a charity are allowable deductions, but not from trading profit. They are deductible from total profits in the main corporation tax computation. Therefore, in the adjustment of profits computation they need to be added back to trading profit.*

2   *The only exception to the non-deductibility of entertainment expenditure is when it is in respect of employees.*

3   *The costs of counselling services for redundant employees are allowable.*

Working – Plant and machinery

	Notes	General pool £	Special rate pool £	Allow-ances £
TWDV b/f		23,600	13,200	
Addition (£3,120 × 100/120)	1, 2	2,600		
		———		
		26,200		
Sale proceeds:	2			
Main pool (£31,200 + £1,800) × 100/120		(27,500)		
Motor car	3		(9,600)	
		———	———	
		(1,300)	3,600	
Balancing charge		1,300		(1,300)
Balancing allowance			(3,600)	3,600
		———	———	———
TWDV c/f		Nil	Nil	
		———	———	
Total allowances				2,300
				———

Tutorial note

1   The annual investment allowance and writing down allowances are not given for the period in which a trade ceases. Therefore the addition is simply added into the general pool.

2   The net cost (excluding VAT) of the addition is added to the general pool as input VAT is recovered on the purchase, and the net sale proceeds (excluding VAT) relating to the sale of general pool items is deducted.

3   Input VAT however would not have been recovered in respect of the motor car as it was not used exclusively for business purposes. Therefore, output VAT is not due on the disposal and the gross sale proceeds are deducted in the capital allowances computation.

Tutor's top tips

Once you have calculated your trading loss in part (a) you have to use it in the calculation of loss relief in part (b). Remember that even if your answer to part (a) is incorrect you will get marks for applying the rules correctly in part (b).

(b)   **Starfish Ltd – Taxable total profits**

	4 m/e 31.3.2011	y/e 31.3.2012	y/e 31.3.2013	y/e 31.3.2014	9 m/e 31.12.2014	3 m/e 31.3.2015
	£	£	£	£	£	£
Trading profit	Nil	64,200	53,900	14,700	49,900	Nil
Less: Loss relief b/f	(–)	(12,600)	(–)	(–)	(–)	(–)
	Nil	51,600	53,900	14,700	49,900	Nil
Bank interest	600	1,400	1,700	Nil	Nil	Nil
	600	53,000	55,600	14,700	49,900	Nil
Less: Loss relief						
– Current period	(Nil)					(Nil)
– Carry back	n/a	(13,250)	(55,600)	(14,700)	(49,900)	
	600	39,750	Nil	Nil	Nil	Nil
Less: QCD relief	(600)	(1,000)	wasted	wasted	wasted	wasted
TTP	Nil	38,750	Nil	Nil	Nil	Nil

Loss working

	£
Tax adjusted trading loss – 3 m/e 31.3.2015	152,650
Relief given in:	
– 3 m/e 31.3.2015	(Nil)
– 9 m/e 31.12.2014	(49,900)
– y/e 31.3.2014	(14,700)
– y/e 31.3.2013	(55,600)
– y/e 31.3.2012 (3/12 × £53,000)	(13,250)
Loss unrelieved	19,200

Tutorial note

1   *Starfish Ltd would not have made a loss relief claim against total profits for the period ended 31 March 2011 as this would have used £600 of the loss, but wasted the qualifying charitable donations (QCDs) for that period and saved no tax as the QCDs already cover the taxable profits.*

2   *The trading loss for the period ended 31 March 2015 is a terminal loss, and can therefore be relieved against total profits:*

       –   *firstly for the period of the loss (£Nil in this case), and then*

       –   *carried back to the previous 36 months prior to the start of the loss-making period, on a LIFO basis.*

    As there is a 9 month CAP in the terminal loss carry back period, the loss can be carried back into the year ended 31 March 2012 computation, but can only be set against 3/12 of the total profits in that year.

3   *Note that the terminal loss is offset against total profits (i.e. before QCDs). The relief for QCDs is therefore wasted in each of the last four CAPs. The loss relief is an all or nothing claim and cannot be restricted to preserve relief for the QCDs.*

Examiner's report

Part (a) was very well answered, with many very good answers.

The only aspect consistently answered incorrectly was the treatment of a purchased asset. In the final capital allowances computation no allowances are given, so the addition should simply have been added to the general pool.

In part (b) many candidates overlooked the trading loss for the final period of trading.

Note: *The examiner's report has been edited to remove comments on elements of the question that have been deleted due to changes to the exam format.*

	ACCA marking scheme	
		Marks
(a)	Depreciation	0.5
	Donations	1.5
	Impairment loss	1.0
	Entertaining customers	0.5
	Entertaining employees	0.5
	Counselling services	0.5
	P & M – WDV brought forward	0.5
	– Addition	1.5
	– General pool proceeds	2.0
	– Special rate pool proceeds	1.0
	– Balancing adjustments	0.5
		10.0
(b)	Trading profit	0.5
	Relief for 2011 loss – Period ended 31 March 2011 (£nil)	0.5
	– Carry forward	0.5
	Bank interest	0.5
	Relief for 2015 loss – Year ended 31 March 2012	1.0
	– Other periods	1.0
	Qualifying charitable donations	1.0
		5.0
Total		**15.0**

64 HEAVY LTD (ADAPTED) *Walk in the footsteps of a top tutor*

Key answer tips

This question required a straight forward corporation tax computation, and easy marks were available for a basic pro forma and straightforward adjustments to trading profits for depreciation, amortisation and capital allowances.

Tutor's top tips

Heavy Ltd owns 100% of the share capital of Soft Ltd, therefore remember to divide the limits by two for the purpose of calculating the corporation tax liabilities.

The period of account straddles FY2014 and FY2015. However as the rates of corporation tax for the two years are assumed to be the same there is no need to time apportion the profits and calculate the tax liability for each financial year.

Heavy Ltd

Corporation tax computation – year ended 31 July 2015

	£
Operating profit	433,100
Add back: Depreciation	12,880
Health and safety fine	9,000
	────────
	454,980
Less: Capital allowances (W1)	(51,370)
	────────
Trading profit	403,610
Chargeable gain (Note 1)	Nil
	────────
TTP	403,610
	────────

	£
Corporation tax (Note 3) (W2)	
(£403,610 × 21%)	84,758
Less: Marginal relief	
1/400 × (£750,000 − £433,610) × £403,610/£433,610	(736)
	────────
	84,022
	────────

Tutorial note

1   *The sale of the office building does not give rise to a chargeable gain as it is an inter-group transfer of a capital asset to Soft Ltd, a 75% group company. The transfer is therefore a nil gain/nil loss event.*

2   *The UK dividends are exempt from UK corporation tax and are therefore excluded from TTP.*

Workings

(W1) Capital allowances

	£	General pool £	SLA (1) £	SLA (2) £	Special rate pool £	Allow-ances £
TWDV b/f		900	15,100	13,200	21,700	
Addition qualifying for AIA						
Office equipment	22,400					
Less: AIA (100%)	(22,400)					22,400
		Nil				
Disposal proceeds				(4,600)	(12,300)	
		900	15,100	8,600	9,400	
Balancing allowance				(8,600)		8,600
Small pool WDA		(900)				900
WDA (18%)			(2,718)			2,718
WDA (8%)					(752)	752
Addition qualifying for FYA						
New low emission car ($CO_2 \leq 95$ g/km)	16,000					
Less FYA (100%)	(16,000)					16,000
		Nil				
TWDV c/f		Nil	12,382	Nil	8,648	
Total allowances						51,370

Tutorial note

1   The balance on the general pool is less than £1,000 so a small pool writing down allowance equal to the unrelieved expenditure can be claimed.

2   Short life asset (1), being an item of plant and machinery, qualifies for a WDA at the rate of 18%. Short life asset (2) was disposed of in the year for proceeds less than its tax written down value and a balancing allowance therefore arises.

3   The motor car acquired on 24 April 2015 is a new low emission car (CO_2 emissions ≤ 95 g/km) and therefore qualifies for a 100% FYA. The private use of the motor car is irrelevant, since such usage will be assessed on the managing director as an employment benefit.

4   Although all of the items included in the special rate pool have been sold, there is no balancing allowance arising as the business is a continuing business which has not ceased.

(W2) Rate of corporation tax

	£
TTP	403,610
Plus: FII (£27,000 × 100/90) (Note)	30,000
Augmented profits	433,610

Heavy Ltd has one associated company; therefore the limits are divided by 2

Upper limit (£1,500,000 ÷ 2)	£750,000
Lower limit (£300,000 ÷ 2)	£150,000

As augmented profits fall between the limits; marginal relief applies.

Tutorial note

UK dividends received are not taxable and do not appear in the TTP computation. However, if they are received from unconnected companies they are treated as Franked Investment Income (FII) for the purposes of determining the correct rate of tax to apply to TTP.

The actual amount received is grossed up at 100/90 to calculate FII.

The dividend from Soft Ltd is however not FII as it is an intra-group dividend and not from an unconnected party.

Examiner's report

There were many very good answers.

The aspects that caused problems were not appreciating that:

1   There was no chargeable gain on a disposal of an office building to Soft Ltd because of the 75% group relationship.

2   The balance on the main capital allowances pool could be fully written off as it was less than £1,000.

3   There was no balancing allowance on the special rate pool despite all the items included therein having been sold.

Note: *The examiner's report has been edited to remove comments on elements of the question that have been deleted due to changes to the exam format.*

ACCA marking scheme	
	Marks
Operating profit	0.5
Depreciation	0.5
Health and safety fine	0.5
Capital allowances – AIA	1.0
– General pool – small pool WDA	1.0
– SLA (1)	1.0
– SLA (2)	2.0
– Special rate pool	2.0
– Low emission car	2.0
Chargeable gain	1.0
Franked investment income	1.5
Corporation tax – Upper limit	0.5
– Main rate	0.5
– Marginal relief	1.0
Total	**15.0**

65 GREENZONE LTD (ADAPTED) *Walk in the footsteps of a top tutor*

Key answer tips

This ten mark question required the computation of a company's tax adjusted trading profit with a number of straightforward adjustments and a detailed capital allowances computation.

It is essential to use the appropriate proformas when attempting this kind of question.

Tutor's top tips

Start your computation with the operating profit figure, as required by the question.

Work through the statement of profit or loss and each of the notes in the question dealing with each piece of information as you go.

Remember to indicate by the use of zero any items for which no adjustment is required.

Tax adjusted trading profit – year ended 31 March 2015

	£
Operating profit	239,700
Depreciation	28,859
Repainting office building	0
New reception area (Note 1)	19,800
Entertaining UK customers (Note 2)	3,600
Entertaining overseas customers (Note 2)	1,840
Political donations	740
Non-qualifying charitable donations (Note 3)	0
Gifts to customers – Pens (Note 4)	660
– Clocks (Note 4)	910
	_____
	296,109
Less: Capital allowances (W)	(18,409)
	_____
Tax adjusted trading profit	277,700
	_____

Tutorial note

1   *The extension of the office building is not deductible, being capital in nature. The building has been improved rather than repaired.*

2   *For corporation tax purposes all entertaining expenditure is disallowed unless it relates to employees.*

3   *The charitable donation is an allowable expense against trading profits as it is local and reasonable in size in relation to the business and is wholly and exclusively incurred for trading purposes (i.e. free advertising). The reference to this being a non-qualifying charitable donation in the question is simply because it will not be deducted from total profits as a qualifying charitable donation (QCD).*

4   *Gifts to customers are only an allowable deduction if they cost less than £50 per recipient per year, are not of food, drink, tobacco or vouchers exchangeable for goods and carry a conspicuous advertisement for the company making the gift.*

Working: Capital allowances

Tutorial note

1   *Motor car (1) is a new car and has CO_2 emissions up to 95 grams per kilometre and therefore qualifies for the 100% first year allowance (FYA).*

2   *Motor car (2) has CO_2 emissions between 95 and 130 grams per kilometre and therefore qualifies for writing down allowances at the rate of 18%.*

3   *The proceeds for motor car (3) are restricted to the original cost figure of £8,500.*

	£	General pool £	Special rate pool £	Allowances £
TWDV b/f		48,150	9,200	
Addition not qualifying for AIA				
Motor car (2)		20,400		
		———		
		68,550		
Proceeds – Motor car (3)		(8,500)		
– Motor car (4)			(12,400)	
		———		
		60,050	(3,200)	
Balancing charge			3,200	(3,200)
			———	
Less: WDA (18%)		(10,809)		10,809
Addition qualifying for FYA				
Motor car (1)	10,800			
Less: FYA (100%)	(10,800)			10,800
	———	Nil		
		———		
TWDV c/f		49,241		
		———		
Total allowances				18,409
				———

ACCA marking scheme	
	Marks
Depreciation	0.5
Repainting office building	0.5
New reception area	0.5
Entertaining UK customers	0.5
Entertaining overseas customers	0.5
Political donations	0.5
Non-qualifying charitable donations	0.5
Gifts to customers – Pens	0.5
– Clocks	0.5
Deducting capital allowances	0.5
Capital allowances:	
TWDVs brought forward	1.0
Addition – Motor car (1)	0.5
Proceeds – Motor car (3)	1.0
– Motor car (4)	0.5
Balancing charge	0.5
WDA – 18%	0.5
Addition qualifying for FYA – Motor car (1)	0.5
FYA – 100%	0.5
Total	**10.0**

66   SOFTAPP LTD (ADAPTED) *Walk in the footsteps of a top tutor*

Key answer tips

This question includes a wide range of corporation tax topics including an adjusted trading profit computation, capital allowances computation, property business income and loan relationships. Originally the question also included the profits of an overseas branch and the calculation of double tax relief, but these are no longer examinable and have therefore been replaced.

Unusually you are instructed to start your computation with the operating profit figure, rather than the more usual approach of starting with the net profit figure. This should not cause any problems but requires care and a slightly different approach.

Tutor's top tips

This corporation tax computation is presented in a familiar format, with a statement of profit or loss followed by a number of notes.

However, note that you are instructed to start your computation with the operating profit figure, rather than the more usual approach of starting with the net profit figure. When adjusting the operating profit for tax purposes note that you will not need to make the 'usual' adjustments for items which appear below operating profit in the statement of profit or loss. For example, you do not need to deduct loan interest receivable from the operating profit as it is not been included in the £1,013,000 figure.

As usual work methodically through the statement, referring to the notes where appropriate, and enter each item in your computation as you go.

The capital additions are slightly unusual but the examiner has given a big clue as to their treatment by indicating which are integral to the building. The question also requires the calculation of property business income from a list of receipts and payments. Care needs to be taken to only include those items which relate to the accounting period.

Corporation tax computation – year ended 31 March 2015

	£	£
Adjustment of profits:		
Operating profit	1,013,000	
Depreciation	8,170	
Amortisation	2,500	
Interest payable (W1)		(62,200)
Capital allowances (W2)		(501,620)
	─────────	─────────
	1,023,670	(563,820)
	(563,820)	─────────
	─────────	
Trading profit	459,850	
Property business profit (W3)	21,800	
Interest income (W4)	3,100	
Chargeable gain	61,300	
	─────────	
Taxable total profits	546,050	
	─────────	
Corporation tax (£546,050 × 21%)	114,670	
Less: Marginal relief (W5)		
1/400 × (£750,000 – £546,050)	(510)	
	─────────	
Corporation tax liability	114,160	
	─────────	
Due payment date	1 January 2016	

Workings

(W1) Loan interest payable for trading purposes

	£
Debenture interest	42,200
Freehold property (£25,000 × 4/5)	20,000
	─────────
	62,200
	─────────

Tutorial note

Interest paid in respect of a loan used for trading purposes is deductible in calculating the trading profit. Only four of the five floors of the office building are used for trading purposes. Therefore 4/5ths of the loan interest is deductible from trading profits.

The remaining 1/5th which relates to the floor which is let out is deductible from interest income under the loan relationship rules. Note that it is not deductible from property income.

(W2) Plant and machinery – Capital allowances

	£	General pool £	Special rate pool £	Allowances £
TWDV b/f		Nil	Nil	
Additions qualifying for AIA				
Integral features (Note):				
Heating system	93,600			
Ventilation system	75,600			
	169,200			
Less: AIA (Max £500,000)	(169,200)			169,200
			Nil	
Additions qualifying for AIA				
Plant and machinery:				
Furniture and furnishings	338,400			
Refrigerator and cooker	1,400			
	339,800			
Less: AIA (remaining max) (£500,000 – £169,200)	(330,800)			330,800
		9,000		
Less: WDA (18%)		(1,620)		1,620
TWDV c/f		7,380	Nil	
Total allowances				501,620

Tutorial note

Note that there are no allowances available for the building costs, only integral features and plant and machinery purchases qualify.

The expenditure which is integral to the building is included in the special rate pool.

It is beneficial to claim the annual investment allowance of £500,000 initially against this expenditure, as it would otherwise only qualify for writing down allowance at the rate of 8%, instead of 18% in the general pool.

(W3) Property business profit

	£
Rent receivable (£15,600 + (15,600 × 2/3))	26,000
Security deposit	0
Less: Allowable expenses	
Advertising	(600)
Insurance (£1,200 × 5/12)	(500)
Repairs (£12,800 – £9,700)	(3,100)
Property business profit	21,800

Tutorial note

1   Property business income is calculated, like trading income, on the accruals basis. The rent receivable for the five months to 31 March 2015 is taxable (and not the actual rent received in the accounting period). Similarly, only the insurance payable for the 5 months to 31 March 2015 is deductible in the year to 31 March 2015.

2   A security deposit, less the cost of making good any damage, is returned to the tenant on the cessation of a letting. It is therefore initially not treated as income.

3   The insurance proceeds relate to the repair costs. As a tax deduction is available from trading profits for the repairs the associated insurance receipt is treated as taxable trading income.

(W4) Interest income

	£
Loan interest receivable (£5,600 + £2,500)	8,100
Less: Non-trading loan interest payable on let property (£25,000 × 1/5)	(5,000)
Interest income	3,100

Tutorial note

Interest paid in respect of a loan used for non-trading purposes (i.e. letting), is deducted from interest income under the loan relationship rules. Note that it is not deductible from property income.

(W5) Upper limit

Softapp Ltd has one associated company, so the upper limit is reduced to £750,000 (£1,500,000 ÷ 2).

Accordingly, the company pays tax at the main rate with marginal relief.

ACCA marking scheme	
	Marks
Trading income	
Operating profit	0.5
Depreciation	0.5
Amortisation	0.5
Chargeable gain	0.5
Corporation tax at main rate	0.5
Marginal relief	0.5
Payment date	1.0
Debenture interest payable deduction	0.5
Freehold property interest payable deduction	1.0
Building costs – not a qualifying addition for capital allowances	0.5
Heating system – special rate (SR) addition	0.5
Ventilation system – SR addition	0.5
AIA firstly against SR additions	0.5
Furniture – general pool addition	0.5
Fridge and cooker – general pool addition	0.5
Balance of AIA	0.5
WDA on general pool	0.5
Rent receivable	0.5
Security deposit – not taxable income	0.5
Advertising	0.5
Insurance	1.0
Repairs net of insurance proceeds	1.0
Interest receivable	0.5
Interest payable re let property	1.0
Upper profits limit	0.5
	——
Total	15.0
	——

RELIEF FOR TRADING LOSSES

67 HALF-LIFE LTD (ADAPTED)

Key answer tips

A loss question which is largely computational but it involves the use of a normal ongoing trading loss, and a terminal loss.

There are two consecutive losses, the first arising from a short three month period. The second is the terminal loss of the last twelve months trading.

Make sure you get the easy marks and give the dates required in part (b).

For ease, use a columnar format to present the loss offset in part (a) and remember to show your record of the losses and their usage.

(a) **Taxable total profits**

	y/e 31.3.12 £	y/e 31.3.13 £	y/e 31.3.14 £	p/e 30.6.14 £	y/e 30.6.15 £
Trading profit	224,000	67,400	38,200	Nil	Nil
Property income	8,200	12,200	6,500	4,400	–
Chargeable gains	–	–	5,600	–	23,700
Total profits	232,200	79,600	50,300	4,400	23,700
Less: Loss relief					
– p/e 30.6.14 loss			(50,300)	(4,400)	
– y/e 30.6.15 loss (W)	(174,150)	(79,600)			(23,700)
	58,050	Nil	Nil	Nil	Nil
Less: QCD relief	(1,200)	wasted	–	–	wasted
Taxable total profits	56,850	Nil	Nil	Nil	Nil

Loss memorandum

	£	£
Loss for the period ended 30 June 2014	61,700	
Loss for the year ended 30 June 2015		308,800
Losses utilised:		
Current period claim		
– Period ended 30 June 2014	(4,400)	
12 month carry back claim		
– y/e 31 March 2014	(50,300)	
Current year claim		
– y/e 30 June 2015		(23,700)
36 month terminal loss carry back claim		
– y/e 31 March 2013		(79,600)
– y/e 31 March 2012 (W)		(174,150)
Losses unrelieved	7,000	31,350

Working: Terminal loss – set off in y/e 31.3.12

For the year ended 31 March 2012, loss relief is restricted to £174,150 (£232,200 × 9/12) as only 9 months of the year falls into the 36 months carry back period from the start of the final loss making accounting period.

Tutorial note

The trading loss for the period ended 30 June 2014 can be relieved against total profits of the current period and the previous 12 months.

The trading loss for the year ended 30 June 2015 can be relieved against total profits of the current year and the previous 36 months because it is a terminal loss.

Unrelieved qualifying charitable donations

Qualifying charitable donations of £1,000 and £700 for respectively the year ended 31 March 2013 and the year ended 30 June 2015 are unrelieved.

(b) **Due date for loss relief claims**

- The loss relief claims against total profits in respect of the loss for the period ended 30 June 2014 must be made by 30 June 2016.
- The loss relief claims against total profits in respect of the loss for the year ended 30 June 2015 must be made by 30 June 2017.

(c) **Corporation tax repayments**

Year ended 31 March 2012 (FY2011)

- Corporation tax of £34,830 (£174,150 at 20%) will be repaid in respect of the year ended 31 March 2012, since the relevant tax rate both before and after the loss relief claim is 20%.

Year ended 31 March 2013 (FY2012)

- Taxable total profits for the year ended 31 March 2013 were originally £78,600 (£79,600 – £1,000 QCD relief)
- Taxable total profits after loss relief is £Nil
- Corporation tax of £15,720 (£78,600 at 20%) will be repaid.

Year ended 31 March 2014 (FY2013)

- Taxable total profits for the year ended 31 March 2014 were originally £50,300
- Taxable total profits after loss relief is £Nil
- Corporation tax of £10,060 (£50,300 at 20%) will be repaid.

Tutorial note

No tax Is repayable in respect of the period ending 30 June 2014 or year ended 30 June 2015 as no tax will have been paid in respect of these periods. The company is not making instalments and the corporation tax return for both periods will show corporation tax payable of nil.

68   LOSER LTD (ADAPTED)

Key answer tips

A tricky question on corporation tax loss reliefs. There are two trading losses to deal with and it is important to deal with the earlier loss first. It is also important to lay out your answer using a standard pro forma.

(a) **Factors influencing the choice of loss reliefs**

- The rate of corporation tax at which relief will be obtained, with preference being given to profits charged at the marginal rate of 21.25% in FY2014, 23.75% in FY2013, (25% in FY2012) and then the main rate of 21% in FY2014, 23% in FY2013, (24% in FY2012).

- The timing of the relief obtained, with a claim against total profits in the current year and previous 12 months resulting in earlier relief than a claim to carry forward the loss against future trading profits.

- The extent to which relief for qualifying charitable donations will be lost, since these cannot be carried forward.

(b) **Loser Ltd – Taxable total profits**

	y/e 30 June 2012 £	p/e 31 March 2013 £	y/e 31 March 2014 £	y/e 31 March 2015 £
Trading profit	86,600	Nil	27,300	Nil
Property profit	–	4,500	8,100	5,600
Total profits	86,600	4,500	35,400	5,600
Less: Loss relief				
– Current period		(4,500)		(5,600)
– 12 months c/b	(21,200)		(35,400)	
	65,400	Nil	Nil	Nil
Less: QCD relief	(1,400)	wasted	wasted	wasted
Taxable total profits	64,000	Nil	Nil	Nil

Loss working

	£	£
Trading loss for the p/e 31.3.13	25,700	
Trading loss for the y/e 31.3.15		78,300
Loss against total profits		
– Current period (p/e 31.3.13)	(4,500)	
12 month carry back (y/e 30.6.12)	(21,200)	
– Current period (y/e 31.3.15)		(5,600)
12 month carry back (y/e 31.3.14)		(35,400)
Loss carried forward	Nil	37,300

(c) **If Loser Ltd ceased to trade on 31 March 2015**

- The whole of the trading loss for the final twelve months of trading can be relieved against total profits for the previous 36 months under the terminal loss relief rules.

- Therefore the unrelieved losses of £37,300 could have been carried back and fully set off in the year ended 30 June 2012.

ACCA marking scheme			Marks
(a)	Rate of corporation tax		1.0
	Timing of relief		1.0
	Qualifying charitable donations		1.0
			3.0
(b)	Trading profit		0.5
	Property business profit		0.5
	Loss relief – current and carry back 12 months		2.0
	QCD relief		1.0
	Unrelieved trading loss		1.0
			5.0
(c)	Terminal loss relief – carry back 36 months		
	Year ended 30 June 2012		2.0
			2.0
Total			10.0

69 SOFA LTD (ADAPTED) *Online question assistance*

Key answer tips

The first part of this question involves a standard adjustment of profit computation where the company is loss making.

The second part is more difficult and requires detailed group relief knowledge and the calculation of the maximum surrender possible to three subsidiaries including one with a non-coterminous year end and another which only joined the group part way through the year.

The part is independent and could be answered first, before part (a), as the question tells you to assume a loss of £200,000.

(a) Trading loss – year ended 31 March 2015

Tutorial note

An adjustment to profits calculation is required and the fact that the company is making a loss should not change your approach in any way.

Just start with a negative figure for the loss, then make the same adjustments as you would make if it were a profit and lay out your answer in the same way.

Remember that it is important to list all the major items indicated in the question requirement, showing a zero (0) for expenditure that is allowable. This is because credit will be given for showing no adjustment where none is needed.

List the adjustments in the order they appear in the question.

If required, also add notes to show why you have not adjusted for an item, or why you have added it back. However, lengthy explanations are not required where the requirement is just to 'calculate' the adjusted profits, rather than to explain them.

Always show your workings if the figure you are adjusting for is not clear from the question.

	£	£
Loss before taxation	(353,810)	
Depreciation	150,820	
Audit and accountancy (Note 1)	0	
Legal fees – issue of share capital (Note 2)	7,800	
Legal fees – renewal of 10 year lease (Note 3)	0	
Legal fees – issue of loan note (Note 2)	0	
Construction of new wall (Note 4)	9,700	
Repairing wall (Note 4)	0	
Entertaining suppliers (Note 5)	1,360	
Entertaining employees (Note 5)	0	
Counselling employee (Note 6)	0	
Health and safety fine (Note 7)	420	
Profit on disposal of shares		4,300
Bank interest received		8,400
Interest payable (Note 8)	0	
Capital allowances (£16,700 × 18%) + (£16,400 × 8%)		4,318
	————	————
	(183,710)	17,018
	(17,018)	————
	————	
Trading loss	(200,728)	
	————	

Tutorial note

1   Audit and accountancy fees are allowable, as they are incurred wholly and exclusively for the purposes of the trade.

2   Legal fees in connection with the issue of share capital are not allowable, being capital in nature. However, the cost of obtaining loan finance is allowable as a trading expense under the loan relationship rules as the loan was used for trading purposes.

3   The cost of renewing a short-lease (less than 50 years) is specifically allowable as a trading expense.

4   The new wall is not allowable, being capital in nature. However, repairing a wall is allowable.

5   The only exception to the non-deductibility of entertainment expenditure is when it is in respect of employees.

6   The costs of counselling services for redundant employees are specifically allowable.

7   Fines for the infringement of laws are not allowable.

8   Interest on a loan used for trading purposes is deductible in calculating the trading loss on an accruals basis.

(b) **Maximum group relief**

Settee Ltd

The accounting periods of Settee Ltd and Sofa Ltd are not coterminous. Therefore, Settee Ltd's taxable total profits and Sofa Ltd's trading loss must be apportioned on a time basis.

Year ended 31 March 2015 and year ended 30 June 2014

The corresponding accounting period is 1 April 2014 to 30 June 2014 (3 months)

Year ended 31 March 2015 and year ended 30 June 2015

The corresponding accounting period is 1 July 2014 to 31 March 2015 (9 months)

Settee Ltd can therefore claim the following group relief:

CAP to 30 June 2014

Sofa Ltd can surrender (3/12 × £200,000)	£50,000
Settee Ltd can accept (3/12 × £240,000)	£60,000

Therefore maximum loss claim is £50,000.

CAP to 30 June 2015

Sofa Ltd can surrender (9/12 × £200,000)	£150,000
Settee Ltd can claim (9/12 × £90,000)	£67,500

Therefore maximum loss claim is £67,500.

Couch Ltd

Couch Ltd is not a 75% subsidiary of Sofa Ltd, so no group relief claim is possible.

Futon Ltd

Futon Ltd did not commence trading until 1 January 2015, so the corresponding accounting period is the 3 months from 1 January 2015 to 31 March 2015.

Sofa Ltd can surrender (3/12 × £200,000)	£50,000
Futon Ltd can claim	£60,000

Therefore maximum loss claim is £50,000.

Examiner's report

Part (a) of this question was very well answered.

A certain amount of bad examination technique was evident as regards the adjustments in computing the trading loss.

Some candidates went into far too much detail explaining the adjustments made, thus wasting time, whilst others produced figures without any workings at all. This was fine for correct answers, but not so for incorrect ones. Where no adjustment was necessary, such as for the interest payable, then this fact should have been clearly shown or stated.

Most candidates did not answer part (b) very well.

Many candidates wasted a lot time by performing detailed calculations showing the amount of group relief that should have been claimed rather than the amount that actually could be claimed.

ACCA marking scheme		
		Marks
(a)	Loss before taxation	0.5
	Depreciation	0.5
	Professional fees	2.5
	Repairs and renewals	1.0
	Other expenses	2.5
	Profit on disposal of shares	0.5
	Bank interest received	0.5
	Interest payable	1.0
	Capital allowances	1.0
		10.0
(b)	Settee Ltd	2.5
	Couch Ltd	1.0
	Futon Ltd	1.5
		5.0
Total		**15.0**

70 VOLATILE LTD (ADAPTED) *Walk in the footsteps of a top tutor*

Key answer tips

A familiar style corporation tax losses question requiring relief to be claimed as soon as possible and a calculation of the loss left to carry forward.

Tutor's top tips

Part (a) requires a purely written answer highlighting the key factors that influence the choice of loss relief.

Only 3 marks are available, suggesting that 3 bullet points will suffice to answer this part.

This requirement is a common request in losses questions and you should learn the factors so that you can jot them down quickly in the exam.

(a) **Factors influencing the choice of loss reliefs**

- Rate of relief

  The rate of corporation tax at which relief will be obtained is an important factor. Preference should be given to profits charged at the marginal rate of 21.25% (23.75% for FY2013 and 25% for FY2012) first, then profits charged at the main rate of 21% (23% for FY2013 and 24% for FY2012) and lastly profits charged at the small profits rate of 20%.

- Cash flow

  The timing of the relief obtained is a key factor. A claim against total profits in the loss making period, then carry back will result in earlier relief than a claim against future trading profits.

- Wastage of qualifying charitable donations

  The extent to which relief for qualifying charitable donations will be lost is another factor, since these cannot be carried forward.

Tutorial note

Remember that for companies, a carry back election cannot be made until the current year total profits have been relieved first.

(b)   **Taxable total profits**

	y/e 31 Dec 2012	9 m/e 30 Sept 2013	y/e 30 Sept 2014
	£	£	£
Trading profit	15,200	78,700	Nil
Property business profit	6,500	–	–
Chargeable gains	–	–	9,700
Total profits	21,700	78,700	9,700
Less: Loss relief (W)			
Current year			(9,700)
Carry back – 12 months	(5,425)	(78,700)	
	16,275	Nil	Nil
Less: QCD relief	(1,200)	wasted	wasted
Taxable total profits	15,075	Nil	Nil

Loss working

	£
Trading loss	101,800
Current year relief (Note)	(9,700)
Carry back relief (previous 12 months)	
– 9 m/e 30 September 2013	(78,700)
	13,400
– y/e 31 December 2012 (£21,700 × 3/12)	(5,425)
Unrelieved loss as at 30 September 2014	7,975

Tutorial note

For the year ended 31 December 2012 loss relief is restricted to the lower of:

(i)   the proportion of the profits of that period of account that falls into the 12 months carry back period preceding 1 October 2013 (i.e. 3 months)

  = (£21,700 × 3/12) = £5,425

(ii)   the remainder of the loss = £13,400

Examiner's report

This question was not particularly well answered.

In part (a) far too many candidates explained the loss reliefs available rather than the factors influencing the choice of claims.

In part (b) many candidates approached this on a year by year basis, rather than one computation with a column for each of the periods. This not only wasted time in having to write out several computations, but also made it very difficult to calculate the correct loss relief claims.

Other common mistakes included treating the chargeable gains separately (rather than as part of the taxable total profits), and deducting qualifying charitable donations from trading profits rather than total income after loss relief.

ACCA marking scheme		
		Marks
(a)	Rate of corporation tax	1.0
	Timing of relief	1.0
	Impact on qualifying charitable donations	1.0
		3.0
(b)	Trading profits	0.5
	Property business profits	0.5
	Chargeable gains	0.5
	Loss relief – Year ended 30 September 2014	1.0
	– Period ended 30 September 2013	1.0
	– Year ended 31 December 2012	2.0
	Qualifying charitable donations	1.0
	Unrelieved trading losses	0.5
		7.0
Total		**10.0**

WITH GROUP ASPECTS

71   ANIMAL LTD (ADAPTED)

Key answer tips

A familiar style of group loss relief question which requires group losses to be allocated to group members in the most beneficial manner.

The group relief calculations are quite tricky, involving companies joining and leaving the group and recognising the different rates of tax paid by the group members. The examiner has however made the question slightly easier by telling you how many associated companies to use when calculating the small profits limits.

Note also that 40% of the marks for this question do not relate to the group relief calculations – so do not get bogged down in these and make sure you pick up the marks for the written sections which were easy marks if the relevant definitions had been learnt.

There were easy marks available for explaining the definition of a group for group loss relief purposes. Note that for 3 marks you would expect to make three separate points.

Similarly there were three easy marks for explaining when companies are associated. The examiner has kindly given you additional guidance by stating how many associates there are in the Animal Ltd group. Again for three marks you would be expected to make three separate points.

(a)   **Group relief group**

- One company must be a 75% subsidiary of the other, or both companies must be 75% subsidiaries of a third company.

- The holding company must have an effective interest of at least 75% of the subsidiary's ordinary share capital.

- The holding company must have the right to receive at least 75% of the subsidiary's distributable profits and net assets on a winding up.

(b)   **Associated companies**

- Bat Ltd, Cat Ltd, Dog Ltd, Fox Ltd and Gnu Ltd are all under the common control (shareholding of over 50%) of Animal Ltd, and are therefore associated companies.

- Where a company such as Elk Ltd has been dormant throughout the accounting period, it does not count as an associated company.

- Companies that are only associated for part of the accounting period, such as Cat Ltd and Dog Ltd, count as associated companies for the whole of the period.

(c) **Taxable total profits – year ended 31 March 2015**

	Animal Ltd £	Bat Ltd £	Cat Ltd £	Dog Ltd £	Fox Ltd £
Trading profit	450,000	65,000	85,000	100,000	60,000
Property income	5,000	15,000			
TTP before group relief	455,000	80,000	85,000	100,000	60,000
Less: Group relief (W)	(95,000)	(30,000)	(35,000)	(25,000)	(15,000)
Taxable total profits	360,000	50,000	50,000	75,000	45,000

Reasons for group relief strategy

- The primary aim for the group is to save as much tax as possible when utilising the loss.

- Gnu Ltd's trading loss is most effectively relieved so as to bring the augmented profits of as many group companies as possible.down to the small profits rate limit (see working below).

- The relevant lower and upper limits for corporation tax purposes are £50,000 (£300,000 ÷ 6) and £250,000 (£1,500,000 ÷ 6) respectively.

Tutorial note

It has been assumed that neither Cat Ltd nor Dog Ltd have any further associated companies arising from the periods when they were not part of the Animal Ltd group of companies.

- Given the level of TTP and FII, Gnu Ltd should bring the augmented profits of Bat Ltd, Cat Ltd, Dog Ltd and Fox Ltd down to £50,000.

  This saves corporation tax at the highest marginal rate of 21.25%.

- As Dog Ltd has only been part of the group for three months of the year, group relief is restricted to a maximum of £25,000, being 3/12ths of its TTP (£100,000 × 3/12).

- Cat Ltd left the group part way through the year, however loss relief given to Cat Ltd is not restricted as the maximum group relief is the lower of the available loss of Gnu Ltd of £150,000 (£200,000 × 9/12) and the available profits of Cat Ltd of £63,750 (£85,000 × 9/12). Only £35,000 loss is required to bring its augmented profits down to £50,000.

- The balance of Gnu Ltd's trading loss of £95,000 (£200,000 – £30,000 – £35,000 – £25,000 – £15,000) is surrendered to Animal Ltd.

  This saves corporation tax at the main rate of 21%.

Working: Augmented profits

	Animal Ltd £	Bat Ltd £	Cat Ltd £	Dog Ltd £	Fox Ltd £
TTP before group relief	455,000	80,000	85,000	100,000	60,000
Plus: FII	20,000				5,000
Augmented profits	475,000	80,000	85,000	100,000	65,000
Lower limit	50,000	50,000	50,000	50,000	50,000
Group relief required to bring to lower limit	425,000	30,000	35,000	50,000	15,000
Rate of tax saving	21%	21.25%	21.25%	21.25%	21.25%

Tutorial note

Strictly, the rate of tax saving in Fox Ltd is not exactly 21.25%, as FII received by a company paying tax at the marginal rate will slightly change the rate of tax in the margin. However, for the purposes of the F6 exam it is perfectly acceptable to assume that the marginal rate applies.

ACCA marking scheme		Marks
(a)	75% subsidiary	1.0
	Ordinary share capital	1.0
	Distributable profits/Net assets	1.0
		3.0
(b)	Identification of companies	1.0
	Dormant companies	1.0
	Associated for part of accounting period	1.0
		3.0
(c)	Trading profits	1.0
	Property business income	0.5
	Group relief – Relevant limits	1.0
	Group relief – Tax rates	1.0
	Group relief – Animal Ltd	1.0
	Group relief – Bat Ltd	0.5
	Group relief – Cat Ltd	1.0
	Group relief – Dog Ltd	1.0
	Group relief – Fox Ltd	1.0
	FII	1.0
		9.0
Total		**15.0**

72   MUSIC PLC (ADAPTED)

Key answer tips

In this question there are 8 marks for written explanations of the gains group and associated company rules. It is important to state the basic rule and then apply to the facts of the question. Be careful with the overseas company, which is included but unable to enjoy the benefits of gains group status.

(a)   **Capital gains group**

- Companies form a capital gains group if at each level in the group structure there is a 75% shareholding, provided the parent company has an effective interest of at least 50%.

- Alto Ltd, Bass Ltd, Cello Ltd, Echo Inc and Flute Ltd are all 75% subsidiaries, and Music plc has an effective interest of 60% (80% × 75%) in Flute Ltd. All of these companies therefore form a capital gains group.

- However, Bass Ltd and Cello Ltd will only be included in respect of assets acquired or disposed of whilst they were members of the group.

- Drum Ltd and Gong Ltd are not included as Drum Ltd is not a 75% subsidiary, and Music plc's effective interest in Gong Ltd is only 48% (80% × 75% × 80%).

- Although Echo Inc is included in the definition of the capital gains group, companies that are resident overseas are not able to take advantage of the provisions applicable to a capital gains group.

(b)   **Associated companies**

- Alto Ltd, Bass Ltd, Cello Ltd, Echo Inc, Flute Ltd and Gong Ltd are all under the common control of Music plc, and are therefore associated companies.

- For associated company purposes, it does not matter where a company is resident. Echo Inc is therefore included despite being resident overseas.

- Companies associated for part of the accounting period, such as Bass Ltd and Cello Ltd, count as associated companies for the whole of the period.

- Drum Ltd is not included as an associated company since Music plc's effective interest in this company is only 45%.

(c)   **Corporation tax liability – year ended 31 March 2015**

	£
Trading profit	92,000
Interest income	12,000
Net chargeable gains (W1)	23,000
Taxable total profits	127,000
Plus: Franked investment income	15,000
Augmented profits	142,000
Corporation tax (£127,000 × 21%) (W2)	26,670
Less: Marginal relief	
1/400 × (£214,286 – £142,000) × £127,000/£142,000	(162)
Corporation tax liability	26,508

Tutorial note

1 The capital gain of £120,000 is included in Music plc's taxable total profits since an appropriate election has been made with Alto Ltd. Capital losses may be set against this gain.

2 Group dividends are not included as franked investment income.

Workings

(W1) Net chargeable gain

	£
Net chargeable gain in the year (by election)	120,000
Less: Capital losses in the year	(65,000)
	———
	55,000
Less: Capital losses b/f	(32,000)
	———
Net chargeable gain	23,000
	———

(W2) Corporation tax rates

		£
Upper limit	(£1,500,000 × 1/7)	214,286
Lower limit	(£300,000 × 1/7)	42,857
Augmented profits		142,000
		Marginal relief applies

There are seven associated companies in the group.

(d) **Bank loan**

Under the loan relationship rules, loans used for non-trade purposes are deductible from interest income. If the loan was used to acquire a property which was to be rented out, the interest would not be deducted from trading income, nor property business income (as for individuals), but from the company's interest income.

Legal fees

Legal fees incurred in relation to the purchase of a capital asset are not deductible from the company's trading profits. They will be deductible in the chargeable gain computation when the building is ultimately sold.

Rent receivable

The rent receivable from letting the property to a tenant will be included on an accruals basis, net of any allowable deductions, in taxable total profits as property income.

73   DEUTSCH LTD (ADAPTED) *Walk in the footsteps of a top tutor*

Key answer tips

This question required a corporation tax computation for a company with shareholdings in a number of other companies. Provided the relevant group definitions had been learnt there were easy marks available for identifying the associated companies in the group and calculating the maximum group relief claim.

The corporation tax calculation required knowledge of the tax treatment of dividend income from both associated and non-associated companies.

(a)   **Associated companies**

- Deutsch Ltd is associated with those companies in which it has a shareholding of over 50%.

- Eins Ltd and Drei Ltd are therefore associated companies.

- For associated company purposes, it does not matter where a company is resident, so Vier Co is also an associated company despite being resident overseas.

(b)   **Maximum amount of group relief**

Tutor's top tips

Your first step should be to identify which companies are in a group relief group with Deutsch Ltd. You can then identify how much group relief is available. Since there are only two marks available for this part you can be confident that a complex working will not be required.

- Deutsch Ltd cannot claim group relief from Eins Ltd as this company is not a 75% subsidiary. However, Drei Ltd and Deutsch Ltd are in a group relief group.

- The maximum amount of group relief that can be claimed is therefore Drei Ltd's trading loss of £64,700.

(c)   **Corporation tax computation – year ended 31 March 2015**

Tutor's top tips

When calculating the corporation tax liability, remember that the tax rate limits must be adjusted to reflect the number of associated companies, and that it is the augmented profits rather than taxable total profits which are compared with those limits.

	£
Trading profit	277,700
Less: Group relief	(64,700)
Taxable total profits	213,000
Plus: FII (W1)	39,000
Augmented profits	252,000
Corporation tax (£213,000 × 21%)	44,730
Less: Marginal relief (W2)	
1/400 × (£375,000 − £252,000) × £213,000/£252,000	(260)
	44,470

Tutorial note

Dividends are not taxable and do not appear in the TTP computation.

However dividends received from non-associated companies are treated as FII for the purposes of determining the correct rate of tax to apply to TTP.

Ignore dividends from associated companies completely as they are not taxable and they are not FII.

Workings

(W1) Franked investment income

Franked investment income is £39,000 (£35,100 × 100/90).

The dividends from Eins Ltd and Drei Ltd are from 51% group companies and are therefore not franked investment income.

(W2) Upper profits limit

Deutsch Ltd has three associated companies, so the limits are reduced to:

Upper limit = (£1,500,000 ÷ 4) = £375,000

Lower limit = (£300,000 ÷ 4) = £75,000

The company's augmented profits of £252,000 are between the reduced limits, therefore marginal relief is available.

Tutorial note

As the company has three associated companies (Eins Ltd, Drei Ltd and Vier Co), the upper and lower limits are divided by four (three associates plus Deutsch Ltd).

(d)   **Time limit for group relief election**

The claim for group relief should be made by Deutsch Ltd (the claimant company) on their corporation tax return by 31 March 2017 (within two years of the end of the chargeable accounting period).

Tutor's top tip

Time limits for claims and elections should represent easy marks provided that you have learnt them prior to the exam.

They often appear at the end of questions so make sure that you leave enough time to answer these sections!

Examiner's report

The first requirement was generally well answered, although some candidates incorrectly applied a 75% threshold.

The second requirement caused more problems, with many candidates including the loss from a group company where the shareholding was only 60%. Some candidates produced confused workings involving all four group companies, and therefore wasted quite a bit of time.

The third requirement was generally well answered, although the franked investment income was often omitted or incorrectly calculated.

Note: *The examiner's report has been edited to remove comments on elements of the question that have been deleted due to changes to the exam format.*

---

74   GASTRON LTD (ADAPTED) *Walk in the footsteps of a top tutor*

Key answer tips

This is a 15 mark corporation tax computational question, requiring a corporation tax computation, and some self-assessment.

Both of these areas are highly likely to be tested and should be well practiced.

Parts (c) and (d) involve capital gains groups, which may be seen as tricky, but most of the marks can be won by simply stating the rules, rather than needing application to the question.

(a)   **Corporation tax computation – year ended 31 March 2015**

	£
Trading profit	516,792
Property business profit (W1)	12,800
Bank interest	12,400
Chargeable gain	74,800
Taxable total profits	616,792
Plus: FII (£36,000 × 100/90) (Note)	40,000
Augmented profits	656,792
Corporation tax	
FY2014: (£616,792 at 21%) (W2)	129,526
Less: Marginal relief	
1/400 × (£750,000 − £656,792) × £616,792/£656,792	(219)
Corporation tax liability	129,307

Tutorial note

Group dividends are not included as franked investment income. Therefore only the dividends received from Tasteless plc, the unconnected company will be grossed up and added to the taxable total profits to calculate augmented profits.

Workings

(W1) Property business profit

	£	£
Rent receivable − First tenant (£1,800 × 9)		16,200
− Second tenant (£1,950 × 2)		3,900
		20,100
Irrecoverable rents (£1,800 × 2) (Note)	3,600	
Decorating costs	3,700	
		(7,300)
Property business profit		12,800

Tutorial note

The rent is taxable on an accruals basis, and therefore all 9 months of rent for the first tenant are included. However, as the tenant left owing two months' rent, the irrecoverable rent is an allowable deduction.

(W2) Corporation tax rate

Gastron Ltd has one associated company, so the upper limit is reduced to £750,000 (£1,500,000 × ½) and the lower limit £150,000 (£300,000 × ½).

Augmented profits fall in between the limits, therefore marginal relief applies.

(b)   **Corporation tax due dates and interest**

Tutor's top tips

Part (b) requires the due date for payments of corporation tax and the interest that will be charged if the tax is paid late.

It is important to actually calculate the interest here, rather than simply stating the way it will be calculated. All calculations should be to the nearest month unless the question says otherwise.

Note that the rates of late payment interest and repayment interest are given in the tax tables.

- Gastron Ltd's corporation tax liability for the year ended 31 March 2015 must be paid by 1 January 2016.
- If the company does not pay its corporation tax until 31 August 2016, then interest of £2,586 (£129,307 at 3% = £3,879 × 8/12) will be charged by HM Revenue and Customs for the period 1 January 2016 to 31 August 2016.

(c)   **Definition of a capital gains group**

Tutor's top tips

This part requires only a definition of a capital gains group for 2 marks.

It is useful to learn this definition, as this is a common requirement in a question involving groups.

- Companies form a capital gains group if at each level in the group structure there is a 75% shareholding.
- However, the parent company must also have an effective interest of over 50% in each group company.

(d) **Gains group election**

Tutor's top tips

Knowledge of time limits and deadlines is very useful for obtaining easy marks.

The most common deadline for claims and elections for corporation tax is two years from the end of the accounting period, and if you don't know the deadline, this can be a good guess to make!

However, it is important to state the actual date, not just the general rule, so you must apply the rule to the dates in the question.

- Gastron Ltd and Culinary Ltd must make the election by 31 March 2017 (i.e. within two years of the end of the accounting period in which the disposal outside of the group occurred).

- Culinary Ltd's otherwise unused capital loss of £66,000 can be set against Gastron Ltd's chargeable gain of £74,800.

- It is beneficial for the balance of the chargeable gain of £8,800 (£74,800 – £66,000) to arise in Culinary Ltd as it will only be taxed at the rate of 20%, instead of at the marginal rate (21.25%) in Gastron Ltd.

Tutorial note

It is not necessary to do a further corporation tax computation in order to calculate the most beneficial way of making this election.

The question states that Culinary is paying tax at 20%, and in part (a) you have calculated that Gastron Ltd is paying tax at 21% less marginal relief. This means that profits falling into the marginal band suffer tax at an effective rate of tax of 21.25%.

It can be useful to learn the effective rate of tax in the margin, as this will help you to quickly calculate the benefit of any tax or loss relief.

Examiner's report

This question was very well answered, with only part (d) consistently causing problems.

In part (b) a disappointing number of candidates gave 31 January as the payment date.

Only a few candidates appreciated that interest would be due, and fewer still correctly calculated the actual amount payable.

In part (c) most candidates appreciated that a 75% shareholding was necessary, but were then often unsure where the 50% limit fitted in. The holding company must have an effective interest of 50%.

In part (d) many candidates simply stated that losses could be set against profits, without making any attempt to use the information given in the question.

Note: *The examiner's report has been edited to remove comments on elements of the question that have been deleted due to changes to the exam format.*

ACCA marking scheme		
		Marks
(a)	Trading profit	0.5
	Property business profit	2.0
	Bank interest	0.5
	Chargeable gain	0.5
	Franked investment income	1.0
	Group dividends	0.5
	Corporation tax	2.0
		7.0
(b)	Due date	1.0
	Interest	2.0
		3.0
(c)	75% shareholding	1.0
	50% effective interest	1.0
		2.0
(d)	Time limit	1.0
	Set off of capital losses	1.0
	Tax rate	1.0
		3.0
Total		**15.0**

75   MICE LTD (ADAPTED) *Walk in the footsteps of a top tutor*

Key answer tips

This 15 mark corporation tax question starts with some detailed property income calculations and then the application of the corporation tax loss rules. With the removal of overseas aspects of corporation tax from the syllabus, this part is now simpler than when the question was originally set.

The examiner has purposely split out the property income into a separate requirement to help you focus on this detailed part in isolation, before moving on to the corporation tax loss section.

Use the appropriate amount of time for the property income in part (a) and then use the figure you have calculated in part (b). Don't worry if you are not confident in your part (a) answer. You can still score full marks in part (b) by carrying forward the property income that you have calculated, even if it is incorrect!

Tutor's top tips

This question can appear daunting on first reading; however it is possible to score very well on this sort of question as long as you do not panic over the quantity of information.

Remember to read the requirements carefully.

The requirements to this question lead you through how to tackle the question in the correct logical order, and it has clear mark allocations, which should be used to allocate the time spent on each section.

The first part requires a calculation of the property business profit before you consider the impact of the losses.

(a)   **Property business profit – year ended 31 March 2015**

Tutor's top tips

Where a company (or individual) has several rental properties, the profits and losses are pooled/aggregated to calculate the net profit or loss (i.e. current period losses are automatically set off against current period profits).

There is no need to do separate calculations of the profit and loss for each property, only one computation is required.

Set up your answer with sub-headings 'Income' and 'Allowable expenses' and leave space underneath to insert the relevant information as you go through each property in the question.

	£	£
Rent accrued – Property 1 (£3,200 × 4)		12,800
– Property 2		6,000
– Property 3		Nil
		———
		18,800
Premium received for sub-lease (Property 2)	18,000	
Less: £18,000 × 2% × (8 – 1)	(2,520)	
	———	
		15,480
		———
		34,280
Business rates	2,200	
Repairs	1,060	
Rent paid	7,800	
Advertising	680	
Insurance (£460 + £310 + (£480 × 3/12))	890	
Loan interest	Nil	
	———	
		(12,630)
		———
Property business profit		21,650
		———

Tutorial note

1   The enlargement of the car park is capital expenditure which cannot be deducted when calculating the property business profit.

2   For Property 2, the rental paid by Mice Ltd for the original lease is an allowable deduction from the income received from the sub-lease.

3   For Property 3, rents accrued up to 31 March are assessed in the year ended 31 March 2015. As the property is not let until 1 April 2015, there is no assessable income. The rent received in advance before 1 April 2015 is not relevant to this question and will be assessed next year.

4   Interest paid in respect of a loan used to purchase a property which is rented out (i.e. non-trade related) by a company is not an allowable deduction against property income, but is an allowable deduction against interest income under the loan relationship rules.

(b)   **Taxable total profits**

Tutor's top tips

Note that the question asks for the taxable total profits of the current year, which is clearly loss making, and the previous years as the loss will be carried back if reliefs are to be claimed as soon as possible.

The examiner's answer did this in two sets of computations; however one set of computations including all of the years would gain equal credit and may save time.

Remember to highlight the 'total profits' subtotal against which the loss is deducted (i.e. total profits before qualifying charitable donations).

	p/e 31.3.12 £	y/e 31.3.13 £	y/e 31.3.14 £	y/e 31.3.15 £
Trading profit	83,200	24,700	51,200	Nil
Property business profit part (a)	2,800	7,100	12,200	21,650
Interest income (Note 1) (£6,400 + £3,200 – £1,800)				7,800
Chargeable gain				10,550
Total profits	86,000	31,800	63,400	40,000
Less: Loss relief (Note 3)				
Current year				(40,000)
Carry back 12 months			(63,400)	
	86,000	31,800	Nil	Nil
Less: QCD relief	(1,000)	(1,500)	–	–
Taxable total profits	85,000	30,300	Nil	Nil

Loss working

	£
Trading loss	180,000
Current year relief – y/e 31 March 2015	(40,000)
Carry back relief (12 months) – y/e 31 March 2014	(63,400)
Unrelieved loss as at 31 March 2014	76,600

Tutorial note

1   Interest income includes all interest received and receivable (i.e. accrued) to 31 March 2015 and interest paid and payable in respect of the loan to purchase Property 3 is deducted.

2   Remember that, for companies, a carry back election for losses cannot be made unless the current year total profits have been relieved first.

3   There is no restriction to the amount of loss relief that can be claimed for carry back to the previous 12 months (i.e. year ended 31 March 2014).

4   Note that the dividend received grossed up by 100/90 is treated as franked investment income when calculating the applicable rate of corporation tax, but this is not part of the requirement of this question.

ACCA marking scheme			
			Marks
(a)	Lease premium received		1.5
	Rent receivable	– Property 1	1.0
		– Property 2 and 3 (0.5 marks each)	1.0
	Business rates		0.5
	Repairs		1.0
	Rent paid		0.5
	Advertising		0.5
	Insurance		1.5
	Loan interest		0.5
			8.0
(b)	Year ended 31 March 2015 –	Property business profit	0.5
		Loan interest	1.5
		Dividend income not taxed	0.5
		Chargeable gain	0.5
		Loss relief	0.5
	Other periods –	Trading profit	0.5
		Property business profit	0.5
		Loss relief	2.0
		QCD relief	0.5
			7.0
Total			**15.0**

76 NEUNG LTD (ADAPTED) *Walk in the footsteps of a top tutor*

Key answer tips

This corporation tax question is a classic question, testing the calculation of a corporation tax liability. There is also a small element of corporation tax groups and group relief for losses.

The bulk of the marks available are for a short adjustment of profits calculation, a fairly detailed capital allowances computation, the calculation of taxable total profits and then the calculation of the corporation tax liability. The question originally contained some overseas income and branch losses, however these aspects are no longer in the syllabus and have been replaced by a trading loss in a group company. This is a relatively straightforward group relief scenario.

You must also be careful to remember the implications of the associated companies on corporation tax limits.

Tutor's top tips

This question can appear daunting on first reading; however it is possible to score very well on this sort of question as long as you do not panic over the group parts where you may be less confident.

Neung Ltd – Corporation tax liability – year ended 31 March 2015

Tutor's top tips

It is important to take a logical step by step approach here. Think through which calculations you will need to do in workings and in particular make sure that your workings for the capital allowances are clearly laid out (on a new sheet of paper) and well referenced.

Remember to consider how to deal with the group loss.

Be careful to consider the impact of the associates on the tax computation – what effect will they have on the limits? Will there be any effect on the FII?

	£
Trading profit (W1)	374,466
Interest income (£25,200 + £12,600)	37,800
Taxable total profits before group relief	412,266
Less: Group relief	(15,700)
Taxable total profits after group relief	396,566
Plus: FII (£37,800 × 100/90)	42,000
Augmented profits	438,566
Corporation tax at marginal rate (W4):	
£396,566 × 21%	83,279
Less: Marginal relief	
1/400 × (£500,000 − £438,566) × £396,566/£438,566	(139)
Corporation tax liability	83,140

Tutorial note

Fifth Ltd's trading loss is available to Neung Ltd as it is a 100% subsidiary and therefore in a group relief group. Since the only other company in the group (Fourth Ltd) is dormant, the whole loss should be surrendered to Neung Ltd.

The dividend received from Second Ltd is grossed up by 100/90 to calculate the FII but the dividend received from Third Ltd is not included as the company is an associate.

Workings

(W1) Trading profit

	£
Operating profit	877,300
Depreciation	11,830
Amortisation	7,000
Less: Lease deduction (W2)	(4,340)
Capital allowances (W3)	(517,324)
Trading profit	374,466

(W2) Lease deduction

	£
Premium paid	140,000
Less: £140,000 × 2% × (20 − 1)	(53,200)
Assessment on landlord	86,800
Allowable deduction per year (£86,800 ÷ 20)	4,340

Tutorial note

Since the property is used for business purposes, a deduction is allowed for the revenue element of the lease premium (which is the amount assessable on the landlord), spread over the life of the lease.

Alternative calculation of the assessment on the landlord:

£140,000 × (51 − 20)/50 = £86,800

(W3) Capital allowances

	£	General pool £	Short life asset £	Special rate pool £	Allowances £
TWDV b/f		4,800	22,800	12,700	
Additions (no AIA)					
Motor car (1)				15,400	
Motor car (2)		28,600			
Additions (with AIA)					
Ventilation system	562,000				
Less: AIA	(500,000)				500,000
	———			62,000	
		33,400	22,800	90,100	
WDA (18%)		(6,012)			6,012
WDA 18%			(4,104)		4,104
WDA (8%)				(7,208)	7,208
		———	———	———	
TWDV c/f		27,388	18,696	82,892	
		———	———	———	
Total allowances					517,324
					———

Tutorial notes

1   *Capital allowances on car purchases are calculated based on the CO_2 emissions of the car as follows:*

–   *New car with CO_2 emissions of ≤ 95 g/km:*

eligible for a FYA of 100% (none in this question)

–   *CO_2 emissions of between 96 – 130 g/km:*

put in general pool and eligible for a WDA at 18% (i.e. Motor Car (2))

–   *CO_2 emissions of > 130 g/km:*

put in special rate pool and eligible for a WDA at 8% (i.e. Motor Car (1))

2   *The short life asset is an item of machinery and is eligible for a WDA at 18%.*

3   *The ventilation system is an integral feature of the freehold office building and is therefore included in the special rate pool. The AIA should always be given against special rate pool expenditure in priority to any other expenditure as it is only eligible for allowances at 8%.*

(W4) Corporation tax rate

Neung Ltd has two associated companies (Third and Fifth) therefore there are three associated companies in total.

		£
Upper limit	(£1,500,000 ÷ 3)	500,000
Lower limit	(£300,000 ÷ 3)	100,000
Augmented profits		438,566
		Marginal relief applies

Tutorial note

Neung Ltd is not associated with Second Ltd as it does not control the company. Fourth Ltd is also excluded as it is dormant.

Examiner's report

This question was generally well answered, and there were many very good answers.

The only aspect which consistently caused problems was the asset that was integral to a building. Although candidates correctly claimed the annual investment allowance against this expenditure, many candidates then claimed the 40% first year allowance on the balance of expenditure, rather than adding it into the special rate pool. [Note that the 40% FYA is no longer available so this would no longer be a potential issue in this question].

Several candidates treated the lease premium as income rather than as a deduction.

Candidates should try to use a new page for large capital allowances computations.

Note: *The examiner's report has been edited to remove comments on elements of the question that have been deleted due to changes to the exam format.*

ACCA marking scheme		Marks
Operating profit		0.5
Depreciation		0.5
Amortisation		0.5
Lease premium	– Assessable amount on landlord	1.5
	– Deduction	1.0
Capital allowances	– AIA	1.5
	– General pool	1.5
	– Short life asset	1.0
	– Special rate pool	1.5
Loan interest		1.0
Group relief		1.0
Franked investment income		1.0
Group dividend		0.5
Corporation tax		2.0
		15.0

77 CLUELESS LTD (ADAPTED) *Walk in the footsteps of a top tutor*

Key answer tips

Part (a) requires the computation of a company's corporation tax liability including an adjustment of trading profits calculation. The information is presented in a slightly unusual format as an existing corporation tax computation that contains numerous errors. However this should not prove a problem for the well prepared student.

Part (b) deals with the administrative aspects of corporation tax. There is an easy mark in part (i). However, part (ii) may cause some students problems if they have not learnt this topic. As all companies must now file their tax returns electronically it is an important and topical area.

Tutor's top tips

Do not be put off by the different format in which the information is presented. Set up your corporation tax computation as usual and work through each of the workings in the question dealing with each piece of information as you go. Remember to indicate by the use of zero any items in the computation of trading profit for which no adjustment is required.

Clueless Ltd has one associated company. Remember that dividends received from this company are not included in either taxable total profits or augmented profits. However also remember to divide the limits by two for the purpose of calculating the rate of tax paid by the company.

(a) **Corporation tax computation – year ended 31 March 2015**

	£
Trading profit (W1)	355,488
Loan interest receivable	32,800
	———
Taxable total profits	388,288
Less: QCD relief	(900)
	———
Taxable total profits	387,388
	———
Corporation tax (£387,388 × 21%)(W3)	81,351
Less: Marginal relief	
1/400 × (£750,000 – £410,388) × 387,388/410,388	(801)
	———
Corporation tax liability	80,550
	———

Tutorial note

Loan interest income is assessed on the amount receivable in respect of the accounting period.

Workings

(W1) Trading profit

	£
Profit before taxation	382,610
Depreciation	15,740
Donations to political parties	400
Qualifying charitable donations	900
Gifts to customers – pens	0
Gifts to customers – food hampers	1,650
	401,300
Less: Capital allowances (W2)	(45,812)
Trading profit	355,488

Tutorial note

1   *Donations to political parties are a disallowable trading expense. Qualifying charitable donations are a disallowable trading expense but are deductible from total profits.*

2   *Gifts to customers are an allowable deduction if they cost less than £50 per recipient per year, are not of food, drink, tobacco or vouchers for exchangeable goods, and carry a conspicuous advertisement for the company making the gift.*

(W2) Capital allowances

	£	General pool £	Special rate pool £	Allowances £
TWDV b/f		12,400	13,500	
Additions not qualifying for AIA				
Motor car			11,800	
Additions qualifying for AIA				
Machinery	42,300			
Less: AIA	(42,300)			42,300
		Nil		
Less: Disposal proceeds			(9,300)	
			16,000	
Less: WDA (18%)		(2,232)		2,232
Less: WDA (8%)			(1,280)	1,280
TWDV c/f		10,168	14,720	
Total allowances				45,812

Tutorial note

1   The motor car has CO_2 emissions over 130 grams per kilometre and therefore qualifies for writing down allowances at the rate of 8%. The private use of a motor car by an employee is irrelevant, since such usage will be assessed on the employee as a benefit.

2   A balancing allowance only arises on the general and special rate pools on the cessation of trade, even where all of the assets in the relevant pool have been disposed of.

(W3) Rate of corporation tax

	£
TTP	387,388
Plus: FII (£20,700 × 100/90)	23,000
Augmented profits	410,388

As Clueless Ltd has one associated company, the limits are divided by 2

Upper limit (£1,500,000 ÷ 2)	£750,000
Lower limit (£300,000 ÷ 2)	£150,000

As augmented profits fall between the limits; marginal relief applies.

The dividends from the 100% subsidiary company are not franked investment income as they are group dividends.

(b)   **Self-assessment return**

Tutor's top tips

For written parts, write short succinct sentences in bullet point form and bear in mind the mark allocation for each sub-section. In general, there is usually one mark allocated for each valid point made. Do not therefore dwell on any one part too much and keep an eye on the clock.

(i)   **Filing date**

- Clueless Ltd's self-assessment tax return for the year ended 31 March 2015 must be submitted by 31 March 2016.

(ii)   **Options for iXBRL format**

- If Clueless Ltd has straightforward accounts, it could use the software provided by HM Revenue and Customs. This automatically produces accounts and tax computations in the iXBRL format.

- Alternatively, other software that automatically produces iXBRL accounts and computations could be used.

- A tagging service could be used to apply the appropriate tags to the accounts and tax computations, or Clueless Ltd could use software to tag documents itself.

Examiner's report

Part (a) was generally very well answered. The only aspect that consistently caused problems was the loan interest with very few candidates appreciating that this is assessed on a receivable basis.

In part (b) it was surprising that only a few candidates were aware of the filing date for a self-assessment corporation tax return, with far too many candidates giving a 31 January date. Despite being covered in the Finance Act 2011 article, hardly any candidates were able to provide relevant details regarding the production of accounts and computations using iXBRL.

Note: *The examiner's report has been edited to remove comments on elements of the question that have been deleted due to changes to the exam format.*

ACCA marking scheme			
			Marks
(a)	Loan interest		0.5
	Qualifying charitable donations		0.5
	Corporation tax at main rate		0.5
	Marginal relief		1.0
	Trading profit		
		Depreciation	0.5
		Donations to political parties	0.5
		Qualifying charitable donations	0.5
		Gifts to customers – pens – no adjustment	0.5
		Gifts to customers – food hampers	0.5
		Capital allowances deducted	0.5
	Capital allowances		
		TWDVs brought forward	0.5
		AIA on machinery	1.0
		Motor car addition in special rate pool	0.5
		Disposal proceeds in special rate pool	0.5
		WDA on general pool at 18%	0.5
		WDA on special rate pool at 8%	0.5
	Rate of corporation tax		
		Limits divided by 2	0.5
	Franked Investment income		
		Dividends from unconnected companies	0.5
		Grossed up at 100/90	0.5
		Excluding dividends from the 100% subsidiary company	0.5
			———
			11.0
			———
(b)	(i)	Submit by 31 March 2016	1.0
			———
	(ii)	HMRC software	1.0
		Other software producing iXBRL accounts	1.0
		Tagging service/software to tag documents	1.0
			———
			3.0
			———
Total			**15.0**
			———

VALUE ADDED TAX

78 CANDY APPLE (ADAPTED) *Walk in the footsteps of a top tutor*

Key answer tips

This question tests knowledge of a number of VAT issues. There were some easy marks to be gained here for a relatively straight forward compulsory registration computation.

The question also covers the ethical issues where a client refuses to disclose information to HM Revenue and Customs.

(a)   **Registration**

- Candy would have been liable to compulsory VAT registration when her taxable supplies during any 12-month period exceeded £81,000.

- This happened on 31 October 2014 when taxable supplies amounted to £84,000 (£10,500 + £10,500 + £10,500 + £10,500 + £14,000 + £14,000 + £14,000).

- Registration is required from the end of the month following the month in which the limit is exceeded, so Candy should have been registered from 1 December 2014.

- If Candy continued to trade after 1 December 2014 without registering for VAT, she would still have to pay the VAT due from the time she should have been registered.

(b)   **Refusal to register – Ethical issues**

- The matter is one of professional judgement, and a trainee Chartered Certified Accountant would be expected to act honestly and with integrity.

- If Candy refuses to register for VAT, then you would be obliged to report under the money laundering regulations.

- You should also cease to act for Candy. HM Revenue and Customs must be notified that you no longer act for Candy although you should not provide any reason for this.

(c)   **Simplified VAT invoices**

Tutor's top tips

Even if you have not learnt the contents of a simplified VAT invoice you should be able to pick up some marks for stating some fundamental information that you would expect to see on all invoices (e.g. retailer's name and address and VAT registration number, tax point).

- A simplified (or less detailed) VAT invoice can be issued where the VAT inclusive total of the invoice is less than £250.

- Such an invoice should be issued when a customer requests a VAT invoice.

- A simplified VAT invoice must show the following information:
    - The retailer's name and address
    - The retailer's VAT registration number
    - The date of supply (the tax point)
    - A description of the goods or services supplied
    - The VAT inclusive total
    - The rate of VAT

79   ASTUTE LTD (ADAPTED)

Key answer tips

A straight forward question on two of the three special accounting schemes available to small businesses, and group VAT registration.

Make sure you illustrate your answer by referring to the numbers in the question and do not just write about the schemes in general.

(a)   **Annual accounting scheme**

- Astute Ltd can apply to use the annual accounting scheme if its expected taxable turnover for the next 12 months does not exceed £1,350,000 exclusive of VAT.

- In addition the company must be up to date with its VAT returns.

- The reduced administration from only having to submit one VAT return each year should mean that default surcharges are avoided in respect of the late submission of VAT returns.

- In addition, making payments on account based on the previous year's VAT liability will improve both budgeting and possibly cash flow where a business is expanding.

(b)   **Cash accounting scheme**

- Clever Ltd can use the cash accounting scheme if its expected taxable turnover for the next 12 months does not exceed £1,350,000 exclusive of VAT.

- In addition, the company must be up to date with its VAT returns and VAT payments.

- Output VAT will be accounted for three months later than at present since the scheme will result in the tax point becoming the date that payment is received from customers.

- The recovery of input VAT on expenses will not be affected as these are paid in cash.

- The scheme will also provide automatic bad debt relief should a customer default on the payment of a debt.

(c)   **Group VAT registration**

- As Talent Limited controls Gifted Limited, it is possible for these two companies to be group VAT registered.

- The effect of a group registration would be that the two companies are effectively treated as a single entity for VAT purposes.

Advantages of Group VAT registration

- One of the companies will be nominated as the representative member and will submit only one VAT return for the group. This can save in administration costs.

- As the two companies trade with each other, output VAT would not be charged on intra-group supplies and therefore the purchasing company would not need to reclaim input VAT. This provides a cash flow advantage.

Tutor's top tips

You were only asked to state one advantage of group VAT registration so don't waste time listing more than one as you will not score more than one mark.

80   VICTOR STYLE (ADAPTED) *Online question assistance*

Key answer tips

This is a question covering the common issues of registration and the flat rate scheme and also asks for the effect of registration on profit. This is unusual because traders usually pass on the cost of VAT to their customers, but in this case the question clearly states that it was not possible to raise prices as a consequence of becoming registered.

Provided you work carefully through the numbers, this should be a straightforward question.

(a)   **VAT payable – y/e 31 December 2015**

- Output VAT will be £19,000 (£9,500 × 12 = £114,000 × 20/120) since Victor must absorb this himself rather than pass it on to his customers.

- Input VAT will be £800 (£400 × 12 = £4,800 × 20/120).

- The total VAT payable by Victor during the year ended 31 December 2015 is therefore £18,200 (£19,000 – £800).

(b)   **Flat rate scheme**

- The main advantage of the flat rate scheme is the simplified VAT administration. Victor will calculate his VAT liability by simply taking a percentage of his turnover rather than having to calculate output tax and input tax separately.

- If Victor had used the flat rate scheme from 1 January 2015, then he would have paid VAT of £14,820 (£114,000 × 13%) during the year ended 31 December 2015.

- This is a saving of £3,380 (£18,200 – £14,820) for the year.

Tutorial note

In the first 12 months of VAT registration, HMRC allow a 1% reduction in the appropriate percentage for that trade group. However, knowledge of this is not required in the exam.

Therefore, the examiner will give you the rate that should apply in the first 12 months and you do not need to deduct 1%, just use the rate given.

(c) **Reduction in net profit**

- If Victor had not increased his prices, his net profit for the year ended 31 December 2015 based on the information given would have been £64,800 (£5,800 – £400 = £5,400 × 12).

- As a result of increasing his prices, Victor's net profit will be as follows:

	£
Sales (£114,000 – £18,200)	95,800
Less: Expenses (£4,800 – £800)	(4,000)
Net profit	91,800

- This is an increase in net profit of £27,000 (£91,800 – £64,800).

Tutorial note

If the flat rate scheme had been used from 1 January 2015 there would have been an increase in net profit of £30,380 (£27,000 + £3,380).

81 LITHOGRAPH LTD (ADAPTED)

Key answer tips

Monthly payments on account under the annual accounting scheme are based on the VAT payable for the previous year.

This first part of the question was only worth two marks and therefore it should be clear that detailed computations are not required and that the reason for the previous year information in the question is for the purposes of this part.

Calculations based on the current year position were not required until the next part of the question, which required a VAT return and should be an expected standard requirement.

(a) **Monthly payments on account of VAT**

- Each payment on account of VAT will be £1,020 (£10,200 × 10%), being 10% of the VAT payable for the previous year.

- Lithograph Ltd will have made nine payments on account, and these will have been paid for the months of April to December 2015, being months 4 to 12 of the annual VAT return period.

(b) (i) **VAT payable – year ended 31 December 2015**

	£	£
Output VAT		
Sales (£160,000 × 20%)		32,000
Motor car scale charge (£2,008 × 20/120)		335
Office equipment (£8,000 × 20%)		1,600
		———
		33,935
Input VAT		
Purchases (£38,000 × 20%)	7,600	
Expenses (Note 1) (£28,000 × 20%)	5,600	
Machinery (£24,000 × 20%)	4,800	
Impaired debt (Note 3) (£4,800 × 20%)	960	
	———	(18,960)
		———
VAT payable		14,975
		———

Tutorial note

1 *Input VAT on business entertainment is not recoverable unless it relates to overseas customers.*

2 *Input VAT cannot be recovered in respect of the motor car as this is not used exclusively for business purposes.*

3 *Relief for the impaired debt is available because the claim is made more than six months from the time that payment was due, and the debt has been written off in the company's books.*

4 *Amounts due from customers are recorded inclusive of VAT. However the question clearly states that all figures are VAT exclusive unless stated otherwise. Hence the impaired debt of £4,800 has been treated as VAT exclusive.*

5 *The tax is calculated as 20/120 for transactions quoted gross, however the use of 1/6 is also acceptable.*

(ii) **Annual VAT return**

- Lithograph Ltd made payments on account totalling £9,180 (£1,020 × 9), so a balancing payment of £5,795 (£14,975 – £9,180) would have been due with the annual VAT return.

- The annual VAT return, along with the balancing payment, would have been due by 28 February 2016, being two months after the end of the annual VAT period.

82   DENZIL DYER (ADAPTED)

Key answer tips

A question ranging over a number of VAT issues. Make sure you consider each part and write enough for each part.

Remember also to relate your answer to the specific circumstances of the business.

Numbered points or bullet points are the best way to make your answer 'marker friendly'.

(a)   **Identification of the type of supply**

- Output VAT is only due in respect of standard rated supplies. Incorrectly classifying a supply as zero-rated would not remove Denzil's liability to pay the output VAT which is calculated on the actual price charged. This would then be an additional cost to the business.

- The type of supply, whether standard rated or zero-rated, has no effect on the recovery of input VAT for Denzil.

(b)   **VAT implications of discounts**

- Where a discount of 5% is given for an order of more than £500 then output VAT is simply calculated on the revised, discounted, selling price.

- As regards the 2.5% discount offered for prompt payment, output VAT is calculated on the selling price less the amount of discount offered.

- There is no amendment to the amount of output VAT charged if the customer does not take the discount but instead pays the full selling price.

(c)   **Conditions for the recovery of input VAT**

- The supply must be made to Denzil since he is the taxable person making the claim.

- The supply must be supported by evidence, normally in the form of a VAT invoice. Denzil will therefore not be able to recover any input VAT in respect of the purchases of office supplies for cash, where there is no invoice.

- Denzil must use the goods or services supplied for business purposes, although an apportionment can be made where supplies are acquired partly for business purposes and partly for private purposes.

(d)   **Circumstances for issuing VAT invoices**

- Denzil must issue a VAT invoice when he makes a standard rated supply to one of his VAT registered customers.

- A VAT invoice is not required if the supply is zero-rated or the supply is to a non-VAT registered customer (e.g. a member of the public) then an invoice need not be issued unless the customer requests

- A simplified invoice can be issued if the supply is less than £250.

- A VAT invoice should be issued within 30 days of the date that the supply of services is treated as being made.

83   ANNE ATTIRE (ADAPTED) *Walk in the footsteps of a top tutor*

Key answer tips

VAT is an important area of the syllabus and you should take care to ensure you have covered all areas.

The question has two independent parts, which have clear requirements and mark allocations. If you do not have the required knowledge to deal with one part do not allow this to put you off attempting the other part.

Tutor's top tips

Part (a) is a standard VAT return, which does not have any particularly difficult items.

Cash and credit sales are both dealt with in the same way, except that the discount is only applicable to the credit sales.

Be careful to ensure you deal with the discounts correctly, in respect of both the credit sales and the impaired debts.

(a)   **VAT return – Quarter ended 31 May 2015**

	£	£
Output VAT		
Cash sales (£28,000 × 20%)		5,600
Credit sales (Note 1) (£12,000 × 95% × 20%)		2,280
		7,880
Input VAT		
Purchases and expenses (£11,200 × 20%)	2,240	
Impairment loss (Note 2) (£800 × 95% × 20%)	152	
		(2,392)
VAT payable		5,488

The VAT return for the quarter ended 31 May 2015 should have been submitted by 7 July 2015, being one month and seven days after the end of the VAT period.

Tutorial note

1   The calculation of output VAT on the credit sales takes into account the discount for prompt payment, even for those 10% of customers that did not take it.

2   Relief for an impairment loss is not given until six months from the time that payment is due. Therefore relief can only be claimed in respect of the invoice due for payment on 10 November 2014. Relief is based on the amount of output VAT that would originally have been paid taking into account the discount for prompt payment.

3   Amounts due from customers are recorded inclusive of VAT. However the question clearly states that all figures are VAT exclusive unless stated otherwise. Hence the impaired debt of £800 has been treated as VAT exclusive.

(b)   (i)   **Sale of assets on a piecemeal basis**

Tutor's top tips

Part (b) concerns the disposal of a VAT registered business.

It is important to make short, clear points, matched to the number of marks available. Therefore two points are required for each part of the answer, although here the same point can be made twice!

If you do not know all the rules, you could still potentially pick up a mark or two, with some sensible comments, such as the need to deregister when you cease trading.

- Upon the cessation of trading Anne will cease to make taxable supplies, so her VAT registration will be cancelled on the date of cessation or an agreed later date.

- Output VAT will be due in respect of the value of the non-current assets at the date of deregistration on which VAT has been claimed (although output VAT is not due if it totals no more than £1,000).

(ii)   **Sale of business as a going concern**

- Since the purchaser is already registered for VAT, Anne's VAT registration will be cancelled as above.

- A sale of a business as a going concern is not treated as a taxable supply, and therefore output VAT will not be due.

Tutorial note

If the purchaser was not already registered for VAT, they could consider taking over Anne's VAT registration. However, that point would not be relevant to this scenario.

Always make your comments relevant to the circumstances in the question.

Examiner's report

This was the first time that VAT has been examined as a separate question, and it was therefore pleasing to see many very good answers.

In part (a) candidates often did not appreciate that output VAT on credit sales had to take account of the discount for prompt payment even if it was not taken by customers.

The same comment applies to part (b). For example, candidates generally appreciated that the taxpayer's VAT registration would be cancelled, but few stated that the reason for the cancellation was the cessation of making taxable supplies.

Many candidates stated that on a sale of the business as a going concern the VAT registration could be taken over by the purchaser despite the question clearly stating that the purchaser was already registered for VAT.

ACCA marking scheme			Marks
(a)	Output VAT – Cash sales		1.0
	– Credit sales		1.5
	Input VAT – Purchases and expenses		1.0
	– Impairment loss		1.5
	Due date		1.0
			6.0
(b) (i)	**Sale of assets on a piecemeal basis**		
	Cancellation of VAT registration		1.0
	Output VAT		1.0
			2.0
(ii)	**Sale of business as a going concern**		
	Cancellation of VAT registration		1.0
	Output VAT not due		1.0
			2.0
Total			**10.0**

84   ASTON MARTYN (ADAPTED)   *Walk in the footsteps of a top tutor*

Key answer tips

This VAT question has a mixture of straightforward and difficult marks to obtain.

The classic popular topics of compulsory registration, contents of a valid invoice and payment dates should not have caused any problems, provided the topics had been revised.

However, the overseas aspects of VAT rules are complicated and difficult to explain succinctly and the penalty regime needed to be applied to the scenario to gain the marks available.

Overall, not an easy question, particularly if the rules have not been learnt, you are not clear in your explanations and do not apply to the facts of the question.

(a) **Compulsory registration**

- Aston would have been liable to compulsory registration for VAT when his taxable supplies at the end of any month exceeded £81,000 for the previous 12-month period (or since the commencement of trade if less than 12 months).

- This occurs on 28 February 2015 when taxable supplies amounted to £81,200 (£2,300 + £6,400 + £25,700 (Note) + £10,700 + £16,100 + £20,000 (Note)).

- Registration is required from the end of the month following the month in which the limit is exceeded.

- Therefore, Aston should have notified HMRC within 30 days (i.e. by 30 March 2015) and registration will have been effective from 1 April 2015 or from an agreed earlier date.

Tutorial note

Taxable supplies include zero-rated supplies.

The notification date is 30 days after the end of the month in which the limit is exceeded.

(b) **Additional pieces of information on VAT invoice**

The following information is required:

(1) Aston's VAT registration number.

(2) An identifying number (invoice number).

(3) The rate of VAT for each supply.

(4) The amount of VAT payable.

Tutor's top tips

There are only 2 marks for this part, and four things to mention. As only half a mark is available for each point you need to be efficient with time and not take too long on this part.

(c) **Supply of services received from EU VAT registered businesses**

- VAT will have to be accounted for according to the time of supply.

- This is the earlier of the date that the service is completed or the date it is paid for.

- The VAT charged at the UK VAT rate should be declared on Aston's VAT return as output VAT, but will then be reclaimed as input VAT on the same VAT return.

- This is known as the reverse charge procedure.

Tutor's top tips

This part is tricky, however marks were given for recognising that there is both input and output VAT to account for on the supply of a service from EU VAT registered businesses.

(d) **Errors on a VAT return**

- Provided Aston has taken reasonable care and informs HMRC promptly of any errors after he has discovered them, HMRC will not charge a penalty.

- However, Aston would be expected to check the VAT classification of each of his supplies when making the supply and invoicing. Therefore, applying the incorrect rate of VAT is more likely to be treated by HMRC as careless, rather than taking reasonable care.

- The maximum amount of penalty for carelessness is 30% of the VAT underpaid.

- However, with unprompted disclosure to HMRC by Aston, the penalty could be reduced to £Nil.

Tutor's top tips

Be careful not to answer this part in general terms. The penalty table could have been presented and would have been mark earning – but only if you then applied the rules to the specific scenario given in the question.

Examiner's report

With the exception of part (b), this question was generally answered quite poorly.

In part (a) most candidates did not appreciate that the zero-rated supplies had to be included when calculating taxable supplies for registration purposes.

Part (b) was well answered, although many candidates wasted time by stating more than four additional pieces of information.

For example, common sense should mean that the business could not possibly state the VAT registration number of the customer.

Many candidates simply ignored part (c), but marks were awarded for any sensible answer such as input VAT and output VAT would contra out.

In part (d) too many candidates simply reproduced the penalty table without relating it to the facts given. Again, marks were awarded for any sensible conclusion.

ACCA marking scheme		
		Marks
(a)	Registration limit	0.5
	28 February 2015	2.0
	Date of registration	0.5
		―――
		3.0
		―――
(b)	Aston's VAT registration number	0.5
	An identifying number	0.5
	The rate of VAT for each supply	0.5
	The amount of VAT payable	0.5
		―――
		2.0
		―――
(c)	Time of supply	1.0
	Entries on VAT return	1.0
		―――
		2.0
		―――
(d)	No penalty if reasonable care	1.0
	Treated as careless	1.0
	Amount of penalty	1.0
		―――
		3.0
		―――
Total		**10.0**
		―――

85 SILVERSTONE LTD (ADAPTED) *Walk in the footsteps of a top tutor*

Key answer tips

This is a classic 10 mark VAT question. A number of easy marks are available for the key facts and advantages of the VAT cash accounting and annual accounting schemes, provided they are related to the particular circumstances of Silverstone Ltd.

Part (b) covers the overseas aspects of VAT which is relatively straightforward provided the rules have been learnt.

Tutor's top tips

Part (a) – Read the requirement carefully – you are required to explain why the company can use the schemes and why they will be beneficial. Make sure that you take account of and refer to the specific circumstances of the company and do not just write about the schemes in general.

In part (b) use headings in your answer so that it is clear which points relate to each type of supplier and remember to deal with both when and how to account for the VAT for each supplier.

(a)   **Cash accounting scheme and Annual accounting scheme**

- Silverstone Ltd can use both schemes because its expected taxable turnover for the next 12 months does not exceed £1,350,000 exclusive of VAT.

- In addition, for both schemes the company is up to date with its VAT payments, and for the cash accounting scheme it is up to date with its VAT returns.

- With the cash accounting scheme, output VAT will be accounted for two months later than at present since the scheme will result in the tax point becoming the date that payment is received from customers.

- The recovery of input VAT on expenses will not be affected as these are paid in cash.

- With the annual accounting scheme, the reduced administration in only having to file one VAT return each year should save on overtime costs.

(b)   **Supplier situated outside the European Union**

- Silverstone Ltd will have to pay VAT of £4,400 (£22,000 at 20%) to HM Revenue and Customs at the time of importation.

- This will then be reclaimed as input VAT on the VAT return for the period during which the machinery is imported.

Supplier situated elsewhere within the European Union

- VAT will have to be accounted for according to the date of acquisition. This will be the earlier of the date that a VAT invoice is issued or the 15th day of the month following the month in which the machinery comes into the UK.

- The VAT charged of £4,400 will be declared on Silverstone Ltd's VAT return as output VAT, but will then be reclaimed as input VAT on the same VAT return. This is known as the reverse charge procedure.

Examiner's report

The first requirement was reasonably well answered, although candidates had a tendency to write everything they knew about the two schemes rather than tailoring their answers to the information given in the question.

The second requirement caused more problems, and there was little appreciation that the two alternatives would effectively leave Silverstone Ltd in the same overall financial position.

ACCA marking scheme			
			Marks
(a)		Both schemes – Expected taxable T/O for next 12 mths ≤ £1,350,000	1.5
		And up to date with VAT payments and returns	1.5
		Cash accounting – output tax accounted for 2 months later	1.0
		Cash accounting – input tax recovery not affected	1.0
		Annual accounting – reduced admin (only one return a year)	1.0
			6.0
(b)	(i)	Supplier situated outside the European Union	
		Pay at time of importation	1.0
		Reclaim as input tax on VAT return in period in which imported	1.0
	(ii)	Supplier situated elsewhere within the European Union	
		Date of acquisition	1.0
		Include as output and input tax on same return	1.0
			4.0
Total			**10.0**

86 THE WHITLOCK SISTERS (ADAPTED) *Walk in the footsteps of a top tutor*

Key Answer Tips

A straightforward computation of the VAT payable using the flat rate scheme percentage, and comparing it with the VAT that would have been payable if the normal basis had been used should have provided easy marks to a well prepared student.

Be careful to read the question carefully though to ascertain whether the figures given are inclusive or exclusive of VAT.

For written parts, write short succinct sentences in bullet point form and bear in mind the mark allocation for each sub-section. In general, there is usually one mark allocated for each valid point made. Do not therefore dwell on any one part too much and keep an eye on the clock.

(a) **VAT flat rate scheme**

- Using the flat rate scheme to calculate its VAT liability the partnership will have paid VAT of £7,761 (£59,700 × 13%) for the quarter ended 31 March 2015.

- If the partnership had used the normal basis it would have paid VAT of £5,400 ((£59,700 − £27,300) = £32,400 × 20/120).

- It was therefore not beneficial to use the flat rate scheme as the additional cost of £2,361 (£7,761 − £5,400) for the quarter would appear to outweigh the advantage of simplified VAT administration.

Tutorial note

Under the flat rate scheme, VAT is calculated by applying a fixed percentage to the sales figure inclusive of VAT.

Calculating the VAT element of VAT inclusive prices using 1/6 rather than 20/120 is an acceptable shortcut.

(b) **Voluntary registration**

- The partnership's sales are all to members of the general public, who cannot recover the input VAT.

- It may not therefore be possible to pass the output VAT on to customers in the prices charged. To the extent this is not possible the partnership would have had to absorb all or some of this amount itself as a cost.

- It was therefore not beneficial for the partnership to have voluntarily registered for VAT from 1 January 2015. For the quarter ended 31 March 2015 voluntary registration reduced the partnership's profits by a maximum of £7,761 (£5,400 if the normal basis had been used).

Tutorial note

Be careful if the customers are members of the public, as they are not allowed to recover the VAT portion of the amount paid.

The VAT inclusive prices may make the product too expensive in the market and in order to remain competitive, the business may need to absorb the VAT as part of their overheads and not pass the price increase on to their customers.

(c) **Tax point date**

- Output VAT must be accounted for according to the VAT period in which the supply is treated as being made. This is determined by the actual tax point date (ATP).

- The basic tax point date (BTP) is the date when the service is completed, which will be the date that the room is used.

- Where payment is received before the BTP, then this date becomes the ATP.

- The ATP for each 25% deposit received is therefore the date that the deposit is actually received.

- Invoices are issued on the same day as the BTP, so this is the ATP for the balancing payments of 75%.

Tutorial note

For services, the basic tax point (BTP) is the date the service is provided/completed.

The actual tax point (ATP) can be either before or after the BTP.

The ATP will be before the BTP if:

- *An invoice is issued before the BTP, or*

- *A payment is received before the BTP (as in this case with the deposit payments).*

The ATP will be after the BTP if:

- *An invoice is issued within 14 days of the BTP, or*

- *The business has an agreement with HMRC for a different date (typically businesses agree a month end invoicing policy so that the invoice date is usually the ATP).*

In this case the invoice for the remaining balance payment is issued on the BTP.

Note however that not all of these rules are relevant to this question and there are not many marks allocated to this part – so only address the rules that apply to the particular scenario given.

Examiner's report

It was disappointing to see a number of candidates deduct inputs when calculating VAT using the flat rate basis, the first requirement was otherwise generally answered very well.

The second requirement caused a lot of confusion, with quite a few candidates discussing VAT registration – the correct answer was simply that voluntary VAT registration reduced the partnership's profits by the amount of VAT payable calculated in the first requirement.

For the final requirement, quite a few candidates just explained the time of supply rules, without relating them to the information given in the question. It was clearly stated that an invoice was issued on the date the room was used – so the 14-day rule for issuing an invoice was irrelevant.

Note: The examiner's report has been edited to remove comments on elements of the question that have been deleted due to changes to the exam format.

ACCA marking scheme			Marks
(a)	Flat rate scheme		1.0
	Normal basis		1.0
	Conclusion		1.0
			3.0
(b)	No recovery of VAT by customers		1.0
	Possible need to absorb output VAT		1.0
	Conclusion		1.0
			3.0
(c)	VAT period		1.0
	Basic tax point		1.0
	Deposit		1.0
	Balance		1.0
			4.0
Total			**10.0**

87   KNIGHT LTD (ADAPTED) *Walk in the footsteps of a top tutor*

Key answer tips

This is a straightforward 10 mark VAT question. A number of easy marks are available in part (a) for calculating the VAT payable for the quarter. You are instructed in the requirement to list all items in notes (1) to (5) in your answer so make sure that you don't miss any out! One way to do this is to tick off each note on your question paper as you deal with each one.

Parts (b) and (c) test the popular topics or VAT penalties and group registration respectively. They are both independent of part (a) and should represent easy marks provided that the rules have been learnt. You may want to attempt parts (b) and (c) before part (a) to make sure you don't run out of time by spending too long on the more time pressured part (a).

(a) **VAT return – quarter ended 31 March 2015**

Tutor's top tips

Marks are available for specifically stating the items for which no adjustment is required, so, as required in the question, remember to indicate these by the use of zero.

	£	£
Output VAT		
Sales (Note 1)		38,210
Group sales		4,330
Fuel scale charge (£328 × 20/120) (Note 2)		55
Input VAT		
Impairment loss (Note 3)	Nil	
Expenses (W)	12,560	
	———	(12,560)
		———
VAT payable		30,035
		———

Tutorial note

1   *The tax point for the deposit is the date of payment, so no adjustment is required to the output VAT figure of £38,210.*

2   *The fuel scale charge is quoted inclusive of VAT. The VAT element can be calculated as 20/120 of the scale figure, or as a short cut, you can use 1/6.*

3   *Relief is not available for the impairment loss as less than six months has passed from the time that payment was due.*

Working: Input tax – Expenses

	£
Total input VAT	12,770
Entertaining UK customers (Note 1)	(210)
Entertaining overseas customers (Note 1)	0
Repainting office building (Note 2)	0
New reception area (Note 2)	0
	———
	12,560
	———

Tutorial note

1   Input VAT on business entertainment is not recoverable unless it relates to the cost of entertaining staff or overseas customers.

2   Input tax is recoverable on both the repairs (revenue expenditure) and the extension (capital expenditure). There is no distinction between capital and revenue for VAT purposes.

(b)   **Default surcharge**

- The late submission for the quarter ended 31 December 2012 is irrelevant, as it was followed by the submission of four consecutive VAT returns on time.

- The late payment for the quarter ended 30 September 2014 results in the issue of a surcharge liability notice for the period up to 30 September 2015.

- The late payment of VAT for the quarter to 31 March 2015 occurs during the surcharge period. Therefore, there will be a surcharge of £601 (£30,035 × 2%).

- In addition, the surcharge period will be extended to 31 March 2016.

Tutorial notes

The surcharge of £601 is payable as it exceeds the de minimis amount of £400.

(c)   **Group registration**

Tutor's top tips

There are only two marks available for this section, indicating that the examiner is probably looking for two advantages and is only expecting a brief statement for each advantage.

- There will be no need to account for VAT on goods and services supplied between group members. Such supplies will simply be ignored for VAT purposes.

- It will only be necessary to complete one VAT return for the three companies, so there could be a saving in administrative costs.

Tutorial notes

Are Ltd and Can Ltd can form a group with Knight Ltd for VAT purposes as they are under the control of Knight Ltd and all of the companies are UK resident.

Examiner's report

The first requirement was generally well answered. Common mistakes included not appreciating that VAT figures were given (rather than supply figures), that no adjustment was required on a deposit (given that the tax point was the date of payment) and that no relief was available for the impairment loss (as less than six months had passed from the time that payment was due).

The second requirement was the one section on this paper that was inadequately answered by the vast majority of candidates, with few being able to explain the correct surcharge position. The third requirement was generally well answered, although many candidates often wrote at length to explain a couple of fairly straightforward points.

Note: *The examiner's report has been edited to remove comments on elements of the question that have been deleted due to changes to the exam format.*

Section 5

SPECIMEN PAPER QUESTIONS

SECTION A – ALL 15 QUESTIONS ARE COMPULSORY AND MUST BE ATTEMPTED

Please use the space provided on the inside cover of the Candidate Answer Booklet to indicate your chosen answer to each multiple-choice question.

Each question is worth 2 marks.

1   During the tax year 2014/15, William was paid a gross annual salary of £82,700. He also received taxable benefits valued at £5,400.

What amount of Class 1 National Insurance contributions (NIC) will have been suffered by William for the tax year 2014/15?

A   £4,994

B   £8,969

C   £4,886

D   £4,069

2   You are a trainee Chartered Certified Accountant and your firm has a client who has refused to disclose a chargeable gain to HM Revenue and Customs (HMRC).

From an ethical viewpoint, which of the following actions could be expected of your firm?

(1)   Reporting under the money laundering regulations

(2)   Advising the client to make disclosure

(3)   Ceasing to act for the client

(4)   Informing HMRC of the non-disclosure

(5)   Warning the client that your firm will be reporting the non-disclosure

(6)   Notifying HMRC that your firm has ceased to act for the client

A   2, 3 and 5

B   1, 2, 3 and 6

C   2, 3 and 4

D   1, 4, 5 and 6

3   Martin was born on 28 June 1965. He is self-employed, and for the year ended 5 April 2015 his trading profit was £109,400. During the tax year 2014/15, Martin made a gift aid donation of £800 (gross) to a national charity.

What amount of personal allowance will Martin be entitled to for the tax year 2014/15?

A   £10,000

B   £5,700

C   £5,300

D   £Nil

4   For the year ended 31 March 2015, Halo Ltd made a trading loss of £180,000.

Halo Ltd has owned 100% of the ordinary share capital of Shallow Ltd since it began trading on 1 July 2014. For the year ended 30 June 2015, Shallow Ltd will make a trading profit of £224,000.

Neither company has any other taxable profits or allowable losses.

What is the maximum amount of group relief which Shallow Ltd can claim from Halo Ltd in respect of the trading loss of £180,000 for the year ended 31 March 2015?

A   £180,000

B   £168,000

C   £45,000

D   £135,000

5   For the year ended 31 March 2014, Sizeable Ltd had a corporation tax liability of £384,000, and for the year ended 31 March 2015 had a liability of £456,000.

Sizeable Ltd is a large company, and is therefore required to make instalment payments in respect of its corporation tax liability.

The company's profits have accrued evenly throughout each year.

What is the amount of each instalment payable by Sizeable Ltd in respect of its corporation tax liability for the year ended 31 March 2015?

A   £228,000

B   £114,000

C   £96,000

D   £192,000

6   For the year ended 31 December 2014, Lateness Ltd had a corporation tax liability of £60,000, which it did not pay until 31 March 2016. Lateness Ltd is not a large company.

How much interest will Lateness Ltd be charged by HM Revenue and Customs (HMRC) in respect of the late payment of its corporation tax liability for the year ended 31 December 2014?

A   £900

B   £2,250

C   £300

D   £450

7   On 26 November 2014 Alice sold an antique table for £8,700. The antique table had been purchased on 16 May 2011 for £3,800.

What is Alice's chargeable gain in respect of the disposal of the antique table?

A   £4,500

B   £1,620

C   £4,900

D   £Nil

8   On 14 November 2014, Jane made a cash gift to a trust of £800,000 (after deducting all available exemptions). Jane paid the inheritance tax arising from this gift. Jane has not made any other lifetime gifts.

What amount of lifetime inheritance tax would have been payable in respect of Jane's gift to the trust?

A   £95,000

B   £190,000

C   £118,750

D   £200,000

9   During the tax year 2014/15, Mildred made the following cash gifts to her grandchildren:

(1)   £400 to Alfred

(2)   £140 to Minnie

(3)   A further £280 to Minnie

(4)   £175 to Winifred

Which of the gifts will be exempt from inheritance tax under the small gifts exemption?

A   1, 2, 3 and 4

B   2, 3 and 4 only

C   2 and 4 only

D   4 only

10 For the quarter ended 31 March 2015, Zim had standard rated sales of £59,700 and standard rated expenses of £27,300. Both figures are inclusive of value added tax (VAT). Zim uses the flat rate scheme to calculate the amount of VAT payable, with the relevant scheme percentage for her trade being 12%.

How much VAT will Zim have to pay to HM Revenue and Customs (HMRC) for the quarter ended 31 March 2015?

A £6,396

B £3,888

C £6,480

D £7,164

11 **Which of the following assets will ALWAYS be exempt from capital gains tax?**

(1) A motor car suitable for private use

(2) A chattel

(3) A UK Government security (gilt)

(4) A house

A 1 and 3

B 2 and 3

C 2 and 4

D 1 and 4

12 Winston has already invested £8,000 into a cash new individual savings account (NISA) during the tax year 2014/15. He now wants to invest into a stocks and shares NISA.

What is the maximum possible amount which Winston can invest into a stocks and shares NISA for the tax year 2014/15?

A £15,000

B £7,000

C £Nil

D £7,500

13 **Ming is self-employed. How long must she retain the business and non-business records used in preparing her self-assessment tax return for the tax year 2014/15?**

	Business records	Non-business records
A	31 January 2017	31 January 2017
B	31 January 2017	31 January 2021
C	31 January 2021	31 January 2021
D	31 January 2021	31 January 2017

14 Moon Ltd has had the following results:

Period	Profit/(loss)
	£
Year ended 31 December 2014	(105,000)
Four-month period ended 31 December 2013	43,000
Year ended 31 August 2013	96,000

The company does not have any other income.

How much of Moon Ltd's trading loss for the year ended 31 December 2014 can be relieved against its total profits of £96,000 for the year ended 31 August 2013?

A £64,000

B £96,000

C £70,000

D £62,000

15 Nigel has not previously been resident in the UK, being in the UK for less than 20 days each tax year. For the tax year 2014/15, he has three ties with the UK.

What is the maximum number of days which Nigel could spend in the UK during the tax year 2014/15 without being treated as resident in the UK for that year?

A 90 days

B 182 days

C 45 days

D 120 days

SECTION B – ALL SIX QUESTIONS ARE COMPULSORY AND MUST BE ATTEMPTED

1 (a) On 10 June 2014, Delroy made a gift of 25,000 £1 ordinary shares in Dub Ltd, an unquoted trading company, to his son, Grant. The market value of the shares on that date was £240,000. Delroy had subscribed for the 25,000 shares in Dub Ltd at par on 1 July 2004. Delroy and Grant have elected to hold over the gain as a gift of a business asset.

Grant sold the 25,000 shares in Dub Ltd on 18 September 2014 for £240,000.

Dub Ltd has a share capital of 100,000 £1 ordinary shares. Delroy was the sales director of the company from its incorporation on 1 July 2004 until 10 June 2014. Grant has never been an employee or a director of Dub Ltd.

For the tax year 2014/15 Delroy and Grant are both higher rate taxpayers. Neither of them has made any other disposals of assets during the year.

Required:

(i) **Calculate Grant's capital gains tax liability for the tax year 2014/15. (3 marks)**

(ii) **Explain why it would have been beneficial for capital gains tax purposes if Delroy had instead sold the 25,000 shares in Dub Ltd himself for £240,000 on 10 June 2014, and then gifted the cash proceeds to Grant.   (2 marks)**

(b) On 12 February 2015, Marlon sold a house for £497,000, which he had owned individually. The house had been purchased on 22 October 1999 for £146,000. Marlon incurred legal fees of £2,900 in connection with the purchase of the house, and legal fees of £3,700 in connection with the disposal.

Throughout the period of ownership the house was occupied by Marlon and his wife, Alvita, as their main residence. One-third of the house was always used exclusively for business purposes by the couple.

Entrepreneurs' relief is not available in respect of this disposal.

For the tax year 2014/15 Marlon is a higher rate taxpayer, but Alvita did not have any taxable income. Neither of them has made any other disposals of assets during the year.

Required:

(i) **Calculate Marlon's chargeable gain for the tax year 2014/15.   (3 marks)**

(ii) **Calculate the amount of capital gains tax which could have been saved if Marlon had transferred 50% ownership of the house to Alvita prior to its disposal.   (2 marks)**

(Total: 10 marks)

2   You should assume that today's date is 15 March 2015.

Opal Elder, aged 71, owns the following assets:

(1)   Two properties respectively valued at £374,000 and £442,000. The first property has an outstanding repayment mortgage of £160,000, and the second property has an outstanding endowment mortgage of £92,000.

(2)   Vintage motor cars valued at £172,000.

(3)   Investments in new individual savings accounts (NISAs) valued at £47,000, savings certificates from NS&I (National Savings and Investments) valued at £36,000, and government stocks (gilts) valued at £69,000.

Opal owes £22,400 in respect of a personal loan from a bank, and she has also verbally promised to pay legal fees of £4,600 incurred by her nephew.

Under the terms of her will, Opal has left all of her estate to her children. Opal's husband is still alive.

On 14 August 2005, Opal had made a gift of £100,000 to her daughter, and on 7 November 2014, she made a gift of £220,000 to her son. Both these figures are after deducting all available exemptions.

The nil rate band for the tax year 2005/06 is £275,000.

Required:

(a)   (i)   **Calculate Opal Elder's chargeable estate for inheritance tax purposes were she to die on 20 March 2015.**   **(5 marks)**

          (ii)   **Calculate the amount of inheritance tax which would be payable in respect of Opal Elder's chargeable estate, and state who will be responsible for paying the tax.**   **(3 marks)**

(b)   **Advise Opal Elder as to why the inheritance tax payable in respect of her estate would alter if she were to live for another seven years until 20 March 2022, and by how much.**

          You should assume that both the value of Opal Elder's estate and the nil rate band will remain unchanged.   **(2 marks)**

                                                                                                            (Total: 10 marks)

3   Glacier Ltd runs a business providing financial services. The following information is available in respect of the company's value added tax (VAT) for the quarter ended 31 March 2015:

(1)   Invoices were issued for sales of £44,600 to VAT registered customers. Of this figure, £35,200 was in respect of exempt sales and the balance in respect of standard rated sales. The standard rated sales figure is exclusive of VAT.

(2)   In addition to the above, on 1 March 2015 Glacier issued a VAT invoice for £8,000 plus VAT of £1,600 to a VAT registered customer. This was in respect of a contract for financial services which will be completed on 15 April 2015. The customer paid for the contract in two instalments of £4,800 on 31 March 2015 and 30 April 2015.

(3)   Invoices were issued for sales of £289,100 to non-VAT registered customers. Of this figure, £242,300 was in respect of exempt sales and the balance in respect of standard rated sales. The standard rated sales figure is inclusive of VAT.

(4) The managing director of Glacier Ltd is provided with free fuel for private mileage driven in her company motor car. During the quarter ended 31 March 2015, this fuel cost Glacier Ltd £260. The relevant quarterly scale charge is £408. Both these figures are inclusive of VAT.

For the quarters ended 30 September 2013 and 30 June 2014, Glacier Ltd was one month late in submitting its VAT returns and in paying the related VAT liabilities. All of the company's other VAT returns have been submitted on time.

Required:

(a) Calculate the amount of output VAT payable by Glacier Ltd for the quarter ended 31 March 2015. **(4 marks)**

(b) Advise Glacier Ltd of the default surcharge implications if it is one month late in submitting its VAT return for the quarter ended 31 March 2015 and in paying the related VAT liability. **(3 marks)**

(c) State the circumstances in which Glacier Ltd is and is not required to issue a VAT invoice, and the period during which such an invoice should be issued. **(3 marks)**

(Total: 10 marks)

4 Sophie Shape has been a self-employed sculptor since 1996, preparing her accounts to 5 April. Sophie's tax liabilities for the tax years 2013/14 and 2014/15 are as follows:

	2013/14	2014/15
	£	£
Income tax liability	5,240	6,100
Class 2 national insurance contributions	143	143
Class 4 national insurance contributions	1,240	1,480
Capital gains tax liability	0	4,880

No income tax has been deducted at source.

Required:

(a) Prepare a schedule showing the payments on account and balancing payment which Sophie Shape will have made, or will have to make, during the period from 1 April 2015 to 31 March 2016.

Your answer should clearly identify the relevant due date of each payment. **(4 marks)**

(b) State the implications if Sophie Shape had made a claim to reduce her payments on account for the tax year 2014/15 to nil without any justification for doing so. **(2 marks)**

(c) Advise Sophie Shape of the latest date by which she can file a paper self-assessment tax return for the tax year 2014/15. **(1 mark)**

(d) State the period during which HM Revenue and Customs (HMRC) will have to notify Sophie Shape if they intend to carry out a compliance check in respect of her self-assessment tax return for the tax year 2014/15, and the possible reasons why such a check would be made.

You should assume that Sophie will file her tax return by the filing date. **(3 marks)**

(Total: 10 marks)

5 On 6 April 2014, Simon Bass, who was born on 14 June 1991, commenced employment with Echo Ltd as a music critic. On 1 January 2015, he commenced in partnership with Art Beat running a small music venue, preparing accounts to 30 April. The following information is available for the tax year 2014/15:

Employment

(1) During the tax year 2014/15, Simon was paid a gross annual salary of £23,700.

(2) During May 2014, Echo Ltd paid £11,600 towards Simon's removal expenses when he permanently moved to take up his new employment with the company, as he did not live within a reasonable commuting distance. The £11,600 covered both his removal expenses and the legal costs of acquiring a new main residence.

(3) Throughout the tax year 2014/15, Echo Ltd provided Simon with living accommodation. The company had purchased the property in 2004 for £89,000, and it was valued at £143,000 on 6 April 2014. The annual value of the property is £4,600. The property was furnished by Echo Ltd during March 2014 at a cost of £9,400.

Partnership

(1) The partnership's tax adjusted trading profit for the four-month period ended 30 April 2015 is £29,700. This figure is before taking account of capital allowances.

(2) The only item of plant and machinery owned by the partnership is a motor car which cost £18,750 on 1 February 2015. The motor car has a CO_2 emission rate of 155 grams per kilometre. It is used by Art, and 40% of the mileage is for private journeys.

(3) Profits are shared 40% to Simon and 60% to Art. This is after paying an annual salary of £6,000 to Art.

Property income

(1) Simon owns a freehold house which is let out furnished. The property was let throughout the tax year 2014/15 at a monthly rent of £660.

(2) During the tax year 2014/15, Simon paid council tax of £1,320 in respect of the property, and also spent £2,560 on purchasing new furniture.

(3) Simon claims the wear and tear allowance.

Required:

(a) Calculate Simon Bass's taxable income for the tax year 2014/15.　　**(13 marks)**

(b) State TWO advantages for the partnership of choosing 30 April as its accounting date rather than 5 April.　　**(2 marks)**

(Total: 15 marks)

6   You are a trainee accountant and your manager has asked you to correct a corporation tax computation which has been prepared by the managing director of Naive Ltd, a company which manufactures children's board games. The corporation tax computation is for the year ended 31 March 2015 and contains a significant number of errors:

Naive Ltd – Corporation tax computation for the year ended 31 March 2015

	£
Trading profit (working 1)	494,200
Loan interest received (working 2)	32,100
	526,300
Dividends received (working 3)	28,700
	555,000
Corporation tax (£555,000 × 21%)	116,550

Working 1 – Trading profit

	£
Profit before taxation	395,830
Depreciation	15,740
Donations to political parties	400
Qualifying charitable donations	900
Accountancy	2,300
Legal fees in connection with the issue of loan notes (the loan was used to finance the company's trading activities)	5,700
Entertaining suppliers	3,600
Entertaining employees	1,700
Gifts to customers (pens costing £40 each and displaying Naive Ltd's name)	920
Gifts to customers (food hampers costing £45 each and displaying Naive Ltd's name)	1,650
Capital allowances (working 4)	65,460
Trading profit	494,200

Working 2 – Loan interest received

	£
Loan interest receivable	32,800
Accrued at 1 April 2014	10,600
Accrued at 31 March 2015	(11,300)
Loan interest received	32,100

The loan was made for non-trading purposes.

Working 3 – Dividends received

	£
From unconnected UK companies	20,700
From a 100% UK subsidiary company	8,000
Dividends received	28,700

These figures were the actual cash amounts received.

Working 4 – Capital allowances

	Main Pool £	Motor car £	Special rate pool £	Allowances £
Written down value (WDV) brought forward	12,400		13,600	
Additions				
Machinery	42,300			
Motor car [1]	13,800			
Motor car [2]		14,000		
	68,500			
Annual investment allowance (AIA)	(68,500)			68,500
Disposal proceeds			(9,300)	
			4,300	
Balancing allowance			(4,300)	(4,300)
Writing down allowance (WDA) – 18% WDA (8%)		(2,520)	x 50%	1,260
WDV carried forward	0	11,480		
Total allowances				65,460

(1)   Motor car [1] has a CO_2 emission rate of 110 grams per kilometre.

(2)   Motor car [2] has a CO_2 emission rate of 155 grams per kilometre. This motor car is used by the sales manager and 50% of the mileage is for private journeys.

(3)   All of the items included in the special rate pool at 1 April 2014 were sold for £9,300 during the year ended 31 March 2015. The original cost of these items was £16,200.

Other information

From your files, you note that Naive Ltd has one associated company (the 100% UK subsidiary company mentioned in working 3).

Required:

Prepare a corrected version of Naive Ltd's corporation tax computation for the year ended 31 March 2015.

You should indicate by the use of zero any items in the computation of the trading profit for which no adjustment is required.   **(15 marks)**

Section 6

ANSWERS TO SPECIMEN PAPER QUESTIONS

SECTION A

1 C

(£33,909 (£41,865 − £7,956) × 12%) + (£40,835 (£82,700 − £41,865) × 2%) = £4,886

2 B

3 B

	£
Personal allowance	10,000
Restriction (£109,400 − £800 − £100,000) = £8,600 ÷ 2	(4,300)
Restricted personal allowance	5,700

4 D

Lower of:

£135,000 (£180,000 × 9/12)

£168,000 (£224,000 × 9/12)

5 B

£456,000/4 = £114,000

6 A

£60,000 × 3% × 6/12 = £900 (period 1 October 2015 to 31 March 2016)

7 A

£2,700 (£8,700 − £6,000) × 5/3 = £4,500

This is less than £4,900 (£8,700 − £3,800)

8   C

   £475,000 (£800,000 − £325,000) × 20/80 = £118,750

9   D

10   D

   £59,700 × 12% = £7,164

11   A

12   B

   £15,000 − £8,000 = £7,000

13   C

14   D

   £105,000 − £43,000 = £62,000

15   A

SECTION B

1 DELROY, GRANT, MARLON AND ALVITA

(a) (i) **Grant – Capital gains tax liability – 2014/15**

	£
Ordinary shares in Dub Ltd:	
Disposal proceeds	240,000
Less: Cost	(25,000)
Chargeable gain	215,000
Less: Annual exempt amount	(11,000)
Taxable gain	204,000
Capital gains tax (£204,000 × 28%)	57,120

Tutorial notes

1   *Because the whole of Delroy's chargeable gain has been held over, Grant effectively took over the original cost of £25,000.*

2   *The disposal does not qualify for Entrepreneurs' relief as Grant was neither an officer nor an employee of Dub Ltd.*

(ii) **Personal sale of shares and gift of cash proceeds**

- The disposal would have qualified for entrepreneurs' relief as Delroy was the sales director of Dub Ltd, and his shareholding of 25% (25,000/100,000 × 100) was more than the minimum required holding of 5%.

- The capital gains tax liability would therefore have been calculated at the rate of 10%.

- There are no capital gains tax implications regarding a gift of cash.

(b) (i) **Marlon – Chargeable gain – 2014/15**

	£	£
House:		
Disposal proceeds		497,000
Less: Cost		(146,000)
Incidental costs (£2,900 + £3,700)		(6,600)
		344,400
Less: Principal private residence exemption (W)		(229,600)
Chargeable gain		114,800

Working: Principal private residence exemption

One-third of Marlon's house was always used exclusively for business purposes.

Therefore, the principal private residence exemption is restricted to £229,600 (£344,400 × 2/3).

(ii) **Capital gains tax saved**

The capital gains tax saving if 50% ownership of the house had been transferred to Alvita prior to its disposal would have been calculated as follows:

	£
Annual exempt amount (£11,000 × 28%)	3,080
Lower rate tax saving (£31,865 × 10% (28% − 18%))	3,186
	———
	6,266
	———

Tutorial note

Transferring 50% ownership of the house to Alvita prior to its disposal would have enabled her annual exempt amount and lower rate tax band of 18% for 2014/15 to be utilised.

---

2 OPAL ELDER

(a) (i) **Chargeable estate**

	£	£
Property (£374,000 + £442,000)		816,000
Repayment mortgage		(160,000)
Endowment mortgage		(Nil)
		———
		656,000
Motor cars		172,000
Investments (£47,000 + £36,000 + £69,000)		152,000
		———
		980,000
Bank loan	22,400	
Legal fees	(Nil)	
	———	(22,400)
		———
Chargeable estate		957,600
		———

Tutorial notes

1   *There is no deduction in respect of the endowment mortgage as this will be repaid upon death by the life assurance element of the mortgage.*

2   *The promise to pay the nephew's legal fees is not deductible as it is not legally enforceable.*

(ii)   **Inheritance tax on death estate**

		£
Chargeable estate		957,600
	£	
IHT liability	105,000 × 0% (W)	Nil
	852,600 × 40%	341,040
	957,600	341,040

The personal representatives of Opal's estate will be responsible for paying the inheritance tax

Working – Available nil rate band

		£
Nil rate band		325,000
Potentially exempt transfers	– 14 August 2005	(Nil)
	– 7 November 2014	(220,000)
		105,000

Tutorial note

The potentially exempt transfer on 14 August 2005 is exempt from inheritance tax as it was made more than seven years before 20 March 2015.

(b)   **If Opal lived seven years longer**

If Opal were to live for another seven years, then the potentially exempt transfer on 7 November 2014 would become exempt.

The inheritance tax payable in respect of her estate would therefore decrease by £88,000 (£220,000 at 40%).

3 GLACIER LTD

(a) Output VAT for the quarter ended 31 March 2015

	£
Sales	
VAT registered customers (£9,400 (£44,600 – £35,200) × 20%)	1,880
Additional contract	1,600
Non-VAT registered customers	
(£46,800 (£289,100 – £242,300) × 20/120)	7,800
Fuel scale charge (£408 × 20/120)	68
	———
	11,348
	———

Tutorial note

The basic tax point for a supply of services is the date when they are completed, but if a VAT invoice is issued or payment received before the basic tax point, then this becomes the actual tax point. Therefore the tax point for the contract is when the VAT invoice was issued on 1 March 2015.

(b) Default surcharge implications

- Glacier Ltd was late in submitting VAT returns and paying the related VAT liability for two previous quarters. The company has not managed to revert to a clean default surcharge record by submitting four consecutive VAT returns on time.

- The late payment of VAT for the quarter ended 31 March 2015 will therefore result in a surcharge of 5% of the VAT liability for that period, although this will not be collected if it is less than £400.

- In addition, the surcharge period will be extended to 31 March 2016.

(c) VAT invoices

- Glacier Ltd must issue a VAT invoice when it makes a standard rated supply to a VAT registered customer.

- However, there is no requirement to do so if the supply is exempt or if the supply is to a non-VAT registered customer.

- A VAT invoice should be issued within 30 days of the date when the supply is treated as being made.

4   SOPHIE SHAPE

(a)   **Schedule of tax payments**

Due date	Tax year	Payment	£
31 July 2015	2014/15	Second payment on account	
		£6,480 (£5,240 + £1,240) × 50%	3,240
31 January 2016	2014/15	Balancing payment	
		£12,460 (£6,100 + £1,480 + £4,880)	
		– £6,480 (£3,240 × 2)	5,980
31 January 2016	2015/16	First payment on account	
		£7,580 (£6,100 + £1,480) × 50%	3,790

Tutorial notes

1   *The second payment on account for 2014/15 is based on Sophie's income tax and class 4 NIC liability for 2013/14.*

2   *The balancing payment for 2014/15 includes the capital gains tax liability for that year.*

3   *The first payment on account for 2015/16 is based on Sophie's income tax and class 4 NIC liability for 2014/15.*

(b)   **Reduction of payments on account**

- If Sophie's payments on account for 2014/15 were reduced to nil, then she would be charged interest on the payments due of £3,240 from the relevant due date to the date of payment.

- A tax-geared penalty will be charged as the claim to reduce the payments on account to nil would appear to be made fraudulently or negligently.

(c)   **Filing a paper tax return**

- Unless the return is issued late, the latest date when Sophie can file a paper self-assessment tax return for 2014/15 is 31 October 2015.

(d)   **Compliance check**

- If HM Revenue and Customs (HMRC) intend to carry out a compliance check into Sophie's 2014/15 tax return they will have to notify her within 12 months of the date when they receive the return.

- HMRC has the right to carry out a compliance check as regards the completeness and accuracy of any return, and such a check may be made on a completely random basis.

- However, compliance checks are generally carried out because of a suspicion that income has been undeclared or because deductions have been incorrectly claimed. For example, where accounting ratios are out of line with industry norms.

5 SIMON BASS

(a) Taxable income – 2014/15

	£
Employment income	
Salary	23,700
Removal expenses (£11,600 – £8,000)	3,600
Living accommodation – Annual value	4,600
– Additional benefit (W1)	2,210
– Furniture (£9,400 × 20%)	1,880
	35,990
Trading profit (W2)	8,220
Property business profit (W4)	5,940
Total income	50,150
Less: Personal allowance	(10,000)
Taxable income	40,150

Tutorial note

Only £8,000 of the relocation costs is exempt.

Workings

(W1) Living accommodation additional benefit

The benefit is based on the market value when first provided

	£
Market value	143,000
Limit	(75,000)
	68,000

The additional benefit is therefore £2,210 (£68,000 × 3·25%).

Tutorial note

The property was purchased more than six years before first being provided, so the benefit is based on the market value when first provided.

(W2) Trading profit

Simon's share of the partnership's trading profit for the period ended 30 April 2015 is £10,960 calculated as follows:

	£
Trading profit	29,700
Capital allowances (W3)	(300)
	29,400
Salary paid to Art (£6,000 × 4/12)	(2,000)
	27,400
Profit share (£27,400 × 40%)	10,960

Simon's trading income assessment for 2014/15 is £8,220 (£10,960 × 3/4).

Tutorial note

Simon's assessment for 2014/15 is for the period 1 January 2015 to 5 April 2015.

(W3) Capital allowances

	Motor car £		Allowances £
Addition	18,750		
WDA (8% × 4/12)	(500)	x 60%	300
WDV carried forward	18,250		

Tutorial note

The partnership's motor car has CO_2 emissions over 130 g/km and therefore qualifies for writing down allowances at the rate of 8%.

(W4) Property business profit

	£	£
Rent receivable (£660 × 12)		7,920
Council tax	1,320	
Wear and tear allowance (W5)	660	
Furniture	Nil	
		(1,980)
Property business profit		5,940

Tutorial note

The cost of purchasing new furniture is irrelevant, since capital allowances are not given in respect of plant and machinery used in a private dwelling.

(W5) Wear and tear allowance

The wear and tear allowance is £660 (£7,920 − £1,320 = £6,600 × 10%) as the rent receivable is reduced by the council tax paid by Simon.

(b) **Advantages of choosing a 30 April accounting date**

- The interval between earning profits and paying the related tax liability will be 11 months longer. This can be particularly beneficial where profits are rising.

- It will be possible to calculate taxable profits well in advance of the end of the tax year, making it much easier to implement tax planning and make pension contributions.

6 NAIVE LTD

Corporation tax computation – year ended 31 March 2015

	£
Trading profit (W1)	369,640
Loan interest	32,800
	402,440
Less: Qualifying charitable donations	(900)
Taxable total profits	401,540
Plus: Franked investment income (W3)	23,000
Augmented profits	424,540
Corporation tax (£424,540 × 21%)	84,323
Less: Marginal relief (W4) 1/400 × (£750,000 − £424,540) × £401,540/£424,540	(770)
Corporation tax liability	83,553

Workings

(W1) Trading profit for the year ended 31 March 2015

	£	£
Profit before taxation	395,830	
Depreciation	15,740	
Donations to political parties	400	
Qualifying charitable donations	900	
Accountancy	0	
Legal fees	0	
Entertaining suppliers	3,600	
Entertaining employees	0	
Gifts to customers – pens	0	
Gifts to customers – food hampers	1,650	
Capital allowances (W2)		48,480
	————	————
	418,120	48,480
	(48,480)	————
	————	
Trading profit	369,640	
	————	

Tutorial notes

1   *The only exception to the non-deductibility of entertainment expenditure is when it is in respect of employees.*

2   *Gifts to customers are an allowable deduction if they cost less than £50 per recipient per year, are not of food, drink, tobacco or vouchers for exchangeable goods, and carry a conspicuous advertisement for the company making the gift.*

(W2)   Capital allowances

		General Pool	Special rate pool	Allowances
	£	£	£	£
TWDV b/f		12,400	13,600	
Additions (no AIA or FYA)				
Motor car 1		13,800		
Motor car 2			14,000	
Additions qualifying for AIA				
Machinery	42,300			
Less: AIA	(42,300)			42,300
	———	Nil		
Disposal proceeds			(9,300)	
		———	———	
		26,200	18,300	
WDA (18%)		(4,716)		4,716
WDA (8%)			(1,464)	1,464
		———	———	
TWDV c/f		21,484	16,836	
		———	———	
Total allowances				48,480
				———

Tutorial notes

1   *Motor car 1 has CO$_2$ emissions between 96 and 130 g/km and therefore qualifies for writing down allowances at the rate of 18%.*

2   *Motor car 2 has CO$_2$ emissions over 130 g/km and therefore qualifies for writing down allowances at the rate of 8%. The private use of the motor car is irrelevant, since such usage will be assessed on the employee as a benefit.*

(W3)   Franked investment income

Franked investment income is £23,000 (20,700 × 100/90).

The dividends from the 100% subsidiary company are not franked investment income as they are group dividends.

(W4)   Upper limit

Naive Ltd has one associated company, so the upper limit is reduced to £750,000 (£1,500,000 ÷ 2).